THE TIMECHART
OF
MILITARY
HISTORY

US Marines landing on the beach at Iwo Jima, one of the bloodiest battles of the Pacific campaign during World War II. In the background can be seen the warships still bombarding the Japanese defences as the Marines advance.

THE TIMECHART
OF
MILITARY
HISTORY

Foreword by David G. Chandler
MA (Oxon), DLitt, FRHist.S, FRGS

PROSPERO
B·O·O·K·S
A DIVISION OF CHAPTERS INC.

The Timechart of Military History
first published 1999 by
The Timechart Company
an imprint of Worth Press Ltd
9 Batchworth Heath, Rickmansworth,
Herts. WD3 1QB, England

This edition produced for Prospero Books,
a division of Chapters Inc.

ISBN 1552672689

British Library Cataloguing in Publication
Data: a catalogue record for this book is
available from the British Library

Designed and edited by
D.A.G. Publications Ltd.
Printed and bound in Hong Kong.

Consultants

Dr Stephen Badsey,
Royal Military Academy, Sandhurst

Dr David Nicolle

Dr Stephen Turnbull

Editorial and Production Team:
Michael Boxall
Roger Chesneau
C. J. Davies
Anthony A. Evans
David Gibbons
John Gilbert
Susie Green
Philip Jarrett
Lynda Jones
Meredith MacArdle
Evgenia North
Jonathan North
Benjamin Yates

With thanks also to
John Walter
Ian V. Hogg

Publisher's Note

With so many facts to marshal into such a confined space, and covering such
a vast range of topics, there will, inevitably, be errors, both of commission and
omission. We will gladly welcome comments and corrections from readers, all
of which will be acknowledged and noted for future editions. Contact us at:
D.A.G. Publications Ltd, 244 Webheath, Netherwood Street, London NW6
2JX, England.

CONTENTS

HOW TO USE THIS BOOK

- **The Timechart History of Warfare** is designed to enable the reader to discover the relationship between individual wars and battles, presenting the overall context of the conflicts and their relative positions in time and space, one to another.

- **The Timechart** (pages 23–49) is a diagram that traces the course of military events from 3000 BC to the present. It shows some 1,000 wars, from the Ancient Egyptians and Sumerians onwards. Having located a battle on this diagram, the reader can turn to the A–Z section and the Chronology to discover further details.

- **The A–Z of Battles** (pages 57–89) lists more than 2,000 individual battles, giving their dates, the names of the victor and the vanquished, and their nationalities. These battles, from their dates, can be located on the Timechart. (But note that, in view of the limitations of space on the Timechart diagram, not all the battles in this list are depicted.)

- **The Chronology** provides more detail to supplement the Timechart diagram, where necessary placing events in context.

- **Battle Maps** presents over 30 battle plans of significant or especially interesting engagements, with statistical and other details.

- More detailed coverage of individual wars or groups of wars are presented between pages 128 and 145.

- Preceding all this is a brief narrative covering the history of warfare with emphasis on the weaponry and technology that has characterised military events and developments through the ages.

FOREWORD

BY DAVID G. CHANDLER

MA (Oxon), D.Litt, FRHist.S
Former Head of Department of War Studies,
Royal Military Academy, Sandhurst

More than a century ago General Sir Edward Hamley (1824–93) wrote in his introduction to *Operations of War* that there is 'no kind of history to fascinate mankind as the history of wars'. Sixty years ago the great Thomas Hardy (1840–1928) declared that, 'War makes rattling good history but Peace is poor reading.' It is now a quarter of a century since I wrote my first book on military history, and I am still as excited by military history as I was then.

Over the past five millennia – three 'BCs' and two 'ADs' – of recorded history, there have been only 290 years free of the horrors of organised armed strife (not including internal guerrilla activities). Between 1740 and 1999 – just some 260 years – 87 million people have died directly from the effects of war. For Great Britain, a relatively small and 'peaceful' island, there has been only one single year (1966) since 1945 in which the British Army has not suffered fatal casualties by enemy action. History, ancient and modern, tells us that wars are probably here to stay well into the foreseeable future.

Napoleon's message to military historians in late 1815 on St. Helena was: 'Peruse again and again the campaigns of Alexander, Hannibal, Caesar, Gustavus Adolphus, Turenne, Eugene and Frederick. Model yourself upon them. This is the only means of gaining the secret of the art of war. Your own genius will be enlightened and improved by this study, and you will learn to reject all maxims foreign to the principles of these great commanders.' This book puts a great deal of such knowledge in your hands.

Whether you are fascinated by the period from Sargon to Schwarzkopf, from Wallenstein to Waterloo, you will find something of interest in this fascinating timechart. At the very least, this book will help the reader to put any given conflict in the wider context of history and to put a clear perspective on our own relatively peaceful times, long may they last.

There have, of course, been earlier attempts at timecharts of their equivalent. For example, Joseph Minard (a French civil servant in Paris, 1869) produced a fascinating drawing entitled *Destruction of an Army in Russia (1812)*. I rather doubt whether this example can be much improved upon for its strategic information at a single glance – even if we had to add more modern battlefield symbols for young officers at Sandhurst in 1986.

This book presents the broader information on the 'great strategical' level. Think of it. We are studying war *over five millennia of history!* Which makes this book's appearance especially timely, as one millennium comes to an end and another begins.

18 June 1999 (the 184th anniversary of Waterloo)

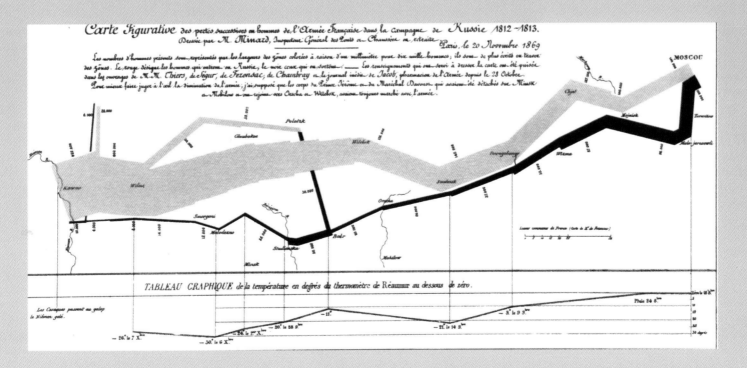

WARFARE AND WEAPONS

A BRIEF HISTORICAL SURVEY

This timechart chronicles the wars and battles of five thousand years of human history – since records began. For four and a half of those millennia, human muscle supplied the power to win wars – with spear, sword, arrow and club. Only in the last half-millennium has muscle power been supplanted by mechanism, and in the last few decades by microchip.

From the ancient Egyptians to the close of the Middle Ages, there are many similarities apparent in the armies and fleets that went to war. Indeed, military styles appeared to have come full circle in the late sixteenth and seventeenth centuries, when bodies of armoured men advanced into combat armed with long pikes not very different from those wielded by the hoplites of ancient Greece. The galleys that fought at Lepanto were powered by oars in much the same way as the triremes that defeated the Persians at Salamis two thousand years before.

Yet from the middle of the fifth millennium in our chronicle to the present, warfare has altered dramatically – to global communications networks, battles and campaigns directed from across the world using computers, satellite surveillance and aircraft capable of delivering cruise missiles from halfway across the earth.

ARMOUR AND CAVALRY

The transition from tribal warfare to organised city-state conflict is not recorded, but the earliest weapons were probably fire-hardened sticks, stone axes, spears, flint daggers, together with slings and primitive bows. By the middle of the third millennium BC, Sumerian smiths were casting socketed axe heads, the axe having developed from the mace, and bronze heads were also being made for spears and javelins (the latter used for throwing as against shock combat). Bas reliefs of Assyrian and Egyptian warfare show regimented warriors, relatively sophisticated in dress and armament, with spears, bows and shields of bronze and wood. Bronze helmets were relatively expensive items. The sword began with the axe, developing into the sickle sword by the middle of the second millennium BC; because of the structural limitations of bronze, only with the coming of iron (about 1200 BC) were long, straight swords possible.

By the time of the Greek–Persian Wars, the Greek phalanx manned by hoplite warriors represented the peak of military organisation. Dressed with bronze helmet and body armour, each man carried a sword, spear and shield. When standing in sixteen-deep phalanx formation, the nine-foot long spears presented a formidable battle front. Philip of Macedon, father of Alexander the Great, equipped his phalanxes with spears more than twice that length, called sarissas. Perceiving that the phalanx was a relatively difficult mass to manoeuvre, Philip and Alexander made the formations smaller and thus more flexible to deploy.

Alexander's great battles were won – in part at least – by the shock effect of cavalry. The first highly mobile shock weapon was the chariot, which was in use by about 1700 BC, the first chariot battle to be recorded being at Meggido in 1457. Around the middle of the second millennium the ridden horse made war chariots redundant, Scythian cavalrymen from the north-east irrupting into the civilised world, as would many other such people in succeeding centuries.

Infantry, however, remained the principal component of armies, the legions of Rome, disciplined, well organised and equipped, becoming supreme on the battlefield for some six hundred years from the middle of the third century BC to the mid-fourth century AD. Organised in smaller sub-units, or cohorts, the legionaries were armed with short stabbing swords and javelins with soft necks behind the points, so that they bent upon impact, catching in opponents' shields. The Roman army was a formidable fighting machine, able to march long distances at speed, make camp for the night, then hurry onwards, the spade being as important as the sword.

During the third century AD, pressure from barbarian tribes upon the borders of the Roman Empire intensified, and warfare was increasingly dominated by cavalry. Mobility was vital to counter the irruptions of tribes along the Rhine–Danube frontier, and during the great crisis of the mid-second century cavalry corps were established at key locations, ready to move against incoming tribal raids. The Battle of Adrianople in 378, at which the Emperor Valens perished, has traditionally been seen as the beginning of the Age of Cavalry. The Roman infantry had long been in decline, a very different instrument of war from Republican days, when it was essentially a citizen army; increasingly the troops were of barbarian origin taken into service by the empire.

The Huns, who terrorised Europe and the Middle East during the middle years of the fifth century, were essentially fast-moving horse archers. Such tribes emerged periodically throughout history, the most dramatic being the Mongols, whose hordes of mounted archers spread terror across the Far East, Asia and the Middle East, and even briefly into Europe during the thirteenth century. Their tactics were not based upon shock. Essentially, they were light cavalry, swarming around an opponent and able to escape before being brought to combat by heavier armed troops. Essentially too they were nomads; they moved quickly, and as quickly disappeared.

The shock effect of cavalry has been ascribed to the introduction of the stirrup during the seventh century, but the breeding of suitable horses was a more important factor, possibly a result of Arab breeds, spread by Islamic conquerors during that century. By the eighth century improved breeds produced heavier war horses that could carry greater weight, making possible the development of the armoured knight. The improved war horses and increasingly sophisticated armour were expensive, so that armies of this period tended to be smaller than those of earlier centuries, consisting of relatively small numbers of 'élite' mounted warriors supported by footmen. The break-up of the Roman Empire ushered in an period of smaller-scale conflicts between the new kingdoms that replaced it, with the rise of feudal states in which tenancy of land was awarded in return for military service. This system, which lasted to the fourteenth century, originated with the Franks in the eighth century and spread to North Italy, Spain and Germany, the Normans taking it to England and southern Italy.

Armour took a variety of forms, evolving over the centuries. Roman armour could be chain mail, scale (overlapping small pieces of metal sewn on to a supporting fabric), lamellar (laced pieces of metal) or laminated (segments of metal bound together) as illustrated on Trajan's Column. Scale and mail were very ancient methods of armouring, dating back to the Assyrians, and lamellar armour was known to the Etruscans. All were relatively expensive to manufacture. During the eleventh century the armour of the Norman knight was typically as depicted in the Bayeux Tapestry: a conical helmet, long hauberk of chain mail, and a kite-shaped shield. Weapons consisted of spear and sword.

Soon after 1200, plate armour began to be manufactured. Helmets with hinged visors appeared about 1300, and the first suits of full armour date from the early years of the fifteenth century. Such suits were heavy and cumbersome, requiring very strong horses to support them; vision was limited and communication made difficult. Arrows and crossbow bolts could be stopped by heavy armour, making the later-period knights the equivalent of modern tanks, powerful shock weapons but requiring support for sustained combat. Ultimately the coming of firearms rendered armour obsolete: plate thick enough to keep out musket balls was impracticable.

FORTIFICATION

Throughout the four and a half of the millennia of warfare chronicled here, fortification and siege warfare remained recognisably the same. Many of the earliest wars recorded are between walled cities, and the bas reliefs of the Ancient Egyptians and Assyrians bear witness to the methods employed to break into fortifications.

Heavy artillery, catapults and battering-rams were used to dislodge part of the city walls, enabling a breach to be made through which an assault might be launched. Such operations took time, and besiegers often looked for the more vulnerable parts of the defences to attack. In particular the city gates would receive attention, and battering rams, often of great size and weight, would be pulled into place under a constant rain of missiles and arrows from the ramparts above. The rams needed to be protected, and these can be seen quite clearly on early bas reliefs. Siege towers, tall mobile structures protected with wood and hides, would also be constructed and hauled into place against the walls, enabling the attackers to reach the ramparts by means of drawbridges and get to grips with the defenders. Such constructions could be huge, requiring the building of long ramps – again under constant enemy harassment – for the approach to the walls, the towers having been fabricated well out of missile range. A further hazard for the besiegers, were the garrison strong enough, was an unexpected sally from the city or fortress to destroy the towers and siege engines under construction.

The relief of besieged places by field armies often made necessary the construction of a double set of siege lines by the attackers – facing outwards (lines of circumvallation)

instead of inwards (lines of contravallation). Sieges were thus lengthy and manpower-consuming – and often awe-inspiring. Caesar's siege of Vercingetorix in Alesia in 52 BC involved the construction of double siege lines some dozen miles in circumference, with towers at intervals and a free, open space between the inward and outward defence lines to enable the speedy reinforcement of threatened zones. In front of the defensive walls, cunning traps – the equivalent of modern minefields – were set for the Gauls: sharpened stakes in concealed pits, blocks of wood with iron hooks, and trenches, all covered by brushwood.

If the walls of a city continued to defy the besiegers, hunger and starvation would eventually succeed in reducing the garrison's ability to resist. The victims 'in the middle' of the combatants were often the civilians living within the walls. The

The ultimate weapon. As the fifth millennium of the timechart draws to a close the risk of nuclear war between superpowers seems to have receded. But stocks of nuclear weapons remain and nuclear technology is now in other hands too. In 1999 India and Pakistan renewed testing, and several other nations are known to have developed them.

fighting men would take priority for food and water; and there are many recorded instances of civilian populations being ruthlessly expelled from besieged towns, to waste away in the no-man's land between besieged and besiegers. In the nineteenth and twentieth centuries this seems less shocking, 'total war' having become a recognised form of warfare, with cities bombarded from the air as well as from the land. During World War II, Leningrad withstood a terrible siege over 29 months, during which the privations of the inhabitants, made worse by the Russian winter, earned them heroic status.

The gunpowder revolution made its impact on siege warfare before having much effect on the battlefield. Large bombards were in use by the last phases of the Hundred Years War and at the Ottoman capture of Constantinople in 1453, and as artillery and small-arms improved, the design of fortifications changed. Previously, it had been enough to build defences thick and high, on hills or crags if possible, giving the defenders the advantage of height as well as the solidity of stone walls. Bastions – towers placed at intervals along the walls, provided extra strength and were a place of refuge for the defenders if the walls were damaged or breached. Gunpowder changed all that. During the Renaissance period a distinct break with previous fortification is apparent, defences becoming lower, rounder and even more massive. But this was not enough. Fortification became a science, the plan of a fortified place being carefully designed to take into account the fields of fire available to both attacker and defender. The bastion became arrow-shaped with a long sloping earthen rampart so that guns could dominate the areas in front of the linking curtain walls. In front of the main defences, ditches and walls were built to impede the approach of infantry – but constructed in such a way as to avoid interfering with defensive fire. Fortifications during the late seventeenth century became ever more complex and effective, featuring outworks such as ravelins and demilunes, the science of fortification being taken to a new level by the works of Vauban, whose fortifications survive in many parts of northern France.

ARMOUR AND EDGED WEAPON

Left: Infantry in ancient times, such as this Roman legionary, carried shields as protection against spear and sword. He carries also the short *gladius*, which the Romans adopted from Spain.

a b c d e

Above: Polearms carried during the la medieval and early modern period: a & halberds; c, partisan which became a sym of rank in the seven teenth century; d, p a weapon that prove deadly in the hands the Swiss; e, sponto which served the sar purpose as the parti

A full suit of armour of the fifteenth century. By this date armour had reached the height of sophistication and design, but, with the introduction of firearms was soon to become redundant

Above: Cataphracts as depicted on Trajan's Column. Roman auxiliaries wearing scale armour and riding armoured horses

Left: Bascinet of the late 14th century with its visor and metal aventail, which protected the neck.

Below: European cavalry mid-seventeenth century wc more open type of helmet, a 'lobster pot'. Body armour both cavalry and infantry wa generally the buff coat of thi leather, which had the advar of lightness and comfort.

Right: A salet as worn during the 15th century. The back of the brim was extended into a pointed tail to protect the neck.

Above: Early to mid-seventeenth century infantryman's helmet as worn by a pikeman. In addition he wore breast- and back-plates and tassets, or metal thigh-guards.

ve: The bayonet originated in Spain in the late sixteenth
tury but did not come into widespread military use for
er century. The advantage was obvious, dispensing with
need to deploy half the infantry in the purely defensive
of pikemen. Now the infantry could fire their muskets,
h their bayonets and be prepared to fight hand-to-hand
o fend off cavalry. The early plug bayonets (above left)
disadvantage in that the musket could not be fired if the
et was fitted. The socket bayonet (above centre), which
in time replaced by the modern knife bayonet (above
), enabled the infantryman to fire his gun and was more
ely fitted. The bayonet later doubled as a combat knife
and a useful tool in addition to its original purpose.

Above: The short, stabbing *gladius* of the Roman army gave way during the age of cavalry dominance to longer, heavier weapons intended to slash and cut. This is a late nineteenth-century cavalry sword.

w: During the seventeenth, eighteenth and nineteenth centuries, infantry had no great
for protective headgear. By the end of the nineteenth century, however, higher-velocity
ns and artillery, with longer-range killing power, meant that infantry could no longer
euvre in line in the open but needed to entrench. During World War I the steel helmet
to evolve. Today's helmets are often made of carbon-fibre materials with housings for
unications equipment. These American infantry wear the standard GI issue steel
ts of World War II.

In addition to artillery fire, the besieged city or fortress would also be threatened – perhaps more insidiously – by the stealthy approach of trenches and tunnels dug by the besiegers. If the underlying geology permitted, one way to bring down a defensive wall was to tunnel beneath it, digging as large a space beneath the wall as possible and shoring up the roof with timbers. When set ablaze, the 'mine' would collapse, bringing down a section of the wall. It was a technique used throughout the history of siege warfare against stone fortifications and even made its contribution to the Vicksburg and later eastern-theatre campaigns of the American Civil War. With the stalemate parallel lines of trenches on the Western Front in World War I, stretching across Belgium and northern France and often no farther apart than a few hundred yards, tunnellers were employed to dig out below no-man's land to beneath the enemy trenches with precisely the same purpose, now using explosives of far greater power. Beneath the trench lines, a dark, horrifying war was waged between the opposing miners, each side listening in the dark for the sounds of enemy digging.

Perhaps the ultimate in fortification, built between World Wars I and II, was the French Maginot Line, a vastly expensive complex with thicker concrete and heavier guns than ever before. Running along France's border with Germany, it was 87 miles in length, permanently manned, with air-conditioned barracks and underground connecting rail lines. Its effectiveness, however, was entirely negative, breeding complacency in the French command that led to disaster in 1940, when the Germans simply outflanked it.

The fortification of towns and cities has now been rendered obsolete by modern weaponry and the speed of communications. A city can be attacked from the air – as was the case during World War II, when London was 'blitzed', and an aerial campaign was waged against Germany's cities. No defence on earth could have prevented the atomic destruction of Hiroshima and Nagasaki.

ARTILLERY

A notable characteristic of warfare has been the increase in the distance at which armies can wage war. In ancient times, the killing range of an army was the length of a sword arm, the distance a spear could be thrown or an arrow shot. Artillery provides a means of extending that distance and increasing the weight of the projectile – and its killing power. Ancient artillery was based upon throwing or slinging projectiles by means of torsion or tension. Ballistae were based upon the latter. Tightly twisted bundles of rope or other fibre provided the energy that, when released, threw the projectile. Tension – as in the bow – was used to power catapults and large horizontal bows. In general these were clumsy and heavy pieces of apparatus, more useful in conducting siege warfare than on the field of battle. Smaller pieces of artillery, however, were useful in defence of fortified lines, typical of Roman warfare.

For siege warfare, the heavier the artillery the better the chance of knocking holes in the defenders' walls. Josephus describes Roman catapults at the siege of Jerusalem in AD 70 as throwing stones of 55 pounds more than 400 yards. With the demise of the Roman Empire, the science of artillery seems to have declined. The trebuchet, however, which appeared about the twelfth century, provided a simple means of propelling large objects considerable distances. They worked by counterpoise, a heavy weight, when released, pulling the launch-arm sharply upwards. Modern experiments indicate the power

FORTIFICATION AND SIEGE WARFARE

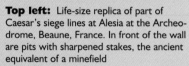

Top left: Life-size replica of part of Caesar's siege lines at Alesia at the Archeo-drome, Beaune, France. In front of the wall are pits with sharpened stakes, the ancient equivalent of a minefield

Above: Model of a Roman siege tower up against a defensive wall, with its drawbridge down ready to disgorge attacking troops on to the enemy rampart

Top right: Conisborough Castle, York-shire, England, built in the late 12th century. This view shows the remains of the curtain wall and the circular keep, with its distinctive buttresses

Centre right: Porchester Castle, Hamp-shire, England, built in the early/mid-12th century. Shown here is the rectangular keep, one of the tallest in England.

Centre, far right: Part of the curtain wall at Carcassonne.

Right: A panoramic view of the restored town of Carcassonne affording an insight into the way medieval walled towns looked

169.   fig. 170.   fig. 171.   fig. 172.

fig. 173.   fig. 174.

fig. 175.

fig. 176.   fig. 177.   fig. 178.

L1.

e: Mid-seventeenth
designs for outworks,
various forms of
. While the bulwark
ended as a strongpoint,
ting the application of
outflank attackers
n bastions, it was itself
ble to being cut off and
ed. These schemes
arious ways of isolating
work so that, even if
ed, the bulwark would
another layer of
es behind it.

e right: A mortar,
seventeenth century
. Mortars were short,
evation guns which
bombs at a high trajec-
er the top of defences.
curate than cannon,
ere nevertheless
tive and could reach
f the defences that
guns could not. Small
mortars, lightweight
n-portable, remain in
h the armies of today.

: Artillery in siege
e as depicted in a
of 1639 demonstrating
e of the bulwark. The
(between the
ks) is protected by
re from the bulwarks;
wer illustration) if the
rs do succeed in taking
wark, its narrow 'neck'
vely easy to seal off
other layer of defence.

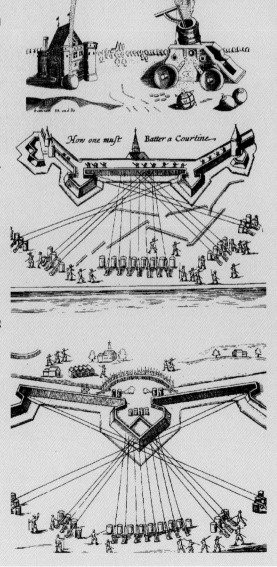

A Morter Shooting upon a Castle

How one must   Batter a Courtine

of such machines: with a ten-ton weight, and an arm about 50 feet long, a 300-pound stone could be lobbed some 300 yards.

Such artillery was only of use in siege warfare, however. Only with the coming of gunpowder did artillery take its place as the arbiter of battles. Early guns were wrought iron tubes, bonded with hoops and loaded at the muzzle end with a spherical stone ball. By the last quarter of the fourteenth century, wrought-iron bombards were capable of projecting 450-pound stone cannonballs. Cast guns were infinitely superior, initially manufactured from brass or bronze, later from iron and steel, and had the advantage of being able to shoot metal cannonballs instead of stone. (Stone anyway was proving too expensive, being too labour-intensive by the fifteenth century.) Gradually the classic artillery piece emerged: a cast metal tube, muzzle-loaded, fired from the breech via a touch-hole, and mounted on a carriage with a pair of wheels and 'cheeks' projecting backwards for training the gun, moving it and absorbing recoil.

By the seventeenth century artillery was becoming lighter and more manoeuvrable, Gustavus Adolphus of Sweden being a particular innovator in designing light battalion guns to support infantry in the field. During the eighteenth century lighter carriages and standardised calibres made manufacture and deployment more practicable. Napoleon (who began his military career as an artilleryman) was able to field 'grand batteries' to blast his opponents' infantry before sending in cavalry and infantry to the attack – at Waterloo his army deployed nearly 250 pieces of artillery.

During the nineteenth century great advances in metallurgy and ballistics improved artillery dramatically, as it did small-arms, and rifling increased accuracy. The gun began to take its modern form, high-velocity, breech loading and rapid firing. By World War I, artillery dominated the battlefield, and during the three and a half years of virtual stalemate on the Western Front, artillery effectively pinned troops to the ground, making infantry assaults almost suicidal. Vast bombardments by huge howitzers failed to cut the barbed wire defending enemy lines and served only to churn up the ground so that it became an almost impassable morass.

Manoeuvre returned in World War II, but the artillery now had new targets: tanks and aircraft. A seesaw development race developed between the tank and the anti-tank gun, tanks becoming bigger and more heavily protected to keep out higher velocity artillery shells designed to penetrate armour. War in the air was contested by fighter aircraft, but anti-aircraft weapons were made more effective by the development of proximity fuzes, which detonated without needing to strike the aircraft. By the end of the war in the Pacific, the US Navy's warships were covered by anti-aircraft guns, in the latter stages to knock down Japan's kamikaze suicide aircraft. Meanwhile the battleships' big guns were now capable of shooting over distances in excess of twenty miles.

Today's artillery has the advantage of satellites and computers to target and range; propellants are many times more powerful than gunpowder; and rockets, tentatively tried by the British Congreve during the Napoleonic Wars, have now come of age, providing power and accuracy that seems set to supplant conventional artillery.

SMALL-ARMS

The so-called 'gunpowder revolution' (c. 1300–1650) brought forth modern artillery, small-arms and bombs. Early 'small-arms were crude and often as dangerous to the user as to the target. In the middle of the fifteenth century the development of slow match and the serpentine made possible the matchlock musket, the first practical firearm. Heavy and cumbersome, it was slow to fire and needed a forked rest to support the muzzle end. Proper gunstocks and butts enabled more accurate and less painful shooting, and during the Dutch War of Independence and the Thirty Years War large formations of musketeers took the field, their slowness of fire requiring them to be protected by bodies of pikeman. With the disappearance of armour towards the end of the sixteenth century, muskets could be lighter and smaller. Also during the sixteenth century, the flintlock was invented, a cheaper, easier to use mechanism for igniting the charge. This came into military use a century later, flintlocks gradually supplanting matchlocks by 1700. In the eighteenth century standardisation of parts and the ability of nation states to manufacture weapons *en masse* made possible large armies of infantry uniformly equipped.

The short range of these weapons, however – much shorter than for the longbow – meant that battles retained the old linear formations and manoeuvres, small-arms being accurate only up to about seventy-five yards, and liable to kill at well under 200 yards. Volley fire increased effectiveness at these short ranges, and battles were often stand-up exchanges of fire between lines of infantry until one side had had enough, the battlefields disappearing into a dense fog of smoke.

The flintlock was the standard infantry weapon of the eighteenth and early nineteenth centuries, but while the method of ignition was relatively reliable, these muzzle-loaders took a long time to load and fire – volley fire probably averaged no more than two or three shots per minute – and the accuracy of the spherical lead balls used, even with rifling, was poor. In 1843 the Prussian army adopted the Dreyse needle-gun, a breech-loader with percussion ignition, and this dramatically increased the rate of fire. The French Minié of 1846/8 extended accuracy to 1,000 yards by means of an improved bullet that expanded on firing, gripping the rifling. By the latter part of the nineteenth century, small-arms had been revolutionised – metallic cartridges and smokeless propellants instead of the old black powder making accurate fire to 1,000 yards while the firer, was virtually undetectable – so that close-order battle formations were suicidal. The major powers were slow to grasp this, as casualties in the Boer War demonstrated.

World War I saw these improved firearms used on a large scale, but it was the machine-gun – notably the recoil-operated Maxim design – that eliminated tactical manoeuvre and set in train the events leading to the 'siege'-line trenches of the Western Front. With a rate of fire of 600 rounds per minute and a range of up to 2,000 yards, they brought unprecedented destructive power to the battlefield.

Modern small-arms include more automatic and semi-automatic weapons of the sort that we see on TV every night. Their firepower is massive, and infantry tactics today emphasise small groups in concealment, working in close cooperation with tanks, artillery and air power.

ARMOURED FIGHTING VEHICLES

With the overwhelming superiority of the defence at the close of the nineteenth century and the beginning of the twentieth, high-velocity firearms and artillery dominating the battlefield at long range, manoeuvre became almost impossible. The

ARTILLERY

mooth bore, muzzle-loading
non, the 12pdr was the heaviest
nch field piece during the
oleonic period.

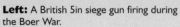

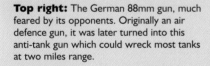

Left: A British 5in siege gun firing during the Boer War.

Top right: The German 88mm gun, much feared by its opponents. Originally an air defence gun, it was later turned into this anti-tank gun which could wreck most tanks at two miles range.

Lower, top right: A German Nebel-werfer during World War II. A simple multiple rocket-launcher, even though not very accurate, this type of artillery proved to be effective when used for area bombardment.

Upper right: The nuclear threat meant that crews needed protection, and self-propelled guns were in demand. The American 155mm M109 howitzer, which became the standard support weapon in most western armies from the 1960s.

Right: Automation extended to towed guns as well: only three men are needed to operate this Swedish 155mm FH-77A howitzer.

opening moves of World War I saw vast armies transported to their staging areas by railway, then advance to meet one-another. After a brief period of manoeuvre, in which the Germans' modified Schlieffen Plan failed at the Battle of the Marne, a virtual stalemate settled across Belgium and north-eastern France, broken by infantry offensives that were unacceptably costly in human lives. Impelled by the idea that, once a breakthrough had been achieved, cavalry would penetrate the breach and 'roll up' the enemy, commanders persisted in throwing attack upon attack against near impervious defences. The Western Front became a giant killing ground, the mud often churned to liquid by the density of artillery fire.

It was in this situation that the tank was conceived and built, its purpose to cross the trenches and penetrate enemy lines. With caterpillar tracks, tanks could indeed cross formidable obstacles, while their armour would keep out small-arms fire, and cannon or machine-guns mounted in the hulls fired back. In time, it had an impact on the course of events on the Western Front, but it was only in World War II that it came of age. Between the wars, such theorists as Fuller, Liddell Hart, Guderian and de Gaulle argued that the tank should be the cutting edge for an attacking army, rather than deployed as infantry support. In this role it brought manoeuvre, shock and speed back into warfare, the German blitzkrieg campaigns in Poland, Belgium, France and Russia demonstrating that properly used tanks were decisive weapons. Since then the tank has been an essential element of land warfare. During World War II the threat of anti-tank artillery was met by heavier armour, and by the time of the epic Battle of Kursk in 1943 each side was fielding thousands of armoured fighting vehicles.

In the last half of the twentieth century the tank has become increasingly sophisticated, with computerised armament able to lock on to targets despite the vehicle's manoeuvres across rough terrain; and modern communications systems have made possible improved coordination of attack. However, the threat from the skies – from jets with 'smart' weapons, attack helicopters that can rise from behind cover to unleash missiles and such aircraft as the heavily armoured A-10 'tankbuster' – many have begun to predict that the tank is obsolete.

WAR AT SEA

For almost four and a half of the millennia covered in this timechart, warships depended on oars for propulsion. During the Ancient period, the Greeks developed a warship that has been considered a classic in ship design: the trireme. Three banks of oars enabled these long, narrow ships to attain bursts of high speed, and the principal method of attack was to ram an opponent. The bows of the ship were sharp and heavily reinforced so as to pierce the side of the victim. This was characteristic of such sea battles from Salamis to Actium and beyond, the ships themselves becoming larger and more powerful over the centuries. However, these were not ocean-going ships, and no complete ancient warship has ever been discovered by archaeologists. Much of the design remains a mystery, but during the 1980s an Anglo-Greek team reconstructed a trireme, using evidence from pottery, bas reliefs, archaeological evidence and the writings of the ancient historians; the result was a convincing warship, but much detail remains conjectural.

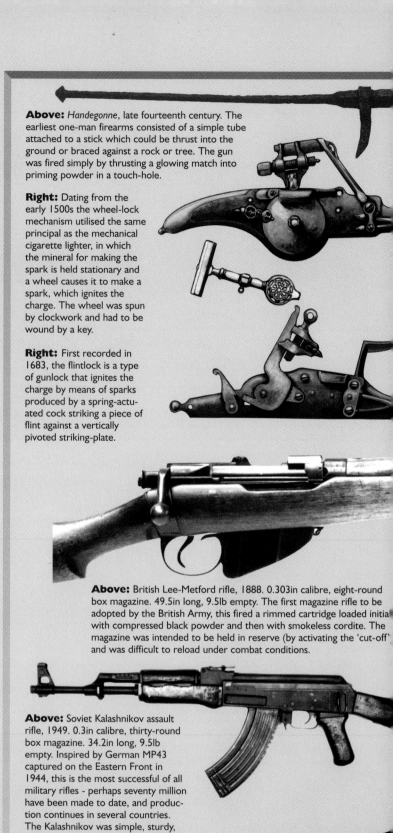

Above: *Handegonne*, late fourteenth century. The earliest one-man firearms consisted of a simple tube attached to a stick which could be thrust into the ground or braced against a rock or tree. The gun was fired simply by thrusting a glowing match into priming powder in a touch-hole.

Right: Dating from the early 1500s the wheel-lock mechanism utilised the same principal as the mechanical cigarette lighter, in which the mineral for making the spark is held stationary and a wheel causes it to make a spark, which ignites the charge. The wheel was spun by clockwork and had to be wound by a key.

Right: First recorded in 1683, the flintlock is a type of gunlock that ignites the charge by means of sparks produced by a spring-actuated cock striking a piece of flint against a vertically pivoted striking-plate.

Above: British Lee-Metford rifle, 1888. 0.303in calibre, eight-round box magazine. 49.5in long, 9.5lb empty. The first magazine rifle to be adopted by the British Army, this fired a rimmed cartridge loaded initial with compressed black powder and then with smokeless cordite. The magazine was intended to be held in reserve (by activating the 'cut-off' and was difficult to reload under combat conditions.

Above: Soviet Kalashnikov assault rifle, 1949. 0.3in calibre, thirty-round box magazine. 34.2in long, 9.5lb empty. Inspired by German MP43 captured on the Eastern Front in 1944, this is the most successful of all military rifles - perhaps seventy million have been made to date, and production continues in several countries. The Kalashnikov was simple, sturdy, efficient and comparatively unsophisticated: an ideal recipe for success. Though accuracy was poor at distances greater than 500 metres, the bullet still retained more than enough energy to kill.

Above: US Garand rifle, 1936. 0.3in calibre, eight-round box magazine. 43.5in long, 9.5lb The 'Rifle M1', better known as the 'Garand', the first semi-automatic to be issued in large numbers. The special cartridge-clip prevented cartridges being loaded singly into the magazin American infantrymen equipped with the Gara had an advantage over their opponents.

SMALL-ARMS

Above: British 'India Pattern Brown Bess', 1802. 0.75in calibre, single shot. 55.5in long, 10.3lb empty. The mainstay of the British infantryman from the campaigns of Marlborough to Waterloo, targets more than 100 yards away were almost impossible to hit unless a volley was fired by flintlock muskets of this general type.

Above: British Enfield rifle-musket, 1853. 0.577in calibre, single shot. 55in long, 8.5lb empty. Similar mechanically to the Brown Bess, misfires were greatly reduced by waterproof percussion caps. Pointed self-expanding bullets extended the effective range and allowed hits to be made at 1,000 yards.

Above: Prussian Dreyse needle rifle, 1860. 0.607in calibre, single shot. 51.2in long, 10.4lb empty. The Prussian army had adopted the Dreyse 'door bolt' breechloading needle rifle in 1840 and had proved its value in battle many times by the time other European armies began to adopt breechloaders of their own.

Above: German Mauser rifle, 1898. 0.311in calibre, five-round box magazine. 49.2in long, 9lb empty. This rejected the compromises popular in Britain and France in the 1890s. The magazine was varied entirely within the stock, the notion of a 'cut off' was rejected, and the gun could be reloaded through the top of the action merely by pressing down with the thumb on a charger-full of cartridges.

Right: Belgian FN Minimi, 1975 0.223in calibre, belt or thirty-round box feed. 40.9in long,15.2lb empty. The Minimi marks a return to the light machine-gun concept pioneered by the Lewis and the Bren. It can be mounted on a tripod and fed with belts, and has a readily exchangeable barrel to allow fire to be sustained. It can also be fitted with a magazine.

Lower right: Maxim Guns, c. 1893. The first automatic machine-gun Maxims have slaughtered millions of men. Designed by an American and subsequently used throughout the world, the Maxim will fire continuously as long the trigger is pressed and ammunition remains in the belt. The one shown here is German, World War I vintage

Above: German Maschinengewehr 42, 1942 0.311in calibre, belt feed. 43in long, 25.5lb empty. Characterised by a high rate of fire which sounded like 'ripping linoleum', this influential and reliable weapon left an indelible impression on those who faced it and pointed to the future of gun-making technology. It was made by production methods which included metal-stamping and welding.

Above: The Heckler and Koch MP5 machine pistol. A favourite of many of the world's police and special forces, this 9mm calibre weapon is one of the most versatile in the world today.

ARMOURED FIGHTING VEHICLE

Above: A typical British tank of World War I, a Mark IV machine-gun armed female, seen in 1917 tackling a slope. The male version was armed with one 6pdr gun in each of two sponsons. Even though slow and vulnerable, these tanks led the way in breaking the stalemate of trench warfare.

Below: Based on the civilian motor-car, a 1920 pattern Rolls-Royce armoured car. Rolls-Royce armoured cars saw extensive use during World War I and the interwar period, with a few remaining in service during the early stages of World War II.

Top right: The principal armoure troop carrier of the US Army and A during World War II, the M3 half-tra This highly successful vehicle can stil found in service in some corners of world, over 50 years after first seein service.

Above: An American M113 armou personnel carrier seen here in Germ service. First entering service in the early 1960s, the M113 is still widely nearly 40 years later, seeing use with 40 countries.

Left: The American Sherman tank the most widely produced and used of the American, British and Wester Allied forces of World War II. Show is a British variant, the Sherman 'Fire armed with the long-barrelled 17pd tank gun.

: Soviet T-54/55 tanks have seen
nsive combat around the world, from
ighting of the Hungarian uprising in
to Kosovo in 1999. Produced in
y variants and in numerous countries,
e of the T-54/55 have been made than
other tank in the post-war world.

ove: The American built M-60 tank
ed the back-bone of the US Army's
forces in the 1960s and 1970s, and is
n service with a number of countries

to date. The Israeli M-60 seen here has
been up-armoured with hi-tech reactive
armour.

Below: Arguably the best tank in the world
today, an American M1 Abrams training in
the USA. During the Gulf War of 1991 the
Abrams proved to be far superior to the
Soviet-built tanks deployed against it. Only a
handful of Abrams were disabled by enemy
action and no crewmen were killed, while
they knocked out hundreds of Iraqi tanks.

The trireme was essentially the warship of the Greek democracies. The galleys of Rome were propelled by slave rowers, and, with the invention of boarding ramps, offensive action depended less upon ramming, the Romans effectively turning sea battles into extensions of war on land.

Slave-propelled galleys remained typical of most navies until the sixteenth century, when the advent of gunpowder revolutionised war at sea just as it did land warfare. Lepanto in 1571 was the last of the great sea battles fought with galleys; seventeen years later the Spanish Armada was a very different type of naval action, fought between fully ocean-going ships propelled by sails and armed with rows of cannon. About the twelfth century, the compass had been discovered, enabling ships to venture more confidently across the seas. By the sixteenth century the earth was being circumnavigated, and war could now be projected across the oceans.

For three and a half centuries, sailing warships ruled the seas, battles and individual combats being characterised by much manoeuvre until the enemies came within cannon range – a few hundred yards – and proceeded to blast broadsides into each others' hulls. Battles between navies were characterised by great fleets in line ahead, carefully manoeuvring to gain advantage and bring the greatest possible number of guns to bear on the enemy.

Trans-oceanic war enabled the conquest of great empires across the globe, wars in Europe now continuing in North America, the Caribbean, India and across the trade routes. By the middle of the nineteenth century, sail power gave way to steam, and the iron-hulled, steam-powered warship, equipped with breech-loading, high velocity weapons, ushered in the age of the battleship. Britain's launch of *Dreadnought* in 1906 set in train a new arms race, and battleships became ever bigger and more powerfully armed. The 18,000-ton *Dreadnought* mounted ten 12-inch guns; during World War II the Japanese had two 70,000-ton giants with nine 18-inch guns.

The age of the battleship did not last long. At sea, as on land, new factors were at hand. Mines and torpedoes were cheap to make and very effective against expensive battleships. Torpedoes fired from submarines brought a new menace to surface fleets as they did to merchantmen. In both World wars, a vast battle was waged across the North Atlantic as Germany's U-boats sought to cut off the supplies to Britain of food, fuel, munitions and men from America.

Most dramatically, it was from the air that came the greatest threat. Aircraft carriers developed between the two wars and during World War II usurped the battleship's place as the capital ship of the world's fleets. The turning-point Battle of Midway in 1942 was fought between fleets that never came within visual distance – they exchanged aerial attacks over a distance of over 100 miles. Air power now dominates sea warfare as it does war on land. The United States, the remaining world superpower, can project its military might across the world by means of vastly powerful carrier battle groups, developed from the great fleets of the World War II in the Pacific. It was from such fleets that the US launched part of the aerial bombardments of Iraq in 1991 and Kosovo in 1999.

MILITARY AVIATION

The impact of aviation has altered warfare almost out of recognition over the last three-quarters of a century. Flight was in its infancy as World War I began, and aircraft were initially deployed for reconnaissance purposes. The elimination of the enemy's reconnaissance aircraft immediately became a prime concern, and the fighter aircraft was the result. The first aerial combats took place between slow aircraft whose pilots sporting pistols and rifles. Machine-guns mounted behind the pilot and operated by a second aviator followed, but fixed forward-firing machine-guns were the true key to fighter effectiveness. The problem of the propeller obstructing forward fire was solved by Fokker, giving the ability to fire through the propeller arc by means of mechanical synchronisation. This made true aerial combat possible, and a series of fighters with improving performance and armament led to the classic 'dogfights' over the trenches. Aerial 'aces' became skilled at manoeuvre, the highest exponent of this new art being Manfred von Richthofen, who scored 80 kills before being brought down, possibly by ground fire, in 1918.

One vital role for the early fighters was shooting down observation balloons and airships. Propelled lighter-than-air craft were deployed as bombers, Zeppelin raids on England – the first planned use of aircraft against civilians – being seen as barbaric. But it was merely a foretaste of what was to come. Between the wars the bomber was seen as the ultimate weapon, with the idea that 'the bomber will always get through' conjuring up to a terrified populace the vision of cities razed to the ground by fleets of aircraft. It was not as simple as that, but ground-attack would come to dominate World War II. During the blitzkrieg campaigns of 1939–41, the Germans used Stuka dive-bombers as close-support 'aerial artillery' for ground troops. In the Far East, the Japanese used air power from their carriers to strike at Pearl Harbor and pre-emptively cripple the US fleet. As Singapore was about to fall, two British capital ships were sunk by Japanese aircraft, proving beyond doubt that at sea as well as on land, air power was now the dominant arm.

Over Europe, bombers struck military and civilian installations indiscriminately, attacked and protected by swarms of fighters, and by the end of the war the Mustang provided the Allies with a long-range fighter that could accompany the bombers on the longest of bombing penetrations. The last, dramatic act of the war came from the air when atomic bombs dropped on two cities finally induced the Japanese to desist in their fanatical resistance to the overwhelming military might of the USA.

The Cold War between the Eastern bloc and the Western powers saw the construction of nuclear bombs sufficient to destroy humanity several times over. The addition of technology developed initially by the Germans as a last-ditch attempt to stave off defeat – the V-2 missile – gave the world the inter-continental ballistic missile, each side targeting the other's cities in a deterrent stand-off. Missiles were, and still are, deployed in land-based silos and at sea in nuclear submarines, each with awesome destructive potential. During the last decades of the twentieth century, however, the Cold War ended; agreements were reached to limit nuclear weapons and the testing of warheads. But many of these terrible weapons remain in being, and nuclear weapons are no longer restricted to the Superpowers.

Air power remains dominant, however. The USA's great aircraft carriers can deploy rapidly to any part of the world, bringing to bear weaponry that is generally far in advance of the potential enemy's. Air power, with new 'smart' weapons and cruise missiles, demonstrated its worth in the Gulf War of 1991 and again in Kosovo in 1999.

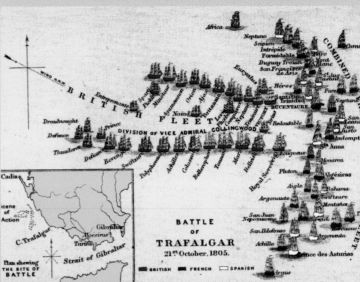

Top: A bas relief of two biremes (each equipped with two banks of oars) from the an⋅ Roman period.

Above: The British victory over the Franco/Spanish fleet at the Battle of Trafalgar, 21 October 1805. One of the most decisive naval victories in history, it secured world supremacy for the British for over a century.

Below: The British-built armoured cruiser *Asama* of the Japanese Navy at the turn of century. It was with ships such as this that Japan defeated Russia during the Russo-Japan War.

Right: Modern submarines, both conventional (diesel/electric) and nuclear powered, have the distinctive teardrop-shaped hull. This is the USS *Blue Back*, one of the last co⋅ tional powered submarines to see service with the US Navy whose submarine fleet is completely nuclear powered.

WARSHIPS

Top: HMS *Hood*, seen here in August 1939, was the pride of the Royal Navy and considered to be one of the most powerful warships in the world. Sadly she was sunk less than two years after this photograph was taken, by the German battleship *Bismarck*.

Above left: German Type VII U-boats seen here after the surrender at the close of World War II. These excellent submarines nearly brought Britain to her knees during the Battle of the Atlantic.

Right: An American Poseidon missile being test launched from a submarine. The successor to the Polaris, missiles such as these maintained the balance of power during the Cold War.

Below: The Aegis-equipped missile cruiser USS *Ticonderoga*, intended to provide anti-aircraft defence for modern carrier battle groups.

NAVAL AIR POWER

Left: Originally a merchant ship, the World War I HMS *Pegasus* was an early 'aircraft carrier'. Here she launches a biplane. Even though she could launch her wheeled aircraft from her short flight deck successfully she did not have the ability to retrieve them - they had to head for shore. But she could operate and retrieve seaplanes.

Above: The US Navy's Douglas Dauntless dive-bomber. In action from the very outset of the Pacific war in World War II, these aircraft participated in all the major battles, dealing the death blows to the Japanese carriers during the crucial US victory at the Battle of Midway, June 1942, and subsequently until the Battle of the Philippine Sea, June 1944.

Left: USS *Essex*, name ship of the excellent class of World War II fleet carriers. Of the 24 ships completed during the early/mid-1940s, six were still retained by the US Navy in the early 1980s, a superb commendation.

Upper right: The escort carrier USS *Croaton* in 1944. Developed during World War II, escort carriers were probably more responsible than any other agency in defeating the submarine menace.

Upper left: Purchased by Canada from the UK in 1952, HMCS *Bonaventure* is seen here in the late 1960s. This class of carrier proved to be very successful during the immediate post-war decades, serving with a number of navies.

Above: The nuclear powered fleet carrier USS *Nimitz*, the ultimate representation of global power projection. Approaching 100,000 tons displacement, these massive ships can each carry nearly 100 of the most capable combat aircraft in the world.

Left: An F-4 Phantom of the US Navy on board USS *Saratoga*, 1964. The Phantom has been one of the most successful combat aircraft of the post-war period, having seen combat from the Vietnam War of the 1960s to the Gulf War of 1991.

TIMECHART

WARS AND BATTLES FROM 3000 BC TO THE PRESENT

The diagram on the following pages presents more than 1,000 wars and their associated battles from the beginnings of recorded history some 5,000 years ago to the present. The dateline is shown at the top and the bottom, and events run laterally, from left to right. Gatefolds on the right-hand pages provide continuity from one spread to the next.

Wars are depicted by deep red bars, battles by crossed swords. For the earlier periods, major states and empires are also shown, as are significant rulers, statesmen and warriors, enabling the reader to view the context of wars and battles within the overall political situation. During these earlier centuries, especially the third and second millennia BC, dates are often uncertain. The reader should, in almost all cases here, insert a mental *circa* before the dates.

The chronological timeline does not run at a consistent pace throughout the diagram. Events move more quickly and more densely in the modern world, so that the later centuries have been given more space. Subject matter, broadly, runs as follows:

3000–500 BC The Ancient world and the great empires of Egypt, Assyria and Persia
500–1 BC The Classical Age of the Greeks and the Roman Republic
AD 1–600 The Roman Empire and its decline and fall
600–1100 The Dark Ages, the Carolingan Empire, the estab-lishment of the Holy Roman Empire and, above all, the impact of the Islamic conquests
1100–1600 The Middle Ages and the Renaissance
1600–1700 From the Thirty Years War to the wars of Louis XIV
1700–1800 Europe's wars of succession, conflict in North America and the French Revolutionary Wars
1800–1900 From the Age of Napoleon to the eve of World War I
1900–1999 The century of World Wars and technological revolution

For context, the historical flowlines have been divided into seven areas of the world:

- **The Americas:** North and South America, including the Caribbean
- **Europe**, including Russia
- **The Middle East:** For contextual reasons, this has been extended to include North Africa and parts of Central Asia, as far as Samarkand and the distant junction with the westernmost extent of China
- **South-East Asia:** The area south of modern China and east of India, including, for context, Australasia and the islands of the central Pacific
- **India:** Including Pakistan, Bangladesh and Sri Lanka
- **China and Japan:** Including Manchuria and Korea
- **Africa** south of the Sahara

KEY TO GEOGRAPHICAL DIVISIONS

HILL FORTS IN WEST

'OLD PALACE' PERIOD   'NEW PALACE' PERIOD   1450-1400 MYCENAEANS MAY HAVE   GREAT INVASIONS OF PE
TAKEN CONTROL OF CRETE   THESSALY, BOE

CRETE   **MINOAN CIVILISATION**   1370 DESTRUCTION OF KNOSSOS

CRETE THE LEADING POWER IN THE AEGEAN   COLLAPSE OF MYCENAE
CIVILISATION BY 1150

GREECE   **MYCENAEAN CIVILISATION**   DESTRUCTION OF
MYCENAEAN CENTRES

GREAT AGE OF MYCENAE

JERICHO IS THE EARLIEST KNOWN FORTIFIED
CITY, DATED VARIOUSLY FROM C. 6800 TO AS
EARLY AS 9000 BC. ITS WALLS WERE FAMOUSLY
BROUGHT DOWN BY JOSHUA'S INVADING
HEBREWS IN THE MID-13TH CENTURY BC

C.2300 FULL EUROPEAN   C. 1700-1200 HEIGHT OF   WARRIOR LEADERS CONSOLIDATE THEIR   ISTHMUS OF CORINTH
BRONZE AGE BEGINS   BRONZE AGE   POWER. SEA-BORNE RAIDS   FORTIFIED AGAINST
NORTHERN INVADERS

Assyrian King   SIEGE OF TROY (ILIAD) POSSIBLY
Tiglath-   DURING THESE CENTURIES
Pileser in war
chariot   1180 PHRYGIANS INVADE
ASIA MINOR

A DOZEN CITY STATES INCLUDING KISH, ERECH,   Assyrian   GREAT INVASIONS INCLUDING POSSIBL
UR, LAGASH COMPETE FOR DOMINATION   2050-1950 UR RECONSTRUCTS THE   turreted   PEOPLES FORMERLY IDENTIFIED BY HI
SUMER-AKKAD EMPIRE   battering ram   'SEA PEOPLES' CAUSE WIDESPREAD D
LAGASH   attacking city   AND FRAGMENTATION THROUGHOUT T
walls   WESTERN WORLD

SUMER   OVERTHROWN BY
ELAMITES AND
KISH   AMORITES - WARRING   1390 - 1364:
WARRING   **AKKAD** **UR**   CITY STATES AGAIN   ERIBA-ADAD WINS   1272-1243:
CITY   URUK   1800: ASSYRIANS   ASSYRIAN INDEPENDENCE   SHALMANESER I
STATES   CONQUER N. BABYLONIANS   FROM MITANNI   BEGINS ASSYRIAN   **ASSYRIA**
EXPANSION AND
CONQUERS
MITANNI

TWO CENTURIES OF CITY-STATE ANARCHY   BY 1450 ASSYRIANS BECOME
VASSALS OF MITANNI

2800   2600   2300-2200   EXPANSION OF UR   1242-1206:   1114-1076:
KISH   URUK   AKKAD - SARGON I   **OLD**   MITANNI   TIKULTI-NINURTA I EXPANDS SOUTH   TIGLATH-PILES
UNITES   OVERTURNS   CONQUERS MESOPOTAMIA, SYRIA, PART OF ASIA   **ASSYRIAN**   DECLINE OF ASSYRIA   BECOMES BUFFER   AND TEMPORARILY (C. 1210) TAKES   ASSYRIAN CON
CITY   KISH   MINOR - THE FIRST GREAT CONQUEROR   **EMPIRE**   STATE BETWEEN   BABYLON   MEDITERRANE
STATES   ASSYRIAN WARS OF CONQUEST   HITTITES AND
GUTI FROM IRAN DESTROY THE   1500:   ASSYRIANS   **ELAM**
AKKADIAN EMPIRE 2150-2050 - THEN   HURRIANS
c. 3000   ARE EXPELLED BY ERECH AND URUK   1747-1717: SHAMSHI-ADAD I WARS   UNITE AS   1124-1103
BEGINNING   OF CONQUEST   MITANNI   1380-1340:   NEBUCHADNEZ
OF THE BRONZE   2270-2230   SUPPILULIAMUS CONQUERS MITANNI   DEFEATS ELAM
AGE   NARAM-SIN RENEWS   **MIDDLE EAST**   C. 1360
AKKADIAN VIGOUR   1190 - 1150:
HITTITE KINGDOM
LATE 3RD MILLENIUM   1620-1590   OVERTHROWN BY
HURRIANS INFILTRATE N.   Hittite   MURSILIS I - 3RD KING OF   PHRYGIANS,
Egyptian Spearmen   MESOPOTAMIA AND SYRIA   bowman   UNITED HITTITE STATE   **HITTITE NEW**   LUVIANS ETC.
FROM THE NORTH
KINGDOM   1200-900 G
1ST HITTITE   HITTITE COLLAPSE ON   2ND HITTITE
EMPIRE   DEATH OF MURSILIS   EMPIRE

MURSILIS DESTROYS ALEPPO,   HITTITE WARS OF   SYRIA   1180s PHILISTINES
RAIDS BABYLON, DEFEATS   CONQUEST   OVERRUN PALESTINE
WARS OF MURSILIS   HURRIANS ON THE EUPHRATES

RISE OF BABYLON TO   1650   FRAGMENTATION OF   1275 QADESH   MID-13TH CENTURY   **PHILIS**
BECOME THE MAIN   KASSITE KINGS   MESOPOTAMIA INTO   FIRST BATTLE IN HISTORY TO   CONQUEST OF
POLITICAL AND   AREAS DOMINATED BY   BE RECORDED IN DETAIL   PALESTINE BY HEBREWS
CULTURAL CENTRE IN   **BABYLON**   HURRIANS, KASSITES   RAMSES II AND MUWATALLI FIGHT AN   - WARS OF JOSHUA   1025-1006 WARS OF
SOUTHERN   AND 'SEALAND' IN THE   INCONCLUSIVE BATTLE A TREATY
MESOPOTAMIA   DECLINE   SOUTH   c. 1263-1258 DIVIDES PALESTINE &
SYRIA BETWEEN EGYPT AND HATTI   **ISRA**
ONGOING WARS WITH KASSITES AND HURRIANS   1427-1400
AMENHOTEP II CAMPAIGNS TO NORTH
1760   1728-1686   OF BYBLOS AND DAMASCUS
KASSITES ENTER   AMORITE HAMMURABI CONQUERS   LATE 16TH CENTURY THUTMOSIS I   BY THE REIGN OF
Egyptian   MESOPOTAMIA INTRODUCING   SOUTHERN MESOPOTAMIA,   DEFEATS HITTITES ON THE EUPHRATES   WARS OF IMPERIAL EGYPT   RAMSES VI (1143-1136)
archers at Deir   HORSE AND CHARIOT   UNITING THE MAIN SIX STATES   EGYPT HAS LOST ITS
el-Bahari   THUTMOSE III   1400-1390 CAMPAIGNS OF THUTMOSIS IV   PALESTINE DOMINIONS
1830   FIGHTS 17   ENDS WITH TREATY WITH MITANNI
SENUSRET III CAMPAIGNS   HYKSOS ENTER NORTH EGYPT IN 18TH CENTURY AND TAKE   CAMPAIGNS INTO   1180-1177 MERENPTAH REPU
TO THE NORTH OF   CONTROL MID-17TH CENTURY. CAPITAL: AVARIS. THEY BRING   PALESTINE   INVASIONS FROM LIBYA AND
BY 2900 NARMER OR   JERUSALEM   TECHNOLOGY OF THE HORSE IN WAR - WITH CHARIOTS, THE   1457 MEGIDDO. THUTMOSIS III DEFEATS   1294-1279 SETI I   PEOPLES' RAIDING ALONG TH
AHA BECOMES KING   COMPOUND BOW, BATTLEAXES AND SKILL IN FORTIFICATION.   CANAANITES AND THEIR ALLIES AND   CAMPAIGNS IN   AND INTO THE NILE DELTA
OF ALL EGYPT.   ADVANCES NORTH TO GALILEE   PALESTINE
CAPITAL: MEMPHIS   **HYKSOS**

1304-1237 RAMSES II
MONJUNOTEP II REUNITES EGYPT   2ND INTERMEDIATE   THE GREAT
PERIOD. EGYPT   1521 HYKSOS
DIVIDED INTO 3   CAPITAL AVARIS
EGYPTIAN   **EGYPTIAN MIDDLE**   GRADUAL   STATES: THEBES, KUSH   FALLS TO THE   **EGYPTIAN EMPIRE**
DISINTEGRATION   AND THE NORTH,   EGYPTIANS
OLD KINGDOM   **KINGDOM**   INTO KINGDOMS OF   CONTROLLED BY THE
AVARIS, THEBES, KUSH   HYKSOS   BY NOW, NUBIAN GOLD (REASON FOR EGYPTIAN
1993 FORTIFICATION   IMPERIALISM TO THE SOUTH) IS EXHAUSTED
OF FIRST AND 2ND CATARACTS

2200 PEPYNAKHT CAMPAIGNS   THEBAN REVOLT   THUTMOSIS III EXTENDS
AGAINST NUBIA   EGYPTIAN CONTROL SOUTH
1573-1550 AHMOSIS   TO 4TH CATARACT
2900 AHA   2064-1990 THEBES   1919-1903   1829-1818 SENUSRET III   EXPELS HYKSOS AND   1184-1153 RAMSES III REPULSES   1087 PAN
ATTACKS   CONQUERS WAWAT   SENUSRET I GAINS   CAMPAIGNS BEYOND 2ND   PURSUES THEM INTO   INVADERS FROM THE SAHARA: NUBIA IN
NUBIA   AND   CONTROL OF WAWAT   CATARACT AND BUILDS A   PALESTINE   DEPICTED ON BAS-RELIEFS AS A   TEMPORA
UPPER EGYPT   (NORTH NUBIA)   SECOND SERIES OF FORTS   NAVAL BATTLE   OCCUPIES
IN 1080 H
SEPARATE
EGYPT

ABOUT 2150   1937-1908
DEATH OF PEPY   AMENEMHAT I BUILDS
II, LAST OF 6TH   THE 'WALLS OF THE
DYNASTY, ENDS   RIVER' FORTIFICATIONS
OLD KINGDOM   ABOUT SUEZ

1500 VEDIC AGE BEGINS
INDUS VALLEY   AFTER 2000 AND BY 1750   INDO-EUROPEAN TRIBES ENTER PUNJAB - SEMI-NOMAD PASTURALIST AND TRIBAL SOCIETIES LED BY
BEGINS   HARAPPAN CULTURE BREAKS   RAJAS (WARRIOR CHIEFS). INTER-TRIBAL CONFLICTS
c. 2500-2300   **HARAPPAN**   DOWN. CITY CIVILISATION
ENDS. CAUSES YET
CIVILISATION   UNKNOWN
MAIN CITIES HARAPPA, MOHENJO-DARO, KALI BANGA. USE OF COPPER AND BRONZE

1500-1200 GANGES VALLEY CIVILISATION

1057 MU Y
OF THE CHOU DECISIVELY DE
CIVILISATION IN THE   AFTER 2500   2200   1760
HUANG HO (YELLOW   WALLED   **YÜ (HSIA OR**
RIVER) VALLEY BY   SETTLEMENTS   **XIA) DYNASTY**   **SHANG(YIN) DYNASTY**   **W**
ABOUT 3000
CONQUER AREA BETWEEN YELLOW RIVER AND YANGTSE

BRONZE AGE IN CHINA   1523 MING CHIAO. SEMI-LEGENDARY SHAO DYNASTY   c.1100 REVOLT AGAINST LAS
DEFEATED AND ELIMINATED BY SHANG   OF THE YIN DYNASTY

Chester William Nimitz (b.1884–1966)

America's greatest admiral, who directed the massive drive across the Pacific to victory against the Japanese in the Second World War. The early part of his career was in submarines, which provided him with the understanding of an element of warfare that would prove crucial during the war – during his command in the Pacific he waged an unrestricted submarine campaign against Japanese merchantmen that crippled the logistics of their wide-spread maritime empire and restricted the deployment of their battlefleet. After the Japanese strike on Pearl Harbor in December 1942 (which he viewed as less of a disaster than many of his colleagues) he was appointed Commander-in-Chief of the US Pacific Fleet. In December 1942 he became C-in-C Pacific Ocean Area, commanding all forces, air, land and sea, for the direct thrust across the Pacific that complemented MacArthur's advance from New Guinea to the Philippines. Making best possible use of ULTRA decrypts, to the value of which he was an early convert, he directed the amphibious landings across the ocean (Tarawa, Kwajalein, Eniwetok, Saipan, Guam, Pelelieu, Iwo Jima, Okinawa). These were often hard-fought battles against fanatical opposition. In support of the Philippine landings, he directed the epic Battle of Leyte Gulf (from Pearl Harbor, a vast distance in pre-satellite days).

George Smith Patton (b.1995–1945)

America's favourite tank general, a charismatic, vigorous but controversial general dubbed by his men 'Old Blood and Guts'. He entered the US cavalry in 1909 and represented his country at the 1912 Olympics. In 1916 he took part in the punitive raid into Mexico and in 1917 joined Pershing's staff on the Western Front. A cavalryman through and through, he immediately saw the significance of the tank and became a vigorous proponent of armoured warfare, of which he became one of the leading exponents. Following the 'Torch' landings, he commanded Western Task Force in North Africa then US II Corps, following the Kasserine disaster. As commander of US Seventh Army, his exploits in Sicily – a dramatic and unplanned thrust to Palermo and Messina before Montgomery arrived – earned him a reputation as a daring, aggressive leader, but his verbal and physical abuse of soldiers suffering from combat exhaustion revealed a darker side to his character and almost ended his military career. As commander of US Third Army, he led the right-flank of the breakout from the Normandy beachhead and advanced across France with spectacular speed, being slowed only by logistics. His redeployment to strike at the southern flank of the German 'bulge' during the Ardennes offensive was brilliant, and his army crossed the Rhine at Mainz and Oppenheim in March 1945. Third Army thereafter sped across southern Germany, ending the war in Czechoslovakia. Shortly after the cessation of hostilities Patton again committed an indiscretion in advocating the employment of ex-Nazi officials in the new administration, and he was relieved of his command. Volatile and pugnacious, he was often unadvisedly outspoken, but his battlefield accomplishments speak for themselves. He died as a result of a minor traffic accident in December 1945.

Erwin Johannes Eugen Rommel (b.1891–1944)

The 'Desert Fox', master of mobile warfare and charismatic leader of armoured troops. Rommel won Prussia's highest decoration, the Pour le Mérite, during the First World War and published *Infantry Attacks* in 1937. He became commander of Hitler's security unit and then made his reputation as commander of 7th Panzer Division during the campaign in the west in 1940. The following year he was appointed to command the German expeditionary force to prop up the Italian régime in North Africa, and, disobeying orders, launched an attack that all but ejected the British from Cyrenaica. His Afrika Korps successfully repulsed two British attacks ('Brevity' and 'Battleaxe') but was forced back to its starting position by 'Crusader' in November 1941. Reinforced, he attacked again in January 1942, capturing Tobruk after an epic battle at Gazala, and pursued the British into Egypt. He was halted at El Alamein; repulsed at Alam Halfa; and defeated by Montgomery's superior forces at Second El Alamein in November. Retreating to Tunisia, to join German reinforcements, he won a tactical success at Kasserine but was repulsed in the Medenine battle, a failed sortie from his Mareth Line defences. From March to May 1943 he was on sick leave but was then sent to take control of the occupation of northern Italy after the Italian surrender to the Allies. He was then placed in charge of the forces defending the coast of north-west France, where he warned the High Command of the need to push an Allied landing immediately back into the sea or risk complete failure. During the Battle for Normandy, he was severely wounded in an air attack (17 July). Implicated in the July bomb plot against Hitler, he was subsequently forced to commit suicide. He remains a legendary figure, seen by the Allies as a chivalric and a worthy opponent. The deserts of North Africa gave him the ideal theatre for demonstrating his great gifts as an audacious commander of armoured troops who led from the front.

H. Norman Schwarzkopf (b.1934)

The first great commander of the 'television age'. Schwarzkopf was highly decorated for his service in Vietnam (1965–6, 1969–70). Rising through the ranks, he commanded the ground forces involved in the invasion of Grenada in 1986. After the Iraqi invasion of Kuwait in 1990, he directed the massive multinational build-up of forces and led them to victory in Operation 'Desert Storm' in February 1991. A natural communicator whose character and charisma immediately won him worldwide fame, he brought to bear a deep understanding of military history and strategy to win a major coalition army victory with minimal casualties.

Isoroku Yamamoto (b.1884–1943)

The man who planned and executed the notorious raid on Pearl Harbor. Yamamoto served in the Russo-Japanese War and was wounded at the battle of Tsushima, losing two fingers from his left hand. Between the wars he studied English at Boston and gained a poor opinion of the US Navy but not of American power. Returning to Japan, he became one of the country's principal experts on military aviation, championing the aircraft carrier as the main naval weapon rather than the battleship, which, he said, was as useful in modern warfare as a samurai sword. He was, however, no warmonger and opposed Japan's bellicose stance, which led to a plot to assassinate him in 1939. In that year he became commander of the Japanese Combined Fleet. If there had to be war, he saw Japan's only hope in a pre-emptive strike at the American fleet. This he planned and carried out with spectacular success. A string of victories followed until the disaster at Midway and Guadalcanal, the naval element of which he directed personally. He was killed on 18 April 1943 when his aircraft was intercepted by US fighters, forewarned by ULTRA decrypts of his flight plan.

possible swift mobile thrusts. Hitler saw the potential and appointed him chief of mobile troops in 1938, in which position he created three armoured divisions. He commanded XIX Panzer Corps in the Polish campaign of 1939, and the western campaign in Belgium and France the following spring. The new blitzkrieg techniques, which also incorporated the use of dive-bombers, was spectacularly successful. In the Russian campaign he commanded 2nd Panzer Group, but fell foul of Hitler after criticising his failure to follow up the initial success by striking directly at Moscow. When he wanted to make a tactical withdrawal Hitler sacked him. In March 1943 he was recalled to become Inspector of Armoured Forces, but again fell out with Hitler and was dismissed after finding the Führer's interference in his activities insupportable. A general of outstanding strategic and tactical vision, his contribution to the development of armoured warfare was crucial.

Douglas, 1st Earl Haig (b.1861–1928)

Principal British land forces commander during the First World War. He fought in the Omdurman campaign of 1898 and in the Boer War of 1899–1902. On the outbreak of war he commanded I Corps, becoming C-in-C First Army in 1915 and then Commander-in-Chief of the British Expeditionary Force at the end of that year. He worked well with Foch during the last year of the war, but his reputation has always been controversial in the light of the devastating number of casualties suffered during the offensives on the Somme in particular. The Somme offensives were, in fact, to relieve pressure on the French at Verdun, but criticism has focused upon the prolonging of these offensives long after – in hindsight – they had proved to have failed. His order of the day to the troops facing the Kaiserschlacht offensive in 1918 is justly famous: 'With our backs to the wall, and believing in the justice of our cause, each one of us must fight on to the end…' In recent years historians have re-evaluated Haig's generalship, and have begun to portray him in a more favourable light. Increasingly he is credited with turning the British Army by 1918 into a superbly trained and equipped war-winning force.

Erich Ludendorff (b.1865–1937)

Strategist responsible for the conduct of German arms during the latter part of the First World War. In the pre-war German Army he rose to command a section of the General Staff and participated in the (ultimately disastrous) revision of the Schlieffen Plan for the invasion of France under Moltke the Younger. Shortly before the outbreak of the First World War his association with extreme nationalists threatened his career, but in 1914 he was appointed Chief of Staff to Hindenburg at Eighth Army on the Eastern front. Ludendorff's triumph at Tannenberg brought his senior great acclaim, and the two generals continued to fight the war on the Eastern Front until 1916. In August of that year the failure of the German assaults on Verdun prompted the Kaiser to bring the duo west, where Hindenburg assumed command of all German armed forces. As before, it was Ludendorff who in fact wielded the power and made the decisions. Eventually he staked all on a general offensive in the west, which opened in March 1918 – the Kaiserschlacht battles. It was a close-run thing, but by autumn the German momentum was spent and the Central Powers' last hope of victory had passed. After the war, Ludendorff did much to foster the 'stab in the back' explanation for the German defeat and served as a National Socialist member of parliament (1924–8). In 1918 his mental state had been strained by the stress of his position; in the inter-war years he became decidedly eccentric in his views, writing in 1935 (in a reversal of Clausewitz) that peace was merely an interval in the natural state of war.

Douglas MacArthur (b.1880–1964)

One of the most controversial generals of the US Army. He graduated with the highest marks ever recorded at West Point and ended the First World War as a highly decorated brigadier. Between the wars he served as Army Chief of Staff (1930), and in 1935 was military advisor in the Philippines, after which he retired in 1937. In July 1941 he was recalled to become commander of US forces in the Far East, just in time to be defeated by the Japanese invasion of December that year. Retreating to Bataan and Corregidor, he was ordered to escape, uttering the famous promise, 'I shall return.' In April 1942 he commanded South West Pacific Area and began an island-hopping offensive that brought US forces back to the Philippines. He took the official surrender of the Japanese aboard USS *Missouri* in Tokyo Bay in September 1945, and thereafter became Supreme Commander Allied Forces, running Japan's transformation to democracy with astonishing success. In 1950 he became Commander-in-Chief of United Nations forces in Korea, stemming the North Korean advance and carrying out a spectacular landing at Inchon to outflank the enemy before driving deep into North Korea. Chinese intervention brought a massive counter-attack that swept the UN forces back south of Seoul, but the line was stabilised farther north. Headstrong and insubordinate, MacArthur refused to countenance Korea as a limited war, and in April 1951 President Truman relieved him of his command. A good planner, and a flamboyant, charismatic personality who knew the value of publicity, MacArthur was also vain, egotistical and contemptuous of his superiors.

Sir Bernard Montgomery, Viscount Montgomery (b.1887–1976)

Principal and most famous British general of the Second World War. Badly wounded in 1914, he was a great student of his profession, dedicating himself to the attainment of victory at the least possible cost in human lives. In 1939 he commanded 3rd Division in the British Expeditionary Force, and after Dunkirk rose rapidly in rank. In August 1942 he was appointed to the command of Eighth Army, facing the triumphant Axis forces of Rommel on the frontier of Egypt. He held Rommel at Alam Halfa; then, patient and careful, insisted on launching an offensive only when he deemed his preparations were fully complete. The result was the victory at El Alamein and the end of the German threat to Egypt. Criticism was made of his pursuit of Rommel to Tunis, but he led Eighth Army through the Tunisian and Sicilian campaigns and into Italy before being appointed land forces commander, under Eisenhower, for the 'Overlord' operation, in December 1943. During the Normandy campaign he was criticised for his difficulty in taking the key town of Caen; and in the subsequent operations in the Low Countries launched the Arnhem airborne operation that ended in failure. By now he had ruffled many feathers among his colleagues and, especially, his American allies, by his conceit and alarming outspokenness. He advocated a narrow-front strategy for the invasion of Germany, but this was rejected by Eisenhower. He took the surrender of enemy forces in north-west Germany at Lüneburg Heath. A great communicator with the ability to inspire his men with confidence, and a great believer in averting casualties, Montgomery's cocky, egocentric character was an unfortunate limitation to his effectiveness as a coalition general.

meet his final defeat at Waterloo. Memoirs written during his years of exile on St Helena helped establish his legend. Beyond that, however, he was a soldier and statesman of towering genius whose impact on the art of war reverberates to this day. Strategically, he emphasised the need to inflict a crushing blow upon an opponent's main army but, rather than being a great innovator, he showed *how* wars should be fought – with speed and decision – and the study of his campaigns and battles resonates with the the intensity of a great mind imposing its will on a volatile and dramatic train of events. Excessive ambition and an inability to recognise the limits of the possible were his undoing. He was very probably murdered, in captivity in the South Atlantic, by the unforgiving Bourbons.

Horatio Nelson, Baron Nelson of the Nile (b.1758–1805)

Arguably the greatest admiral in history, Nelson became a popular hero in his lifetime, and the circumstances of his death at the hour of victory at Trafalgar made him a legend. Entering the Royal Navy in 1770, he fought during the American Revolutionary War in the West Indies. In 1797 he played a crucial part at the Battle of Cape St. Vincent. His great victories began in 1798 at the Nile (Aboukir Bay) where he destroyed Bonaparte's Egyptian invasion fleet. At Copenhagen in 1801 he disobeyed his superior admiral's order and won a victory that effectively ended the anti-British league of Armed Neutrality. At Trafalgar in 1805 he destroyed the combined fleets of France and Spain, the long-term results of which were to establish British naval supremacy for a century. During his career he was badly injured twice, losing the sight of his right eye during operations on Corsica, and losing his right arm at Tenerife in 1797. Laying emphasis especially on individual initiative, his influence on the Royal Navy was profound.

Shaka kaSenzagakhona (c.1787–1828)

Founder of the Zulu empire of the nineteenth century. In 1816 he usurped the chieftaincy of the Zulus and embarked upon wars of conquest with an army that he designed to be the most efficient fighting machine in Africa. Regiments were age-graded (*amabutho*) and made up of conscripts under forty years of age. Drill, discipline and mobility were the hallmarks of Shaka's military system, together with surprise tactics. A favourite stratagem involved encirclement by the *impondo zankomo* ('horns of the beast') attack formation. His conquests over a decade included most of Natal and modern Zululand. Among his principal battles were KwaGqoki (1816), where he survived attack by a superior force of Ndwande; Mhlatuze, when he inflicted the final defeat on the Ndwande, eliminating the last major rival to Zulu supremacy in southern Africa; and inDolowane, in 1826, when he brought an end to the Ndwande kingdom. He was assassinated by his half-brothers in 1828. His legacy was a powerful and proud military nation, which was to make its mark in history in the epic battles of 1879.

Arthur Wellesley, Duke of Wellington (b.1769–1852)

Victor of the Peninsular War, Wellington – the 'Iron Duke' – was rather more than the 'Sepoy General' Napoleon considered him. He made his name in India with victories in the Maratha War at Assaye and Argaon. In 1807 he took part in the Copenhagen expedition, then defeated Junot at Vimiero in Portugal. Returning to Portugal in 1809, he fought a 5-year war to drive the French from the Peninsular. In 1809 he defeated Jourdan at Talavera. Outnumbered by Masséna's army in 1810, he defeated

the French at Busaco before falling back behind his fortified Lines of Torres Vedras north of Lisbon. These foiled the French, who were eventually forced to retreat. In a series of victories – Fuentes de Oñoro (1811), Salamanca (1812) and Vitoria (1813), he drove the French over the Pyrenees, inflicting a final defeat at Toulon in 1814. Despite these huge achievements, he is best remembered for the victory at Waterloo (1815) which brought Napoleon's Hundred Days to an end. In the post-war era he was famous throughout Europe. Less successful was his Prime Ministership of Britain in 1828–30 and his legacy of opposition to the modernisation of the army can be seen to have contributed to the deficiencies made apparent in the British army's performance during the Crimean War. During the Napoleonic Wars however, he proved himself Britain's greatest general since Marlborough. Patience, an eye for terrain and an ability to use British troops in line to destroy attacking French columns were the essentials of his generalship.

Sir Garnet, later Lord, Wolseley (b.1833–1913)

The greatest of Britain's generals during the colonial wars of the nineteenth century. He fought in the Second Burma War, in the Crimea and the Indian Mutiny, where he lost the sight of an eye. In 1870 he led the Red River expedition in Canada; in 1873 the Ashanti campaign; in 1875 the campaign in Natal; and he took command in the later stages of the Anglo–Zulu War of 1879. In 1882 he led the conquest of Egypt, winning the Battle of Tel el-Kebir, and two years later led the abortive Gordon rescue mission to Khartoum. His reforms of the British Army were significant in preparing it for the larger-scale operations of the Second Boer War and the First World War.

GREAT COMMANDERS OF THE TWENTIETH CENTURY

Ferdinand Foch (b.1851–1929)

First World War Commander of Allied Forces from March 1918. An artilleryman, then professor of tactics, he wrote a number of works on the theory and practice of war. In 1914 he commanded XX Corps in Nancy, his tenacity contributing to the victory of the Marne. After two years commanding Northern Army Group, he was made Chief of the general Staff to the French Minister of War, effectively 'advisor' to the Allied armies. He advocated a unified command but was not listened to until the German spring 1918 offensive struck. On 26 March he became generalissimo of the Allied armies to coordinate the Allied armies on the Western Front. In a titanic battle of wills with the effective commander of the German armies, Ludendorff, he reacted to each of the German offensives until, in Champagne, the German offensive ran out of steam. Now it was the Allies' turn to attack, this time advancing until the signing of the Armistice in November 1918. The man who brought the war to a victorious conclusion after four years of practical stalemate, Foch was the greatest French soldier of the twentieth century.

Heinz Wilhelm Guderian (b.1888–1954)

German pioneer of armoured warfare and creator of the blitzkrieg. After service in the First World War, he wrote *Achtung Panzer!* in 1937 advocating the use of tanks as spearhead elements rather than as support for the infantry. In this he incorporated the ideas of other inter-war military theorists, notably Liddell Hart, Fuller and de Gaulle. He realised that the use of radio would facilitate the coordination of tank formations, and proposed that tanks with armoured infantry would make eastern Baltic provinces. With the Knights of the Sword he fought in Estonia, winning control of the area at the Battle of Tallinn. The Danish Empire was now huge; but in 1281 he was surprised and imprisoned by his enemies, with the result that he lost much of the territory he had gained. In 1227 he took the field to restore his empire but met decisive defeat at the battle of Bornhöved in 1227. All prospects of a Danish north German empire were dashed, although he did retain part of Estonia. For a time, however, he had made Denmark the greatest power in the Baltic region.

FROM 1600–1700 BC SPREAD:

Gustavus II Adolphus (1611–1632)

One of the Great Captains of History and often considered the 'father of modern warfare', he created the first truly 'modern' army, which became the model for all the other powers of Europe. Succeeding to the Swedish throne in 1611, he re-organised the country's armed forces, adopting a regional regimental system (supported by mercenaries) and using the Dutch linear tactics to defeat mass tercios. His three-deep infantry formation gave increased flexibility of manoeuvre, combining shock effect with firepower. Shorter (eight-foot) pikes were easier to handle and deploy; lighter muskets with pre-packed cartridges increased the rate of fire. His artillery too became a vital tactical factor on the battlefield: 'leather' guns and light brigade artillery were more mobile and gave close support to the infantry. After early campaigns in the Baltic area, capturing Riga and taking possession of the Prussian ports, he became involved in the Thirty Years War. Breitenfeld (1631) signalled the emergence of Sweden as a major military power; but he met his death at Lützen the following year, at the head of his cavalry.

Maurice, Count of Nassau, Prince of Orange (1587–1625)

One of the major military innovators of his time, Maurice succeeded, in a series of victories, in securing the area that is today the Kingdom of the Netherlands, his campaigns of 1587 to 1609 being remembered in Dutch history as 'the closing of the garden'. In these years he took Sluys (1587), Breda (1590), Zutpen (1591), Nijmegen (1591) and inflicted defeats on the Spanish at Turnhout (1597) and Nieuport (1600). As Stadthouder and Captain-General of the United Provinces (from 1588) he reorganised and revitalised the Dutch army, introducing the battalion (550 men) to face the Spanish tercios, paying his troops properly and instilling improved discipline with regular drill. His scientific methods of siege warfare were based upon sound mathematical and engineering principles in a period when firearms and artillery were fast coming of age. The results of his campaigns were the recognition of the Netherlands as an independent state. When war began again in 1621 after the Twelve Years Truce he was less successful and died just weeks before the Spaniards retook Breda for Spain.

Prince Rupert of the Rhine, Duke of Cumberland (b.1619–1682)

The quintessential dashing cavalier of romance, Prince Rupert was the third son of Frederick of the Palatinate. Joining his uncle at the outbreak of the English Civil War, he led the Royalist cavalry at Edgehill and First Newbury, captured Bristol in 1643 and carried out a spectacularly successful campaign in the North the following year. After relieving York, however, he demonstrated the impetuous side of his nature and ventured a battle against the odds at Marston Moor. This defeat lost the North for the King. As Commander-in-Chief of the Royalist army he found dissent among his fellow commanders preventing effective coordination . He took Leicester in 1645 but was defeated at Naseby and subsequently surrendered Bristol, to the anger of the King. From 1649 to 1652 he led a small squadron of Royalist buccaneers in *a guerre de course* against the new régime but was tirelessly pursued and worn down by Blake. After the Restoration he served as an admiral with Albemarle and the Duke of York in the Second and Third Anglo-Dutch wars, fighting at Southwold Bay (1665), the Four Days Fight (1667) and North Foreland (1667).

Michiel Adriaanzoon de Ruyter (b.1607–1676)

The Netherlands' greatest admiral, de Ruyter's naval victories against England did much to maintain Dutch power and prestige. After serving under Tromp in the First Anglo-Dutch War, he fought with the Danes in the First Northern War and defeated the Swedes at Nyborg in 1659. He then campaigned off the Guinea coast and in the West Indies before leading major fleet actions in the Second Anglo-Dutch War, including the Four Days Fight in 1666. The following year his audacious invasion of the Medway, destroying much of the English fleet and capturing the English flagship, was spectacular. His greatest battles were fought during the Third Anglo-Dutch War (1672–4) and included victories at Sole Bay (1672), Ostend (1623) and Kijduin in 1673. Subsequently redeploying to the Mediterranean, he was mortally wounded off Sicily.

Henri de la Tour d'Auvergne Turenne (b.1611–1675)

France's most successful soldier of the seventeenth century, Turenne learnt the art of war from his uncle, Maurice of Nassau, and entered the French service in 1630. He rose to command France's armies during the Thirty Years War, reconquering Roussillon, winning battles at Freiburg (1644) and Zusmarshausen in 1648, and often sharing the command with Condé. During the two French civil wars known as the *Fronde*, he found himself each time on the side opposite to Condé. He was defeated at Rethel in 1650, but was later reconciled with the court. During the second Fronde he had the better of Condé and subsequently defeated him at the Dunes in 1658 after having conquered much of the Spanish Netherlands. In 1677 he commanded in the wars against the Dutch, leading the triumphant campaign of 1675. His glorious career was cut short by a cannon ball that year. A master of strategy and tactics, he is one of the Great Captains of History, and his remains lie near to those of Napoleon in Les Invalides, Paris.

FROM 1700–1800 BC SPREAD:

George Brydges Rodney, 1st Baron Rodney (b.1719–1792)

One of the Royal Navy's greatest admirals of the 18th century. Rodney was present at Hawke's victory at Ushant in 1747 and fought with distinction during the Seven Years War. During the American Revolutionary War he won the battle of Cape St. Vincent, fought an indecisive battle off Martinique, and captured the island of St. Eustatius. Rodney's greatest victory at the Saintes in 1782 came at a crucial time in Britain's fortunes. It could not reverse the outcome of the American Revolutionary War, but it did avert the French threat to Britain's possessions in the West Indies and won back British control of the seas.

FROM 1800–1900 BC SPREAD:

[Napoleon I continued] brought down and forced to abdicate. A year later he returned dramatically from exile on Elba only to

Italian conflicts in 951 and assuming the title of King of the Lombards. He was obliged to make two more expeditions to Italy (962 and 966), and also subdued the tribes of the middle Elbe and middle Oder. His main achievement was the consolidation of the Reich, bringing peace and security to Germany and establishing it as Europe's greatest power for several hundred years.

William I the Conqueror (b.1027–1087)

Initially facing serious threats to his dukedom, by 1066 he had annexed Maine and the Vexin and was laying claim to the throne of England. He defeated his rival, Harold Godwinson, at Hastings (Senlac) in 1066, and was crowned King of England on Christmas Day of that year. He spent the years from 1067 to 1071 consolidating his conquests before invading Scotland in 1072 and Wales in 1081, creating marches, or buffer areas. These activities in the British Isles led to the loss of Maine in 1077.

FROM 1100–1600 BC SPREAD:

[Edward III continued] his early years he had been a knight of outstanding vigour and energy, with a brilliant court. He instigated the Order of the Garter and in 1348 was offered the imperial crown of the Holy Roman Empire.

Genghis Khan (1206–1277)

By violence he overcame rivals to become ruler of all the Mongolian steppe peoples. One of the great conquerors of history, whose armies of fast-moving horse archers everywhere outmatched their opponents, the vast campaigns of conquest he set in motion are awe-inspiring. In 1215 he captured Beijing and began the subjugation of China. During 1210 to 1223 he devastated Muslim Kwarzm. His successors continued the great conquests, which were universally destructive. They did not result in a truly unified empire, and Europe was saved from the full force of the Mongol terror by succession crises in distant Asia. Nevertheless the thirteenth century was dominated by the impact of the Mongols, whose empire at its peak extended from the Mediterranean to the Pacific and the Baltic.

Henry V (1413–1422)

Famed as Shakespeare's heroic victor of Agincourt, Henry's star blazed bright and died quickly. The victory at Agincourt was against the odds and justifiably takes its place as one of the great battles of the Middle Ages. Less well known are his subsequent operations in France, leading to the Treaty of Troyes and his recognition as next King of France. In three well-planned campaigns he conquered Normandy, but before his monarchial aim could be realised he died, just two months before his father in law, Charles VI of France. His courage and determination in the face of seemingly impossible odds remains a model of English cool-headed pluck.

Mehmet II the Conqueror (Mehmed Fatih) (1451–1481)

Ottoman sultan who ended the Byzantine Empire by taking Constantinople in 1453. During the following two decades he campaigned in the Balkans, conquering the Morea, Serbia and Bosnia, Wallachia and, later, Moldavia. A war with Venice (1463–79) brought Negroponte and northern Albania, and in 1473 he repulsed an invasion of Turkomen at Otluk Beli. Otranto fell in 1480, but in the same year Ottoman forces failed to take Rhodes from the Knights of St. John. He took measures to repopulate Constantinople, now Istanbul, and reorganised the Ottoman army to incorporate increased use of cannon. Ushering in an golden age, he made the Ottoman Empire a major power in both Europe and the Middle East.

Philip II Augustus (1180–1223)

King of France and principal founder of French monarchical power. As much Machiavellian statesman as soldier, he took considerable areas of the Angevin empire while his most worthy opponent, Richard I, was in the Holy Land on a crusade from which Philip returned early. Richard's brother John was no match for him. The Battle of Bouvines (1214) against John's allies of Flanders and Germany sealed the fate of the Angevin possessions in France, enabling France to become the greatest power in Western Europe.

Richard I the Lionheart (1189–1199)

The model Crusader and a great romantic hero, Richard led the Third Crusade to the Holy Land in the wake of the disasters that had befallen the Christians after the Battle of Hattin. The Battle of Arsuf (1191) was Richard's greatest victory against Saladin, but in the end he failed to retake Jerusalem. Returning to England (where the misgovernment of his brother John provided the background to the legend of Robin Hood) he was captured by his arch-enemy and held for ransom for two years (1192–4). Less glorious than his Middle Eastern adventure was his struggle against Philip Augustus of France, who took advantage of his absence to conquer much of his possessions in France.

Saladin (Salah al-Din) (1169–1193)

Zangid Sultan of Egypt, he ended the Fatimid regime there and fought during 1184–1187 in Mesopotamia to reconstruct the empire of Nur al-Din. His realm eventually surrounded the Crusader states, and for once the Christians were facing an enemy united and led by one man. From 1169 onwards Saladin engaged in desultory operations against the Crusader states until in 1187 he won a truly decisive victory at Hattin. This broke the power of the Crusader states, and Jerusalem soon fell, as did Acre. In 1189 a new Crusade laid siege to Acre, and it was taken two years later by Richard the Lionheart. Saladin's attempts to expel the invaders was repulsed at Arsuf in 1191, but this was not decisive, and the campaign ended with Jerusalem still in Muslim hands. His Ayyubid dynasty lasted until 1250.

Timur (Tamerlane, Timur lenk) (b.1336–1405)

Last great Asiatic conqueror of the Mongol line, a military adventurer who erupted from his Transoxanian realm in the 1370s, dynamically filling the power vacuum in the area resulting form the decline of Il-Khanate. For over thirty years his armies of mounted archers spread terror and destruction far and wide – in Iran, against the Golden Horde (he held Moscow for a year in 1385) and against the Mamelukes, sacking Damascus in 1401 and taking Baghdad the same year. During 1398–9 he invaded India and sacked Delhi; and in 1402 defeated the Ottomans at Ankara, taking Bayazid I prisoner. The vast empire he created was ruled from his tent, constantly on the move, his administration an uneasy compromise between this Turko–Mongol style and settled Islam. He died preparing to invade China.

Valdemar II the Victorious / the Conqueror (1202–1241)

After involvement in the politics of the Holy Roman Empire, he was one of the Northern Crusaders, fighting to Christianise the empire in the east, about 304 BC he ceded his Indian provinces to Chandragupta, founder of the Mauryan Empire. He was assassinated while embarking on a campaign to win Macedonia; his dynasty lasted for two centuries.

Quintus Sertorius (c.122–72 BC)
Roman general who allied with Marius and Cinna against Sulla; he fled to Spain after the Battle of the Colline Gate. Brave and resourceful, he proved brilliant in irregular warfare. With Lusitanians and an army of exiles from Sullan Rome, he defied the best efforts even of Pompey until being assassinated in 72 BC.

Lucius Cornelius Sulla (138–78 BC)
Second of Rome's great warlords during the 1st century BC and dictator of Rome 81–79 BC. Rivalry with Marius over command in the 1st Mithridatic War led to his march on Rome and seizure of power. He defeated Mithridates and returned to civil war in Rome. The issue was settled in 82 BC at the Battle of the Colline Gate and he took control of Rome. His régime restored the power of the *Optimates*, but Rome was now set for a half-century of civil strife that would be ended by the rule of one man.

FROM AD 1–600 SPREAD:

[Euric continued] conquered much of the Iberian peninsula, where his successors were to rule a prosperous kingdom until the early 8th century.

Gaiseric (428–477)
King of the Vandals who led his people from Spain to establish a kingdom in North Africa. Advancing from the Strait of Gibraltar, he took the Roman province of Africa (essentially Tunisia) by 439 when Carthage fell. Alone of the barbarian chiefs who set up kingdoms in the wreckage of the Western Roman Empire, he constructed a considerable fleet, which raided widely in the central Mediterranean. In 455 an expedition arrived at the mouth of the Tiber and proceeded to sack Rome. The activities of the Vandal pirates provoked the Empire into two major attempts to destroy the Vandals. These, in 460 and 468, were foiled, and the Vandals extended their control to the Balearic Islands, Sardinia, Corsica and Sicily (which was subsequently passed to the Ostrogothic Kingdom of Italy). Gaiseric's Vandal kingdom lasted until 533 when Belisarius reconquered North Africa for the Byzantine Emperor Justinian.

Lucius Septimius Severus (193–211)
Founder of the Severan dynasty, and African by birth, Septimius had to fight for the throne, overcoming Didius Julianus in 193, Pescennius Niger in 194 and Clodius Albinus in 196. He understood the importance of the army and provoked the hostility of the senate by stationing troops near to the capital. He conquered Mesopotamia (195–202), taking Ctesiphon and annexing the area. In 208 he visited Britain and mounted an expedition against the Caledonians, after which, understanding that the Antonine Wall was a defence-line too far north, ordered the upgrading of Hadrian's Wall. He died at Eburacum (York, England) leaving the empire to his unbalanced megalomaniac son Caracalla, who proceeded to undo much of the good work Septimius had done.

Flavius Stilicho (395–408)
Rome's chief general during the reign of the Emperor Honorius, and by strength of character an important stabiliser during a difficult period following the disaster of Adrianople and break-in of the Goths under Alaric. He manoeuvred with them in Greece and foiled their invasion of Italy in 401–3, winning an incomplete victory at Pollentia. In 406 at Florence he destroyed a large number of invaders. Two years later, however, he was murdered by Honorius, leaving Italy leaderless and open to further invasion. The result was the first sack of Rome in 800 years.

Theodosius the Great (379–395)
Last ruler of a united Roman Empire, Theodosius succeeded in avoiding total disaster for the empire after the massive defeat at Adrianople and the death of his predecessor in the East, Valens. He was forced to defeat two usurpers, Maximus and Eugenius, and temporarily ended the continuing conflict with Persia.

Marcus Ulpius Traianus, Trajan (98–117)
Of Iberian origin, Trajan was the epitome of Rome's great soldier-emperors, famous above all for his conquest of Dacia, which is commemorated on Trajan's Column in Rome. Provoked by the activities of the Dacian King Decebalus, Trajan conquered the area in two campaigns, establishing a dramatic salient resting on the Carpathian Mountains. This acted as a strategic shield for the Danube and its region until the crisis of the 3rd century, when Aurelian abandoned the province. Dacia also had the advantage of containing gold and silver deposits. Less lasting was Trajan's conquest of Armenia and Mesopotamia, provoked by one of many succession crises in Armenia and the interference of the Parthians. The Romans took the Parthian capital, Ctesiphon, and reached the mouth of the Tigris, but the area proved too difficult to hold and Trajan's successor, Hadrian, withdrew the frontier.

FROM 600–1100 SPREAD:

[Mahmud of Ghazna continued] Punjab. The effects of his campaigns were to weaken the hold of the Hindu rulers in northern India and to prepare the way for subsequent Muslim invasions.

Charles Martel (c.688–741)
Mayor of Austrasia, Charles was the victor at the Battle of Tours (or possibly Poitiers, the location being uncertain) in 732, famously defeating the last significant Muslim expedition from Spain to penetrate deep into France. (Modern historians, however, dispute the size and significance of the battle.) As a result of this he received the nickname 'Martel' (the Hammer). After a civil war following the death of his father, Pepin, in 714, he had established control of the Frankish realms and subsequently campaigned tirelessly against Bavaria, Burgundy, Aquitaine and the Saxons. In 737 he took Avignon from the Muslims and in 739 drove them out of Provence. The fiction of Merovingian rule was maintained, but power rested firmly in his hands and was passed at his death to his two legitimate sons, following the Franks' lamentable custom of dividing the inheritance. However, he laid the foundations upon which his illustrious grandson Charlemagne would build a great empire.

Otto the Great (936–973)
German king from 936 and creator of the German Holy Roman Empire. He defeated the Magyars on the Lech River in 955, ending their career of penetrating raids that had terrorised central and western Europe for more than half a century. In 962 he was crowned Emperor in Rome after having been drawn into

GREAT COMMANDERS

FROM 300–500 BC SPREAD:

{Thutmosis III continued] Syria and Palestine, while campaigns up the Nile extended Egyptian control as far as the 4th cataract.

Tiglath-Pileser (745–727 BC)

Founder of the Neo-Assyrian Empire after a period of relative weakness. Campaigned against Urartu, Aramaeans, in Palestine, Syria, Iran and Babylonia, extending Assyrian domination to the Egyptian frontier and the Persian Gulf. 729 annexed Babylon. 732 took Damascus. Replaced militia system with a standing army and began cruel policy of mass deportations (today euphemised as 'ethnic cleansing'), such as that of the 'lost ten tribes' of Israel in 722.

FROM 500–1 BC SPREAD:

Hannibal (247–183 BC)

One of the Great Captains of History, famous for crossing the Alps into Italy with an army that included elephants. He took command of the Carthaginian army in Spain in 221 BC and captured Saguntum two years later, precipitating the 2nd Punic War with Rome. He devised the bold strategy of invading Italy (from Spain, via the Alps) to raise revolt among Rome's allies in the peninsula. Principal battles were Ticinus (218 BC), the Trebbia (218 BC), Lake Trasimeno (217 BC), Cannae (216 BC) and Zama (202 BC). The victory at Cannae stands as one of the classic battles of history, exemplar of double envelopment. However, despite divided command, the strategy of Fabius (avoiding set-piece battles to wear down the Carthaginian army) and the reluctance of Rome's allies to join the Carthaginian cause, led to the gradual erosion of his army. After 16 years of campaigning without a decisive result, Hannibal returned to defend Carthage in 203 BC. The following year he was defeated by Scipio at Zama.

Caius Marius (157–86 BC)

First of the great Roman warlords whose ambitions and rivalries brought about the fall of the Roman Republic. He rose to prominence during the Jugurthine War, revolutionising the composition of the Roman army by taking volunteers irrespective of the established property qualifications, creating a semi-professional army more apt to be loyal to its general than to the state. He defended Italy from the invasion of the Cimbri and Teutones, defeating them at Aquae Sextiae (102 BC) and Vercellae (101 BC). He was consul for an unprecedented six times and subsequently became involved in the political struggle between the *Optimates* and *Equites* in alliance with Saturninus and, later, Cinna, and in opposition to Sulla. He died before Sulla triumphed. He was, by marriage, the uncle of Julius Caesar.

Mithridates VI the Great (120–63 BC)

King of Pontus and implacable enemy of Rome. In 88 BC he seized Cappadocia, Bithynia and the Roman province of Asia, but was defeated and expelled by Sulla by 84 BC. He defeated the activities of Sulla's lieutenant Murena (83–82 BC) and invaded Bithynia again (bequeathed to Rome in 74 BC). The Roman general Lucullus's successful campaigns against Pontus were frustrated by politics, and Mithridates was finally driven from his kingdom by Pompey.

Pompey the Great (Gnaeus Pompeius Magnus) (106–48 BC)

Dominant Roman general between the régimes of Sulla and Caesar. Rose to prominence with his father, Strabo, during the Social War. Aided Sulla (83–82 BC) and helped put down revolt of Lepidus in 77 BC. Campaigned in Spain against Sertorius, then returned to Italy at the end of the rebellion of Spartacus. With Crassus, overawed Rome to become consul for 70 BC. Undertook vast campaign against pirates in the Mediterranean (67 BC) then took command of the war against Mithridates, thereafter settling Roman affairs in the east. Returned to Rome to form 1st Triumvirate with Crassus and Caesar. Fought Caesar (49–48 BC) in the Roman Civil War (War of the 1st Triumvirate), meeting defeat at Pharsalus (48 BC) and assassination in Egypt.

Ptolemy I Soter (c.367–282/3 BC)

Friend, general and biographer of Alexander the Great, and founder of the Macedonian dynasty that ruled Egypt from 305/4 BC to the death of Cleopatra in 30 BC. During the wars of Alexander's successors he established himself as king of Egypt and extended his dominion to Palestine, Cyprus and parts of the Aegean.

Publius Cornelius Scipio Africanus Major (c.236–184 BC)

One of Rome's greatest generals, who led the Republic to victory in the 2nd Punic War. Elected to an unprecedented proconsular imperium at the age of 25, he revised legionary tactics and proceeded to defeat Hannibal's brother Hasdrubal at Baecula. His victory at Ilipa effectively decided the course of the war in Spain. He was consul in 205 BC, then led the invasion of the Carthaginian homeland, capturing Utica and Tunis before defeating Hannibal at Zama. His triumphant campaign won him the appelation 'Africanus'.

Pyrrhus (319–272 BC)

King of Epirus who aspired to be 'the Alexander of the west'. His Italian campaigns (281–275 BC) were initially to aid Tarentum against Rome. Principal battles were Heraclea (280 BC), Ausculum (279 BC) and Beneventum (275 BC). He also fought the Carthaginians in Sicily, inconclusively. His 'Pyrrhic victories' (as at Heraclea, won at an unsupportable cost) gained no lasting success, however.

Seleucus I Nicator (c.358–280 BC)

The most successful of Alexander the Great's generals competing to reunite and rule his huge empire after his death. By 312 BC Seleucus controlled Babylon and much of Mesopotamia. Victory at Ipsus (301 BC) brought control of Syria and (in 296 BC) Cilicia. He founded Antioch in 300 BC and Seleuceia on the Tigris in 312 BC. The Battle of Corupedium (281 BC) won Asia Minor, so that at his death he had reunited most of Alexander's empire in Asia. Recognising the limits of his

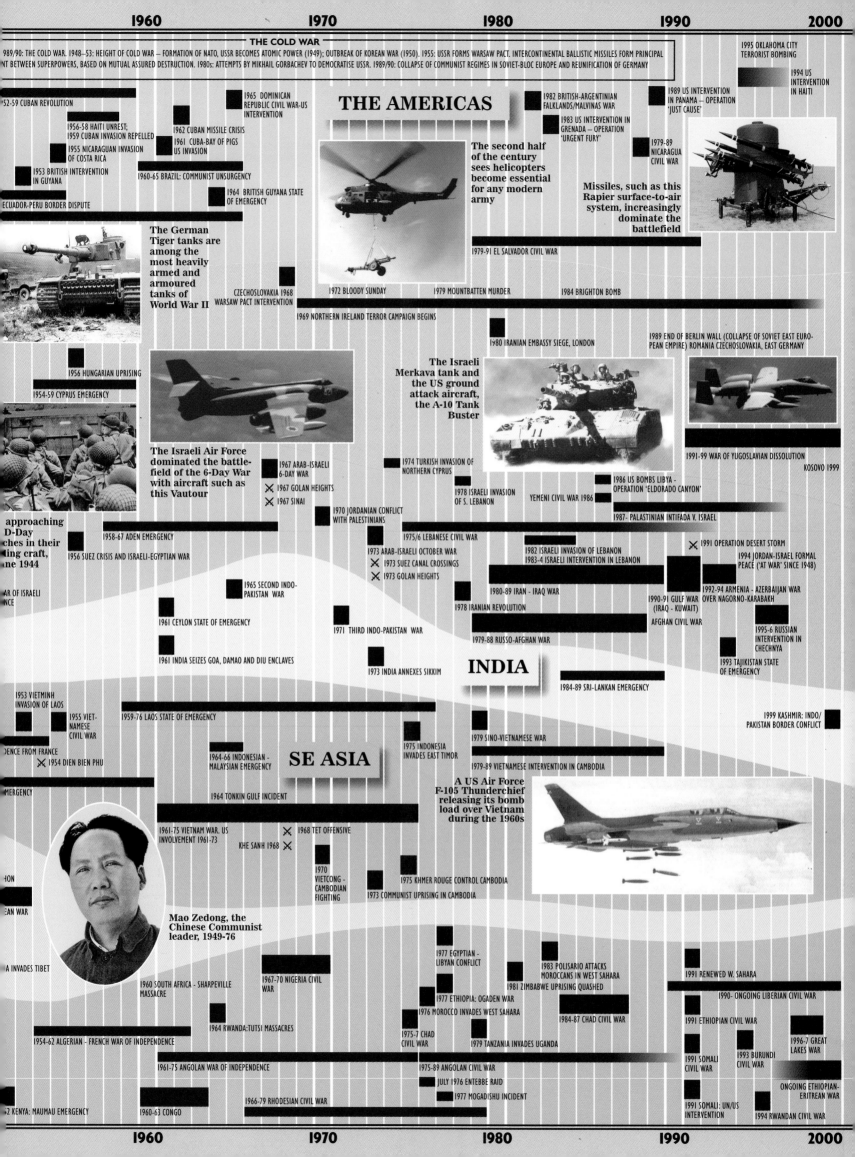

THE COLD WAR

989/90: THE COLD WAR. 1948–53: HEIGHT OF COLD WAR – FORMATION OF NATO, USSR BECOMES ATOMIC POWER (1949); OUTBREAK OF KOREAN WAR (1950). 1955: USSR FORMS WARSAW PACT. INTERCONTINENTAL BALLISTIC MISSILES FORM PRINCIPAL NT BETWEEN SUPERPOWERS, BASED ON MUTUAL ASSURED DESTRUCTION. 1980s: ATTEMPTS BY MIKHAIL GORBACHEV TO DEMOCRATISE USSR. 1989/90: COLLAPSE OF COMMUNIST REGIMES IN SOVIET-BLOC EUROPE AND REUNIFICATION OF GERMANY

THE AMERICAS

1995 OKLAHOMA CITY TERRORIST BOMBING

1994 US INTERVENTION IN HAITI

52-59 CUBAN REVOLUTION

1965 DOMINICAN REPUBLIC CIVIL WAR-US INTERVENTION

1982 BRITISH-ARGENTINIAN FALKLANDS/MALVINAS WAR

1989 US INTERVENTION IN PANAMA – OPERATION 'JUST CAUSE'

1956-58 HAITI UNREST; 1959 CUBAN INVASION REPELLED

1962 CUBAN MISSILE CRISIS

1961 CUBA-BAY OF PIGS US INVASION

1983 US INTERVENTION IN GRENADA – OPERATION 'URGENT FURY'

1979-89 NICARAGUA CIVIL WAR

1955 NICARAGUAN INVASION OF COSTA RICA

The second half of the century sees helicopters become essential for any modern army

1953 BRITISH INTERVENTION IN GUYANA

1960-65 BRAZIL: COMMUNIST UNSURGENCY

Missiles, such as this Rapier surface-to-air system, increasingly dominate the battlefield

ECUADOR-PERU BORDER DISPUTE

1964 BRITISH GUYANA STATE OF EMERGENCY

The German Tiger tanks are among the most heavily armed and armoured tanks of World War II

1979-91 EL SALVADOR CIVIL WAR

CZECHOSLOVAKIA 1968 WARSAW PACT INTERVENTION

1972 BLOODY SUNDAY

1979 MOUNTBATTEN MURDER

1984 BRIGHTON BOMB

1969 NORTHERN IRELAND TERROR CAMPAIGN BEGINS

1956 HUNGARIAN UPRISING

1980 IRANIAN EMBASSY SIEGE, LONDON

1989 END OF BERLIN WALL (COLLAPSE OF SOVIET EAST EURO-PEAN EMPIRE) ROMANIA CZECHOSLOVAKIA, EAST GERMANY

1954-59 CYPRUS EMERGENCY

The Israeli Merkava tank and the US ground attack aircraft, the A-10 Tank Buster

approaching D-Day ches in their ing craft, ne 1944

The Israeli Air Force dominated the battle-field of the 6-Day War with aircraft such as this Vautour

1967 ARAB-ISRAELI 6-DAY WAR

✕ 1967 GOLAN HEIGHTS

✕ 1967 SINAI

1974 TURKISH INVASION OF NORTHERN CYPRUS

1986 US BOMBS LIBYA – OPERATION 'ELDORADO CANYON'

1991-99 WAR OF YUGOSLAVIAN DISSOLUTION

KOSOVO 1999

1978 ISRAELI INVASION OF S. LEBANON

YEMENI CIVIL WAR 1986

1970 JORDANIAN CONFLICT WITH PALESTINIANS

1987- PALASTINIAN INTIFADA V. ISRAEL

1958-67 ADEN EMERGENCY

1975/6 LEBANESE CIVIL WAR

✕ 1991 OPERATION DESERT STORM

1982 ISRAELI INVASION OF LEBANON
1983-4 ISRAELI INTERVENTION IN LEBANON

1994 JORDAN-ISRAEL FORMAL PEACE ('AT WAR' SINCE 1948)

1956 SUEZ CRISIS AND ISRAELI-EGYPTIAN WAR

1973 ARAB-ISRAELI OCTOBER WAR

✕ 1973 SUEZ CANAL CROSSINGS

✕ 1973 GOLAN HEIGHTS

AR OF ISRAELI NCE

1965 SECOND INDO-PAKISTAN WAR

1980-89 IRAN - IRAQ WAR

1978 IRANIAN REVOLUTION

1992-94 ARMENIA - AZERBAIJAN WAR OVER NAGORNO-KARABAKH

1961 CEYLON STATE OF EMERGENCY

1971 THIRD INDO-PAKISTAN WAR

1990-91 GULF WAR (IRAQ - KUWAIT)

AFGHAN CIVIL WAR

1995-6 RUSSIAN INTERVENTION IN CHECHNYA

1961 INDIA SEIZES GOA, DAMAO AND DIU ENCLAVES

1973 INDIA ANNEXES SIKKIM

INDIA

1979-88 RUSSO-AFGHAN WAR

1993 TAJIKISTAN STATE OF EMERGENCY

1953 VIETMINH INVASION OF LAOS

1984-89 SRI-LANKAN EMERGENCY

1955 VIET-NAMESE CIVIL WAR

1959-76 LAOS STATE OF EMERGENCY

1979 SINO-VIETNAMESE WAR

1999 KASHMIR: INDO/ PAKISTAN BORDER CONFLICT

DENCE FROM FRANCE

✕ 1954 DIEN BIEN PHU

1964-66 INDONESIAN - MALAYSIAN EMERGENCY

1975 INDONESIA INVADES EAST TIMOR

SE ASIA

1979-89 VIETNAMESE INTERVENTION IN CAMBODIA

A US Air Force F-105 Thunderchief releasing its bomb load over Vietnam during the 1960s

ERGENCY

1964 TONKIN GULF INCIDENT

1961-75 VIETNAM WAR. US INVOLVEMENT 1961-73

✕ 1968 TET OFFENSIVE

KHE SANH 1968 ✕

1970 VIETCONG - CAMBODIAN FIGHTING

1975 KHMER ROUGE CONTROL CAMBODIA

1973 COMMUNIST UPRISING IN CAMBODIA

Mao Zedong, the Chinese Communist leader, 1949-76

1977 EGYPTIAN - LIBYAN CONFLICT

1983 POLISARIO ATTACKS MOROCCANS IN WEST SAHARA

1991 RENEWED W. SAHARA

A INVADES TIBET

1981 ZIMBABWE UPRISING QUASHED

1960 SOUTH AFRICA - SHARPEVILLE MASSACRE

1967-70 NIGERIA CIVIL WAR

1977 ETHIOPIA: OGADEN WAR

1990- ONGOING LIBERIAN CIVIL WAR

HON

1976 MOROCCO INVADES WEST SAHARA

1991 ETHIOPIAN CIVIL WAR

EAN WAR

1964 RWANDA:TUTSI MASSACRES

1975-7 CHAD CIVIL WAR

1984-87 CHAD CIVIL WAR

1996-7 GREAT LAKES WAR

1954-62 ALGERIAN - FRENCH WAR OF INDEPENDENCE

1979 TANZANIA INVADES UGANDA

1993 BURUNDI CIVIL WAR

1961-75 ANGOLAN WAR OF INDEPENDENCE

1975-89 ANGOLAN CIVIL WAR

1991 SOMALI CIVIL WAR

ONGOING ETHIOPIAN-ERITREAN WAR

JULY 1976 ENTEBBE RAID

52 KENYA: MAUMAU EMERGENCY

1960-63 CONGO

1966-79 RHODESIAN CIVIL WAR

1977 MOGADISHU INCIDENT

1991 SOMALI: UN/US INTERVENTION

1994 RWANDAN CIVIL WAR

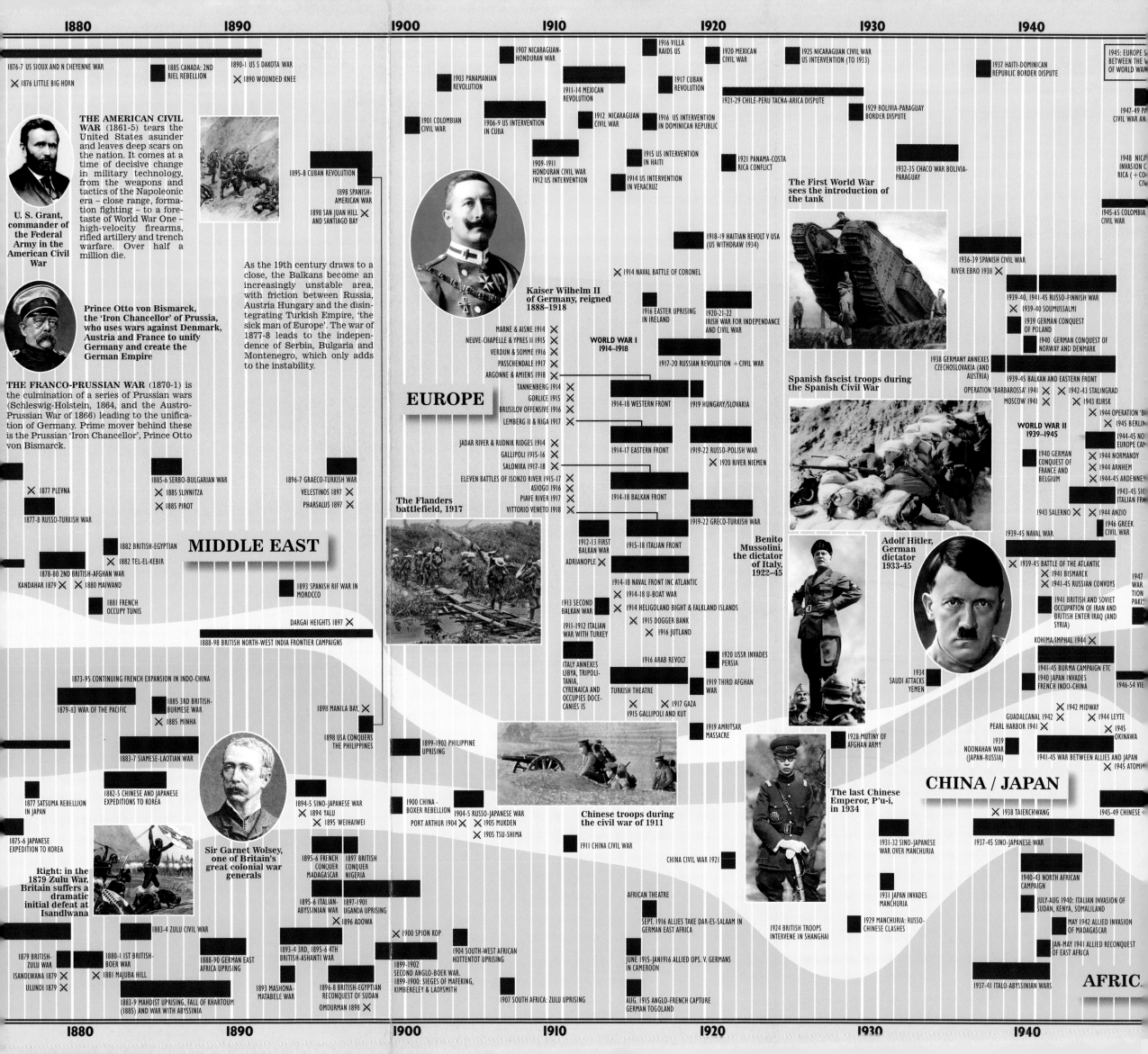

U. S. Grant, commander of the Federal Army in the American Civil War

THE AMERICAN CIVIL WAR (1861-5) tears the United States asunder and leaves deep scars on the nation. It comes at a time of decisive change in military technology, from the weapons and tactics of the Napoleonic era – close range, formation fighting – to a foretaste of World War One – high-velocity firearms, rifled artillery and trench warfare. Over half a million die.

Prince Otto von Bismarck, the 'Iron Chancellor' of Prussia, who uses wars against Denmark, Austria and France to unify Germany and create the German Empire

THE FRANCO-PRUSSIAN WAR (1870-1) is the culmination of a series of Prussian wars (Schleswig-Holstein, 1864, and the Austro-Prussian War of 1866) leading to the unification of Germany. Prime mover behind these is the Prussian 'Iron Chancellor', Prince Otto von Bismarck.

As the 19th century draws to a close, the Balkans become an increasingly unstable area, with friction between Russia, Austria Hungary and the disintegrating Turkish Empire, 'the sick man of Europe'. The war of 1877-8 leads to the independence of Serbia, Bulgaria and Montenegro, which only adds to the instability.

EUROPE

MIDDLE EAST

CHINA / JAPAN

AFRIC.

Kaiser Wilhelm II of Germany, reigned 1888–1918

The First World War sees the introduction of the tank

Spanish fascist troops during the Spanish Civil War

Benito Mussolini, the dictator of Italy, 1922–45

Adolf Hitler, German dictator 1933-45

The Flanders battlefield, 1917

Sir Garnet Wolsey, one of Britain's great colonial war generals

Chinese troops during the civil war of 1911

The last Chinese Emperor, P'u-i, in 1934

Right: in the 1879 Zulu War, Britain suffers a dramatic initial defeat at Isandlwana

WORLD WAR I 1914–1918

WORLD WAR II 1939–1945

1876-7 US SIOUX AND N CHEYENNE WAR
✕ 1876 LITTLE BIG HORN
1885 CANADA: 2ND RIEL REBELLION
1890-1 US S DAKOTA WAR
✕ 1890 WOUNDED KNEE
1895-8 CUBAN REVOLUTION
1898 SPANISH-AMERICAN WAR
1898 SAN JUAN HILL AND SANTIAGO BAY ✕

1901 COLOMBIAN CIVIL WAR
1903 PANAMANIAN REVOLUTION
1907 NICARAGUAN-HONDURAN WAR
1906-9 US INTERVENTION IN CUBA
1911-14 MEXICAN REVOLUTION
1912 NICARAGUAN CIVIL WAR
1916 VILLA RAIDS US
1917 CUBAN REVOLUTION
1916 US INTERVENTION IN DOMINICAN REPUBLIC
1920 MEXICAN CIVIL WAR
1925 NICARAGUAN CIVIL WAR US INTERVENTION (TO 1933)
1937 HAITI-DOMINICAN REPUBLIC BORDER DISPUTE
1909-1911 HONDURAN CIVIL WAR 1912 US INTERVENTION
1915 US INTERVENTION IN HAITI
1914 US INTERVENTION IN VERACRUZ
1921 PANAMA-COSTA RICA CONFLICT
1921-29 CHILE-PERU TACNA-ARICA DISPUTE
1929 BOLIVIA-PARAGUAY BORDER DISPUTE
1932-35 CHACO WAR BOLIVIA-PARAGUAY
1918-19 HAITIAN REVOLT V USA (US WITHDRAW 1934)
1936-39 SPANISH CIVIL WAR RIVER EBRO 1938 ✕

1945: EUROPE S BETWEEN THE W OF WORLD WAR
1947-49 PA CIVIL WAR AN
1948 NIC INVASION C RICA (+ CO CIW
1945-65 COLOMBIA CIVIL WAR

1914 NAVAL BATTLE OF CORONEL ✕
1916 EASTER UPRISING IN IRELAND
1920-21-22 IRISH WAR FOR INDEPENDENCE AND CIVIL WAR
1917-20 RUSSIAN REVOLUTION + CIVIL WAR
1938 GERMANY ANNEXES CZECHOSLOVAKIA (AND AUSTRIA)
1939-40 SOUMUSSALMI
1939-40, 1941-45 RUSSO-FINNISH WAR
✕ 1939-40 SOUMUSSALMI
1939 GERMAN CONQUEST OF POLAND
1940 GERMAN CONQUEST OF NORWAY AND DENMARK

MARNE & AISNE 1914 ✕
NEUVE-CHAPELLE & YPRES II 1915 ✕
VERDUN & SOMME 1916 ✕
PASSCHENDALE 1917 ✕
ARGONNE & AMIENS 1918 ✕
TANNENBERG 1914 ✕
GORLICE 1915 ✕
BRUSILOV OFFENSIVE 1916 ✕
LEMBERG II & RIGA 1917 ✕
JADAR RIVER & RUDNIK RIDGES 1914 ✕
GALLIPOLI 1915-16 ✕
SALONIKA 1917-18 ✕
ELEVEN BATTLES OF ISONZO RIVER 1915-17 ✕
ASIOGO 1916 ✕
PIAVE RIVER 1917 ✕
VITTORIO VENETO 1918 ✕

1914-18 WESTERN FRONT
1919 HUNGARY/SLOVAKIA
1914-17 EASTERN FRONT
1919-22 RUSSO-POLISH WAR
1920 RIVER NIEMEN ✕
1914-18 BALKAN FRONT
1919-22 GRECO-TURKISH WAR

1939-45 BALKAN AND EASTERN FRONT OPERATION 'BARBAROSSA' 1941 ✕
✕ 1942-43 STALINGRAD
MOSCOW 1941 ✕ ✕ 1943 KURSK
✕ 1944 OPERATION 'B
✕ 1945 BERLIN
WORLD WAR II 1939–1945
1944-45 NO EUROPE CA
1940 GERMAN CONQUEST OF FRANCE AND BELGIUM
✕ 1944 NORMANDY
✕ 1944 ARNHEM
1944-45 ARDENNE
1943-45 SIC ITALIAN FR
1943 SALERNO ✕ ✕ 1944 ANZIO
1946 GREEK CIVIL WAR
1939-45 NAVAL WAR
✕ 1939-45 BATTLE OF THE ATLANTIC
✕ 1941 BISMARCK
✕ 1941-45 RUSSIAN CONVOYS
1941 BRITISH AND SOVIET OCCUPATION OF IRAN AND BRITISH ENTER IRAQ (AND SYRIA)
1947 WAR TION PAKI
KOHIMA/IMPHAL 1944 ✕
1941-45 BURMA CAMPAIGN ETC
1940 JAPAN INVADES FRENCH INDO-CHINA
1946-54 VIE

1912-13 FIRST BALKAN WAR
ADRIANOPLE ✕
1913 SECOND BALKAN WAR
1915-18 ITALIAN FRONT
1914-18 NAVAL FRONT INC ATLANTIC
1914-18 U-BOAT WAR
1914 HELIGOLAND BIGHT & FALKLAND ISLANDS
✕ 1915 DOGGER BANK
✕ 1916 JUTLAND
1911-1912 ITALIAN WAR WITH TURKEY
ITALY ANNEXES LIBYA, TRIPOLITANIA, CYRENAICA AND OCCUPIES DODECANIES IS
1916 ARAB REVOLT
1920 USSR INVADES PERSIA
1919 THIRD AFGHAN WAR
TURKISH THEATRE
✕ 1917 GAZA
1915 GALLIPOLI AND KUT
1919 AMRITSAR MASSACRE
1928 MUTINY OF AFGHAN ARMY
1934 SAUDI ATTACKS YEMEN
1942 MIDWAY
GUADALCANAL 1942 ✕ 1944 LEYTE
PEARL HARBOR 1941 ✕ ✕ 1945 OKINAWA
1939 NOONAHAN WAR (JAPAN-RUSSIA)
1941-45 WAR BETWEEN ALLIES AND JAPAN
✕ 1945 ATOMI

1885-6 SERBO-BULGARIAN WAR
✕ 1885 SLIVNITZA
✕ 1885 PIROT
1896-7 GRAECO-TURKISH WAR
VELESTINOS 1897 ✕
PHARSALUS 1897 ✕
✕ 1877 PLEVNA
1877-8 RUSSO-TURKISH WAR

1882 BRITISH-EGYPTIAN
✕ 1882 TEL-EL-KEBIR
1878-80 2ND BRITISH-AFGHAN WAR
KANDAHAR 1879 ✕ ✕ 1880 MAIWAND
1881 FRENCH OCCUPY TUNIS
1893 SPANISH RIF WAR IN MOROCCO
DARGAI HEIGHTS 1897 ✕
1888-98 BRITISH NORTH-WEST INDIA FRONTIER CAMPAIGNS

1873-95 CONTINUING FRENCH EXPANSION IN INDO-CHINA
1879-83 WAR OF THE PACIFIC
1885 3RD BRITISH-BURMESE WAR
✕ 1885 MINHA
1898 MANILA BAY. ✕
1898 USA CONQUERS THE PHILIPPINES
1883-7 SIAMESE-LAOTIAN WAR
1899-1902 PHILIPPINE UPRISING
1900 CHINA - BOXER REBELLION
PORT ARTHUR 1904 ✕
1904-5 RUSSO-JAPANESE WAR
✕ 1905 MUKDEN
✕ 1905 TSU-SHIMA
1911 CHINA CIVIL WAR
CHINA CIVIL WAR 1921
1938 TAIERCHWANG ✕
1945-49 CHINESE

1877 SATSUMA REBELLION IN JAPAN
1882-5 CHINESE AND JAPANESE EXPEDITIONS TO KOREA
1894-5 SINO-JAPANESE WAR
✕ 1894 YALU
✕ 1895 WEIHAIWEI
1875-6 JAPANESE EXPEDITION TO KOREA
1895-6 FRENCH CONQUER MADAGASCAR
1897 BRITISH CONQUER NIGERIA
1931-32 SINO-JAPANESE WAR OVER MANCHURIA
1937-45 SINO-JAPANESE WAR
1924 BRITISH TROOPS INTERVENE IN SHANGHAI
1931 JAPAN INVADES MANCHURIA
1929 MANCHURIA: RUSSO-CHINESE CLASHES

1879 BRITISH-ZULU WAR
ISANDLWANA 1879 ✕
ULUNDI 1879 ✕
1880-1 1ST BRITISH-BOER WAR
✕ 1881 MAJUBA HILL
1883-4 ZULU CIVIL WAR
1888-90 GERMAN EAST AFRICA UPRISING
1893-4 3RD, 1895-4 4TH BRITISH-ASHANTI WAR
1895-6 ITALIAN-ABYSSINIAN WAR
1897-1901 UGANDA UPRISING
✕ 1896 ADOWA
✕ 1900 SPION KOP
✕ 1900 SPION KOP
1904 SOUTH-WEST AFRICAN HOTTENTOT UPRISING
AFRICAN THEATRE
SEPT. 1916 ALLIES TAKE DAR-ES-SALAAM IN GERMAN EAST AFRICA
1940-43 NORTH AFRICAN CAMPAIGN
JULY-AUG 1940: ITALIAN INVASION OF SUDAN, KENYA, SOMALILAND
MAY 1942 ALLIED INVASION OF MADAGASCAR
JAN-MAY 1941 ALLIED RECONQUEST OF EAST AFRICA
1937-41 ITALO-ABYSSINIAN WARS
1883-9 MAHDIST UPRISING, FALL OF KHARTOUM (1885) AND WAR WITH ABYSSINIA
1893 MASHONA-MATABELE WAR
1896-8 BRITISH-EGYPTIAN RECONQUEST OF SUDAN OMDURMAN 1898 ✕
1899-1902 SECOND ANGLO-BOER WAR. 1899-1900: SIEGES OF MAFEKING, KIMBERELEY & LADYSMITH
1907 SOUTH AFRICA: ZULU UPRISING
JUNE 1915-JAN1916 ALLIED OPS. V. GERMANS IN CAMEROON
AUG. 1915 ANGLO-FRENCH CAPTURE GERMAN TOGOLAND

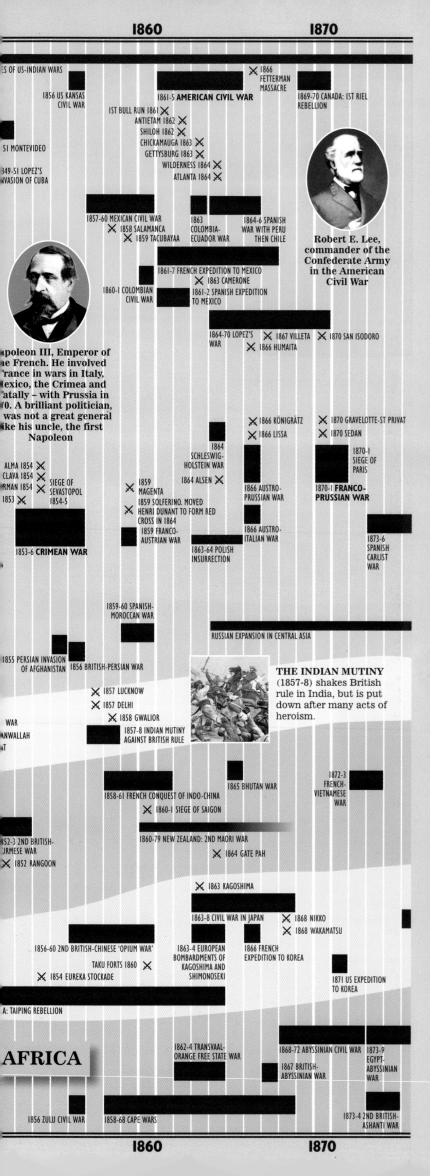

GREAT COMMANDERS

Simon Bolivar (b.1783–1830) The Liberator
Revolutionary hero of the Latin-American Wars of Independence. From a wealthy Creole family in Venezuela, he was much influenced by the Napoleonic idea of destiny and the ethos of the French Revolution. In 1805 he vowed to liberate his homeland. He participated in Miranda's ill-fated first attempt, then became leader of the movement. The early years were unsuccessful, but in 1816 he began a two-year campaign that established the independence of Venezuela. He then entered Colombia and Ecuador to organise the new nation of Gran Colombia. Two years fighting in Peru and Bolivia followed, the Spanish surrendering to his chief of staff, Sucre in 1824. The work for which he is remembered was now complete. There followed political and constitutional wrangles, fuelled by his own authoritarian republicanism, which presaged the civil wars that have bedevilled South America.

Ulysses S. Grant 1822–1885
The North's greatest general during the American Civil War. Grant fought in the Mexican War, and served in the western theatre of operations, capturing Fort Donelson 1862. He won at Shiloh (1862) and after a lengthy campaign captured Vicksburg in 1863. In March 1864 he was given command of all the Union armies and devised the North's winning strategy. The decisive thrusts were made in the west, while Grant pressed Lee back on Petersburg and Richmond, conditions of combat eventually becoming almost static, a foretaste of the First World War. He receiving the Confederate general's surrender at Appomattox Court House on 9 April 1865. Grant went on to serve two terms as the 18th President of the USA from 1869 to 1877.

Thomas 'Stonewall' Jackson 1824–1863
The ablest of Lee's generals, Jackson's sobriquet stems from his stolid defence at the first battle of the American Civil War, First Bull Run (1861). His partnership with Robert E. Lee in the Army of Northern Virginia was all but unbeatable, and he played vital roles at Second Bull Run (1862), Antietam (1862), Fredericksburg (1862) and Chancellorsville (1863). His masterpiece Shenandoah Valley campaign of summer 1862 remains a of model of the art of war. Jackson was killed accidentally by his own men during the Battle of Chancellorsville.

Robert E. Lee 1807–1870
Legendary commander-in-chief of the Confederate Army during the American Civil War, Lee was possibly the greatest soldier since Napoleon. He served in the Mexican War and suppressed John Brown's insurrection at Harper's Ferry in 1859. Appointed C-in-C of Virginia's army on the outbreak of the Civil war, he attained field command in March 1862, organising the famed Army of Northern Virginia, which he led to a string of victories, including The Seven Days Battles (1862), Second Bull Run (1862), Fredericksburg (1862) and Chancellorsville (1863). His invasions of the North met with failure at Antietam (1862) and Gettysburg (1863), and his later campaigns defending Petersburg and Richmond were fought against impossible odds. He was much loved by his men and remains an enduring symbol of the South.

Helmuth von Moltke 1800–1891
Architect of Prussian victories against Denmark (1864), Austria (1866) and France (1870-1). After serving on the Prussian military mission to Turkey in 1832–9, he became Chief of the Prussian General Staff in 1858. He was the first soldier to recognise the importance of railways in the deployment of troops and munitions, and reorganised the Prussian army and its General Staff, making it a model for all other Western armies. His greatness lies not in being a field commander but rather the virtual creator of the military machine that united Germany and fought the First World War.

Napoleon I (Napoleon Bonaparte) (b.1769–1821)
The greatest general of modern times, who lent his name to an age. When the French Revolution broke out he was a lieutenant of artillery in the French Army. He made his mark in 1793 directing the artillery at the siege of Toulon. A general three years later, he began a series of spectacular campaigns: 1796–7 in Italy; 1798–9 in Egypt; 1800 in Italy again, after a daring trans-Alpine march; 1805 in Germany (the lightening Ulm–Austerlitz campaign); 1807 in Germany (the Jena campaign); and the 1807 Eylau–Friedland campaign against Russia. In 1799 a coup d'etat (18th *Brumaire*) brought him to power in France as First Consul; five years later he crowned himself Emperor of the French. 1807 was perhaps the zenith of his career. The Peninsular War, which began in 1808, became a steady drain on French resources and the crowned heads of Europe, always encouraged and often financed by his intransigent British enemies, were never reconciled to his imperial domination of Europe. In 1809 war with Austria was dearly brought to a victorious conclusion at Wagram. In 1812 he began his war to enforce the Tsar's compliance with his anti-British Continental System. The result was an epic invasion of Russia and a catastrophic retreat. From this point Napoleon was essentially always on the defensive against an ever-growing ring of opponents. In 1813 the Battle of Leipzig lost him control of Germany. In 1814, despite a brilliant campaign against impossible odds, Napoleon was

Continued on page 50

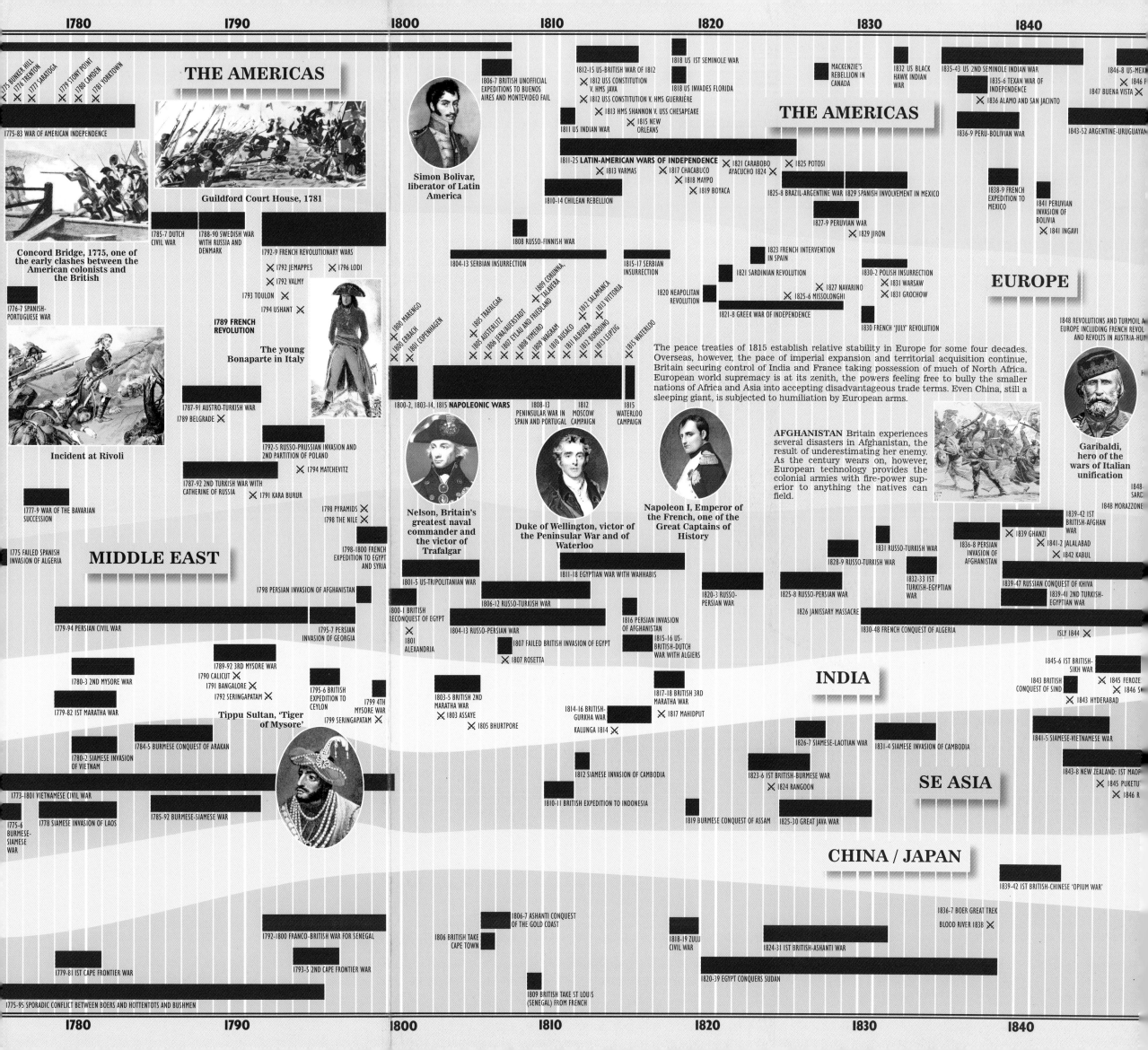

THE AMERICAS

1780 · 1790 · 1800 · 1810 · 1820 · 1830 · 1840

1775 BUNKER HILL · 1776 TRENTON · 1777 SARATOGA · 1779 STONY POINT · 1780 CAMDEN · 1781 YORKTOWN

1775-83 WAR OF AMERICAN INDEPENDENCE

Guildford Court House, 1781

Concord Bridge, 1775, one of the early clashes between the American colonists and the British

1785-7 DUTCH CIVIL WAR

1788-90 SWEDISH WAR WITH RUSSIA AND DENMARK

1792-9 FRENCH REVOLUTIONARY WARS

✕ 1792 JEMAPPES · ✕ 1796 LODI
✕ 1792 VALMY
1793 TOULON ✕
1794 USHANT ✕

1776-7 SPANISH-PORTUGUESE WAR

Incident at Rivoli

1789 FRENCH REVOLUTION

The young Bonaparte in Italy

1787-91 AUSTRO-TURKISH WAR
1789 BELGRADE ✕

1792-5 RUSSO-PRUSSIAN INVASION AND 2ND PARTITION OF POLAND
✕ 1794 MATCHEVITZ

1787-92 2ND TURKISH WAR WITH CATHERINE OF RUSSIA
✕ 1791 KARA BURUR

1777-9 WAR OF THE BAVARIAN SUCCESSION

1798 PYRAMIDS ✕
1798 THE NILE ✕

1798-1800 FRENCH EXPEDITION TO EGYPT AND SYRIA

1775 FAILED SPANISH INVASION OF ALGERIA

MIDDLE EAST

1798 PERSIAN INVASION OF AFGHANISTAN

Simon Bolivar, liberator of Latin America

1806-7 BRITISH UNOFFICIAL EXPEDITIONS TO BUENOS AIRES AND MONTEVIDEO FAIL

1812-15 US-BRITISH WAR OF 1812
✕ 1812 USS CONSTITUTION V. HMS JAVA
✕ 1812 USS CONSTITUTION V. HMS GUERRIÈRE
✕ 1813 HMS SHANNON V. USS CHESAPEAKE
✕ 1815 NEW ORLEANS

1811 US INDIAN WAR

1818 US 1ST SEMINOLE WAR
1818 US INVADES FLORIDA

THE AMERICAS

1811-25 LATIN-AMERICAN WARS OF INDEPENDENCE
✕ 1813 VARMAS · ✕ 1817 CHACABUCO · ✕ 1821 CARABOBO · AYACUCHO 1824 · ✕ 1825 POTOSI
✕ 1818 MAYPO
✕ 1819 BOYACA

1810-14 CHILEAN REBELLION

1808 RUSSO-FINNISH WAR

1804-13 SERBIAN INSURRECTION

1815-17 SERBIAN INSURRECTION

1825-8 BRAZIL-ARGENTINE WAR · 1829 SPANISH INVOLVEMENT IN MEXICO

1827-9 PERUVIAN WAR
✕ 1829 JIRON

1823 FRENCH INTERVENTION IN SPAIN

1821 SARDINIAN REVOLUTION

1820 NEAPOLITAN REVOLUTION

1821-8 GREEK WAR OF INDEPENDENCE
✕ 1827 NAVARINO
✕ 1825-6 MISSOLONGHI

1830-2 POLISH INSURRECTION
✕ 1831 WARSAW
✕ 1831 GROCHOW

1830 FRENCH 'JULY' REVOLUTION

EUROPE

✝ 1800 MARENGO · ✝ 1805 TRAFALGAR · ✝ 1805 AUSTERLITZ · ✝ 1806 JENA/AUERSTADT · ✝ 1807 EYLAU AND FRIEDLAND · ✝ 1808 VIMEIRO · ✝ 1809 CORUNNA, TALAVERA · ✝ 1809 WAGRAM · ✝ 1810 BUSACO · ✝ 1811 ALBUERA · ✝ 1812 SALAMANCA · ✝ 1812 BORODINO · ✝ 1813 VITTORIA · ✝ 1813 LEIPZIG · ✝ 1815 WATERLOO
✝ 1800 ERBACH · ✝ 1801 COPENHAGEN

1800-2, 1803-14, 1815 NAPOLEONIC WARS
1808-13 PENINSULAR WAR IN SPAIN AND PORTUGAL · 1812 MOSCOW CAMPAIGN · 1815 WATERLOO CAMPAIGN

Nelson, Britain's greatest naval commander and the victor of Trafalgar

Duke of Wellington, victor of the Peninsular War and of Waterloo

Napoleon I, Emperor of the French, one of the Great Captains of History

The peace treaties of 1815 establish relative stability in Europe for some four decades. Overseas, however, the pace of imperial expansion and territorial acquisition continue, Britain securing control of India and France taking possession of much of North Africa. European world supremacy is at its zenith, the powers feeling free to bully the smaller nations of Africa and Asia into accepting disadvantageous trade terms. Even China, still a sleeping giant, is subjected to humiliation by European arms.

AFGHANISTAN Britain experiences several disasters in Afghanistan, the result of underestimating her enemy. As the century wears on, however, European technology provides the colonial armies with fire-power superior to anything the natives can field.

Garibaldi, hero of the wars of Italian unification

1848 REVOLUTIONS AND TURMOIL A... EUROPE INCLUDING FRENCH REVOL... AND REVOLTS IN AUSTRIA-HUN...
1848 SARD...
1848 MORAZZONE

1811-18 EGYPTIAN WAR WITH WAHHABIS

1801-5 US-TRIPOLITANIAN WAR

1800-1 BRITISH RECONQUEST OF EGYPT
✕ 1801 ALEXANDRIA

1806-12 RUSSO-TURKISH WAR

1804-13 RUSSO-PERSIAN WAR
✕ 1807 FAILED BRITISH INVASION OF EGYPT
✕ 1807 ROSETTA

1816 PERSIAN INVASION OF AFGHANISTAN

1815-16 US-BRITISH-DUTCH WAR WITH ALGIERS

1820-3 RUSSO-PERSIAN WAR

1825-8 RUSSO-PERSIAN WAR

1828-9 RUSSO-TURKISH WAR · 1831 RUSSO-TURKISH WAR

1826 JANISSARY MASSACRE

1832-33 1ST TURKISH-EGYPTIAN WAR

1836-8 PERSIAN INVASION OF AFGHANISTAN

1839-42 1ST BRITISH-AFGHAN WAR
✕ 1839 GHANZI
✕ 1841-2 JALALABAD
✕ 1842 KABUL

1839-47 RUSSIAN CONQUEST OF KHIVA
1839-41 2ND TURKISH-EGYPTIAN WAR

1830-48 FRENCH CONQUEST OF ALGERIA
ISLY 1844 ✕

INDIA

1779-94 PERSIAN CIVIL WAR
1795-7 PERSIAN INVASION OF GEORGIA

1789-92 3RD MYSORE WAR
1790 CALICUT ✕
1791 BANGALORE ✕
1792 SERINGAPATAM ✕

1780-3 2ND MYSORE WAR

1779-82 1ST MARATHA WAR

1795-6 BRITISH EXPEDITION TO CEYLON
1799 4TH MYSORE WAR
1799 SERINGAPATAM ✕

Tippu Sultan, 'Tiger of Mysore'

1784-5 BURMESE CONQUEST OF ARAKAN

1780-2 SIAMESE INVASION OF VIETNAM

1803-5 BRITISH 2ND MARATHA WAR
✕ 1803 ASSAYE
✕ 1805 BHURTPORE

1814-16 BRITISH-GURKHA WAR
KALUNGA 1814 ✕

1817-18 BRITISH 3RD MARATHA WAR
✕ 1817 MAHIDPUT

1826-7 SIAMESE-LAOTIAN WAR · 1831-4 SIAMESE INVASION OF CAMBODIA

1841-5 SIAMESE-VIETNAMESE WAR

1845-6 1ST BRITISH-SIKH WAR
1843 BRITISH CONQUEST OF SIND
✕ 1845 FEROZE
✕ 1846 S...
✕ 1843 HYDERABAD

1773-1801 VIETNAMESE CIVIL WAR

1775-6 BURMESE-SIAMESE WAR

1778 SIAMESE INVASION OF LAOS

1785-92 BURMESE-SIAMESE WAR

1812 SIAMESE INVASION OF CAMBODIA

1810-11 BRITISH EXPEDITION TO INDONESIA

1823-6 1ST BRITISH-BURMESE WAR
✕ 1824 RANGOON

1819 BURMESE CONQUEST OF ASSAM

1825-30 GREAT JAVA WAR

SE ASIA

1843-8 NEW ZEALAND: 1ST MAORI...
✕ 1845 PUKETU...
✕ 1846 R...

CHINA / JAPAN

1839-42 1ST BRITISH-CHINESE 'OPIUM WAR'

1792-1800 FRANCO-BRITISH WAR FOR SENEGAL

1806-7 ASHANTI CONQUEST OF THE GOLD COAST

1806 BRITISH TAKE CAPE TOWN

1818-19 ZULU CIVIL WAR

1824-31 1ST BRITISH-ASHANTI WAR

1836-7 BOER GREAT TREK
BLOOD RIVER 1838 ✕

1779-81 1ST CAPE FRONTIER WAR

1793-5 2ND CAPE FRONTIER WAR

1820-39 EGYPT CONQUERS SUDAN

1775-95 SPORADIC CONFLICT BETWEEN BOERS AND HOTTENTOTS AND BUSHMEN

1809 BRITISH TAKE ST LOUIS (SENEGAL) FROM FRENCH

MACKENZIE'S REBELLION IN CANADA

1832 US BLACK HAWK INDIAN WAR

1835-43 US 2ND SEMINOLE INDIAN WAR

1846-8 US-MEX...
1847 BUENA VISTA

1835-6 TEXAN WAR OF INDEPENDENCE
✕ 1836 ALAMO AND SAN JACINTO

1836-9 PERU-BOLIVIAN WAR

1843-52 ARGENTINE-URUGUAYAN...

1838-9 FRENCH EXPEDITION TO MEXICO
1841 PERUVIAN INVASION OF BOLIVIA
✕ 1841 INGAVI

1780 · 1790 · 1800 · 1810 · 1820 · 1830 · 1840

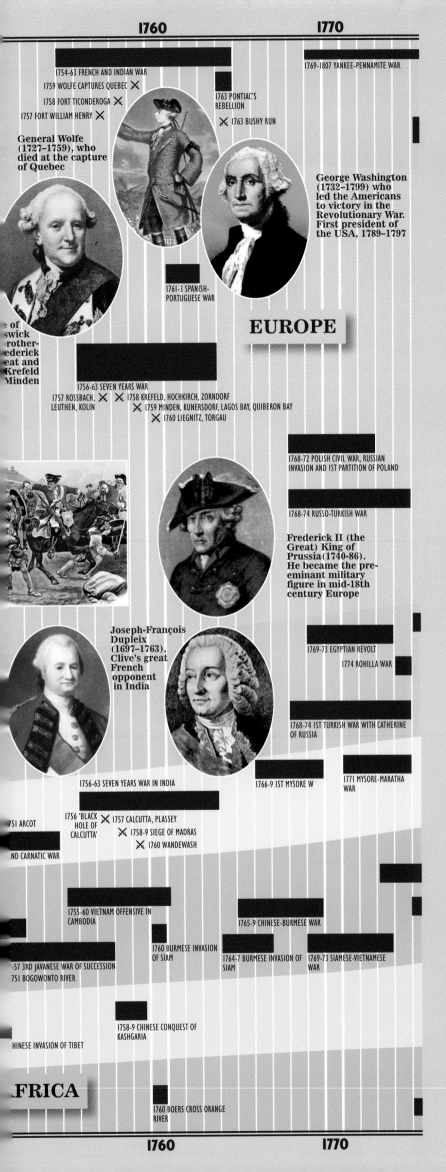

1754–63 FRENCH AND INDIAN WAR
1769–1807 YANKEE–PENNAMITE WAR
1759 WOLFE CAPTURES QUEBEC ✕
1758 FORT TICONDEROGA ✕
1757 FORT WILLIAM HENRY ✕
1763 PONTIAC'S REBELLION
✕ 1763 BUSHY RUN

General Wolfe (1727–1759), who died at the capture of Quebec

George Washington (1732–1799) who led the Americans to victory in the Revolutionary War. First president of the USA, 1789–1797

1761–3 SPANISH–PORTUGUESE WAR

EUROPE

e of swick rother- ederick eat and Krefeld Minden

1756–63 SEVEN YEARS WAR
1757 ROSSBACH, LEUTHEN, KOLIN ✕   ✕ 1758 KREFELD, HOCHKIRCH, ZORNDORF
✕ 1759 MINDEN, KUNERSDORF, LAGOS BAY, QUIBERON BAY
✕ 1760 LIEGNITZ, TORGAU

1768–72 POLISH CIVIL WAR, RUSSIAN INVASION AND 1ST PARTITION OF POLAND

1768–74 RUSSO-TURKISH WAR

Frederick II (the Great) King of Prussia (1740–86). He became the pre-eminent military figure in mid-18th century Europe

Joseph-François Dupleix (1697–1763), Clive's great French opponent in India

1769–73 EGYPTIAN REVOLT
1774 ROHILLA WAR

1768–74 1ST TURKISH WAR WITH CATHERINE OF RUSSIA

1756–63 SEVEN YEARS WAR IN INDIA
1766–9 1ST MYSORE W
1771 MYSORE-MARATHA WAR

751 ARCOT
1756 'BLACK HOLE OF CALCUTTA'   ✕ 1757 CALCUTTA, PLASSEY
✕ 1758-9 SIEGE OF MADRAS
✕ 1760 WANDEWASH

ND CARNATIC WAR

1755–60 VIETNAM OFFENSIVE IN CAMBODIA
1765–9 CHINESE-BURMESE WAR
1760 BURMESE INVASION OF SIAM
1764-7 BURMESE INVASION OF SIAM
1769-73 SIAMESE-VIETNAMESE WAR

–57 3RD JAVANESE WAR OF SUCCESSION
751 BOGOWONTO RIVER

1758-9 CHINESE CONQUEST OF KASHGARIA
HINESE INVASION OF TIBET

FRICA

1760 BOERS CROSS ORANGE RIVER

GREAT COMMANDERS

Charles XII (1697–1728)

Like Napoleon, Charles XII found nemesis in Russia. A brilliant tactician, he led Sweden to victory in a series of encounters in the first decade of the 18th century. When the Great Northern War began in 1700, a coalition of Denmark, Saxony and Russia attacked Sweden's Baltic and north German possessions. At the age of 19 Charles established his reputation at Narva in 1700, driving the Russians back from Sweden's Baltic provinces. His generals had already forced Denmark out of the war; in a succession of campaigns following Narva, by 1706 Charles thrashed all his opponents. The Swedish–Russian enmity continued however and in 1707 he invaded Russia, winning a battle at Holowczyn, but gradually being drawn deeper into Russia. Eventually at Poltava in 1709 his army, worn down by the long campaign far from home, was confronted by Peter the Great's far superior numbers and destroyed. Charles spent an astonishing 5 years in Turkey before returning to Sweden incognito through hostile Germany. He at once set about defending the beleaguered Swedish Empire, but it was too late. In 1718 he died of a head wound at the siege of Fredrikshald, Sweden's status as a great power dying with him. Brilliant as a tactician, he improved platoon firing and as at Narva made shock his chief weapon. But he was no logistician. He was also headstrong, restless, impulsive and lacking in strategic judgement.

John Churchill, Duke of Marlborough (b.1650–1722)

One of Britain's greatest generals, Marlborough won a series of epic victories in the War of the Spanish Succession that turned the tide against the expansionism of Louis XIV's France. In 1685 he served at Sedgemoor during the Monmouth Rebellion but deserted James II in 1688 to welcome William of Orange as King of England. He served in Ireland and Flanders before becoming Captain General of the Allied armies in Flanders, at the head of the coalition created by William to counter the aggression of France in the Low Countries. In 10 successive campaigns he proved his skills as strategist, tactical and logistical organiser – and as soldier-diplomat. His greatest victories were Blenheim (1704), Ramillies (1706), Oudinarde (1708) and Malplaquet (1709). Well-loved by his troops, rewarded with a dukedom and the palace of Blenheim in Oxfordshire, he retired in 1711 the victim of shifting political sands.

Robert, Lord Clive of Plassey (b.1725–1774)

The founder of the British Empire in India, Clive rose from humble beginnings as a clerk in the East India Company. In 1747 he became an ensign and began an unlikely military-political career. With audacity and much luck he was involved in numerous military expeditions against the Indians and French during the 2nd Carnatic War (1751–3). His defence of Arcot, which won Britain control of the Carnatic, made his reputation. His Bengal campaign of 1757 began as a response to the seizure of Calcutta by Nawab Siraj-ud-Daula and the story of the 'Black Hole' atrocity. Clive led the recapture of the city and defeated the Nawab at Plassey in a battle won by will-power and nerve against enormous odds. The result was British domination of Bengal. The establishment of the British Empire in India was to take many years, but his great victory had laid the foundation and Clive's subsequent role in extending and organising British India was profound.

Frederick II the Great (1740–96)

One of the Great Captains of History, Frederick was the man who turned Prussia into a major military power. Surviving a terrible early life with a violent, bullying father, Frederick inherited a highly organised military state – a machine he 'perfected' and took to war. In 1740 he seized Silesia and his battles to defend it proclaimed Prussia's new aggressive stance in Germany. During the Seven Years War his greatest battles were at Rossbach and Leuthen in 1757, but by 1759 he was beset by the converging forces of Austria, Russia and Sweden. The fact that Prussia survived is testimony to fast marching, hard fighting and Frederick's own indomitable genius. His influence on the conduct of war was of the greatest significance. His principles of war were fourfold – harsh discipline that reduced the individual soldier virtually to an automaton; great attention to prepared logistics; a stress on the offensive; and what he termed 'practicability' – which encompassed the use of the oblique order and aimed at local superiority on the battlefield. He was also an intellectual, the model of 'enlightened despotism' in the Age of Reason, a patron of Voltaire and an accomplished musician.

Maurice, Comte de Saxe (b.1696–1750)

Significant for his writings as much as for his deeds, de Saxe fought for the French in the War of the Austrian Succession, taking Tournai in 1745 after defeating the allies (Dutch, British, Austrians) at Fontenoy. This led to the conquest of much of the Spanish Netherlands; in 1746 he took Brussels and two years later Maastricht. His *Mes Rêveries* (1732) was the most important and forward-thinking military treatise of the early 18th century. Maurice stressed the need for officer responsibility, uniform drill and training. Light infantry were to be used in large numbers; and de Saxe also proposed an all-arms formation that was the precursor of the Napoleonic corps d'armeé.

Continued on page 50

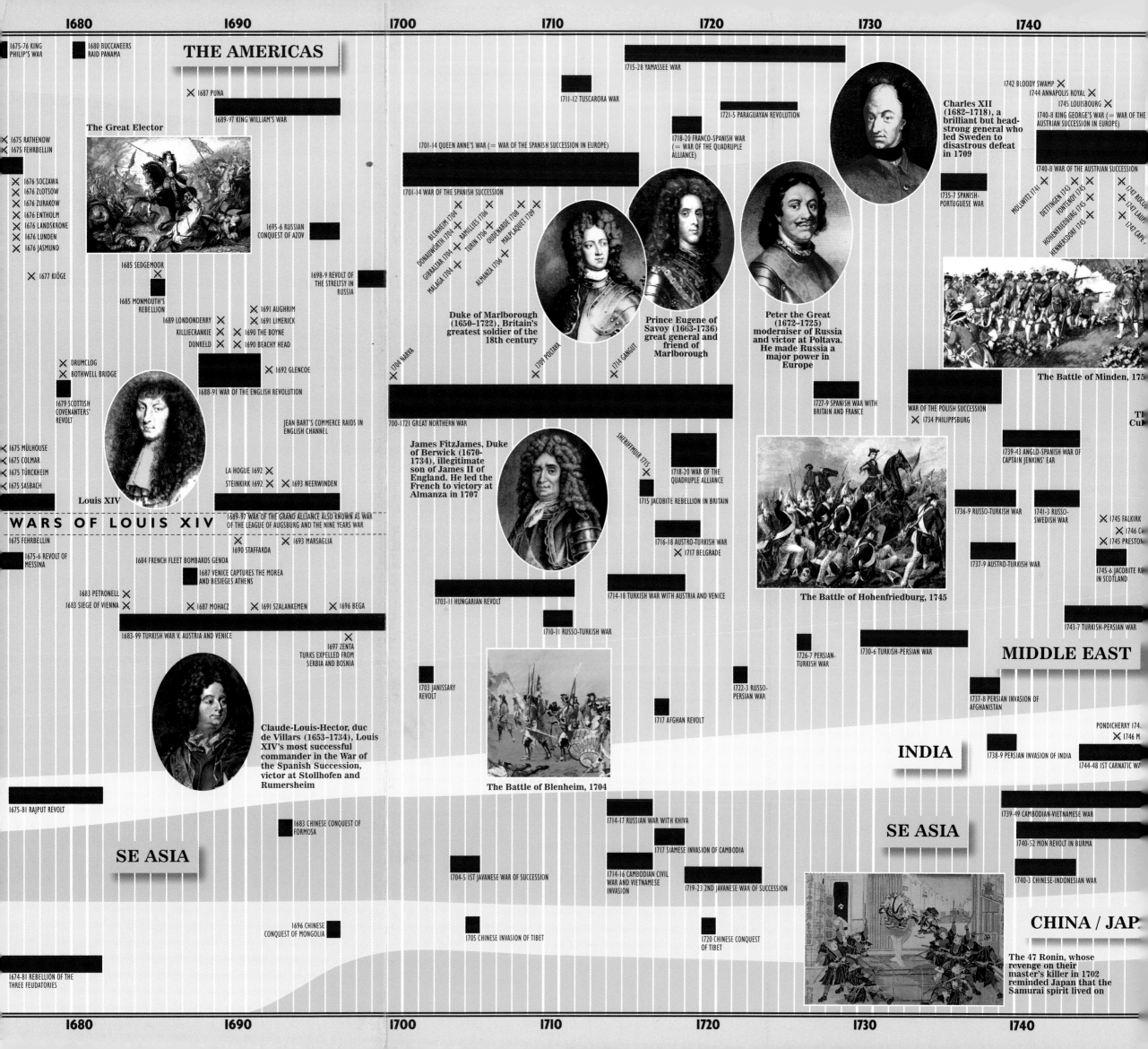

THE AMERICAS

1675-76 KING PHILIP'S WAR
1680 BUCCANEERS RAID PANAMA
✕ 1687 PUNA
1689-97 KING WILLIAM'S WAR
1715-28 YAMASSEE WAR
1711-12 TUSCARORA WAR
1721-5 PARAGUAYAN REVOLUTION
1742 BLOODY SWAMP ✕
1744 ANNAPOLIS ROYAL ✕
1745 LOUISBOURG ✕
1740-8 KING GEORGE'S WAR (= WAR OF THE AUSTRIAN SUCCESSION IN EUROPE)

The Great Elector

1695-6 RUSSIAN CONQUEST OF AZOV

Charles XII (1682–1718), a brilliant but head-strong general who led Sweden to disastrous defeat in 1709

1701-14 QUEEN ANNE'S WAR (= WAR OF THE SPANISH SUCCESSION IN EUROPE)

1718-20 FRANCO-SPANISH WAR (= WAR OF THE QUADRUPLE ALLIANCE)

1740-8 WAR OF THE AUSTRIAN SUCCESSION

1701-14 WAR OF THE SPANISH SUCCESSION

1735-7 SPANISH-PORTUGUESE WAR

MOLLWITZ 1741 ✕
DETTINGEN 1743 ✕
FONTENOY 1745 ✕
HOHENFRIEDBURG 1745 ✕
HENNERSDORF 1745 ✕
1742 ROCOU...
1745 LAUF...
1747 CAPE...

✕ 1675 RATHENOW
✕ 1675 FEHRBELLIN
✕ 1676 SOCZAWA
✕ 1676 ZLOTSOW
✕ 1676 ZURAKOW
✕ 1676 ENTHOLM
✕ 1676 LANDSKRONE
✕ 1676 LUNDEN
✕ 1676 JASMUND
✕ 1677 KIÖGE

BLENHEIM 1704 ✕
DONAUWÖRTH 1704 ✕
GIBRALTAR 1704 ✕
MALAGA 1704 ✕
RAMILLIES 1706 ✕
TURIN 1706 ✕
ALMANZA 1706 ✕
OUDENARDE 1708 ✕
MALPLAQUET 1709 ✕

✕ 1704 NARVA
✕ 1709 POLTAVA
✕ 1714 GANGUT

1685 SEDGEMOOR
1698-9 REVOLT OF THE STRELTSY IN RUSSIA

Duke of Marlborough (1650–1722), Britain's greatest soldier of the 18th century

Prince Eugene of Savoy (1663-1736) great general and friend of Marlborough

Peter the Great (1672–1725) moderniser of Russia and victor at Poltava. He made Russia a major power in Europe

1685 MONMOUTH'S REBELLION
1689 LONDONDERRY ✕   ✕ 1691 AUGHRIM
KILLIECRANKIE   ✕ 1691 LIMERICK
DUNKELD   ✕ 1690 THE BOYNE
✕ 1690 BEACHY HEAD
✕ 1692 GLENCOE

✕ DRUMCLOG
✕ BOTHWELL BRIDGE
1688-91 WAR OF THE ENGLISH REVOLUTION

The Battle of Minden, 175...

1679 SCOTTISH COVENANTERS' REVOLT

1727-9 SPANISH WAR WITH BRITAIN AND FRANCE
WAR OF THE POLISH SUCCESSION
✕ 1734 PHILIPPSBURG

✕ 1675 MÜLHOUSE
✕ 1675 COLMAR
✕ 1675 TÜRCKHEIM
✕ 1675 SASBACH

Louis XIV

JEAN BART'S COMMERCE RAIDS IN ENGLISH CHANNEL

700-1721 GREAT NORTHERN WAR

James FitzJames, Duke of Berwick (1670-1734), illegitimate son of James II of England. He led the French to victory at Almanza in 1707

SHERIFFMUIR 1715 ✕

1739-43 ANGLO-SPANISH WAR OF CAPTAIN JENKINS' EAR

LA HOGUE 1692 ✕
STEINKIRK 1692 ✕   ✕ 1693 NEERWINDEN

1718-20 WAR OF THE QUADRUPLE ALLIANCE

1715 JACOBITE REBELLION IN BRITAIN

The Battle of Hohenfriedburg, 1745

WARS OF LOUIS XIV

1689-97 WAR OF THE GRAND ALLIANCE ALSO KNOWN AS WAR OF THE LEAGUE OF AUGSBURG AND THE NINE YEARS WAR

1675 FEHRBELLIN
✕ 1690 STAFFARDA   ✕ 1693 MARSAGLIA
1684 FRENCH FLEET BOMBARDS GENOA
1687 VENICE CAPTURES THE MOREA AND BESIEGES ATHENS

1716-18 AUSTRO-TURKISH WAR
✕ 1717 BELGRADE

1736-9 RUSSO-TURKISH WAR
1741-3 RUSSO-SWEDISH WAR
✕ 1745 FALKIRK
✕ 1746 C...
✕ 1745 PRESTON...

1675-6 REVOLT OF MESSINA

1737-9 AUSTRO-TURKISH WAR

1745-6 JACOBITE R... IN SCOTLAND

1683 PETRONELL ✕
1683 SIEGE OF VIENNA ✕
✕ 1687 MOHACZ   ✕ 1691 SZALANKEMEN   ✕ 1696 BEGA

1714-18 TURKISH WAR WITH AUSTRIA AND VENICE

Claude-Louis-Hector, duc de Villars (1653–1734), Louis XIV's most successful commander in the War of the Spanish Succession, victor at Stollhofen and Rumersheim

1683-99 TURKISH WAR V. AUSTRIA AND VENICE
✕ 1697 ZENTA
TURKS EXPELLED FROM SERBIA AND BOSNIA

1703-11 HUNGARIAN REVOLT

1710-11 RUSSO-TURKISH WAR

1726-7 PERSIAN-TURKISH WAR
1730-6 TURKISH-PERSIAN WAR

1743-7 TURKISH-PERSIAN WAR

MIDDLE EAST

1703 JANISSARY REVOLT

1722-3 RUSSO-PERSIAN WAR

1737-8 PERSIAN INVASION OF AFGHANISTAN

1717 AFGHAN REVOLT

1675-81 RAJPUT REVOLT

The Battle of Blenheim, 1704

PONDICHERRY 174...
✕ 1746 M...

INDIA

1738-9 PERSIAN INVASION OF INDIA
1744-48 1ST CARNATIC WAR

1683 CHINESE CONQUEST OF FORMOSA

1714-17 RUSSIAN WAR WITH KHIVA

1739-49 CAMBODIAN-VIETNAMESE WAR

1717 SIAMESE INVASION OF CAMBODIA

1740-52 MON REVOLT IN BURMA

SE ASIA

1704-5 1ST JAVANESE WAR OF SUCCESSION

1714-16 CAMBODIAN CIVIL WAR AND VIETNAMESE INVASION

1719-23 2ND JAVANESE WAR OF SUCCESSION

1740-3 CHINESE-INDONESIAN WAR

1696 CHINESE CONQUEST OF MONGOLIA

1705 CHINESE INVASION OF TIBET

1720 CHINESE CONQUEST OF TIBET

CHINA / JAP...

The 47 Ronin, whose revenge on their master's killer in 1702 reminded Japan that the Samurai spirit lived on

1674-81 REBELLION OF THE THREE FEUDATORIES

GREAT COMMANDERS

Robert Blake (b.1599–1657)

One of England's greatest admirals, Blake fought for the Parliament in the defence of Bristol, Lyme Regis and Taunton during the English Civil war. In 1644 he became Parliament's General at Sea, in which role he hounded Prince Rupert's Royalist fleet to destruction (1650). The result was the recovery of the Scillies and Jersey. He fought during the First Anglo-Dutch War, defeating Tromp off Dover (1652) and Kentish Knock (1652), losing off Dungeness but winning again off Portland in 1653. In 1655 he campaigned against the Barbary pirates; in 1656–7 blockaded Spain over the winter; and in 1657 carried out a spectacular raid on Santa Cruz in the Canaries. He was instrumental in creating the new British navy and in the creation of *Fighting Instructions* in 1653, crucial to the development of the organisation and tactical handling of fleets in battle. From this time onwards, Britain's navy was to become one of the great military forces on the world stage.

The Great Condé, Louis II de Bourbon, Prince de Condé, Duc d'Enghien (b.1621–1686)

Of French royal blood, Condé was, with Turenne, the greatest general of his time. His first victory came at Rocroi in 1643, when he was just 21 years of age. It was the greatest French victory for a century and marked the end of Spanish tercio supremacy and the rise of French military power. A series of victories followed with Turenne, including Freiburg, Philippsburg, Mainz and Nördlingen in 1645. His campaign in Flanders in 1646 was a brilliant success, as was his victory at Lens in 1648, following a brief campaign in Spain and defeat at Lérida the previous year. He was on Mazarin's side during the first *parliamentaire Fronde* of 1648–9 but turned against the Cardinal and was imprisoned in 1650, setting in motion the *Fronde* of the Princes – a major crisis for the regency of Anne of Austria and Mazarin. Released in 1651, he went into open rebellion until his position became untenable and he left France to fight for Spain. During this time he met defeat at the Battle of the Dunes in 1658. He was reconciled to Louis XIV the following year, thereafter invading Franche Comté in 1668 and invading the Netherlands with Turenne in 1672. At Seneffe two years later he halted the advance of the Prince of Orange. His personality was marked by princely arrogance coupled with an unrestrained temper, which must have been exacerbated in later life by crippling gout. He retired in 1675, the year in which his friend and colleague Turenne was killed.

Oliver Cromwell (b.1599–1658)

Arguably the greatest Englishman of the seventeenth century, Cromwell was essentially a politician and statesman, whose generalship was forced upon him by circumstance, revealing a soldier of genius. A Member of Parliament before and during the English Civil war, he raised his own regiment of 'Ironsides' and served as second-in-command of the Eastern Association army. Impatience with the lacklustre prosecution of the war by the Parliament's military leaders, he led the creation of the new Model Army, in which he soon became second-in-command. At Naseby the charge of his cavalry won the day. As an independent commander he proved his abilities at Preston, then at Dunbar (1650) and Worcester (1651). His campaign in Ireland (1649–50) earned him notoriety in Irish history for massacres following the capture of Drogheda and Wexford, but recent research has begun to absolve him. Essentially a moderate, he was driven to extreme measures by the duplicity and intransigence of the King, and took the lead in bringing Charles to trial and execution. Subsequent attempts to settle the government of the country proved tiresome and fruitless, and he soon became frustrated. His role as Lord Protector (1653 to his death) verged on monarchy. A central figure in British history, he was one of the great generals of the seventeenth century. He was also the statesman whose foreign policy marked a turning-point, leading to the nation's emergence as a world power.

Sir Thomas Fairfax (b.1612–1671)

Captain-General of Parliament's New Model Army during the English Civil War, 'Black Tom' was a brave cavalryman and a skilled general. His apprenticeship to war was in 1629–31 in the Netherlands, and in 1640 he fought at Newburn in the Bishops' Wars. During the early years of the English Civil War he commanded the cavalry under his father in Yorkshire, taking Leeds and Wakefield in 1643, but being defeated at Adwalton Moor. He shared the victory at Winceby and in 1644 laid siege to York. At the Battle of Marston Moor he commanded the right wing of the Roundhead army. In 1645 Parliament appointed him Captain-General of the New Model Army, with which he won at Naseby and Langport, cleared the Royalist West and in 1646 entered the Royalist capital of Oxford. In 1648 he crushed the Royalists at Maidstone and Colchester during the Second Civil War. Essentially a moderate man without the political motivation of many of his colleagues, he increasingly distanced himself from the victorious Parliament leadership and retired in 1651. Although he has often been eclipsed by Cromwell in accounts of the English Civil war, it was the military partnership of the two men that proved the war-winning factor in the Roundhead victory.

Continued on page 50

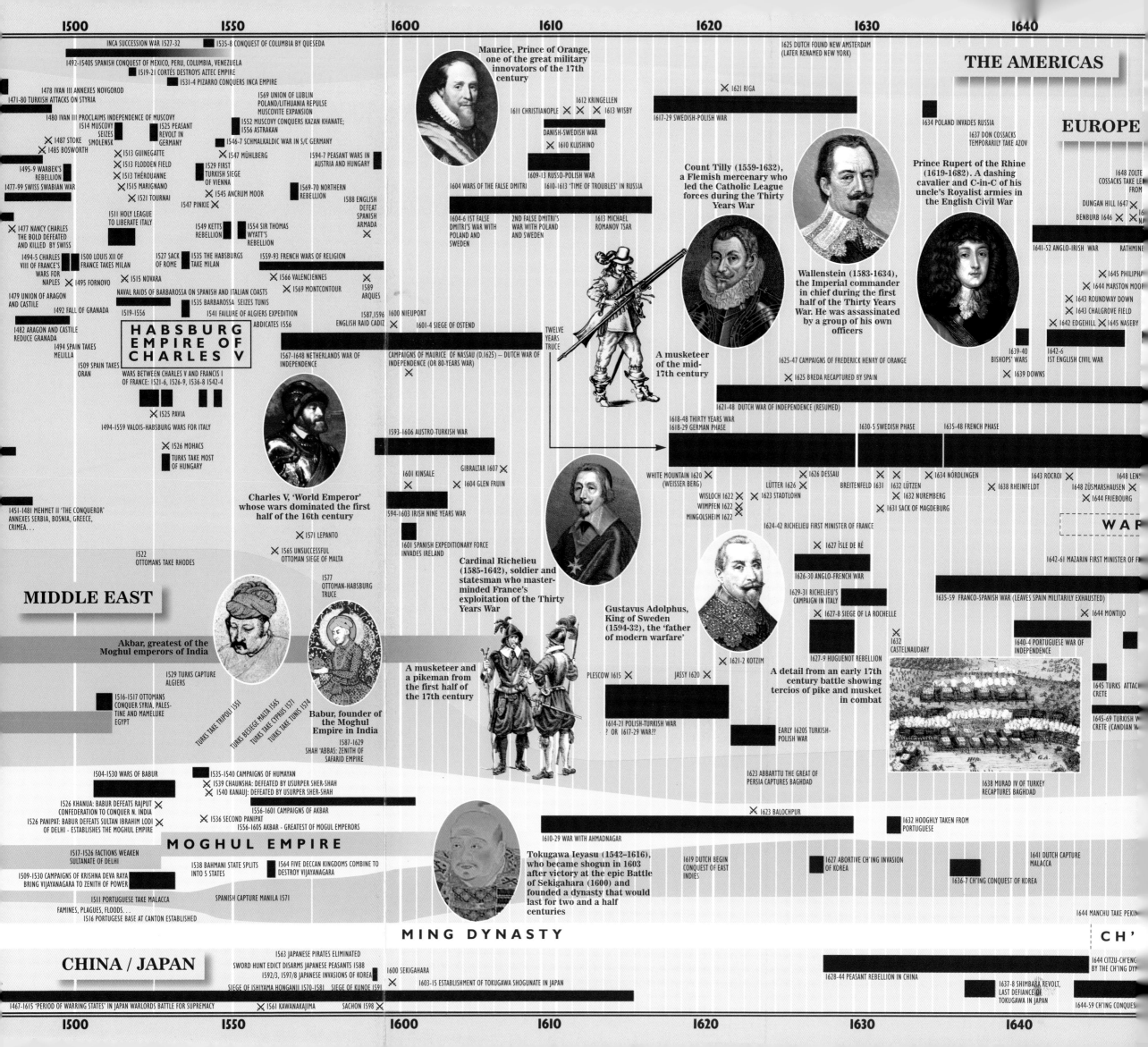

Timeline 1500–1640

Axis: 1500 · 1550 · 1600 · 1610 · 1620 · 1630 · 1640

THE AMERICAS

- INCA SUCCESSION WAR 1527-32
- 1535-8 CONQUEST OF COLUMBIA BY QUESEDA
- 1492-1540s SPANISH CONQUEST OF MEXICO, PERU, COLUMBIA, VENEZUELA
- 1519-21 CORTÉS DESTROYS AZTEC EMPIRE
- 1531-4 PIZARRO CONQUERS INCA EMPIRE
- 1625 DUTCH FOUND NEW AMSTERDAM (LATER RENAMED NEW YORK)

Maurice, Prince of Orange, one of the great military innovators of the 17th century

EUROPE

- 1478 IVAN III ANNEXES NOVGOROD
- 1471-80 TURKISH ATTACKS ON STYRIA
- 1480 IVAN III PROCLAIMS INDEPENDENCE OF MUSCOVY
- 1514 MUSCOVY SEIZES SMOLENSK
- 1525 PEASANT REVOLT IN GERMANY
- 1552 MUSCOVY CONQUERS KAZAN KHANATE; 1556 ASTRAKAN
- 1546-7 SCHMALKALDIC WAR IN S/C GERMANY
- 1569 UNION OF LUBLIN POLAND/LITHUANIA REPULSE MUSCOVITE EXPANSION
- 1611 CHRISTIANOPLE ✕ ✕ 1612 KRINGELLEN ✕ 1613 WISBY
- ✕ 1621 RIGA
- 1617-29 SWEDISH-POLISH WAR
- DANISH-SWEDISH WAR
- ✕ 1610 KLUSHINO
- 1609-13 RUSSO-POLISH WAR
- 1604 WARS OF THE FALSE DMITRI
- 1610-1613 'TIME OF TROUBLES' IN RUSSIA
- 1604-6 1ST FALSE DMITRI'S WAR WITH POLAND AND SWEDEN
- 2ND FALSE DMITRI'S WAR WITH POLAND AND SWEDEN
- 1613 MICHAEL ROMANOV TSAR
- 1634 POLAND INVADES RUSSIA
- 1637 DON COSSACKS TEMPORARILY TAKE AZOV
- 1648 ZOLTE COSSACKS TAKE LE... FROM
- 1487 STOKE ✕
- 1485 BOSWORTH ✕
- ✕ 1513 GUINEGATTE
- ✕ 1513 FLODDEN FIELD
- ✕ 1513 THÉROUANNE
- 1495-9 WARBEK'S REBELLION
- 1477-99 SWISS SWABIAN WAR
- 1529 FIRST TURKISH SIEGE OF VIENNA
- 1547 MÜHLBERG ✕
- 1594-7 PEASANT WARS IN AUSTRIA AND HUNGARY
- ✕ 1515 MARIGNANO
- 1545 ANCRUM MOOR
- ✕ 1521 TOURNAI
- 1547 PINKIE
- 1569-70 NORTHERN REBELLION
- 1588 ENGLISH DEFEAT SPANISH ARMADA
- DUNGAN HILL 1647
- BENBURB 1646
- 1641-52 ANGLO-IRISH WAR
- RATHMIN...
- 1511 HOLY LEAGUE TO LIBERATE ITALY
- 1549 KETTS REBELLION
- 1554 SIR THOMAS WYATT'S REBELLION
- 1645 PHILIPHA...
- 1477 NANCY CHARLES THE BOLD DEFEATED AND KILLED BY SWISS
- 1494-5 CHARLES VIII OF FRANCE'S WARS FOR NAPLES
- ✕ 1495 FORNOVO
- 1500 LOUIS XII OF FRANCE TAKES MILAN
- 1527 SACK OF ROME
- 1535 THE HABSBURGS TAKE MILAN
- 1559-93 FRENCH WARS OF RELIGION
- ✕ 1644 MARSTON MOO...
- ✕ 1643 ROUNDWAY DOWN
- ✕ 1643 CHALGROVE FIELD
- ✕ 1515 NOVARA
- ✕ 1566 VALENCIENNES
- ✕ 1569 MONTCONTOUR
- 1589 ARQUES
- ✕ 1642 EDGEHILL ✕ 1645 NASEBY
- 1479 UNION OF ARAGON AND CASTILE
- 1492 FALL OF GRANADA
- 1482 ARAGON AND CASTILE REDUCE GRANADA
- 1509 SPAIN TAKES ORAN
- 1519-1556
- Naval raids of Barbarossa on Spanish and Italian coasts
- 1535 BARBAROSSA SEIZES TUNIS
- 1541 FAILURE OF ALGIERS EXPEDITION
- 1587,1596 ENGLISH RAID CADIZ
- 1600 NIEUPORT
- 1601-4 SIEGE OF OSTEND
- 1639-40 BISHOPS' WARS
- 1642-6 1ST ENGLISH CIVIL WAR
- ✕ 1639 DOWNS
- 1494 SPAIN TAKES MELILLA
- 1625-47 CAMPAIGNS OF FREDERICK HENRY OF ORANGE
- ✕ 1625 BREDA RECAPTURED BY SPAIN

HABSBURG EMPIRE OF CHARLES V

- ABDICATES 1556
- 1567-1648 NETHERLANDS WAR OF INDEPENDENCE
- CAMPAIGNS OF MAURICE OF NASSAU (D.1625) – DUTCH WAR OF INDEPENDENCE (OR 80-YEARS WAR)
- TWELVE YEARS TRUCE
- 1621-48 DUTCH WAR OF INDEPENDENCE (RESUMED)
- WARS BETWEEN CHARLES V AND FRANCIS I OF FRANCE: 1521-6, 1526-9, 1536-8 1542-4
- ✕ 1525 PAVIA
- 1494-1559 VALOIS-HABSBURG WARS FOR ITALY
- 1593-1606 AUSTRO-TURKISH WAR
- 1618-48 THIRTY YEARS WAR
- 1618-29 GERMAN PHASE
- 1630-5 SWEDISH PHASE
- 1635-48 FRENCH PHASE
- ✕ 1526 MOHACS
- TURKS TAKE MOST OF HUNGARY
- 1601 KINSALE ✕
- GIBRALTAR 1607 ✕
- ✕ 1604 GLEN FRUIN
- 1594-1603 IRISH NINE YEARS WAR
- WHITE MOUNTAIN 1620 ✕✕ (WEISSER BERG)
- ✕ 1626 DESSAU
- ✕ 1634 NÖRDLINGEN
- 1643 ROCROI ✕
- 1648 LEN...
- LÜTTER 1626 ✕
- BREITENFELD 1631 ✕
- 1632 LÜTZEN ✕
- ✕ 1638 RHEINFELDT
- 1648 ZÜSMARSHAUSEN
- WISLOCH 1622 ✕
- ✕ 1623 STADTLOHN
- 1632 NUREMBERG
- 1644 FRIEBOURG
- WIMPFEN 1622 ✕
- MINGOLSHEIM 1622 ✕
- 1631 SACK OF MAGDEBURG
- 1624-42 RICHELIEU FIRST MINISTER OF FRANCE
- ✕ 1627 ÎSLE DE RÉ
- 1626-30 ANGLO-FRENCH WAR
- 1629-31 RICHELIEU'S CAMPAIGN IN ITALY
- ✕ 1627-8 SIEGE OF LA ROCHELLE
- 1627-9 HUGUENOT REBELLION
- 1635-59 FRANCO-SPANISH WAR (LEAVES SPAIN MILITARILY EXHAUSTED)
- ✕ 1644 MONTIJO
- 1642-61 MAZARIN FIRST MINISTER OF F...
- 1632 CASTELNAUDARY
- 1640-4 PORTUGUESE WAR OF INDEPENDENCE

Count Tilly (1559-1632), a Flemish mercenary who led the Catholic League forces during the Thirty Years War

Wallenstein (1583-1634), the Imperial commander in chief during the first half of the Thirty Years War. He was assassinated by a group of his own officers

Prince Rupert of the Rhine (1619-1682). A dashing cavalier and C-in-C of his uncle's Royalist armies in the English Civil War

A musketeer of the mid-17th century

Charles V, 'World Emperor' whose wars dominated the first half of the 16th century

Cardinal Richelieu (1585-1642), soldier and statesman who masterminded France's exploitation of the Thirty Years War

Gustavus Adolphus, King of Sweden (1594-32), the 'father of modern warfare'

A detail from an early 17th century battle showing tercios of pike and musket in combat

MIDDLE EAST

- 1451-1481 MEHMET II 'THE CONQUEROR' ANNEXES SERBIA, BOSNIA, GREECE, CRIMEA...
- 1522 OTTOMANS TAKE RHODES
- ✕ 1571 LEPANTO
- ✕ 1565 UNSUCCESSFUL OTTOMAN SIEGE OF MALTA
- 1601 SPANISH EXPEDITIONARY FORCE INVADES IRELAND
- 1577 OTTOMAN-HABSBURG TRUCE
- 1529 TURKS CAPTURE ALGIERS
- 1516-1517 OTTOMANS CONQUER SYRIA, PALESTINE AND MAMELUKE EGYPT
- TURKS TAKE TRIPOLI 1551
- TURKS BESIEGE MALTA 1565
- TURKS TAKE CYPRUS 1571
- TURKS TAKE TUNIS 1574
- PLESCOW 1615 ✕
- JASSY 1620 ✕
- 1614-21 POLISH-TURKISH WAR ? OR 1617-29 WAR??
- ✕ 1621-2 KOTZIM
- EARLY 1620s TURKISH-POLISH WAR
- 1623 ABBARTTU THE GREAT OF PERSIA CAPTURES BAGHDAD
- 1638 MURAD IV OF TURKEY RECAPTURES BAGHDAD
- 1645 TURKS ATTACK CRETE
- 1645-69 TURKISH W... CRETE (CANDIAN W...
- 1587-1629 SHAH 'ABBAS: ZENITH OF SAFARID EMPIRE

Akbar, greatest of the Moghul emperors of India

Babur, founder of the Moghul Empire in India

A musketeer and a pikeman from the first half of the 17th century

MOGHUL EMPIRE

- 1504-1530 WARS OF BABUR
- 1535-1540 CAMPAIGNS OF HUMAYAN
- ✕ 1539 CHAUNSHA: DEFEATED BY USURPER SHER-SHAH
- ✕ 1540 KANAUJ: DEFEATED BY USURPER SHER-SHAH
- 1526 KHANUA: BABUR DEFEATS RAJPUT CONFEDERATION TO CONQUER N. INDIA ✕
- ✕ 1536 SECOND PANIPAT
- 1556-1601 CAMPAIGNS OF AKBAR
- 1526 PANIPAT: BABUR DEFEATS SULTAN IBRAHIM LODI OF DELHI - ESTABLISHES THE MOGHUL EMPIRE ✕
- 1556-1605 AKBAR - GREATEST OF MOGUL EMPERORS
- ✕ 1623 BALOCHPUR
- 1610-29 WAR WITH AHMADNAGAR
- 1517-1526 FACTIONS WEAKEN SULTANATE OF DELHI
- 1538 BAHMANI STATE SPLITS INTO 5 STATES
- 1564 FIVE DECCAN KINGDOMS COMBINE TO DESTROY VIJAYANAGARA
- 1509-1530 CAMPAIGNS OF KRISHNA DEVA RAYA BRING VIJAYANAGARA TO ZENITH OF POWER
- 1511 PORTUGUESE TAKE MALACCA
- SPANISH CAPTURE MANILA 1571
- FAMINES, PLAGUES, FLOODS...
- 1516 PORTUGESE BASE AT CANTON ESTABLISHED
- 1619 DUTCH BEGIN CONQUEST OF EAST INDIES
- 1627 ABORTIVE CH'ING INVASION OF KOREA
- 1636-7 CH'ING CONQUEST OF KOREA
- 1632 HOOGHLY TAKEN FROM PORTUGUESE
- 1641 DUTCH CAPTURE MALACCA

Tokugawa Ieyasu (1542–1616), who became shogun in 1603 after victory at the epic Battle of Sekigahara (1600) and founded a dynasty that would last for two and a half centuries

CHINA / JAPAN

MING DYNASTY | **CH'...**

- 1563 JAPANESE PIRATES ELIMINATED
- SWORD HUNT EDICT DISARMS JAPANESE PEASANTS 1588
- 1592/3, 1597/8 JAPANESE INVASIONS OF KOREA
- 1600 SEKIGAHARA ✕
- 1603-15 ESTABLISHMENT OF TOKUGAWA SHOGUNATE IN JAPAN
- 1628-44 PEASANT REBELLION IN CHINA
- 1637-8 SHIMBARA REVOLT, LAST DEFIANCE OF TOKUGAWA IN JAPAN
- SIEGE OF ISHIYAMA HONGANJI 1570-1581   SIEGE OF KUNOE 1591
- 1467-1615 'PERIOD OF WARRING STATES' IN JAPAN WARLORDS BATTLE FOR SUPREMACY
- ✕ 1561 KAWANAKAJIMA
- SACHON 1598
- 1644 MANCHU TAKE PEKIN...
- 1644 CITZU-CH'ENG... BY THE CH'ING DY...
- 1644-59 CH'ING CONQUE...

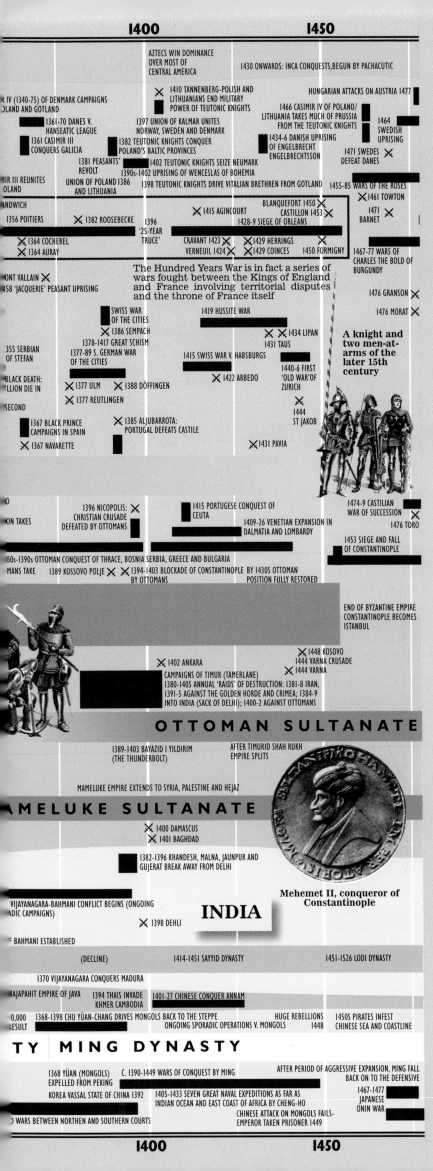

GREAT COMMANDERS

Babur (Zahir ad-Din Muhammad) (1494/1526–1530)

Founder of the Mogul Empire in India. A descendant of the great Mongol conquerors (including Genghis Khan and Timur), he succeeded to the throne of the insignificant kingdom of Fargana in 1494. His ambitions lay towards Samarkand (which had been Timur's capital), but here he found only frustration. His great enterprise to India met with spectacular success, striking against a Sultanate of Delhi riven and weakened by factionalism. His key victories at Panipat and Khanua in 1526 secured Delhi and Agra, and he subsequently extended his conquests to the frontier of Bengal. Cultured and convivial, he was a great poet and sportsman and conversationalist. His memoirs, *Babur-nameh*, are a classic.

Baybars I (1260–1277)

Founder of the Mameluke Sultanate of Egypt and Syria. After fighting in the campaign against Louis IX's crusade during 1249–50, and participating in the victory over the Mongols at Ayn Jalut in 1260, he usurped the throne and began a vigorous campaign to eliminate the remaining crusader states in Syria. In 1268 he took Antioch and in 1271 captured the impressive Christian castle of Krak des Chevaliers. A truce with the Christians was followed by campaigns against the Armenians in 1266, 1275 and 1277. Throughout his reign he was in almost constant conflict with the crusaders and the Mongols, against whom he fought nine battles. He united Syria and Egypt into one state and pursued an intelligent foreign policy, establishing good relations with the Byzantines. He died accidentally of poison intended for another victim.

Robert I (the Bruce) (1306–1329)

Scotland's greatest warrior hero, who won independence from England. Of essentially Anglo-Norman lineage, he became leader of the anti-English party in 1306, after years of service to Edward I. His murder of John Comyn allowed him to proclaim himself King of Scotland, but long campaigning was necessary to make this a reality. In 1306 he was defeated at Methven and Dalry, becoming a fugitive (from which grew the famous legend of his taking new heart from the efforts of a spider repairing its web). Taking full advantage of the weak reign of Edward II, he achieved a major victory at Bannockburn. Even so, another fourteen years of fighting were necessary to bring English recognition of Scottish independence. The romance of his life continued after his death, his heart being taken in pilgrimage for burial in the Holy Land.

Charles V (1519–1558)

Habsburg monarch whose reign dominated the first half of the sixteenth century. His vast inheritance – Spain in 1516, Austria and the Holy Roman Empire in 1519 – constituted a 'monarchia' of unprecedented proportions, taking in Spain, parts of Italy, the Netherlands, Germany and the Habsburg lands in the New World. His reign was coloured by three main themes: the Reformation and his attempts to defeat Protestantism in Germany; the aggressive expansionism of the Ottoman Turks in Hungary and the Mediterranean; and a continuing feud with Francis I of France, the French seeing themselves as encircled and threatened by the huge empire of the Habsburgs. Charles was forced to travel constantly in Europe to deal with a succession of crises. His army defeated the French at Pavia in 1525, ensuring Spanish supremacy in Italy. In 1547 at Mühlberg he defeated the German Protestants. But his incessant wars outran his credit, the silver mines of South America yet to come into production and provide the massive quantity of bullion that would enrich Spain during his son's reign. The responsibilities of state weighed heavily upon him, for ruling an empire this colossal in the sixteenth century was beyond the capability of one man. He abdicated in 1555/6, splitting the empire into its Spanish and Austrian components.

Edward I (1272–1307)

One of England's greatest soldier-kings, who emerged from the civil wars of thirteenth-century England by his victory at Evesham in 1265 to become virtual ruler of the county. In two campaigns he conquered Wales (1277 and 1282), subsequently building massive and beautiful castles to overawe the Welsh. His wars in Scotland met with less success. In 1296 he conquered Scotland but immediately provoked uprisings, including that of Sir William Wallace. He died on campaign in Scotland.

Edward III (1327–1377)

The first half of Edward's long reign were years of dazzling success. In 1333 at Halidon Hill he took revenge upon the Scots for Bannockburn. In 1337 disputes with the King of France over English possessions led to the outbreak of the Hundred Years War, the first phase of which Edward won in style. At Sluys in 1340 he achieved a major naval victory, practically annihilating the French fleet. In 1347 his celebrated victory at Crécy led to the capture of Calais. As the Black Death made its terrible impact upon Europe, only sporadic operations followed both in France and Scotland, until the victory at Poitiers in 1356 where the Black Prince captured the French king. A subsequent campaign was needed to bring peace on English terms, the zenith of Edward's reign, in 1360, by which Edward gained all Aquitaine. The remainder of his reign was

Continued on page 50

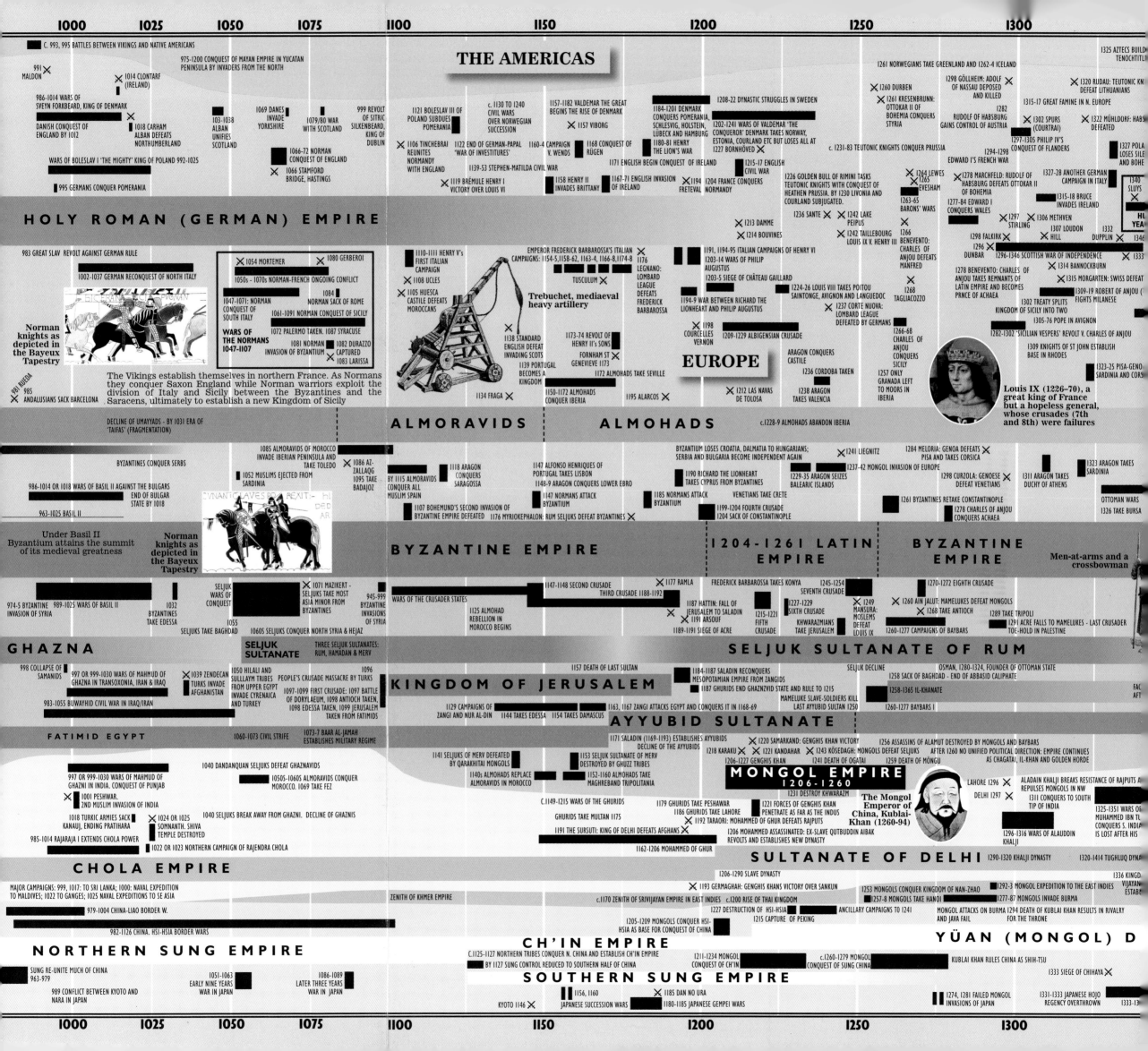

1000 | 1025 | 1050 | 1075 | 1100 | 1150 | 1200 | 1250 | 1300

THE AMERICAS

C. 993, 995 BATTLES BETWEEN VIKINGS AND NATIVE AMERICANS

975-1200 CONQUEST OF MAYAN EMPIRE IN YUCATAN PENINSULA BY INVADERS FROM THE NORTH

1325 AZTECS BUILD TENOCHTITL[AN]

991 MALDON

1014 CLONTARF (IRELAND)

986-1014 WARS OF SVEYN FORKBEARD, KING OF DENMARK

DANISH CONQUEST OF ENGLAND BY 1012

1018 CARHAM ALBAN DEFEATS NORTHUMBERLAND

1034-1038 ALBAN UNIFIES SCOTLAND

1069 DANES INVADE YORKSHIRE

1079/80 WAR WITH SCOTLAND

999 REVOLT OF SITRIC SILKENBEARD, KING OF DUBLIN

1066-72 NORMAN CONQUEST OF ENGLAND

1066 STAMFORD BRIDGE, HASTINGS

WARS OF BOLESLAV I 'THE MIGHTY' KING OF POLAND 992-1025

995 GERMANS CONQUER POMERANIA

1121 BOLESLAV III OF POLAND SUBDUES POMERANIA

c. 1130 TO 1240 CIVIL WARS OVER NORWEGIAN SUCCESSION

1157-1182 VALDEMAR THE GREAT BEGINS THE RISE OF DENMARK

1157 VIBORG

1184-1201 DENMARK CONQUERS POMERANIA, SCHLESWIG, HOLSTEIN, LÜBECK AND HAMBURG

1208-22 DYNASTIC STRUGGLES IN SWEDEN

1202-1241 WARS OF VALDEMAR 'THE CONQUEROR' DENMARK TAKES NORWAY, ESTONIA, COURLAND ETC BUT LOSES ALL AT 1227 BORNHÖVED

1180-81 HENRY THE LION'S WAR

1261 NORWEGIANS TAKE GREENLAND AND 1262-4 ICELAND

1260 DURBEN

1261 KRESENBRUNN: OTTOKAR II OF BOHEMIA CONQUERS STYRIA

1298 GÖLLHEIM: ADOLF OF NASSAU DEPOSED AND KILLED

1282 RUDOLF OF HABSBURG GAINS CONTROL OF AUSTRIA

1320 RUDAU: TEUTONIC KN[IGHTS] DEFEAT LITHUANIANS

1315-17 GREAT FAMINE IN N. EUROPE

1302 SPURS (COURTRAI)

1322 MÜHLDORF: HABS[BURGS] DEFEATED

1297-1305 PHILIP IV'S CONQUEST OF FLANDERS

1294-1298 EDWARD I'S FRENCH WAR

1327 POLA[ND] LOSES SILE[SIA] AND BOHE[MIA]

c. 1231-83 TEUTONIC KNIGHTS CONQUER PRUSSIA

1106 TINCHEBRAI REUNITES NORMANDY WITH ENGLAND

1122 END OF GERMAN-PAPAL 'WAR OF INVESTITURES'

1160-4 CAMPAIGN V. WENDS

1168 CONQUEST OF RÜGEN

1171 ENGLISH BEGIN CONQUEST OF IRELAND

1215-17 ENGLISH CIVIL WAR

1139-53 STEPHEN-MATILDA CIVIL WAR

1119 BRÉMULE HENRY I VICTORY OVER LOUIS VI

1158 HENRY II INVADES BRITTANY

1167-71 ENGLISH INVASION OF IRELAND

1194 FRETEVAL

1204 FRANCE CONQUERS NORMANDY

1226 GOLDEN BULL OF RIMINI TASKS TEUTONIC KNIGHTS WITH CONQUEST OF HEATHEN PRUSSIA. BY 1230 LIVONIA AND COURLAND SUBJUGATED.

1264 LEWES

1265 EVESHAM

1263-65 BARONS' WARS

1278 MARCHFELD: RUDOLF OF HABSBURG DEFEATS OTTOKAR II OF BOHEMIA

1327-28 ANOTHER GERMAN CAMPAIGN IN ITALY

1315-18 BRUCE INVADES IRELAND

1277-84 EDWARD I CONQUERS WALES

1340 SLUYS

HU[NDRED] YEA[RS]

HOLY ROMAN (GERMAN) EMPIRE

1236 SANTE

1242 LAKE PEIPUS

1213 DAMME

1214 BOUVINES

1242 TAILLEBOURG LOUIS IX V. HENRY III

1297 STIRLING

1306 METHVEN

1307 LOUDON HILL

1332 DUPPLIN

1346

1298 FALKIRK

1296 DUNBAR

1296-1346 SCOTTISH WAR OF INDEPENDENCE

1333

983 GREAT SLAV REVOLT AGAINST GERMAN RULE

1002-1037 GERMAN RECONQUEST OF NORTH ITALY

1054 MORTEMER

1080 GERBEROI

1050s - 1070s NORMAN-FRENCH ONGOING CONFLICT

1047-1071: NORMAN CONQUEST OF SOUTH ITALY

1084 NORMAN SACK OF ROME

1061-1091 NORMAN CONQUEST OF SICILY

WARS OF THE NORMANS 1047-1107

1072 PALERMO TAKEN. 1087 SYRACUSE

1081 NORMAN INVASION OF BYZANTIUM

1082 DURAZZO CAPTURED

1083 LARISSA

Norman knights as depicted in the Bayeux Tapestry

1110-1111 HENRY V's FIRST ITALIAN CAMPAIGN

1108 UCLES

1105 HUESCA CASTILE DEFEATS MOROCCANS

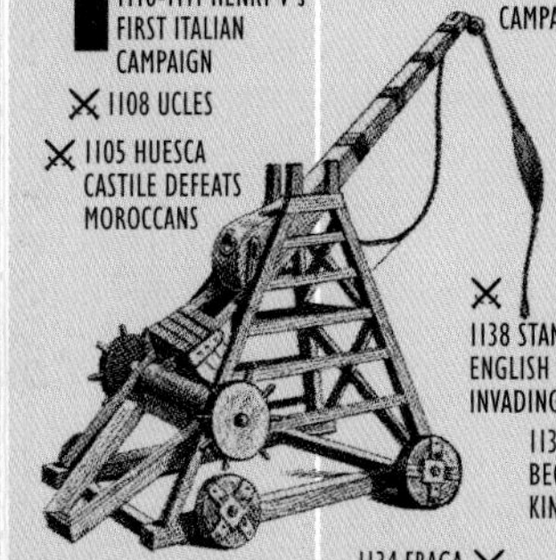

Trebuchet, mediaeval heavy artillery

EMPEROR FREDERICK BARBAROSSA'S ITALIAN CAMPAIGNS: 1154-5,1158-62, 1163-4, 1166-8,1174-8

1176 LEGNANO: LOMBARD LEAGUE DEFEATS FREDERICK BARBAROSSA

TUSCULUM

1191, 1194-95 ITALIAN CAMPAIGNS OF HENRY VI

1203-14 WARS OF PHILIP AUGUSTUS

1203-5 SIEGE OF CHÂTEAU GAILLARD

1224-26 LOUIS VIII TAKES POITOU SAINTONGE, AVIGNON AND LANGUEDOC

1194-9 WAR BETWEEN RICHARD THE LIONHEART AND PHILIP AUGUSTUS

1237 CORTE NUOVA: LOMBARD LEAGUE DEFEATED BY GERMANS

1266 BENEVENTO: CHARLES OF ANJOU DEFEATS MANFRED

1268 TAGLIACOZZO

1278 BENEVENTO: CHARLES OF ANJOU TAKES REMNANTS OF LATIN EMPIRE AND BECOMES PRNCE OF ACHAEA

1314 BANNOCKBURN

1315 MORGARTEN: SWISS DEFEAT

1309-19 ROBERT OF ANJOU FIGHTS MILANESE

1302 TREATY SPLITS KINGDOM OF SICILY INTO TWO

1305-76 POPE IN AVIGNON

1138 STANDARD ENGLISH DEFEAT INVADING SCOTS

1139 PORTUGAL BECOMES A KINGDOM

1173-74 REVOLT OF HENRY II's SONS

FORNHAM ST GENEVIEVE 1173

1198 COURCELLES VERNON

1209-1229 ALBIGENSIAN CRUSADE

1266-68 CHARLES OF ANJOU CONQUERS SICILY

1282-1302 'SICILIAN VESPERS' REVOLT V. CHARLES OF ANJOU

1309 KNIGHTS OF ST JOHN ESTABLISH BASE IN RHODES

EUROPE

ARAGON CONQUERS CASTILE

1236 CORDOBA TAKEN

1257 ONLY GRANADA LEFT TO MOORS IN IBERIA

1323-25 PISA-GENO[A] SARDINIA AND COR[SICA]

1172 ALMOHADS TAKE SEVILLE

1150-1172 ALMOHADS CONQUER IBERIA

1134 FRAGA

1195 ALARCOS

1212 LAS NAVAS DE TOLOSA

1238 ARAGON TAKES VALENCIA

Louis IX (1226–70), a great king of France but a hopeless general, whose crusades (7th and 8th) were failures

The Vikings establish themselves in northern France. As Normans they conquer Saxon England while Norman warriors exploit the division of Italy and Sicily between the Byzantines and the Saracens, ultimately to establish a new Kingdom of Sicily

981 RUEDA

985 ANDALUSIANS SACK BARCELONA

DECLINE OF UMAYYADS - BY 1031 ERA OF 'TAIFAS' (FRAGMENTATION)

ALMORAVIDS

ALMOHADS

c.1228-9 ALMOHADS ABANDON IBERIA

1085 ALMORAVIDS OF MOROCCO INVADE IBERIAN PENINSULA AND TAKE TOLEDO

1086 AZ-ZALLAQG

1095 TAKE BADAJOZ

BYZANTINES CONQUER SERBS

1052 MUSLIMS EJECTED FROM SARDINIA

BY 1115 ALMORAVIDS CONQUER ALL MUSLIM SPAIN

1118 ARAGON CONQUERS SARAGOSSA

1147 ALFONSO HENRIQUES OF PORTUGAL TAKES LISBON

1148-9 ARAGON CONQUERS LOWER EBRO

BYZANTIUM LOSES CROATIA, DALMATIA TO HUNGARIANS; SERBIA AND BULGARIA BECOME INDEPENDENT AGAIN

1241 LIEGNITZ

1237-42 MONGOL INVASION OF EUROPE

1284 MELORIA: GENOA DEFEATS PISA AND TAKES CORSICA

1190 RICHARD THE LIONHEART TAKES CYPRUS FROM BYZANTINES

1229-35 ARAGON SEIZES BALEARIC ISLANDS

1298 CURZOLA: GENOESE DEFEAT VENETIANS

1311 ARAGON TAKES DUCHY OF ATHENS

1323 ARAGON TAKES SARDINIA

986-1014 OR 1018 WARS OF BASIL II AGAINST THE BULGARS

END OF BULGAR STATE BY 1018

963-1025 BASIL II

1147 NORMANS ATTACK BYZANTIUM

1185 NORMANS ATTACK BYZANTIUM

VENETIANS TAKE CRETE

1261 BYZANTINES RETAKE CONSTANTINOPLE

OTTOMAN WARS

1326 TAKE BURSA

1107 BOHEMUND'S SECOND INVASION OF BYZANTINE EMPIRE DEFEATED

1176 MYRIOKEPHALON: RUM SELJUKS DEFEAT BYZANTINES

1199-1204 FOURTH CRUSADE

1204 SACK OF CONSTANTINOPLE

1278 CHARLES OF ANJOU CONQUERS ACHAEA

Norman knights as depicted in the Bayeux Tapestry

Under Basil II Byzantium attains the summit of its medieval greatness

BYZANTINE EMPIRE

1204-1261 LATIN EMPIRE

BYZANTINE EMPIRE

Men-at-arms and a crossbowman

974-5 BYZANTINE INVASION OF SYRIA

989-1025 WARS OF BASIL II

1032 BYZANTINES TAKE EDESSA

SELJUK WARS OF CONQUEST

1055 SELJUKS TAKE BAGHDAD

1071 MAZIKERT - SELJUKS TAKE MOST ASIA MINOR FROM BYZANTINES

945-999 BYZANTINE INVASIONS OF SYRIA

1060s SELJUKS CONQUER NORTH SYRIA & HEJAZ

WARS OF THE CRUSADER STATES

1147-1148 SECOND CRUSADE

THIRD CRUSADE 1188-1192

1177 RAMLA

1125 ALMOHAD REBELLION IN MOROCCO BEGINS

1187 HATTIN: FALL OF JERUSALEM TO SALADIN

1191 ARSOUF

1189-1191 SIEGE OF ACRE

FREDERICK BARBAROSSA TAKES KONYA

1215-1221 FIFTH CRUSADE

1227-1229 SIXTH CRUSADE

KHWARAZMIANS TAKE JERUSALEM

1245-1254 SEVENTH CRUSADE

1249 MANSURA: MOSLEMS DEFEAT LOUIS IX

1270-1272 EIGHTH CRUSADE

1260 AIN JALUT: MAMELUKES DEFEAT MONGOLS

1268 TAKE ANTIOCH

1260-1277 CAMPAIGNS OF BAYBARS

1289 TAKE TRIPOLI

1291 ACRE FALLS TO MAMELUKES - LAST CRUSADER TOE-HOLD IN PALESTINE

GHAZNA

SELJUK SULTANATE

THREE SELJUK SULTANATES: RUM, HAMADAN & MERV

SELJUK SULTANATE OF RUM

998 COLLAPSE OF SAMANIDS

997 OR 999-1030 WARS OF MAHMUD OF GHAZNA IN TRANSOXONIA, IRAN & IRAQ

1039 ZENDECAN TURKS INVADE AFGHANISTAN

1050 HILALI AND SULLAYM TRIBES FROM UPPER EGYPT INVADE CYRENAICA AND TURKEY

1096 PEOPLE'S CRUSADE MASSACRE BY TURKS

1097-1099 FIRST CRUSADE: 1097 BATTLE OF DORYLAEUM, 1098 ANTIOCH TAKEN, 1098 EDESSA TAKEN, 1099 JERUSALEM TAKEN FROM FATIMIDS

983-1055 BUWAYHID CIVIL WAR IN IRAQ/IRAN

KINGDOM OF JERUSALEM

1157 DEATH OF LAST SULTAN

1184-1187 SALADIN RECONQUERS MESOPOTAMIAN EMPIRE FROM ZANGIDS

1187 GHURIDS END GHAZNAVID STATE AND RULE TO 1215

SELJUK DECLINE

OSMAN, 1280-1324, FOUNDER OF OTTOMAN STATE

1258 SACK OF BAGHDAD - END OF ABBASID CALIPHATE

1258-1365 IL-KHANATE

MAMELUKE SLAVE-SOLDIERS KILL LAST AYYUBID SULTAN 1250

1260-1277 BAYBARS I

1129 CAMPAIGNS OF ZANGI AND NUR AL-DIN

1144 TAKES EDESSA

1154 TAKES DAMASCUS

1163, 1167 ZANGI ATTACKS EGYPT AND CONQUERS IT IN 1168-69

AYYUBID SULTANATE

FATIMID EGYPT

1060-1073 CIVIL STRIFE

1073-7 BAAR AL-JAMAH ESTABLISHES MILITARY REGIME

1171 SALADIN (1169-1193) ESTABLISHES AYYUBIDS

DECLINE OF THE AYYUBIDS

1220 SAMARKAND: GENGHIS KHAN VICTORY

1218 KARAKU

1221 KANDAHAR

1243 KÖSEDAGH: MONGOLS DEFEAT SELJUKS

1256 ASSASSINS OF ALAMUT DESTROYED BY MONGOLS AND BAYBARS

AFTER 1260 NO UNIFIED POLITICAL DIRECTION: EMPIRE CONTINUES AS CHAGATAI, IL-KHANATE AND GOLDEN HORDE

1206-1227 GENGHIS KHAN

1241 DEATH OF OGATAI

1259 DEATH OF MÖNGU

1141 SELJUKS OF MERV DEFEATED BY QARAKHITAI MONGOLS

1153 SELJUK SULTANATE OF MERV DESTROYED BY GHUZZ TRIBES

1140s ALMOHADS REPLACE ALMORAVIDS IN MOROCCO

1152-1160 ALMOHADS TAKE MAGHREBAND TRIPOLITANIA

1040 DANDANQUAN SELJUKS DEFEAT GHAZNAVIDS

997 OR 999-1030 WARS OF MAHMUD OF GHAZNI IN INDIA. CONQUEST OF PUNJAB

1050S-1060S ALMORAVIDS CONQUER MOROCCO. 1069 TAKE FEZ

MONGOL EMPIRE 1206-1260

1231 DESTROY KHWARAZM

The Mongol Emperor of China, Kublai-Khan (1260-94)

LAHORE 1296

DELHI 1297

ALADAIN KHALJI BREAKS RESISTANCE OF RAJPUTS A[ND] REPULSES MONGOLS IN NW

1311 CONQUERS TO SOUTH TIP OF INDIA

1325-1351 WARS OF MUHAMMED IBN T[UGHLUQ] CONQUERS S. INDIA IS LOST AFTER HIS

1001 PESHWAR. 2ND MUSLIM INVASION OF INDIA

1018 TURKIC ARMIES SACK KANAUJ, ENDING PRATIHARA

1024 OR 1025 SOMNANTH. SHIVA TEMPLE DESTROYED

1040 SELJUKS BREAK AWAY FROM GHAZNI. DECLINE OF GHAZNIS

C.1149-1215 WARS OF THE GHURIDS

GHURIDS TAKE MULTAN 1175

1179 GHURIDS TAKE PESHAWAR

1186 GHURIDS TAKE LAHORE

1192 TARAORI: MOHAMMED OF GHUR DEFEATS RAJPUTS

1221 FORCES OF GENGHIS KHAN PENETRATE AS FAR AS THE INDUS

1206 MOHAMMED ASSASSINATED: EX-SLAVE QUTBUDDIN AIBAK REVOLTS AND ESTABLISHES NEW DYNASTY

1296-1316 WARS OF ALAUDDIN KHALJI

985-1014 RAJARAJA I EXTENDS CHOLA POWER

1022 OR 1023 NORTHERN CAMPAIGN OF RAJENDRA CHOLA

1191 THE SURSUTI: KING OF DELHI DEFEATS AFGHANS

1162-1206 MOHAMMED OF GHUR

SULTANATE OF DELHI

1290-1320 KHALJI DYNASTY

1320-1414 TUGHLUQ DYNA[STY]

CHOLA EMPIRE

1206-1290 SLAVE DYNASTY

1336 KINGD[OM OF] VIJAYAN[AGAR] ESTAB[LISHED]

MAJOR CAMPAIGNS: 999, 1017: TO SRI LANKA; 1000: NAVAL EXPEDITION TO MALDIVES; 1022 TO GANGES; 1025 NAVAL EXPEDITIONS TO SE ASIA

ZENITH OF KHMER EMPIRE

1193 GERMAGHAH: GENGHIS KHANS VICTORY OVER SANKUN

c.1170 ZENITH OF SRIVIJAYAN EMPIRE IN EAST INDIES

c.1200 RISE OF THAI KINGDOM

1253 MONGOLS CONQUER KINGDOM OF NAN-ZHAO

1257-8 MONGOLS TAKE HANOI

1292-3 MONGOL EXPEDITION TO THE EAST INDIES

1277-87 MONGOLS INVADE BURMA

979-1004 CHINA-LIAO BORDER W.

1227 DESTRUCTION OF HSI-HSIA

1215 CAPTURE OF PEKING

ANCILLARY CAMPAIGNS TO 1241

MONGOL ATTACKS ON BURMA AND JAVA FAIL

1294 DEATH OF KUBLAI KHAN RESULTS IN RIVALRY FOR THE THRONE

982-1126 CHINA. HSI-HSIA BORDER WARS

1205-1209 MONGOLS CONQUER HSI-HSIA AS BASE FOR CONQUEST OF CHINA

NORTHERN SUNG EMPIRE

CH'IN EMPIRE

YÜAN (MONGOL) D[YNASTY]

C.1125-1127 NORTHERN TRIBES CONQUER N. CHINA AND ESTABLISH CH'IN EMPIRE

BY 1127 SUNG CONTROL REDUCED TO SOUTHERN HALF OF CHINA

1211-1234 MONGOL CONQUEST OF CH'IN

c.1260-1279 MONGOL CONQUEST OF SUNG CHINA

KUBLAI KHAN RULES CHINA AS SHIH-TSU

SUNG RE-UNITE MUCH OF CHINA 963-979

1051-1063 EARLY NINE YEARS WAR IN JAPAN

1086-1089 LATER THREE YEARS WAR IN JAPAN

1333 SIEGE OF CHIHAYA

SOUTHERN SUNG EMPIRE

989 CONFLICT BETWEEN KYOTO AND NARA IN JAPAN

KYOTO 1146

1156, 1160 JAPANESE SUCCESSION WARS

1185 DAN NO URA

1180-1185 JAPANESE GEMPEI WARS

1274, 1281 FAILED MONGOL INVASIONS OF JAPAN

1331-1333 JAPANESE HOJO REGENCY OVERTHROWN

1333-13[...]

1000 | 1025 | 1050 | 1075 | 1100 | 1150 | 1200 | 1250 | 1300

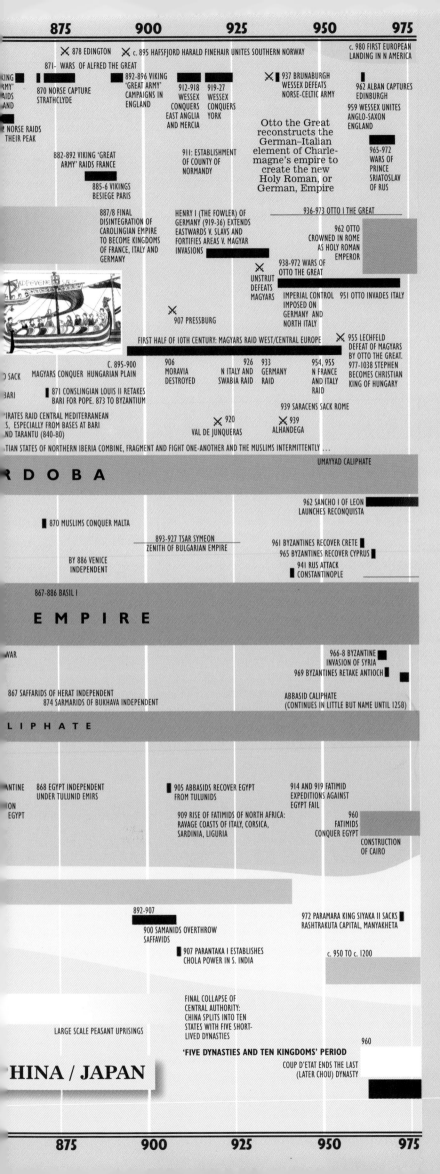

c. 980 FIRST EUROPEAN LANDING IN N AMERICA

✕ 878 EDINGTON ✕ c. 895 HAFSFJORD HARALD FINEHAIR UNITES SOUTHERN NORWAY

871- WARS OF ALFRED THE GREAT

870 NORSE CAPTURE STRATHCLYDE

892-896 VIKING 'GREAT ARMY' CAMPAIGNS IN ENGLAND

912-918 WESSEX CONQUERS EAST ANGLIA AND MERCIA

919-27 WESSEX CONQUERS YORK

✕ 937 BRUNABURGH WESSEX DEFEATS NORSE-CELTIC ARMY

962 ALBAN CAPTURES EDINBURGH

959 WESSEX UNITES ANGLO-SAXON ENGLAND

NORSE RAIDS THEIR PEAK

882-892 VIKING 'GREAT ARMY' RAIDS FRANCE

885-6 VIKINGS BESIEGE PARIS

887/8 FINAL DISINTEGRATION OF CAROLINGIAN EMPIRE TO BECOME KINGDOMS OF FRANCE, ITALY AND GERMANY

911: ESTABLISHMENT OF COUNTY OF NORMANDY

Otto the Great reconstructs the German–Italian element of Charlemagne's empire to create the new Holy Roman, or German, Empire

965-972 WARS OF PRINCE SRIATOSLAV OF RUS

HENRY I (THE FOWLER) OF GERMANY (919-36) EXTENDS EASTWARDS V. SLAVS AND FORTIFIES AREAS V. MAGYAR INVASIONS

936-973 OTTO I THE GREAT

962 OTTO CROWNED IN ROME AS HOLY ROMAN EMPEROR

✕ 938-972 WARS OF OTTO THE GREAT

UNSTRUT DEFEATS MAGYARS

IMPERIAL CONTROL IMPOSED ON GERMANY AND NORTH ITALY

951 OTTO INVADES ITALY

✕ 907 PRESSBURG

FIRST HALF OF 10TH CENTURY: MAGYARS RAID WEST/CENTRAL EUROPE

✕ 955 LECHFELD DEFEAT OF MAGYARS BY OTTO THE GREAT.

977-1038 STEPHEN BECOMES CHRISTIAN KING OF HUNGARY

906 MORAVIA DESTROYED

926 N ITALY AND SWABIA RAID

933 GERMANY RAID

954, 955 N FRANCE AND ITALY RAID

MAGYARS CONQUER HUNGARIAN PLAIN

939 SARACENS SACK ROME

... SACK

BARI

871 CONSLINGIAN LOUIS II RETAKES BARI FOR POPE. 873 TO BYZANTIUM

✕ 920 VAL DE JUNQUERAS

✕ 939 ALHANDEGA

PIRATES RAID CENTRAL MEDITERRANEAN ..S., ESPECIALLY FROM BASES AT BARI AND TARANTU (840-80)

..TIAN STATES OF NORTHERN IBERIA COMBINE, FRAGMENT AND FIGHT ONE-ANOTHER AND THE MUSLIMS INTERMITTENTLY ...

..RDOBA

UMAYYAD CALIPHATE

962 SANCHO I OF LEON LAUNCHES RECONQUISTA

870 MUSLIMS CONQUER MALTA

893-927 TSAR SYMEON ZENITH OF BULGARIAN EMPIRE

961 BYZANTINES RECOVER CRETE

965 BYZANTINES RECOVER CYPRUS

941 RUS ATTACK CONSTANTINOPLE

BY 886 VENICE INDEPENDENT

867-886 BASIL I

E M P I R E

..WAR

966-8 BYZANTINE INVASION OF SYRIA

969 BYZANTINES RETAKE ANTIOCH

867 SAFFARIDS OF HERAT INDEPENDENT
874 SARMARIDS OF BUKHAVA INDEPENDENT

ABBASID CALIPHATE (CONTINUES IN LITTLE BUT NAME UNTIL 1258)

..LIPHATE

868 EGYPT INDEPENDENT UNDER TULUNID EMIRS

..ANTINE ..ION EGYPT

905 ABBASIDS RECOVER EGYPT FROM TULUNIDS

914 AND 919 FATIMID EXPEDITIONS AGAINST EGYPT FAIL

909 RISE OF FATIMIDS OF NORTH AFRICA: RAVAGE COASTS OF ITALY, CORSICA, SARDINIA, LIGURIA

960 FATIMIDS CONQUER EGYPT

CONSTRUCTION OF CAIRO

892-907

900 SAMANIDS OVERTHROW SAFFAVIDS

907 PARANTAKA I ESTABLISHES CHOLA POWER IN S. INDIA

972 PARAMARA KING SIYAKA II SACKS RASHTRAKUTA CAPITAL, MANYAKHETA

c. 950 TO c. 1200

FINAL COLLAPSE OF CENTRAL AUTHORITY: CHINA SPLITS INTO TEN STATES WITH FIVE SHORT-LIVED DYNASTIES

960

LARGE SCALE PEASANT UPRISINGS

'FIVE DYNASTIES AND TEN KINGDOMS' PERIOD

COUP D'ETAT ENDS THE LAST (LATER CHOU) DYNASTY

..HINA / JAPAN

GREAT COMMANDERS

Alfred the Great (839–858)
Legendary king of Wessex and energetic defender against the seemingly invincible Danes. Despite great setbacks, he ultimately succeeded in driving the Vikings back to a line between London and Chester. He established a semi-professional army and began the construction of the West Saxon fleet. He also refortified London, which had been effectively abandoned for several centuries.

Basil II Bulgaroctonus (Slayer of the Bulgars) (963–1025)
One of the greatest soldier-emperors of Byzantium. He had to defeat internal opposition (by 989) before he could pursue his policy of extending and consolidating Byzantine authority. He expanded the empire in Syria, but his principal achievement, as his name suggests, was the conquest of Bulgaria (986–1018). After his victory at Ochrida (the Bulgarian capital), he blinded the whole of the surviving Bulgarian army, leaving but one man in a hundred with eyes to lead the rest home. (The Bulgarian king immediately expired in shock.) Basil never married or had children, so that on his death his achievements were rapidly frittered away.

Boleslav the Mighty (or the Brave) (992–1025)
First king of Poland. He subjugated the West Slav tribes and worked to unify Poland. In 996 he conquered Pomerania and then Cracow. From 1003 to 1018 he was in conflict with the German Empire, but succeeded in increasing the size of his realm at the expense of all his neighbours. He made Poland a major European state, but his conquests were not lasting.

Charlemagne (768–814)
One of the great, towering figures of the Middle Ages, Charlemagne (Charles the Great) reunited the Frankish realms by 771 and by many wars of conquest welded almost all Western Europe (save the Iberian peninsula) into a Christian polity. He was crowned Holy Roman Emperor by the Pope in Rome on Christmas Day 800 and, initially at least, used military force as a means of spreading Christianity among the heathen tribes of Germany. His campaigns are too many to list here, often taking the form of annual expeditions. In 773 he invaded Italy and put an end to the Lombard kingdom after besieging Pavia. In 778 he crossed the Pyrenees without intending permanent conquest. The rearguard battle (actually little more than a skirmish) of Roncesvalles during the withdrawal from Spain has passed into heroic legend. Subsequent invasions of Spain were to create (by 795) a Spanish march, or buffer state. Longer-term campaigns took place in Germany, deposing Duke Tassilo of Bavaria (787–8), defeating the Avars (788–796) and a long series of bitter wars in Saxony.

Sveyn Haraldsson (Forkbeard) (986–1014)
After overthrowing his father, Harold Bluetooth, Sveyn extended Danish rule in Scandinavia and conquered England, founding an Anglo-Danish empire that continued under his son and grandson. He was acknowledged as King of England in 1013 and died a year later, being succeeded by his son Canute.

Robert de Hauteville (Guiscard) (b.1015–1085)
Epitome of the heroic, larger-than-life characters that strode through these centuries, Guiscard was a man of action but shrewd too, an immediate predecessor of the leaders who would cut their way to Jerusalem at the end of the 11th century. In 1047 joining his Norman brothers (including William de Hautevile, elected count of Apulia after defeating the Byzantines), Robert carved out a major kingdom in the south of Italy and Sicily. In 1059 the Pope enfeofed him with the duchy of Apulia, Calabria and Sicily, the last-named being yet unwon. In 1061 he conquered Calabria; in 1071 Bari, the Byzantines' last city in Italy, fell to him; and in 1076 he took Salerno and made it his capital. With his brother Roger, and with Papal support, he conquered Sicily from 1081. Ambitious to the end, he died campaigning against the Byzantines on Cephalonia.

Heraclius I (610–641)
Byzantine emperor who restored the fortunes of the empire after a period of civil war and military defeat. In 610 he took power in Constantinople following a major mutiny of the army and virtual anarchy in the capital. Initial failures in Syria and Palestine were met by major campaigns into Armenia and Mesopotamia, leading to the downfall of the Persian king, Chosroes. He reformed the Byzantine army, creating a regional system of local farmer-soldiers to replace the previous reliance on irregular recruiting and mercenaries. This gave the defences of the empire a new lease of life. However, Heraclius's declining years saw the whirlwind of Muslim conquest begin to blow through the empire.

Mahmud of Ghazna (999–1030)
Sultan of Ghazna, an Afghan Muslim ruler who was the first Muslim invader of India, mounting some seventeen expeditions into northern India (1001–1026) and winning a great battle against a confederacy of Hindu states in 1008. His last raid resulted in the sack of the Hindu temple at Somnath. He conquered most of Iran and ruled an empire that included Kashmir and the

Continued on page 50

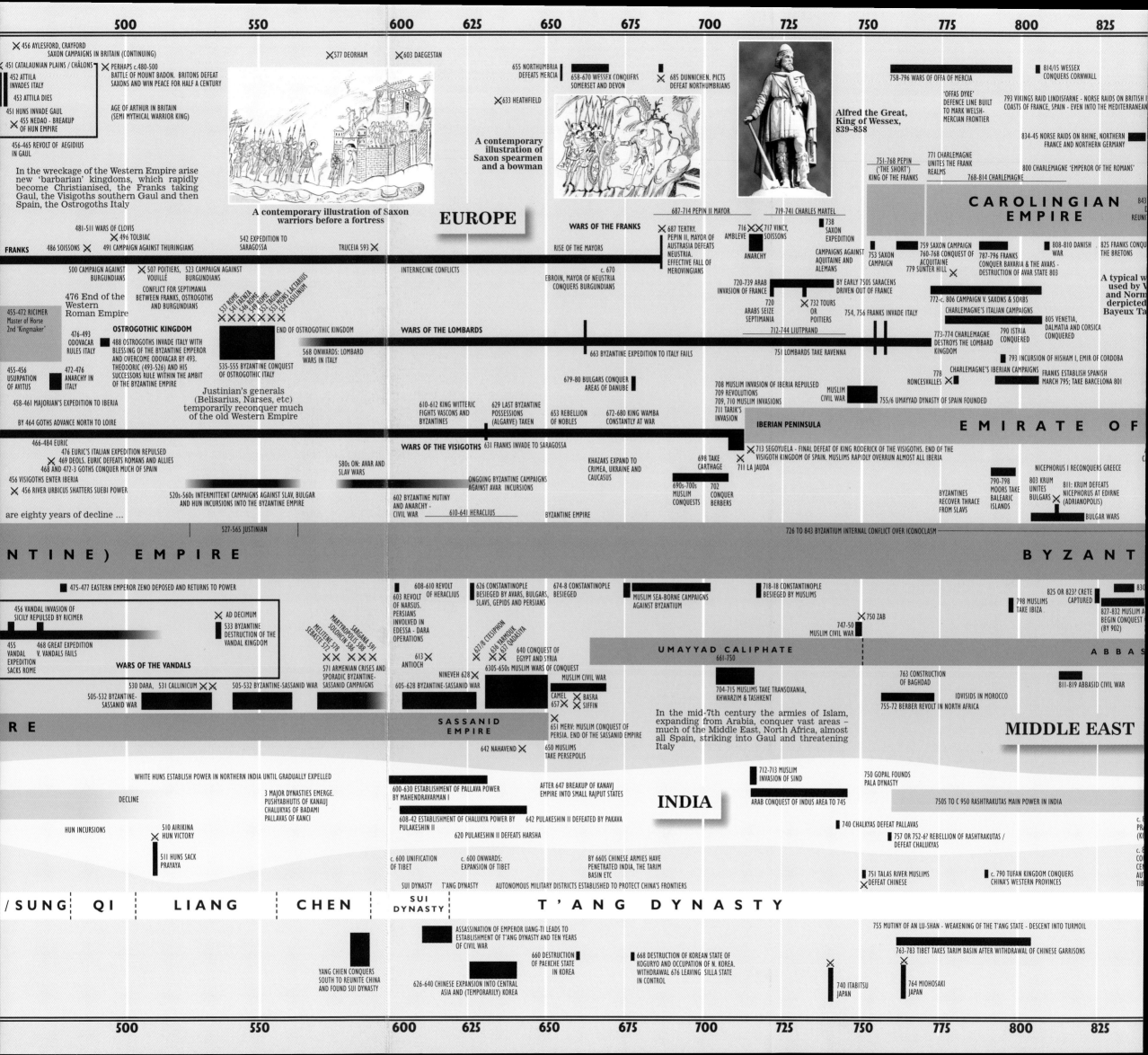

Timeline chart

Top scale: 500 · 550 · 600 · 625 · 650 · 675 · 700 · 725 · 750 · 775 · 800 · 825

Top box (Britain / Huns)

- 456 AYLESFORD, CRAYFORD
- SAXON CAMPAIGNS IN BRITAIN (CONTINUING)
- 451 CATALAUNIAN PLAINS / CHÂLONS
- 452 ATTILA INVADES ITALY
- 453 ATTILA DIES
- 451 HUNS INVADE GAUL
- 455 NEDAO - BREAKUP OF HUN EMPIRE
- 454-465 REVOLT OF AEGIDIUS IN GAUL
- PERHAPS c.480-500 BATTLE OF MOUNT BADON. BRITONS DEFEAT SAXONS AND WIN PEACE FOR HALF A CENTURY
- AGE OF ARTHUR IN BRITAIN (SEMI MYTHICAL WARRIOR KING)

In the wreckage of the Western Empire arise new 'barbarian' kingdoms, which rapidly become Christianised, the Franks taking Gaul, the Visigoths southern Gaul and then Spain, the Ostrogoths Italy

- ✕577 DEORHAM
- ✕603 DAEGESTAN
- 655 NORTHUMBRIA DEFEATS MERCIA
- 658-670 WESSEX CONQUERS SOMERSET AND DEVON
- 685 DUNNICHEN. PICTS DEFEAT NORTHUMBRIANS
- ✕633 HEATHFIELD

A contemporary illustration of Saxon spearmen and a bowman

Alfred the Great, King of Wessex, 839–858

- 758-796 WARS OF OFFA OF MERCIA
- 814/15 WESSEX CONQUERS CORNWALL
- 'OFFA'S DYKE' DEFENCE LINE BUILT TO MARK WELSH-MERCIAN FRONTIER
- 793 VIKINGS RAID LINDISFARNE - NORSE RAIDS ON BRITISH COASTS OF FRANCE, SPAIN - EVEN INTO THE MEDITERRANEAN
- 834-45 NORSE RAIDS ON RHINE, NORTHERN FRANCE AND NORTHERN GERMANY

A contemporary illustration of Saxon warriors before a fortress

EUROPE

WARS OF THE FRANKS

- 771 CHARLEMAGNE UNITES THE FRANK REALMS
- 800 CHARLEMAGNE 'EMPEROR OF THE ROMANS'
- 751-768 PEPIN ('THE SHORT') KING OF THE FRANKS
- 768-814 CHARLEMAGNE

CAROLINGIAN EMPIRE

- 843 REUNI...

Franks row

- 481-511 WARS OF CLOVIS
- 496 TOLBIAC
- 486 SOISSONS ✕
- 491 CAMPAIGN AGAINST THURINGIANS
- 542 EXPEDITION TO SARAGOSSA
- TRUCEIA 593 ✕
- RISE OF THE MAYORS
- INTERNECINE CONFLICTS
- 687-714 PEPIN II MAYOR
- 687 TERTRY. PEPIN II, MAYOR OF AUSTRASIA DEFEATS NEUSTRIA. EFFECTIVE FALL OF MEROVINGIANS
- 719-741 CHARLES MARTEL
- 716 AMBLEVE ✕✕ 717 VINCY, SOISSONS
- ANARCHY
- 738 SAXON EXPEDITION
- 753 SAXON CAMPAIGN
- 759 SAXON CAMPAIGN
- 760-768 CONQUEST OF ACQUITAINE
- CAMPAIGNS AGAINST AQUITAINE AND ALEMANS
- 779 SÜNTER HILL ✕
- 787-796 FRANKS CONQUER BAVARIA & THE AVARS - DESTRUCTION OF AVAR STATE 803
- 808-810 DANISH WAR
- 825 FRANKS CONQU... THE BRETONS

Middle Europe

- 500 CAMPAIGN AGAINST BURGUNDIANS
- 507 POITIERS, VOUILLÉ
- 523 CAMPAIGN AGAINST BURGUNDIANS
- CONFLICT FOR SEPTIMANIA BETWEEN FRANKS, OSTROGOTHS AND BURGUNDIANS
- 476 End of the Western Roman Empire
- c. 670 EBROIN, MAYOR OF NEUSTRIA
- 720-739 ARAB INVASION OF FRANCE
- BY EARLY 750s SARACENS DRIVEN OUT OF FRANCE
- 720 ARABS SEIZE SEPTIMANIA
- 732 TOURS OR POITIERS
- 754, 756 FRANKS INVADE ITALY
- 772-c. 806 CAMPAIGN V. SAXONS & SORBS
- CHARLEMAGNE'S ITALIAN CAMPAIGNS
- 805 VENETIA, DALMATIA AND CORSICA CONQUERED
- A typical w... used by V... and Norm... depicted... Bayeux Ta...

Ostrogoths / Lombards

- 455-472 RICIMER Master of Horse 2nd 'Kingmaker'
- 476-493 ODOVACAR RULES ITALY
- 476-493 OSTROGOTHIC KINGDOM
- 488 OSTROGOTHS INVADE ITALY WITH BLESSING OF THE BYZANTINE EMPEROR AND OVERCOME ODOVACAR BY 493. THEODORIC (493-526) AND HIS SUCCESSORS RULE WITHIN THE AMBIT OF THE BYZANTINE EMPIRE
- 455-456 USURPATION OF AVITUS
- 472-476 ANARCHY IN ITALY
- 458-461 MAJORIAN'S EXPEDITION TO IBERIA
- BY 464 GOTHS ADVANCE NORTH TO LOIRE
- 537 ROME, 541 GENOA, 546 ROME, 549 ROME, 552 TAGINA, 553 HUNS LACTARIUS, 554 CASILINUM
- END OF OSTROGOTHIC KINGDOM
- 535-555 BYZANTINE CONQUEST OF OSTROGOTHIC ITALY
- Justinian's generals (Belisarius, Narses, etc) temporarily reconquer much of the old Western Empire
- 568 ONWARDS: LOMBARD WARS IN ITALY
- WARS OF THE LOMBARDS
- 663 BYZANTINE EXPEDITION TO ITALY FAILS
- 712-744 LIUTPRAND
- 751 LOMBARDS TAKE RAVENNA
- 773-774 CHARLEMAGNE DESTROYS THE LOMBARD KINGDOM
- 790 ISTRIA CONQUERED
- 793 INCURSION OF HISHAM I, EMIR OF CORDOBA

Visigoths / Iberia

- 466-484 EURIC
- 476 EURIC'S ITALIAN EXPEDITION REPULSED
- 469 DEOLS. EURIC DEFEATS ROMANS AND ALLIES
- 468 AND 472-3 GOTHS CONQUER MUCH OF SPAIN
- 456 VISIGOTHS ENTER IBERIA
- 456 RIVER URBICUS SHATTERS SUEBI POWER
- 580s ON: AVAR AND SLAV WARS
- 610-612 KING WITTERIC FIGHTS VASCONS AND BYZANTINES
- WARS OF THE VISIGOTHS
- 629 LAST BYZANTINE POSSESSIONS (ALGARVE) TAKEN
- 631 FRANKS INVADE TO SARAGOSSA
- 653 REBELLION OF NOBLES
- 672-680 KING WAMBA CONSTANTLY AT WAR
- 679-80 BULGARS CONQUER AREAS OF DANUBE
- 708 MUSLIM INVASION OF IBERIA REPULSED
- 709 REVOLUTIONS
- 709, 710 MUSLIM INVASIONS
- 711 TARIK'S INVASION
- MUSLIM CIVIL WAR
- 778 RONCESVALLES ✕
- CHARLEMAGNE'S IBERIAN CAMPAIGNS
- FRANKS ESTABLISH SPANISH MARCH 795; TAKE BARCELONA 801
- 755/6 UMAYYAD DYNASTY OF SPAIN FOUNDED
- 713 SEGOYUELA - FINAL DEFEAT OF KING RODERICK OF THE VISIGOTHS. END OF THE VISIGOTH KINGDOM OF SPAIN. MUSLIMS RAPIDLY OVERRUN ALMOST ALL IBERIA
- 698 TAKE CARTHAGE
- 711 LA JAUDA ✕
- IBERIAN PENINSULA

EMIRATE OF...

Byzantine

- KHAZAKS EXPAND TO CRIMEA, UKRAINE AND CAUCASUS
- 690s-700s MUSLIM CONQUESTS
- 702 CONQUER BERBERS
- ONGOING BYZANTINE CAMPAIGNS AGAINST AVAR INCURSIONS
- 602 BYZANTINE MUTINY AND ANARCHY - CIVIL WAR
- 610-641 HERACLIUS
- BYZANTINE EMPIRE
- 520s-560s INTERMITTENT CAMPAIGNS AGAINST SLAV, BULGAR AND HUN INCURSIONS INTO THE BYZANTINE EMPIRE
- are eighty years of decline ...
- BYZANTINES RECOVER THRACE FROM SLAVS
- 790-798 MOORS TAKE BALEARIC ISLANDS
- 803 KRUM UNITES BULGARS
- 811: KRUM DEFEATS NICEPHORUS AT EDIRNE (ADRIANOPLIS)
- NICEPHORUS I RECONQUERS GREECE
- BULGAR WARS
- 726 TO 843 BYZANTIUM INTERNAL CONFLICT OVER ICONOCLASM
- 527-565 JUSTINIAN

...NTINE) EMPIRE

BYZANT...

Eastern Empire / Middle East

- 475-477 EASTERN EMPEROR ZENO DEPOSED AND RETURNS TO POWER
- 608-610 REVOLT OF HERACLIUS
- 603 REVOLT OF NARSUS. PERSIANS INVOLVED IN EDESSA - DARA OPERATIONS
- 626 CONSTANTINOPLE BESIEGED BY AVARS, BULGARS, SLAVS, GEPIDS AND PERSIANS
- 674-8 CONSTANTINOPLE BESIEGED
- MUSLIM SEA-BORNE CAMPAIGNS AGAINST BYZANTIUM
- 718-18 CONSTANTINOPLE BESIEGED BY MUSLIMS
- 825 OR 823? CRETE CAPTURED
- 798 MUSLIMS TAKE IBIZA
- 827-832 MUSLIM A... BEGIN CONQUEST... (BY 902)
- 456 VANDAL INVASION OF SICILY REPULSED BY RICIMER
- AD DECIMUM ✕
- 533 BYZANTINE DESTRUCTION OF THE VANDAL KINGDOM
- 613 ✕ ANTIOCH
- 627/8 ✕ CTESIPHON
- 636 YARMOUK ✕✕ 637 QADASIYA
- 640 CONQUEST OF EGYPT AND SYRIA
- 747-50 MUSLIM CIVIL WAR
- 750 ZAB ✕
- 455 VANDAL EXPEDITION SACKS ROME
- 468 GREAT EXPEDITION V. VANDALS FAILS
- WARS OF THE VANDALS
- 571 ARMENIAN CRISES AND SPORADIC BYZANTINE-SASSANID CAMPAIGNS
- MARTYROPOLIS 588, SANGARA 591, MELITENE 578, SOLOCHON 586, SEBASTI 572
- NINEVEH 628 ✕
- 630s-650s MUSLIM WARS OF CONQUEST
- MUSLIM CIVIL WAR
- CAMEL 657 ✕✕ BASRA, SIFFIN
- 704-715 MUSLIMS TAKE TRANSOXANIA, KHWARZIM & TASHKENT
- **UMAYYAD CALIPHATE** 661-750
- 763 CONSTRUCTION OF BAGHDAD
- 811-819 ABBASID CIVIL WAR
- **ABBAS...**
- 530 DARA, 531 CALLINICUM ✕✕
- 505-532 BYZANTINE-SASSANID WAR
- 605-628 BYZANTINE-SASSANID WAR
- 642 NAHAVEND
- 650 MUSLIMS TAKE PERSEPOLIS
- 651 MERV: MUSLIM CONQUEST OF PERSIA. END OF THE SASSANID EMPIRE
- 755-72 BERBER REVOLT IN NORTH AFRICA
- IDVISIDS IN MOROCCO
- 505-532 BYZANTINE-SASSANID WAR
- **SASSANID EMPIRE**
- In the mid-7th century the armies of Islam, expanding from Arabia, conquer vast areas – much of the Middle East, North Africa, almost all Spain, striking into Gaul and threatening Italy

...RE **MIDDLE EAST**

India

- WHITE HUNS ESTABLISH POWER IN NORTHERN INDIA UNTIL GRADUALLY EXPELLED
- DECLINE
- HUN INCURSIONS
- 510 AIRIKINA HUN VICTORY ✕
- 511 HUNS SACK PRAYAYA
- 3 MAJOR DYNASTIES EMERGE. PUSHYABHUTIS OF KANAUJ CHALUKYAS OF BADAMI PALLAVAS OF KANCI
- 600-630 ESTABLISHMENT OF PALLAVA POWER BY MAHENDRAVARMAN I
- 608-42 ESTABLISHMENT OF CHALUKYA POWER BY PULAKESHIN II
- 620 PULAKESHIN II DEFEATS HARSHA
- AFTER 647 BREAKUP OF KANAVJ EMPIRE INTO SMALL RAJPUT STATES
- 642 PULAKESHIN II DEFEATED BY PAKAVA
- 712-713 MUSLIM INVASION OF SIND
- ARAB CONQUEST OF INDUS AREA TO 745
- 750 GOPAL FOUNDS PALA DYNASTY
- 750S TO C 950 RASHTRAKUTAS MAIN POWER IN INDIA
- 740 CHALKYAS DEFEAT PALLAVAS
- 757 OR 752-6? REBELLION OF RASHTRAKUTAS / DEFEAT CHALUKYAS
- **INDIA**

China / Far East

- c. 600 UNIFICATION OF TIBET
- c. 600 ONWARDS: EXPANSION OF TIBET
- BY 660S CHINESE ARMIES HAVE PENETRATED INDIA, THE TARIM BASIN ETC
- AUTONOMOUS MILITARY DISTRICTS ESTABLISHED TO PROTECT CHINA'S FRONTIERS
- 751 TALAS RIVER MUSLIMS ✕ DEFEAT CHINESE
- c. 790 TUFAN KINGDOM CONQUERS CHINA'S WESTERN PROVINCES
- SUI DYNASTY
- T'ANG DYNASTY

/SUNG QI LIANG CHEN SUI DYNASTY T'ANG DYNASTY

- YANG CHIEN CONQUERS SOUTH TO REUNITE CHINA AND FOUND SUI DYNASTY
- ASSASSINATION OF EMPEROR UANG-TI LEADS TO ESTABLISHMENT OF T'ANG DYNASTY AND TEN YEARS OF CIVIL WAR
- 626-640 CHINESE EXPANSION INTO CENTRAL ASIA AND (TEMPORARILY) KOREA
- 660 DESTRUCTION OF PAEKCHE STATE IN KOREA
- 668 DESTRUCTION OF KOREAN STATE OF KOGURYO AND OCCUPATION OF N. KOREA. WITHDRAWAL 676 LEAVING SILLA STATE IN CONTROL
- 755 MUTINY OF AN LU-SHAN - WEAKENING OF THE T'ANG STATE - DESCENT INTO TURMOIL
- 763-783 TIBET TAKES TARIM BASIN AFTER WITHDRAWAL OF CHINESE GARRISONS
- 740 ITABITSU JAPAN
- 764 MIOHOSAKI JAPAN

Bottom scale: 500 · 550 · 600 · 625 · 650 · 675 · 700 · 725 · 750 · 775 · 800 · 825

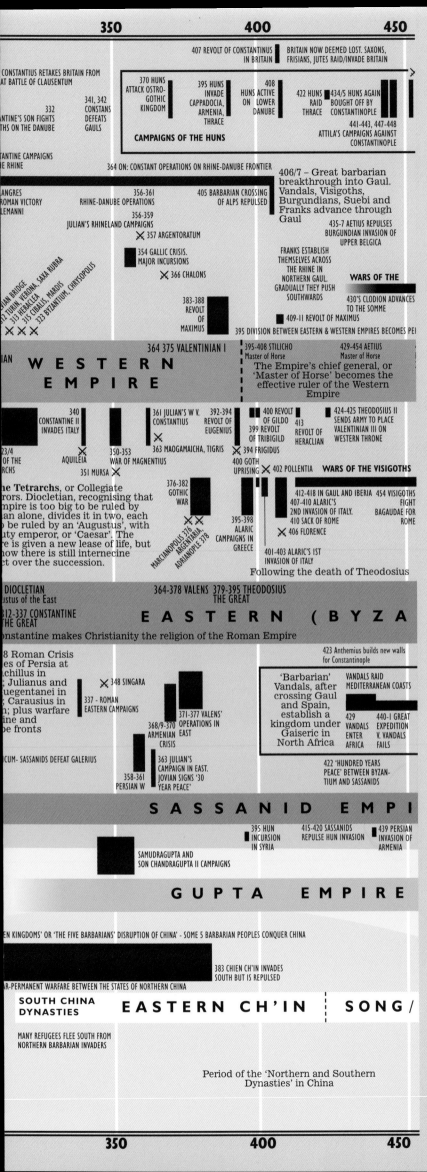

GREAT COMMANDERS

Flavius Aetius (390–545)

Master of Horse (general in chief) for the Roman Emperor Valentinian III, Aetius fought a series of campaigns to reassert Roman authority in the West against Visigoths, Franks and Burgundians, the latter being destroyed during 435–7. His greatest battle was in 451 at the Catalaunian Fields, where, with Visigoth help, he defeated Attila's Huns. Aetius was murdered by his ungrateful emperor in 454.

Attila (434–453)

'The Scourge of God' succeeded his father as king of the Hun confederacy in 434 with his brother, whom he soon murdered. The Huns were nomadic peoples from central Asia, who had migrated gradually from the steppe to create a vast empire that encompassed much of Germany and east to the Caspian. From here Attila's horsemen terrorised their neighbouring tribes and raided the frontier territories of the Roman Empire. Dramatic incursions were wholly destructive, each time the Huns returning home with vast booty and often considerable subsidies from Constantinople, the walls of which, however, defied them. Nevertheless great cities, such as Singidunum, Sirmium, Naissus, Serdica and Aquileia, were destroyed, and large areas of the Danube provinces laid waste. His defeat in 451 saved Gaul, but Attila was yet capable of a subsequent invasion of Italy which appeared unstoppable. His death ended the unity of the Hun confederacy and the great threat to Western civilisation faded away.

Belisarius (c.505–565)

Byzantine Emperor Justinian's greatest general, and a legendary figure thanks to the writings of Procopius and, in the twentieth century, Robert Graves. After fighting in the wars against Persia, he quelled the Nika Insurrection in Constantinople, which was dangerous to the imperial régime. He led the expeditionary force that destroyed the Vandal kingdom in 533. Two years later he was sent to retake Italy from the Ostrogoths and was initially successful, but inadequately supported by Constantinople. After being besieged in Rome during 537–8, he advanced north and accepted the Ostrogoth surrender, at the same time refusing their offer of the Italian throne. This made Justinian suspicious; Belisarius was recalled, and thereafter his military career was sporadic and at the mercy of court intrigue, made worse by the scandalous activities of his wife.

Clovis I (481–511)

Merovingian founder of the Frankish kingdom. Under his leadership the Franks advanced ever deeper into Gaul, defeating Syagrius, the last Roman ruler in Gaul, at Soissions in 486. He fought campaigns against the Burgundians and German tribes in Thuringia, and at Vouillé, near Poitiers, he defeated the Visigoths, subsequently taking temporary possession of their capital, Toulouse. He adopted Catholicism (in contrast to the Arian Christianity of his southern foes, the Visigoths) and established his capital at Paris. One of the great, central figures of French history, he established an enduring dynasty and the beginnings of a power-base for the future Carolingian Empire.

Flavius Valerius Constantinus, Constantine the Great (306–337)

First Christian emperor of Rome, who fought rivals for six years (306–312), then in 323 eliminated his colleague Licinius (Augustus of the East) to become sole ruler of the Roman Empire. Recognising that Rome was no longer the strategic capital of the empire, he established a new capital at Byzantium, renaming it Constantinople. According to legend, a vision before the decisive Battle of the Milvian Bridge led to his adoption of Christianity, and his military standard incorporated the *Labarum*, a monogram combining the first two letters of the word 'Christ' in Greek.

Gaius Aurelius Valerius Diocletianus, Diocletian (284–305)

After two decades of short-lived emperors, Dalmatian-born Diocletian stabilised and reformed the Roman system of government to take account of the demands on the ruler imposed by the continuing wars against barbarian invasions and the threat of usurpers being raised up by the various armies deployed about the empire. Two senior and two junior emperors, with adoptive succession, were to rule the empire. It did not work completely, but it did provide a more sound, structured government that would in essence survive to the middle of the next century. Effectively (and with the subsequent contribution of Constantine) he re-founded the empire. Discipline was restored to the army, which included a larger standing force as well as local defence units within smaller provinces to guard the frontiers.

Euric (466–484)

Founder of the Visigothic kingdom in Spain, Euric altered Visigoth policy by setting out to make his Kingdom of Toulouse independent of Rome rather than a federate. Threatened by the Franks to his north, the Burgundians to the east and Roman attempts to reimpose control on Gaul, Euric went on the offensive. At Deols on the Indre he won a shattering victory over a coalition of Romans, the independent Syagrius, Bretons, Franks and Burgundians. In 472–3 his armies

Continued on page 50

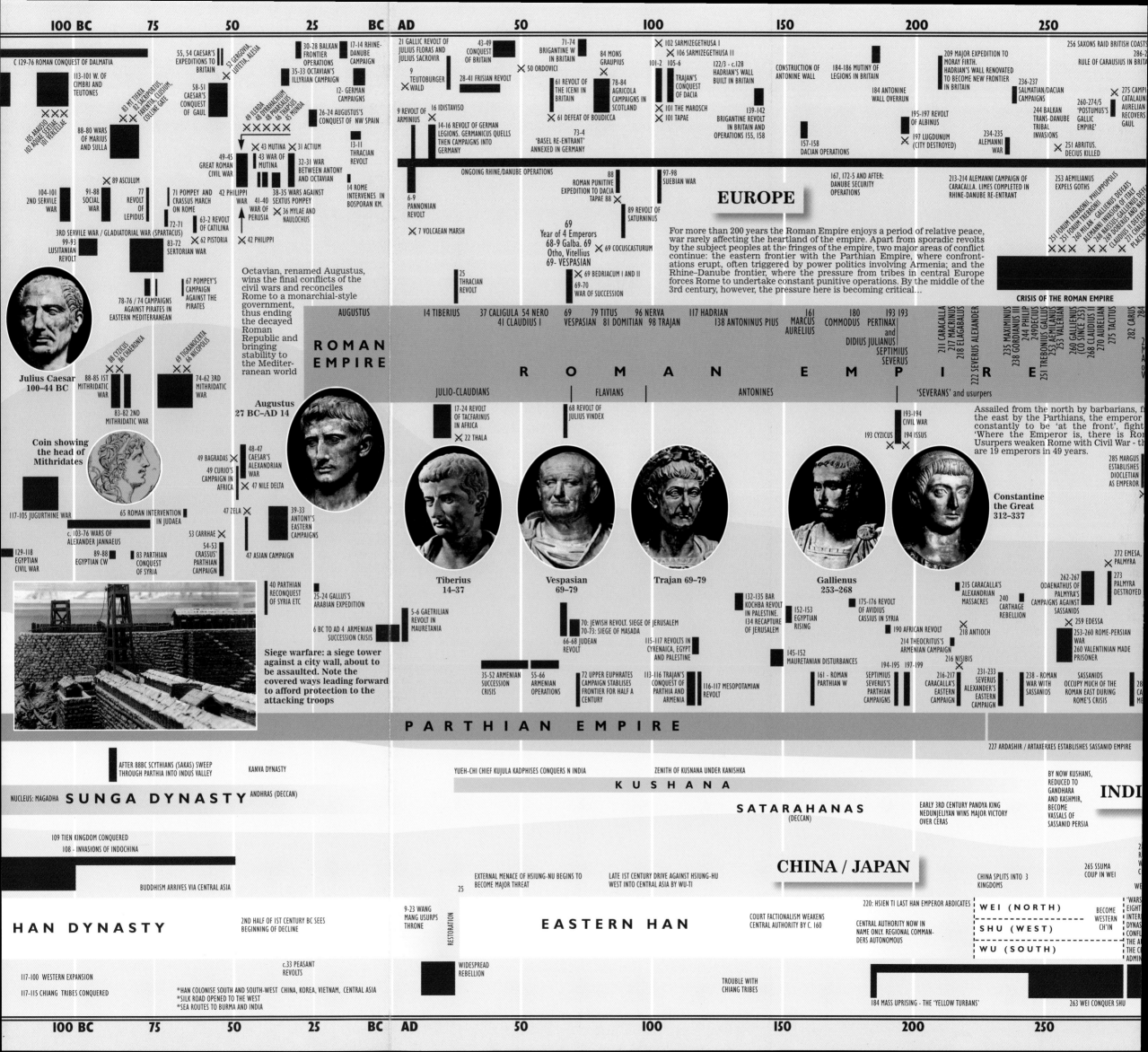

Timeline scale (top)

100 BC — 75 — 50 — 25 — BC | AD — 50 — 100 — 150 — 200 — 250

EUROPE

C 129-76 ROMAN CONQUEST OF DALMATIA

113-101 W. OF CIMBRI AND TEUTONES

105 ARAUSIO
102 AQUAE SEXTIAE
101 VERCELLAE

88-80 WARS OF MARIUS AND SULLA

104-101 2ND SERVILE WAR

91-88 SOCIAL WAR

77 REVOLT OF LEPIDUS

89 ASCULUM

71 POMPEY AND CRASSUS MARCH ON ROME

72-71 3RD SERVILE WAR / GLADIATORIAL WAR (SPARTACUS)

63-2 REVOLT OF CATILINA

62 PISTORIA

99-93 LUSITANIAN REVOLT

83-72 SERTORIAN WAR

78-76 / 74 CAMPAIGNS AGAINST PIRATES IN EASTERN MEDITERRANEAN

67 POMPEY'S CAMPAIGN AGAINST THE PIRATES

55, 54 CAESAR'S EXPEDITIONS TO BRITAIN

52 GERGOVIA, LUTETIA, ALESIA

83 MT TIFATA
82 SACRIPONTUS, FAVENTIA, CLUSIUM, COLLINE GATE

58-51 CAESAR'S CONQUEST OF GAUL

35-33 OCTAVIAN'S ILLYRIAN CAMPAIGN

52 GERGOVIA

12- GERMAN CAMPAIGNS

26-24 AUGUSTUS'S CONQUEST OF NW SPAIN

49 ILERDA
48 DYRRHACHIUM
48 PHARSALUS
48 THAPSUS
45 MUNDA

43 MUTINA

31 ACTIUM

49-45 GREAT ROMAN CIVIL WAR

43 WAR OF MUTINA

32-31 WAR BETWEEN ANTONY AND OCTAVIAN

71 POMPEY WAR

42 PHILIPPI

41-40 WAR OF PERUSIA

36 MYLAE AND NAULOCHUS

35-38 WARS AGAINST SEXTUS POMPEY

13-11 THRACIAN REVOLT

14 ROME INTERVENES IN BOSPORAN KM.

30-28 BALKAN FRONTIER OPERATIONS

17-14 RHINE-DANUBE CAMPAIGN

21 GALLIC REVOLT OF JULIUS FLOROS AND JULIUS SACROVIR

9 TEUTOBURGER WALD

28-41 FRISIAN REVOLT

9 REVOLT OF ARMINIUS

16 IDISTAVISO

14-16 REVOLT OF GERMAN LEGIONS. GERMANICUS QUELLS THEN CAMPAIGNS INTO GERMANY

43-49 CONQUEST OF BRITAIN

50 ORDOVICI

71-74 BRIGANTINE W IN BRITAIN

84 MONS GRAUPIUS

78-84 AGRICOLA CAMPAIGNS IN SCOTLAND

61 REVOLT OF THE ICENI IN BRITAIN

61 DEFEAT OF BOUDICCA

73-4 'BASEL RE-ENTRANT' ANNEXED IN GERMANY

102 SARMIZEGETHUSA I

106 SARMIZEGETHUSA II

101-2 105-6

TRAJAN'S CONQUEST OF DACIA

101 THE MAROSCH

101 TAPAE

122/3 - c.128 HADRIAN'S WALL BUILT IN BRITAIN

139-142 BRIGANTINE REVOLT IN BRITAIN AND OPERATIONS 155, 158

CONSTRUCTION OF ANTONINE WALL

157-158 DACIAN OPERATIONS

184-186 MUTINY OF LEGIONS IN BRITAIN

184 ANTONINE WALL OVERRUN

209 MAJOR EXPEDITION TO MORAY FIRTH.
HADRIAN'S WALL RENOVATED TO BECOME NEW FRONTIER IN BRITAIN

195-197 REVOLT OF ALBINUS

197 LUGDUNUM (CITY DESTROYED)

234-235 ALEMANNI WAR

236-237 SALMATIAN/DACIAN CAMPAIGNS

244 BALKAN TRANS-DANUBE TRIBAL INVASIONS

251 ABRITUS. DECIUS KILLED

256 SAXONS RAID BRITISH COASTS

286-2 RULE OF CARAUSIUS IN BRITA

260-274/5 'POSTUMUS'S' GALLIC 'EMPIRE'

275 CAMPI CATALAUN AURELIAN RECOVERS GAUL

ONGOING RHINE/DANUBE OPERATIONS

6-9 PANNONIAN REVOLT

7 VOLCAEAN MARSH

88 ROMAN PUNITIVE EXPEDITION TO DACIA TAPAE 88

69 COCUSCASTURUM

89 REVOLT OF SATURNINUS

97-98 SUEBIAN WAR

167, 172-5 AND AFTER: DANUBE SECURITY OPERATIONS

213-214 ALEMANNI CAMPAIGN OF CARACALLA. LIMES COMPLETED IN RHINE-DANUBE RE-ENTRANT

253 AEMILIANUS EXPELS GOTHS

251 FORUM TREBONNI, PHILIPPOLIS
251 FORUM TREBONI
260 MILAN - GALLIENUS DEFEATS ALEMANNI INVASION OF ITALY
268 NAISSUS-GALLIENUS DEFE
268 UUBERUS AND NAIS
CLAUDIUS II DEFEAT
271 PLACEN

EUROPE

For more than 200 years the Roman Empire enjoys a period of relative peace, war rarely affecting the heartland of the empire. Apart from sporadic revolts by the subject peoples at the fringes of the empire, two major areas of conflict continue: the eastern frontier with the Parthian Empire, where confrontations erupt, often triggered by power politics involving Armenia; and the Rhine–Danube frontier, where the pressure from tribes in central Europe forces Rome to undertake constant punitive operations. By the middle of the 3rd century, however, the pressure here is becoming critical…

CRISIS OF THE ROMAN EMPIRE

Assailed from the north by barbarians, f[rom] the east by the Parthians, the emperor constantly to be 'at the front', fight[ing] 'Where the Emperor is, there is Rom[e]'. Usurpers weaken Rome with Civil War - th[ere] are 19 emperors in 49 years.

285 MARGUS ESTABLISHES DIOCLETIAN AS EMPEROR

ROMAN EMPIRE

AUGUSTUS

14 TIBERIUS — 37 CALIGULA — 54 NERO — 69 — 79 TITUS — 96 NERVA — 117 HADRIAN — 161 MARCUS AURELIUS — 180 COMMODUS — 193 193 PERTINAX and DIDIUS JULIANUS SEPTIMIUS SEVERUS — 211 CARACALLA — 217 MACRINUS — 218 ELAGABALUS — 222 SEVERUS ALEXANDER — 235 MAXIMINUS — 238 GORDIANUS III — 244 PHILIP — 249 DECIUS — 251 TREBONIUS GALLUS — 253 AEMILIANUS — 253 VALERIAN — 260 GALLIENUS (CO SINCE 253) — 268 CLAUDIUS II — 270 AURELIAN — 275 TACITUS — 282 CARUS — 284

41 CLAUDIUS I — VESPASIAN — 81 DOMITIAN — 98 TRAJAN — 138 ANTONINUS PIUS

ROMAN EMPIRE

JULIO-CLAUDIANS — FLAVIANS — ANTONINES — 'SEVERANS' and usurpers

Augustus 27 BC–AD 14

Julius Caesar 100–44 BC

Coin showing the head of Mithridates

117-105 JUGURTHINE WAR

129-118 EGYPTIAN CIVIL WAR

c. 103-76 WARS OF ALEXANDER JANNAEUS

89-88 EGYPTIAN CW

83 PARTHIAN CONQUEST OF SYRIA

88 CYZICUS
86 CHAERONEA

69 TIGRANOCERTA
68 NICOPOLIS

88-85 1ST MITHRIDATIC WAR

74-62 3RD MITHRIDATIC WAR

83-82 2ND MITHRIDATIC WAR

65 ROMAN INTERVENTION IN JUDAEA

49 BAGRADAS

48-47 CAESAR'S ALEXANDRIAN WAR

49 CURIO'S CAMPAIGN IN AFRICA

47 NILE DELTA

47 ZELA

53 CARRHAE

54-53 CRASSUS' PARTHIAN CAMPAIGN

47 ASIAN CAMPAIGN

39-33 ANTONY'S EASTERN CAMPAIGNS

40 PARTHIAN RECONQUEST OF SYRIA ETC

25-24 GALLUS'S ARABIAN EXPEDITION

6 BC TO AD 4 ARMENIAN SUCCESSION CRISIS

5-6 GAETRILIAN REVOLT IN MAURETANIA

17-24 REVOLT OF TACFARINAS IN AFRICA

22 THALA

68 REVOLT OF JULIUS VINDEX

193-194 CIVIL WAR

193 CYZICUS

194 ISSUS

Tiberius 14–37

Vespasian 69–79

Trajan 69–79

Gallienus 253–268

Constantine the Great 312–337

70. JEWISH REVOLT. SIEGE OF JERUSALEM
70-73: SIEGE OF MASADA

66-68 JUDEAN REVOLT

72 UPPER EUPHRATES CAMPAIGN STABLISES FRONTIER FOR HALF A CENTURY

113-116 TRAJAN'S CONQUEST OF PARTHIA AND ARMENIA

115-117 REVOLTS IN CYRENAICA, EGYPT AND PALESTINE

116-117 MESOPOTAMIAN REVOLT

132-135 BAR KOCHBA REVOLT IN PALESTINE.
134 RECAPTURE OF JERUSALEM

152-153 EGYPTIAN RISING

145-152 MAURETANIAN DISTURBANCES

175-176 REVOLT OF AVIDIUS CASSIUS IN SYRIA

190 AFRICAN REVOLT

194-195 197-199

161 - ROMAN PARTHIAN W

SEPTIMIUS SEVERUS'S PARTHIAN CAMPAIGNS

214 THEOCRITUS'S ARMENIAN CAMPAIGN

216 NISIBIS

215 CARACALLA'S ALEXANDRIAN MASSACRES

218 ANTIOCH

240 CARTHAGE REBELLION

231-233 SEVERUS ALEXANDER'S EASTERN CAMPAIGN

238 - ROMAN WAR WITH SASSANIDS

216-217 CARACALLA'S EASTERN CAMPAIGN

262-267 ODAENATHUS OF PALMYRA'S CAMPAIGNS AGAINST SASSANIDS

259 EDESSA

253-260 ROME-PERSIAN WAR
260 VALENTIAN MADE PRISONER

SASSANIDS OCCUPY MUCH OF THE ROMAN EAST DURING ROME'S CRISIS

272 EMESA, PALMYRA

273 PALMYRA DESTROYED

28 CA

35-52 ARMENIAN SUCCESSION CRISIS

55-66 ARMENIAN OPERATIONS

25 THRACIAN REVOLT

PARTHIAN EMPIRE

227 ARDASHIR / ARTAXERXES ESTABLISHES SASSANID EMPIRE

Siege warfare: a siege tower against a city wall, about to be assaulted. Note the covered ways leading forward to afford protection to the attacking troops

Octavian, renamed Augustus, wins the final conflicts of the civil wars and reconciles Rome to a monarchial-style government, thus ending the decayed Roman Republic and bringing stability to the Mediterranean world

INDIA

AFTER 88BC SCYTHIANS (SAKAS) SWEEP THROUGH PARTHIA INTO INDUS VALLEY

KANVA DYNASTY

NUCLEUS: MAGADHA — SUNGA DYNASTY — ANDHRAS (DECCAN)

YUEH-CHI CHIEF KUJULA KADPHISES CONQUERS N INDIA

ZENITH OF KUSNANA UNDER KANISHKA

KUSHANA

SATARAHANAS (DECCAN)

EARLY 3RD CENTURY PANDYA KING NEDUNJELIYAN WINS MAJOR VICTORY OVER CERAS

BY NOW KUSHANS, REDUCED TO GANDHARA AND KASHMIR, BECOME VASSALS OF SASSANID PERSIA

CHINA / JAPAN

109 TIEN KINGDOM CONQUERED

108 - INVASIONS OF INDOCHINA

BUDDHISM ARRIVES VIA CENTRAL ASIA

25 EXTERNAL MENACE OF HSIUNG-NU BEGINS TO BECOME MAJOR THREAT

LATE 1ST CENTURY DRIVE AGAINST HSIUNG-HU WEST INTO CENTRAL ASIA BY WU-TI

CHINA SPLITS INTO 3 KINGDOMS

265 SSUMA COUP IN WEI

HAN DYNASTY

2ND HALF OF 1ST CENTURY BC SEES BEGINNING OF DECLINE

9-23 WANG MANG USURPS THRONE

RESTORATION

EASTERN HAN

COURT FACTIONALISM WEAKENS CENTRAL AUTHORITY BY C. 160

220: HSIEN TI LAST HAN EMPEROR ABDICATES

CENTRAL AUTHORITY NOW IN NAME ONLY. REGIONAL COMMANDERS AUTONOMOUS

WEI (NORTH)

SHU (WEST)

WU (SOUTH)

BECOME WESTERN CH'IN

117-100 WESTERN EXPANSION

117-115 CHIANG TRIBES CONQUERED

c.33 PEASANT REVOLTS

WIDESPREAD REBELLION

*HAN COLONISE SOUTH AND SOUTH-WEST CHINA, KOREA, VIETNAM, CENTRAL ASIA
*SILK ROAD OPENED TO THE WEST
*SEA ROUTES TO BURMA AND INDIA

TROUBLE WITH CHIANG TRIBES

184 MASS UPRISING - THE 'YELLOW TURBANS'

263 WEI CONQUER SHU

Timeline scale (bottom)

100 BC — 75 — 50 — 25 — BC | AD — 50 — 100 — 150 — 200 — 250

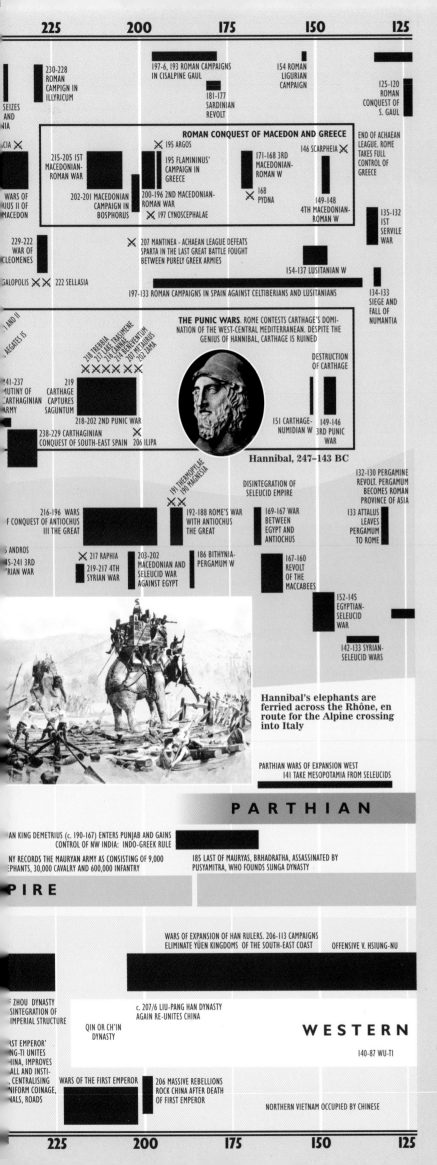

230-228 ROMAN CAMPIGN IN ILLYRICUM

SEIZES AND ...HIA

...CIA

197-6, 193 ROMAN CAMPAIGNS IN CISALPINE GAUL

181-177 SARDINIAN REVOLT

154 ROMAN LIGURIAN CAMPAIGN

125-120 ROMAN CONQUEST OF S. GAUL

END OF ACHAEAN LEAGUE. ROME TAKES FULL CONTROL OF GREECE

ROMAN CONQUEST OF MACEDON AND GREECE

× 195 ARGOS

195 FLAMININUS' CAMPAIGN IN GREECE

171-168 3RD MACEDONIAN-ROMAN W

146 SCARPHEIA ×

215-205 1ST MACEDONIAN-ROMAN WAR

202-201 MACEDONIAN CAMPAIGN IN BOSPHORUS

200-196 2ND MACEDONIAN-ROMAN WAR

× 168 PYDNA

× 197 CYNOSCEPHALAE

149-148 4TH MACEDONIAN-ROMAN W

WARS OF ...IUS II OF ...ACEDON

135-132 1ST SERVILE WAR

229-222 WAR OF ...CLEOMENES

207 MANTINEA - ACHAEAN LEAGUE DEFEATS SPARTA IN THE LAST GREAT BATTLE FOUGHT BETWEEN PURELY GREEK ARMIES

154-137 LUSITANIAN W

...GALOPOLIS × × 222 SELLASIA

197-133 ROMAN CAMPAIGNS IN SPAIN AGAINST CELTIBERIANS AND LUSITANIANS

134-133 SIEGE AND FALL OF NUMANTIA

THE PUNIC WARS. ROME CONTESTS CARTHAGE'S DOMINATION OF THE WEST-CENTRAL MEDITERRANEAN. DESPITE THE GENIUS OF HANNIBAL, CARTHAGE IS RUINED

DESTRUCTION OF CARTHAGE

218 TREBBIA
217 LAKE TRASIMENE
216 CANNAE
214 BENEVENTUM
207 METAURUS
202 ZAMA

219 CARTHAGE CAPTURES SAGUNTUM

151 CARTHAGE-NUMIDIAN W

149-146 3RD PUNIC WAR

...41-237 ...UTINY OF ...ARTHAGINIAN ...RMY

218-202 2ND PUNIC WAR

238-229 CARTHAGINIAN CONQUEST OF SOUTH-EAST SPAIN 206 ILIPA

Hannibal, 247-143 BC

...1 AND II

...AGATES IS

...5-241 3RD ...RIAN WAR

191 THERMOPYLAE 190 MAGNESIA

DISINTEGRATION OF SELEUCID EMPIRE

132-130 PERGAMINE REVOLT. PERGAMUM BECOMES ROMAN PROVINCE OF ASIA

216-196 WARS ...F CONQUEST OF ANTIOCHUS III THE GREAT

192-188 ROME'S WAR WITH ANTIOCHUS THE GREAT

169-167 WAR BETWEEN EGYPT AND ANTIOCHUS

133 ATTALUS LEAVES PERGAMUM TO ROME

× 217 RAPHIA

219-217 4TH SYRIAN WAR

203-202 MACEDONIAN AND SELEUCID WAR AGAINST EGYPT

186 BITHYNIA-PERGAMUM W

167-160 REVOLT OF THE MACCABEES

...S ANDROS

...5-241 3RD ...RIAN WAR

152-145 EGYPTIAN-SELEUCID WAR

142-133 SYRIAN-SELEUCID WARS

Hannibal's elephants are ferried across the Rhône, en route for the Alpine crossing into Italy

PARTHIAN WARS OF EXPANSION WEST 141 TAKE MESOPOTAMIA FROM SELEUCIDS

PARTHIAN

...AN KING DEMETRIUS (c. 190-167) ENTERS PUNJAB AND GAINS CONTROL OF NW INDIA: INDO-GREEK RULE

...NY RECORDS THE MAURYAN ARMY AS CONSISTING OF 9,000 ...EPHANTS, 30,000 CAVALRY AND 600,000 INFANTRY

185 LAST OF MAURYAS, BRHADRATHA, ASSASSINATED BY PUSYAMITRA, WHO FOUNDS SUNGA DYNASTY

...PIRE

WARS OF EXPANSION OF HAN RULERS. 206-113 CAMPAIGNS ELIMINATE YÜEN KINGDOMS OF THE SOUTH-EAST COAST

OFFENSIVE V. HSIUNG-NU

...ZHOU DYNASTY ...SINTEGRATION OF ...IMPERIAL STRUCTURE

c. 207/6 LIU-PANG HAN DYNASTY AGAIN RE-UNITES CHINA

QIN OR CH'IN DYNASTY

WESTERN

...RST EMPEROR' ...ING-TI UNITES ...HINA, IMPROVES ...ALL AND INSTI-...CENTRALISING ...NIFORM COINAGE, ...ALS, ROADS

140-87 WU-TI

WARS OF THE FIRST EMPEROR

206 MASSIVE REBELLIONS ROCK CHINA AFTER DEATH OF FIRST EMPEROR

NORTHERN VIETNAM OCCUPIED BY CHINESE

GREAT COMMANDERS

Marcus Vipsanius Agrippa (c.63–12 BC)
Associate and general of Augustus, 44–30 BC, victor at Actium (31 BC) over Antony and Cleopatra.

Alexander the Great (Alexander III of Macedon) (356–323 BC)
Perhaps the greatest warrior-hero of all time, a military genius, whose legend persists to this day in folklore throughout the vast empire he conquered in the Middle East. He was the son of Philip II (380–336 BC), who created an élite military force and won control of the Greek city states. Alexander participated in his father's victory at Chaeronea in 338 and succeeded to the throne of Macedon upon Philip's assassination two years later. He invaded Asia in 334, aiming at nothing less than the conquest of the Persian Empire. This he accomplished in four years of campaigning, proclaiming himself Great King in 331. His principal battles were the Granicus (334 BC), Issus (333), Gaugamela (331) and the Hydaspes (327). As much explorer as soldier, he led his army east and north, into modern Afghanistan and to the frontier of India until his troops refused to march farther. He died at Babylon before his plans for conquests in the west could be undertaken.

Mark Antony (Marcus Antonius) (c.82–30 BC)
Penultimate in the line of warlords whose rivalries led to the fall of the Roman Republic. Served with Caesar in Gaul and during the Civil War (War of the 1st Triumvirate). Allied with Octavian and Lepidus after the failure of the Mutina War to form 2nd Triumvirate (43 BC). Defeated Caesar's assassins at Philippi (42 BC). Divided the Roman world with Octavian and attempted unsuccessfully to conquer Parthia. Fell out with Octavian and, in alliance with Cleopatra of Egypt, was defeated at Actium (31 BC), subsequently committing suicide.

Antiochus III the Great (241–187 BC)
Seleucid king whose expansionist ambitions led, after much success, to the eventual downfall of the Seleucid kingdom at the hand of Rome. After restoring lost parts of his empire in the east (Armenia, Parthia, Bactria), he conspired with Philip V of Macedon against Egypt. In 202–198 BC he conquered Ptolemaic Syria and Palestine, then came up against Roman interests in Greece (192 BC). At Thermopylae (191 BC) and Magnesia (189 BC) he was defeated by Rome, ending the Seleucid kingdom as a major power in the Mediterranean.

Augustus (C. Octavius/Octavian) (63 BC–AD14)
Heir to Julius Caesar and founder of the Roman Empire. A statesman rather than a general (see Agrippa). With Antony and Lepidus formed 2nd Triumvirate; defeated Pompey's son Sextus by 36 BC and Antony at Actium in 31 BC. Subsequently campaigned in Illyricum and in north-west Spain. Secured Rome's northern frontiers and stabilised the administration of Rome and her overseas relationships, ushering in a long period of relative peace and Roman domination of Western Europe and the Mediterranean.

C. Julius Caesar (100–44 BC)
One of the greatest generals in history, Caesar conquered Gaul for Rome, invaded Britain twice, and defeated his enemies, led by Pompey the Great, in the Roman Civil War of 49–45 BC. Assuming the dictatorship of Rome, he effectively brought the Roman Republic to an end, ushering in an imperial regime, the founder of which was his adopted nephew Octavius (later known as Augustus). With Pompey and Crassus, he had formed an alliance (the 1st Triumvirate) and after his consulship assumed the governorship of Gaul, then a small part of the area that is modern France. Between 58 and 52 he systematically conquered the rest of Gaul, pausing in 55 and 54 to invade, but not conquer, Britain. A full-scale revolt in Gaul was suppressed after hard fighting in 52–1. Tension with the Senate and his erstwhile ally Pompey led to Civil War in 49. Caesar invaded Italy, defeated a Pompeian army in Spain, then faced Pompey at Dyrrhachium before defeating him at Pharsalus in Greece (48 BC). His pursuit of Pompey to Egypt led to a campaign in Alexandria and on the Nile, after which he returned to Rome, defeating Pontic forces at Zama in modern Turkey (47). His enemies had meanwhile rallied in Africa, where Caesar defeated them at Thapsus (47–46) before tracking down Pompey's last supporters at Munda in Spain (45). Caesar was assassinated while planning a new campaign against the Parthians.

Demetrius I Poliorcetes (336–283 BC)
Son of Antigonus Monopthalmus, one of Alexander's successors competing for control of the Macedonian Empire, whose appellation Poliorcetes means 'the Besieger'. Principal battles were Gaza (312 BC), Salamis/Cyprus (306 BC), Ipsus (301 BC). More ambitious and energetic than successful, his resilience and ability to rebound vigorously from one defeat to another are impressive. He campaigned widely, gaining control of Greece (293–289 BC) but lost Macedon in 288 BC, ending his career trapped with a small force of mercenaries by Seleucus in Cilicia. Rather than execute him, his captor encouraged him to drink himself to death.

Continued on page 50

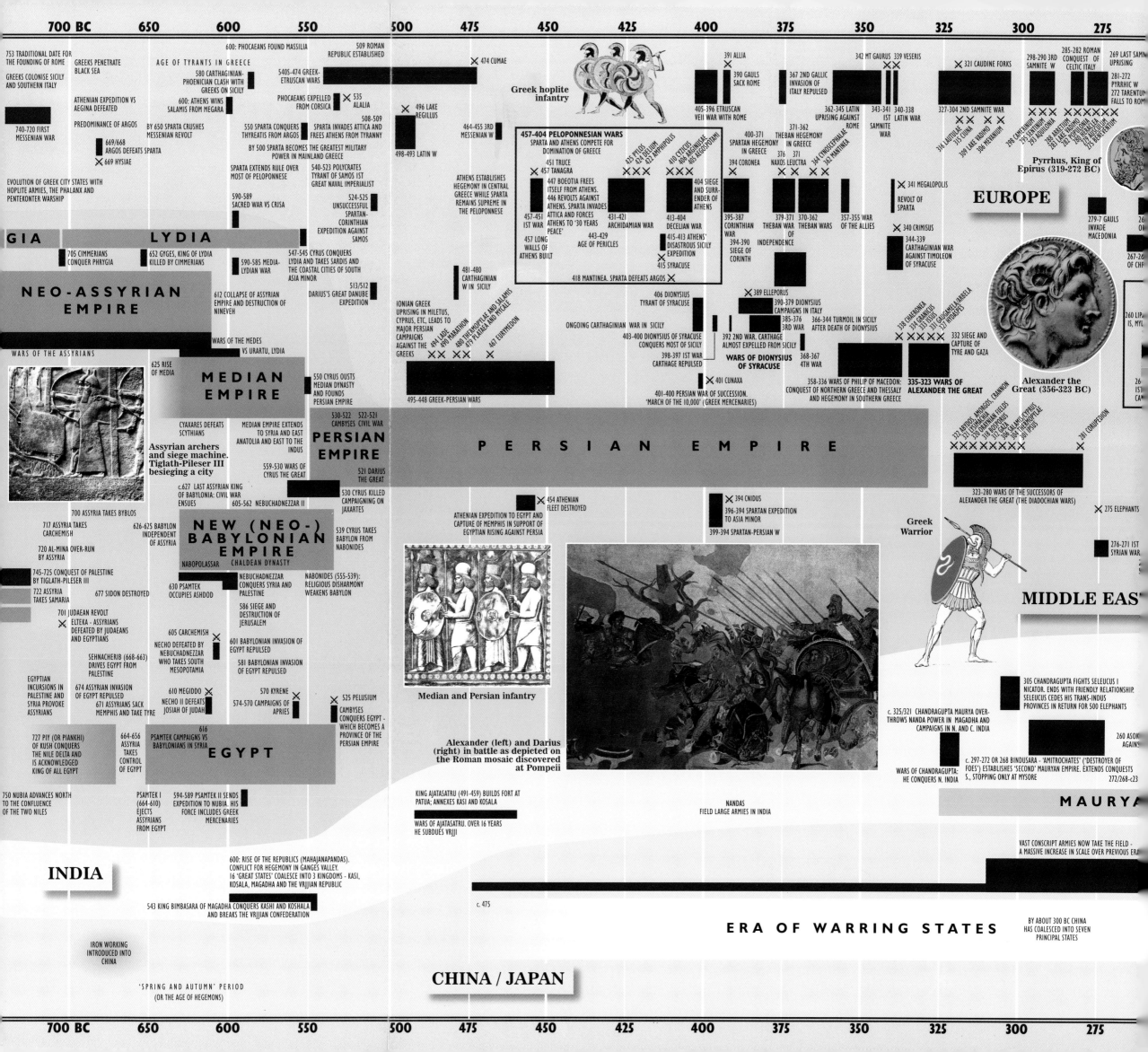

Greek hoplite infantry

Median and Persian infantry

Alexander (left) and Darius (right) in battle as depicted on the Roman mosaic discovered at Pompeii

Greek Warrior

Pyrrhus, King of Epirus (319–272 BC)

Alexander the Great (356–323 BC)

EUROPE

MIDDLE EAST

INDIA

MAURYA

CHINA / JAPAN

ERA OF WARRING STATES

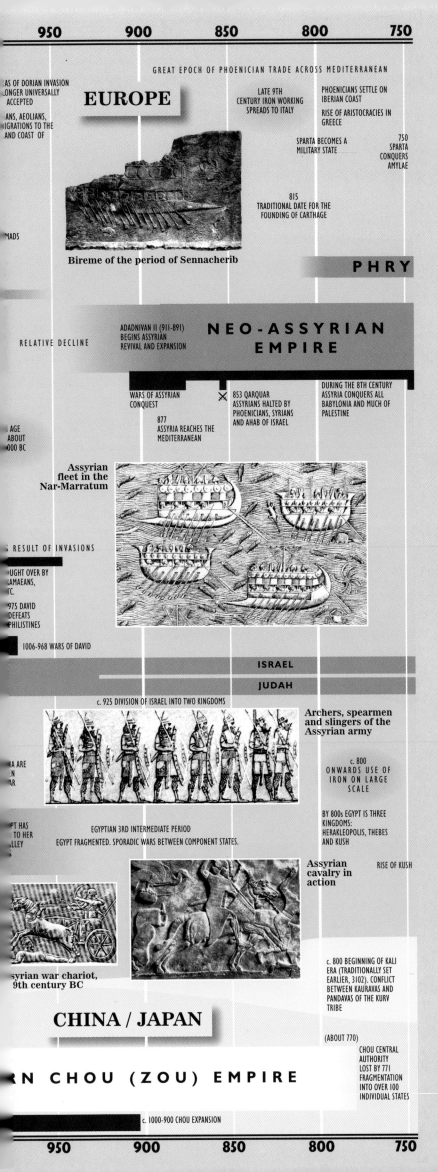

GREAT EPOCH OF PHOENICIAN TRADE ACROSS MEDITERRANEAN

AS OF DORIAN INVASION LONGER UNIVERSALLY ACCEPTED

ANS, AEOLIANS, MIGRATIONS TO THE AND COAST OF

MADS

LATE 9TH CENTURY IRON WORKING SPREADS TO ITALY

PHOENICIANS SETTLE ON IBERIAN COAST

RISE OF ARISTOCRACIES IN GREECE

SPARTA BECOMES A MILITARY STATE

750 SPARTA CONQUERS AMYLAE

815 TRADITIONAL DATE FOR THE FOUNDING OF CARTHAGE

Bireme of the period of Sennacherib

PHRY

RELATIVE DECLINE

ADADNIVAN II (911–891) BEGINS ASSYRIAN REVIVAL AND EXPANSION

NEO-ASSYRIAN EMPIRE

WARS OF ASSYRIAN CONQUEST

853 QARQUAR ASSYRIANS HALTED BY PHOENICIANS, SYRIANS AND AHAB OF ISRAEL

DURING THE 8TH CENTURY ASSYRIA CONQUERS ALL BABYLONIA AND MUCH OF PALESTINE

877 ASSYRIA REACHES THE MEDITERRANEAN

AGE ABOUT 000 BC

Assyrian fleet in the Nar-Marratum

RESULT OF INVASIONS

UGHT OVER BY AMAEANS, C.

975 DAVID DEFEATS PHILISTINES

1006-968 WARS OF DAVID

ISRAEL

JUDAH

c. 925 DIVISION OF ISRAEL INTO TWO KINGDOMS

Archers, spearmen and slingers of the Assyrian army

NA ARE N AR

c. 800 ONWARDS USE OF IRON ON LARGE SCALE

PT HAS TO HER LLEY

EGYPTIAN 3RD INTERMEDIATE PERIOD
EGYPT FRAGMENTED. SPORADIC WARS BETWEEN COMPONENT STATES.

BY 800s EGYPT IS THREE KINGDOMS: HERAKLEOPOLIS, THEBES AND KUSH

Assyrian cavalry in action

RISE OF KUSH

syrian war chariot, 9th century BC

c. 800 BEGINNING OF KALI ERA (TRADITIONALLY SET EARLIER, 3102). CONFLICT BETWEEN KAURAVAS AND PANDAVAS OF THE KURV TRIBE

(ABOUT 770)

CHOU CENTRAL AUTHORITY LOST BY 771 FRAGMENTATION INTO OVER 100 INDIVIDUAL STATES

N CHOU (ZOU) EMPIRE

c. 1000-900 CHOU EXPANSION

GREAT COMMANDERS

Ashurbanipal (668–627 BC)
The last great king of Assyria. Quelled two revolts in Egypt, but was unable to hold the province after 655. In 648 conquered Babylonia from his brother. In 642 invaded Elam and destroyed Susa.

Ashurnasirpal II (883–859 BC)
Assyrian king of particular cruelty. Extended Assyrian power to the shores of the Mediterranean. He founded Nimrud, to become the military capital of the empire. He reorganised the army, the first great power to use iron weapons en masse, and his annual campaigns spread terror far and wide.

Cyrus the Great (559–530 BC)
Founder of the Achaemenid, or Persian, Empire. After defeating his Median overlord by 550, he conquered Media, Assyria and part of Asia Minor before taking Lydia and the Ionian cities. In 539 he captured Babylon. His empire, 4,000km in width and 1,500km from north to south, was vast, with a population of some 35 millions. His son, Cambyses, conquered Egypt and Cyprus.

Darius I (The Great) (521–486 BC)
Aided by his predecessor, Cambyses' bodyguard (the Ten Thousand Immortals), he ousted the usurper Bardiya and then set about expanding the already huge Persian Empire. By 513 he had conquered east as far as the Indus. In 510 he launched a major expedition in the Balkans against the Scythians and encroached upon the city states of mainland Greece. The revolt of the Ionian Greeks was met with the destruction of Miletus and deportations, but this sparked full-scale war with the Greeks. Defeated at Marathon, and with a rebellion in Egypt, Darius died before he could counter-attack.

Esarhaddon (680–669 BC)
Assyrian king who repulsed Scythian and Cimmerian invaders from the north and north-east. 671 crushed revolt in Sidon, took Tyre and invaded Egypt, taking Memphis in 671. His campaigns brought the Assyrian Empire to its greatest territorial extent.

Nebuchadnezzar II (605–562 BC)
Son of the founder of the Chaldean Empire, he was a brilliant tactician and strategist who pursued a policy aiming at having 'no opponent from horizon to sky'. He smashed the Egyptian army at Carchemish and Hamath, thereby gaining control of Syria. Subsequent campaigns in Palestine culminated in the capture of Jerusalem in 597 and 586. His attempted invasion of Egypt in 568/7 was not successful.

Ramses II the Great (1304–1237 BC)
One of the greatest of Egypt's rulers, who fought a series of campaigns against the Hittites in Syria and Palestine. The Battle of Qadesh (Kadesh) against the Hittites is the first great battle in history to be recorded in detail. Other campaigns were generally punitive expeditions in outlying provinces, in addition to the defence of Egypt against invaders from Libya. His reign marks the last peak of Egypt as a military power.

Sargon of Akkad (c.2334–2279 BC)
The first great empire-builder, he rose from being a servant of the king of Kish to found his own state around the city of Agade. He may have conquered all southern Mesopotamia and south-west Persia as well as parts of Lebanon. His successors were continually at war defending the empire, which finally succumbed to the Guti by about 2050.

Sargon II (721–705 BC)
Assyrian king who spent much of his reign crushing rebellions and reconquering lost territories, Egypt, Elam and Urartu all fostering resistance to Assyrian rule. 714 invaded and crushed Urartu. Reconquered Babylon 710 (which had been taken by Chaldeans in 720).

Sennacherib (705–681 BC)
Quelled revolt in Palestine and Phoenicia; ended Babylonian revolts by recapturing and sacking the city in 689. Attacked Elam. Enlarged and rebuilt Nineveh.

Shamshi-Adad I (c.1814–1781 BC)
Founder of the first Assyrian Empire. Conquered all northern Mesopotamia.

Suppuliuliamus (1380–1340)
Founder of the Hittite Empire. Conquered Mitanni c.1360 and invaded Syria. Captured Carchemish c.1354 and reduced Mitanni to vassalage.

Thutmosis I (1525–1512 BC)
Pharaoh of 18th Dynasty Egypt, he campaigned deep into Nubia, beyond the 4th cataract, securing Nubia's rich gold mines. He pursued the Hyksos to the Euphrates, which he claimed as the boundary of the Egyptian Empire.

Thutmosis III (1504–1450 BC)
One of the greatest pharaohs of Egypt. Faced with a major revolt in Syria, he won the Battle of Meggido (1457), the first military engagement of recorded history. Seventeen subsequent campaigns subjugated

Continued on page 50

A–Z OF GREAT NAVAL BATTLES

OF THE MODERN ERA

Battle	Date	Result
...cudi	8 Jan 1676	**de Ruyter [Dutch]** - Duquesne [F]
...gusta	22 Aug 1676	**Duquesne [F]** - de la Cerda [Sp/Dut Allies]
...achy Head	10 July 1690	**de Tourville [F]** - Torrington [Br/Dut]
...smarck	18-27 May 1941	**Tovey [Br]** - Lütjens [Ger]
...diz	19 April 1587	**Francis Drake [Eng]** - Spanish
...diz	June-July 1596	**Howard/Essex [Eng/Dut]** - Spanish
...mperdown	11 Oct 1797	de Winter [Bat] - **Duncan [Br]**
...Esperance	11-12 Oct 1942	Japanese - USA
...Finisterre I	3 May 1747	Anson [Br] - de la Jonquière [F]
Finisterre II	14 Oct 1747	Hawke [Br] - de Letenduère [F]
Finisterre III	22 July 1805	Calder [Br] - Villeneuve [Fr/Sp]
...Passaro	31 July 1718	**Byng [Br/Allies]** - Castañeta [Sp]
St. Vincent	16 Jan 1780	**Rodney [Br]** - Langara [Sp]
St. Vincent	14 Feb 1797	**Jervis [Br]** - Cordova [Sp]
...esapeake Bay	5 Sept 1781	**de Grasse [F]** - Graves [Br]
...esme	6-7 July 1770	**Orlov [R]** - Turks
...ios I	9 Feb 1695	Venice - Turks
...ios II	5 July 1770	**Orlov [R]** - Turks
...penhagen	2 April 1801	**Parker/Nelson [Br]** - Fischer [Dan]
...ral Sea	7-8 May 1942	Fletcher [US] - Inouye [Jap]
...rfu	8 July 1716	Andrea Corner [Venice] - Turks
...ronel	1 Nov 1914	**Spee [Ger]** - Cradock [Br]
...rdanelles I	26 June 1656	**Lorenzo Marcello [Venice]** - Turks
...rdanelles II	17 July 1657	**Turks** - Lazaro Mocenigo [Venice]
...rdanelles III	20 Sept 1698	Venice - Turks
...rdanelles IV	18 March 1915	**von Sanders [Tu]** - Sackville Carden [Br]/ de Robeck [F]
...ieper	28-29 June 1788	Nassau-Siegen [R] - el Ghazi [Tu]
...gger Bank	24 Jan 1915	Hipper [Ger] - **Beatty [Br]**
...ver	29 May 1652	Blake [Eng] - Tromp [Dutch]
...wns, The	21 Oct 1639	**Tromp [Dutch]** - de Oquendo [Sp]
...ngeness	10 Dec 1652	**Tromp [Dutch]** - Robert Blake [Eng]
...stern	23-25 Aug 1942	Japanese - USA
...Solomans		
...kland	8 Dec 1914	**Sturdee [Br]** - Spee [Ger]
...slands		
...cchies	12 May 1649	**Giacomo Riva [Venice]** - Turks
...ur Days Fight	11-14 June 1666	**de Ruyter [Dutch]** - Albemarle/ Monck/
...Dover Strait		Prince Rupert [Eng]
...bbard Bank	12-13 June 1653	**Monck/Deane [Eng]** - Martin Van
...North Foreland/Nieuport		Tromp/Witte de With [Dutch]
...orious lst June	1 June 1794	Howe [Br] - Villaret-Joyeuse [F]
...Ushant II		
...enada	6 July 1779	d'Estaing [F] - Byron [Br]
...adalcanal	12-15 Nov 1942	USA - Japanese
...eligoland Bight	28 Aug 1914	**Beatty [Br]** - Germans
...glund	17 July 1788	Greig [R] - Sudermanland [Swe]
...panese Sea	14 Aug 1904	**Kamimura [Jap]** - Yessen [R]
...va Sea	27-28 Feb 1942	**Takagi [Jap]** - Doorman
...rba	1560	**Piali Pasha [Tu]** - Doria [Sp/Genoa]
...tland	31 May-1 June 1916	**Scheer [Ger]** - Jellicoe [Br]
...ntish Knock	8 Oct 1652	**Blake [Eng]** - Witte de With [Dutch]
...öge Bay I	11 July 1677	**Juel [Dan/Dutch Allies]** - Horn [Swe]
...öge Bay II	4 Oct 1710	Gyldenlove [Dan] - Wachmeister [Swe]
...mandorski Is.	26 March 1943	McMorris [US] - Hosagaya [Jap]
...onstadt	3-4 June 1790	**Kruse [R]** - Swedish
...Hogue	19-20 May 1692	**Russell/Allemande [Br/Dut]** - **de Tourville [F]**
...gos Bay	18-19 Aug 1759	**Boscawen [Br]** - De la Clue [F]
...mnos I	12 + 16 July 1717	Venice - Turks
...mnos II	30 June 1807	**Seniavin [R]** - Turks
...panto	7 Oct 1571	**Don John of Austria [Sp/Papal/Ven Alliance]** - Ali Pasha [Tu/Algerians]
...yte Gulf	23-26 Oct 1944	**Nimitz [US]** - Toyoda [Jap]
...ssa (Vis)	20 July 1866	**Tegetthoff [A]** - Persano [It]
...westoft	13 June 1665	**Duke of York/Prince Rupert [Eng]** - Wassenaer van Obdam [Dutch]
...Solebay		
...alaga I	13 Aug 1704	**Rooke [Br/Dut]** - de Toulouse [F]
...alaga II	24 Aug 1704	Shovell [Br] - Saint-Aubin [F]
...artinique	17 April 1780	Rodney [Br] - de Guichen [F]
...atapan I	19 July 1717	**Diedo [Venice]** - Turks
...atapan II	20-22 July 1718	**Diedo [Venice]** - Turks
...atapan III	26-29 March 1941	**Cunningham [Br]** - Iachino [It]
...idway	4-6 June 1942	**Nimitz [US]** - Yamamoto [Jap]
...inorca	20 May 1756	Blakeney/Byng [Br] - **de la Galissonière [F]**
...obile Bay	5 Aug 1864	**Farragut [Fed]** - Buchanon [Con]
...avarino Bay	20 Oct 1827	**Codrington/de Rigny/Heiden [Br/Fr/R]** - Ibrahim Pasha [Tu/Eg]
...le (Aboukir Bay)	1 Aug 1798	**Nelson [Br]** - Brueys [F]
...orth Cape	26 Dec 1943	**Fraser [Br]** - Bey [Ger]
North Foreland II	25 July 1666	**Albemarle/Prince Rupert [Eng]** - de Ruyter/Tromp [Dutch]
Noryang	Nov 1598	**Yi Sun-sin [Kor]** - Japanese
Oeland I	11 June 1676	**Tromp [Dan/Dut Allies]** - Creutz [Swe]
Oeland II	26 July 1789	**Duke Carl [Swe]** - Chichagov [Ru]
Okpo	May 1592	**Yi Sun-sin [Kor]** - Japanese
Palermo	2 June 1676	**Comte de Vivonne [F]** - Spanish/Dutch
Paros Island	July 1651	Mocenigo [Venice] - Turks
Pearl Harbor	7 Dec 1941	**Nagumo [Jap]** - USA
Philippine Sea	19-20 June 1944	**Mitscher [US]/Allies** - Toyoda [Jap]
Portland /Beachey Head	28 Feb-2 March 1653	**Blake [Eng]** - Tromp [Dut]
Punta Delgada	1582	**Marquis of Santa Cruz [Sp]** - Philip Strozzi [F]
Pusan	Aug 1592	**Yi Sun-sin [Kor]** - Japanese
Quiberon Bay	20 Nov 1759	**Hawke [Br]** - Conflans [F]
River Plate	13 Dec 1939	**Harwood [Br]** - Langsdorff [Ger]
Romerswael	29 Jan 1574	**Boisot ['Beggars of the Sea']** - Romero [Sp]
Rügen	8 Aug 1715	**Raben [Dan]** - Sparre [Swe]
Santa Cruz	20 April 1657	**Blake [Br]** - Spanish
Santa Cruz Is.	25-26 Oct 1942	**USA** - **Japanese**
Santiago	3 July 1898	**Schley/Sampson [US]** Cervera [Sp]
Savo Island	8/9 Aug 1942	**Japanese** - USA
Scheveningen /Texel I	8-10 Aug 1653	**Monck [Eng]** - Tromp [Dut]
Schooneveldt I	7 June 1673	de Ruyter [Dutch] - Prince Rupert/d'Estrées [Eng/F]
Schooneveldt II	14 June 1673	de Ruyter [Dutch] - Prince Rupert/d'Estrées [Eng/F]
Southwold /Solebay	28 May 1672	**de Ruyter [Dutch]** - York/d'Estrées [Eng/F]
Spanish Armada	31 July-8 Aug 1588	**Howard of Effingham [Eng]** - Medina Sidonia [Sp]
St. Kitts	25-26 Jan 1782	Hood [Br] - de Grasse [F]
Svensksund I	24 Aug 1789	**Nassau-Siegen [R]** - Ehrensvärd [Swe]
Svensksund I	9-10 July 1790	**Swedes** -Russians
Syrte I	17 Dec 1941	Iachino [It] - Vian [Br]
Syrte II	22 March 1942	**Vian [Br]** - Iachino [It]
Tanhangpo	June 1592	**Yi Sun-sin [Kor]** - Japanese
Taranto	12 Nov 1940	**Cunningham [Br]** - Italians
Tassafaronga	30 Nov 1942	**Japanese** - USA
Tendra	8-9 Sept 1790	**Ushakov [R]** - Said Bey [Tu]
Texel II /Camperdown	21 Aug 1673	**de Ruyter [Dutch]** - Prince Rupert/d'Estrées [Eng/F]
The Saints	12 April 1782	**Rodney [Br]** -de Grasse [F]
The Sound	8 Nov 1658	**van Obdam [Dut]** - Wrangel [Swe]
Trafalgar	21 Oct 1805	**Nelson [Br]** - Villeneuve [F/Sp]
Tsushima	27-28 May 1905	**Togo [Jap]** - Rozhdestvenski [R]
Ushant	27 July 1778	**Keppel [Br]** - d'Estaing [F]
Yalu River	17 Sept 1894	**Ito [Jap]** - Ting [China]
Yellow Sea	10 Aug 1904	**Togo [Jap]** - Russians

KEY TO NATIONALITIES

Abbr	Nationality	Abbr	Nationality	Abbr	Nationality	Abbr	Nationality
[A-H]	Austria-Hungary	[Dut]	Dutch	[Lith]	Lithuania	[Rhod]	Rhodes
[A-S]	Anglo-Saxons	[E Ang]	East Anglia	[Lyd]	Lydians	[Rep]	Republic
[A]	Austria	[Eg]	Egypt	[Mac]	Macedonia	[Rom]	Rome
[Af]	Afghanistan	[Emp East]	Eastern Roman East. Empire	[Mahd]	Mahdists	[Roy]	Royalists
[Afg]	Afghanistan	[Emp West]	Western Roman West. Empire	[Malt]	Malta	[Roy]	Royalist
[Alb]	Albania	[Eng]	England	[Mam]	Mamelukes	[High]	Highlanders
[Alg]	Algeria	[F]	France	[Man]	Mantua	[Rep]	Republic
[Amer]	USA/ America	[Arg] Argentina	[F] France	[Mar]	Marathas	[S Emp]	Southern Empire (Japan)
[Arg]	Argentina	[Fed]	Federals	[Merc]	Mercia	[SA]	South Africa
[Ath]	Athens	[Fin]	Finland	[Mex]	Mexico	[Sab]	Sabines
[Aust]	Austria	[Flem]	Flemish	[Mex Lib]	Mexican Liberals	[Sar]	Saracens
[Bat]	Batavian Republic - Dutch	[Flem]	Flemish	[Mold]	Moldavia	[Sara]	Saracens
[Bav]	Bavaria	[Prot]	Protestants	[Mo]	Moldavia	[Sard]	Sardinia
[Bel]	Belgium	[Fr]	France	[Mog]	Moghuls	[Sax]	Saxony
[Boh]	Bohemia	[Gari]	Garibaldians	[Mogh]	Moghuls	[Scots]	Scotland
[Bohem]	Bohemia	[GB]	Britain	[Mon]	Mongols	[Serb]	Serbia
[Bol]	Bolivia	[Gen]	Genoa	[Mos]	Muslims	[Sic]	Sicily
[Bos]	Bosnia	[Ger]	German	[Mus]	Muslims	[Sp]	Spain
[Br]	Britain	[Ger]	Germany	[Mys]	Mysore	[Spar]	Sparta
[Bran]	Brandenburg	[Ghib]	Ghibellines	[N Emp]	Northern Empire (Japan)	[Sud]	Sudan
[Brand]	Brandenburg	[Govt]	Government	[Neap]	Naples	[Swe]	Sweden
[Braz]	Brazil	[Gr]	Greece	[New Eng]	New Englanders	[Swed]	Sweden
[Brit]	Britain	[Han]	Hanover	[Nor]	Normans	[Syr]	Syria
[Bul]	Bulgaria	[Hess]	Hesse	[Nor]	Norway	[Syrac]	Syracuse
[Bulg]	Bulgaria	[High]	Highlanders	[Northum]	Northumbria	[T]	Turks
[Burg]	Burgundy	[HRE]	Holy Roman Empire			[Tar]	Tartars
[Burm]	Burma	[Hu]	Huguenots	[NZ]	New Zealand	[Teu]	Teutonic Knights
[Byz]	Byzantium	[Hug]	Huguenots	[P]	Prussia	[Tex]	Texas
[Cæs]	Cæsarians	[Hun]	Hungary	[Palat]	Palatinate	[Trans]	Transylvania
[Can]	Canada	[Hung]	Hungary	[Pann]	Pannonian Legions	[Tu]	Turks
[Carl]	Carlists	[Huss]	Hussites	[Pap]	Papal States	[Tur]	Turkey
[Carth]	Carthage	[Imp]	Empire (Roman) Byzantine/	[Para]	Paraguay	[Ulst]	Ulster
[Cast]	Castile	[Cav] Cavalry	Japanese/ Holy Roman)	[Parl]	Parliament	[Prot]	Protestants
[Cat]	Catalan	[Imp/ Pret]	Imperial Pretender	[Parth]	Parthians	[UN]	United Nations
[Cath]	Catholics	[Ind]	Indians	[Pat]	Patriots	[Uru]	Uruguay
[Chil]	Chile	[Ion]	Ionians	[Pelo]	Peloponnesians	[US]	USA
[Chin]	China	[Ir]	Ireland	[Per]	Persia	[Van]	Vandals
[Christ]	Christians	[Isr]	Israel	[Peruv]	Peruvians	[Ven]	Venice
[Col]	Columbia	[It]	Italy	[Pied]	Piedmont	[Ven]	Venetians
[Con]	Confederate States	[Jacob]	Jacobites	[Pol]	Poland	[Viet]	Vietnam
[Cong]	Congressists	[Jap]	Japan	[Pomp]	Pompeians	[Virg]	Virginia
[Cov]	Covenanters	[Kor]	Korea	[Pon]	Pontics	[Vis]	Visigoths
[Cris]	Cristinos	[R]	Russia	[Port]	Portugal	[York]	Yorkists
[Crus]	Crusaders	[reb]	rebels	[Prot]	Protestants	[W Sax]	West Saxons
[Dan]	Denmark	[Lanc]	Lancastrians			[Wall]	Walloons
[Du]	Dutch					[Wall]	Wallachians
						[Wes]	Wessex
						[Würt]	Württemberg

CHRONOLOGY

WARS AND BATTLES OF HISTORY

Middle East

By beginning of 3rd Millennium a dozen city states including Kish, Erech, Ur, Lagash compete for domination

By 2900 Narmer or Aha becomes King of all Egypt

2800 Kish unites city states of Sumer

2600 Uruk overthrows Kish

2300-2200 Akkad. Sargon I, the first great conqueror of history, conquers Mesopotamia, Syria, part of Asia Minor.

About 2000 Expansion of Ur

Mid-20th century Ur overthrown by Elamites and Amorites. Two centuries of city-state anarchy follow

2270-2230 Naram-Sin renews Akkadian vigour. Late third millennium Hurrians infiltrate northern Mesopotamia and Syria from the north

2200 Pharaoh Pepynakht campaigns against Nubia

About 2150 death of Pepy II, last of 6th Dynasty, ends Old Kingdom of Egypt

2150-2050 Guti from Iran destroy the Akkadian Empire, then are expelled by Erech and Uruk

1st Intermediate period, after which Monjunotep II reunites Egypt. Beginning of the Egyptian Middle Kingdom. Fragmentation of Egypt

Gradual disintegration into Kingdoms of Avaris, Thebes, Kush

2064-1990 Thebes conquers Wawat and upper Egypt

2050-1950 Ur reconstructs the Sumer-Akkad empire

1993 fortification of 1st and 2nd cataracts of the Nile

1937-1908 Amenemhat I builds the 'Walls of the River' about Suez

1919-1903 Senuset I gains control of Wawat (north Nubia)

19th century Rise of Babylon to become the main political and cultural centre in Southern Mesopotamia

1830 Senusret III campaigns to the north of Jerusalem

1829-1818 Senuset III

campaigns beyond 2nd cataract of the Nile and builds a second series of forts

18th-early 17th centuries Assyrian wars of conquest

1800 Assyrians conquer northern Babylonians. Foundation of 'Old Assyrian Empire'

1760 Kassites enter Mesopotamia introducing horse and chariot

1728-1686 Amorite Hammurabi of Babylon conquers southern Mesopotamia, uniting the six main states

Late 18th to mid-17th centuries gradual disintegration of Egypt into Kingdoms of Avaris, Thebes and Kush

18th century Hyksos enter north Egypt and take control during the mid-17th century. Capital: Avaris. They bring technology of the horse in war - with chariots, the compound bow, battleaxes and skill in fortification.

Late 16th century Thutmose I defeats Hittites on the Euphrates

Egyptian 2nd Intermediate Period. Egypt divided into three states: Thebes, Kush and the North, controlled by the Hyksos

1650 Kassite kings

17th-16th centuries Babylon fights continuously with Kassites and Hurrians

1573-1550 Pharaoh Ahmose expells Hyksos and pursues them into Palestine. Foundation of the Egyptian Empire

1521 Avaris falls to Egyptians

1500 Hurrians unite as Mitanni

Late 17th century Mursilis, 3rd king of united Hittite state, destroys Aleppo, raids Babylon, defeats Hurrians on the Euphrates. First Hittite Empire

Europe

Crete: Minoan civilisation may have begun as early as 3000. 2200-1400 Crete is leading power in the Aegean

2000 arrival of Greek-speaking peoples in mainland Greece: Mycenaean warriors consolidate power in Greece and raid overseas

2000-1600 Minoan 'Old Palace' period

1600-1400s Minoan 'New Palace' period until a wave of destruction about 1425 leaves only Knossos intact

1450-1400 Probable Mycenean conquest of Crete; 1370 destruction of Knossos. 14th and 13th centuries are the great age of Mycenae

13th century: more massive fortifications are built and the Isthmus of Corinth fortified against invaders from the north

Mid-14th to mid-12th centuries: period during which the siege and fall of Troy is thought to have taken place, according to the account of Homer's *Iliad*, which did not exist in written form until the 8th or 7th centuries

13th century General breakdown of settled conditions and overall decline; by 1150 Mycenaean civilisation collapses; from 1100 to 800 a dark age descends on the Aegean and the coast of Asia Minor, as invaders from the north (Ionians, Aeolians, Dorians, etc.) enter the area in the 11th and 10th centuries. There remains much uncertainty about this period

India

About the beginning of the 3rd Millennium to c.2300 Harrapan Civilisation begins in Indus Valley. After 2000 and by 1750 Harappan culture breaks down, with collapse of city civilisation, causes yet unknown

1500 Vedic Age begins. Indo-European (Aryan) tribes enter Punjab, semi-nomad pasturalists and tribal societies led by rajas (warrior chiefs). Inter-tribal conflicts ensue

1500-1200 Ganges Valley Civilisation

China

By about 3000 Civilisation in the Huang Ho (Yellow River) valley appears; after 2500 walled settlements appear

2200-1760 Yü (Hsia or Xia) Dynasty

1760-1100 Shang (Yin) Dynasty. They conquer the area between the Yellow River and the Yangtse

1100 Revolt against last of the Yin Dynasty, Zhouxin, and foundation of Western Chou (Zou) Empire. Wars of expansion c.1000-900

By 771 Chou central authority overall is lost. Fragmentation into more than 100 individual states

770-475 'Spring and Autumn' Period (or The Age of Hegemons)

Middle East

By 1600 Fragmentation of Mesopotamia into areas dominated by Hurrians, Kassites and 'Sealand' in the south

1457 Battle of Megiddo. Pharaoh Thutmosis III defeats Canaanites and their allies and advances north to Galilee

By 1450 Assyrians become vassals of Mittani

15th century Thutmosis III fights 17 campaigns into Palestine

1427-1400 Pharaoh Amenhotep II campaigns to north of Byblos and Damascus

Late 16th century to early 12th century Wars of Imperial Egypt

Thutmosis III extends Egyptian control south to 4th cataract of the Nile

Hittite wars of conquest. Foundation of second Hittite Empire, the 'Hittite New Kingdom'

1400-1390 campaigns of Pharaoh Thutmosis IV ends with treaty with Mitanni

1390-1364 Eriba-Adad wins Assyrian independence from Mitanni

1380-1340 Hittite King Suppiluliamnus. He conquers the Mitanni (c.1360), which becomes a buffer state betwen the Hittites and the Assyrians

1294-1279 Pharaoh Seti I campaigns in Palestine

c.1275 Battle of Qadesh. First battle in history to be recorded in detail. Ramses II and Muwatalli fight an inconclusive battle. A treaty c.1263-1258 divides Palestine and Syria between Egypt and Hatti

By 13th-12th centuries, Nubian gold (reason for Egyptian imperialism to the south) is exhausted Shalmaneser I

1272-1243 begins Assyrian expansion and conquers Mitanni

1242-1206 Tukulti-Ninurta I, Assyrian dominion expands south and temporarily (c.1210) takes Babylon

1200-900 General decline in face of invasions

Europe

End of 2nd millennium: hill forts are being constructed in Western Europe

815 Foundation of Carthage (traditional date)

By 800 Sparta has emerged as a military state in the Peloponnese

8th century Phoenicians, already trading widely in the Mediterranean, establish outposts on the Iberian coast

8th century Rise of aristocracies in Greece. Evolution of city-states, with hoplite armies, the phalanx battle formation and pentekonter warships

753 Foundation of Rome (traditional date)

750 Sparta conquers Amylae

8th century Greeks colonise Sicily and southern Italy

735 Syracuse founded by Corinthians

730-710 Spartan conquest of Messenia

About 700 Greeks penetrate the Black Sea

Early 7th century Predominance of Argos in the Peloponnese

669 Battle of Hysiae. Argos defeats Sparta

By 650 Sparta defeats Messenian revolt

Mid-7th to mid-6th

centuries Age of Tyrants in Greece
580 Carthaginian/ Phoenician clashes with Greeks begin on Sicily
600 Phocaeans found Massilia (modern Marseilles)
600 Athens takes Salamis from Megara
600-550 Sparta extends dominion over most of the Peloponnese
570 War between Athens and Megara
560-550 War between Sparta and Tegea
550 Sparta takes Thyreatis from Argos
546-5 Persia conquers the Greek city-states on the Aegean coast of Asia Minor
540-523 Polycrates, Tyrant of Samos, is the first great naval imperialist
535 Battle of Alalia. Phocaeans expelled from Corsica by Etruscans and Phoenicians
525-524 Unsuccessful Spartan-Corinthian expedition against Samos
509-508 Sparta invades Attica and frees Athens from tyranny
By 500 Sparta is established as the greatest military power in mainland Greece. 494 Cleomenes, King of Sparta (520-490), crushes the revival of Argos

Middle East
Mid-13th century Conquest of Palestine by Hebrews. Wars of Joshua (including fall of Jericho)
1190-1150 Hittite Kingdom overthrown by Phrygians, Luvians etc.
1184-1153 Pharaoh Ramses III repulses invaders from the Sahara: depicted on bas-reliefs is a naval battle
1180 Phrygians invade Asia Minor
Great invasion including possibly those of peoples formerly identified by historians as the 'sea peoples' cause widespread disruption and fragmentation
1180-1177 Pharaoh Merenptah repulses invasions from Libya and 'Sea Peoples' in raiding along the coast and into the Nile delta
By the reign of Ramses VI (1143-1136) Egypt has lost her Palestine dominions
Late 13th to 12th centuries Rise of Elam
1124-1103 Nebuchadnezzar

I defeats Elam
1114-1076 Tiglath-Pileser expands Assyrian control to Mediterranean coast
Late 12th to early 10th century Philistines dominate Palestine
1087 King Panehsy of Nubia invades and temporarily occupies Thebes. In 1080 his regime separates from Egypt
By 1060 Egypt has withdrawn to her original valley boundaries. End of Egyptian Empire
1025-1006 Wars of Israelite King Saul
1006-968 Wars of Israelite King David. He captures Jerusalem
975 Shoshek I reasserts Egyptian authority vs Israel - split
975 David defeats Philistines
11th and 10th centuries Babylonia fought over by Assyrians, Aramaeans, Chaldeans etc.
925 Division of Kingdom of Israel into Israel (north) and Judah (south)
Egyptian 3rd Intermediate Period. Egypt fragmented. Sporadic wars between component states
911-891 Adadnivan II begins Assyrian revival and expansion. Foundation of 'Neo-Assyrian Empire'
9th to 7th centuries Constant warfare waged by Assyrians, based on terror to dominate Mesopotamia and beyond
877 Assyria reaches the Mediterranean
853 Battle of Quaquar. Assyrians halted by Phoenicians, Syrians and Ahab of Israel
8th century Assyria conquers all Babylonia and much of Palestine
By 800 Egypt is three kingdoms: Herakleopolis, Thebes and Kush
Mid 8th century Rise of Kush
750 Nubia advances north to the confluence of the two Niles
745-725 Conquest of Palestine by Tiglath-Pileser III of Assyria
Late 8th century Egyptian incursions in Palestine and Syria provoke Assyrians
727 Piy (or Piankhi) of Kush conquers the Nile Delta and is acknowledged King of all Egypt

722 Assyria takes Samaria
720 Al-Mina overrun by Assyria
717 Assyria takes Carchemish
705 Cimmerians conquer Phrygia
701 Judaean revolt Battle of Elteka. Assyrians defeated by Judaeans and Egyptians
700 Assyria takes Byblos
688-663 Sennacherib drives Egypt from Palestine
677 Sidon destroyed
674 Assyrian invasion of Egypt repulsed
671 Assyrians sack Memphis and take Tyre
664-656 Assyria takes control of Egypt
664-610 Psamtek I ejects Assyrians from Egypt
652 Gyges, King of Lydia, killed by Cimmerians
630 Psamtek occupies Ashdod
c.627 Last Assyrian King of Babylonia dies: Civil War ensues. Nabopolassar New (Neo-) Babylonian Empire Nabopolassar
626-625 Babylon independent of Assyria
625 Rise of Media Empire
625-539 Chaldean dynasty reinstates Babylon as the dominant power in Mesopotamia, the 'Neo-Babylonian Empire'
Cyaxares defeats Scythians
616 Psamtek campaigns v. Babylonians in Syria
612 Collapse of Assyrian Empire and destruction of Nineveh
Late 7th to mid 6th centuries War of the Medes v. Urartu, Lydia, etc., the Media Empire extends to Syria and East Anatolia and East to the Indus
610 Battle of Megiddo. Egyptian Neko II defeats Josiah of Judah
By 610 Saite dynasty rules Egypt
605-562 Nebuchadnezzar II conquers Syria and Palestine
605 Battle of Carchemish. Neko defeated by Nebuchadnezzar who takes southern Mesopotamia
601 Babylonian invasion of Egypt repulsed
c.600 Lydia introduces world's first coinage
597 Nebuchadnezzar captures Jerusalem
594-589 Psamtek II sends expedition to Nubia (or 594-589). His force includes Greek mercenaries
590-589 Sacred War v. Crisa

590-585 Media-Lydian War
586 Siege and destruction of Jerusalem by Nebuchadnezzar
581 Babylonian invasion of Egypt repulsed
574-570 Campaigns of Apries
570 Battle of Kyrene
561-547 Croesus King of Lydia
560 Ahmose II asserts Egyptian domination of Syria and Palestine and occupies Cyprus
555-539 Nabonides last king of Babylon
550 Cyrus the Great (559-530) ousts Median dynasty and founds Persian Empire
547-545 Cyrus conquers Lydia and takes Sardis and the coastal cities of South Asia Minor
539 Cyrus takes Babylon from NabonidesCyrus the Great
530 Cyrus killed campaigning on Jaxertes
530-522 522-521 Cambyses Civil War
525 Battle of Pelusium. Babylonian king Cambyses conquers Egypt, which becomes a province of the Persian Empire
513 Darius of Persia's great Danube expedition

India
c.800 Beginning of Kali era (traditionally set earlier, 3102). Conflict between Kauravas and Pandavas of the Kurv tribe
600 Rise of the Republics (Mahajanapandas). Conflict for hegemony in Ganges Valley. 16 'great states' coalesce into 3 kingdoms - Kashi, Koshala, Magadha, and the Vrjjian Republic
543 King Bimbasara of Magadha conquers Kashi and Koshala and breaks the Vrjjian confederation
537 Darius of Persia conquers Indus Valley
491 King Ajatasatru (491-459) builds fort at Patua; annexes Kasi and Kosala Wars of Ajatasatru. Over 16 years he subdues Vrjji
By about 400 Nandas field large armies

495-448 Greek-Persian Wars
497 Greek uprisings against Persians in Miletus, Cyprus etc
494 Battle of Lade Persians defeat Ionian fleet
492 1st Campaign. Thracians repel Persians
490 2nd Campaign. Battle

of Marathon. Greeks defeat Persians
480 3rd Campaign. Battle of Thermopylae
480 Battle of Cape Artemisium. Sack of Athens by Persians
480 Battle of Salamis
479 Persians re-occupy Athens. Battle of Plataea
479 Battle of Mycale and Greek liberation of Asia Minor city states
478 Greeks capture Byzanatium and Cyprus under Pausanias. Athens organises Delian League against Persia
476.7 Battle of Eurymedon. Athens defeats Persians
458 Battle of Aegina
459 Greek fleet supports Egyptian uprising. Expeditions to Memphis
454 Greek fleet annihilated by Persians
449 Battle of Salamis/Cyprus
448 Treaty of Callias ends war

Greek-Etruscan Wars (W. Mediterranean)
540 Battle of Alalia
535 Greeks expelled from Corsica
474 Battle of Cyme/Cumae

481-480 Carthage in Sicily
480 Battle of Himena (Syracuse, Carthage)

509 Revolution v. Tarquinius Superbus in Rome

China
475-221 Era of the Warring States.
By about 300 China has coalesced into seven principal states; vast conscript armies now take the field, a massive increase in scale over previous eras of war
c.255 End of Zhou Dynasty and final disintegration of any sort of imperial structure

431-404 Peloponnesian Wars
457-1 1st War, Athens defeated
457 Athens conquers Aegina. Battle of Tangra
451 Truce
447 Boeotia frees itself from Athens
446 Euboea and Magara. Revolt against Athens. '30 Years Peace'. Athens returns war gains
431-21 2nd War, indecisive
431-421 Archidamian War Sparta devastates Attica; plague in Athens
425 Battle of Pylos. Athens

BC

victory. Sphacteria capitulates
424 Thracian campaign. Battle of Amphipolis
421 Battle of Niceas
Sparta dominates the land; Athens the sea
430-427 Plague weakens Athens
428-7 Revolt of Mytilene
425 Battle of Pylos. Athens victorious
424 Battle of Delium. Athens defeated
421 Treaty of Nicias, resulting from war-weariness
418 Battle of Mantinea. Sparta defeats Argos
415-413 Athens' disastrous expedition to Sicily. Fleet annihilated
413-404 Decelian War
410 Battle of Cyzicus. Athens regains naval supremacy
407 Sparta gains Persian cooperation
406 Battle of Arginusae. Athens victorious. But internal dissention
405 Battle of Aegospotania. Athens fleet destroyed
404 Siege and surrender of Athens

409 Carthage advances towards Syracuse
401-400 'March of the 10,000'

Continuing expansion of Rome in Italy
431 Battle of Algidus
498-493 Latin Wars
403-400 Dionysus of Syracuse conquers most of Sicily
401-400 March of the 10,000. During Persian Civil War (Artaxerxes II v. Cyrus the Younger), Greek mercenaries win Battle of Cunaxa, but then make epic retreat across mountains in winter

Sparta
399-394 SPARTA-PERSIAN WAR
396-394 SPARTAN EXPEDITION TO ASIA MINOR
395-387 CORINTHIAN WAR
395 Battle of Haliartus
394 Siege of Corinth (to 390)
394 Battle of Coronea
394 Battle of Cnidus. Spartan fleet defeated by Persia
382 Sparta occupies Thebes citadel
379-371 THEBAN BATTLE OF INDEPENDENCE
379 Thebes expels Spartan garrison
376 Battle of Naxos.

Athens defeats Sparta at sea
371 Battle of Leuctra. Thebes defeats Sparta

370-362 Theban Wars
370 Theban invasion of Peleponnese and Laconia
364 Theban naval expedition to Byzantium
364 Battle of Cynoscephalae
363 Thebans defeat Thessalians
362 Thebes invades Peloponnese again
362 Battle of Mantinea

Dionysian Wars v. Carthage
398-397 1st War. Carthage pushed back from Syracuse
392 2nd War. Carthage almost ejected from Sicily
390-379 Dionysius conquers part of S. Italy
389 Battle of Elleponus. Dionysius defeats Italians
385-376 3rd War
368-367 4th War
366-344 Turmoil in Syracuse after 367 death of Dionysius

Roman conquest of Italy
405-396 Etruscan Veii besiege Rome
391 Gauls besiege Clusium
391 Gauls defeat Rome at Battle of Allia 3 and sack Rome
367 2nd Gallic invasion repulsed
362-345 Rome contains Latin uprisings
343-341 1ST SAMNITE WAR
343 Battles of Astura, Suessula, Salicula
342 Battle of Mt Gaurus
341 Battles of Veseris, Tifernum; Roman conquest of Campania
340-338 LATIN WARS
338 Battles of Sinnessa, Pedum
360-1, 350-349 Gauls raid to the Tiber valley

Carthage v. Syracuse
344-339 Carthaginian war v. Timoleon of Syracuse. Siege of Syracuse
340 Battle of Crimissus

Wars of Philip of Macedon
358 Philip unifies Macedon
357-355 War of the Allies
357, 356 Philip expands to Chaldice
355-346 Philip seizes much of Thessaly
355-346 2nd Holy War. Philip is drawn into central Greek conflict
352 Battle of Crocus Field
348 Philip conquers of Chaldice, Thrace
345-339 Philip consolidates

hold on north of Greece
342 Persia meanwhile regains control of Egypt
341-338 Macedonian war v. Hellenic League
338 Battle of Chaeronaea. Philip defeats Hellenic League
337 Philip's general Parmenion leads vanguard for projected invasion of Persia
336 Philip assassinated

335-323 Wars of Alexander the Great
335 Campaign v. Danube tribes: suppresses revolts in Thessaly, Athens, Thebes
334-331 CONQUEST OF PERSIA
334 Battle of Granicus
333 Battle of Issus
332-331 Conquest of Syria
332 Siege of Tyre, siege of Gaza and conquest of Egypt
331 Spartan uprising. Battle of Megalopolis. Antipater defeats Agis
331 Battle of Gaugamela/Arbela
330 Occupation of Mesopotamia
331-323 CONQUESTS OF E. PERSIA TO HYDASPES
326 Battle of the Hydaspes
323 Death of Alexander

327/6-304 2nd Samnite War against Rome
323 Carthage begins reconquest of Sicily
321 Battle of Caudine Forks/Passes. Humiliating Roman defeat by Sabines

India
c.325/321 Chandragupta Maurya overthrows Nanda power in Magadha and campaigns in northern and central India
Wars of Chandragupta: he conquers northern India and founds Mauryan Empire
305 Chandragupta fights Seleucus I Nicator. Ends with friendly relationship. Seleucus cedes his trans-Indus provinces in return for 500 elephants
c.297-272 or 268 Bindusara - 'Amitrochates' ('Destroyer of Foes') establishes 'Second' Mauryan Empire, which he extends south, stopping only at Mysore
272/268-c.231 Asoka
Pliny records the Mauryan army as consisting of 9,000 elephants, 30,000 cavalry and 600,000 infantry
260 Asoka campaigns

against Kalinga
Baetrian King Demetrius (c.190-167) enters Punjab and gains control of north-west India: Indo-Greek rule
185 Last of Mauryas, Brhadratha, assassinated by Pusyamitra, who founds Sunga Dynasty, with its nucleus as Magadha
After 88 Scythians (Sakas) sweep through Parthia into Indus valley
Kanva Dynasty and Aandhras (Deccan)

323-280 Diadochian Wars: the Wars of Alexander's Successors
323-322 LAMIAN WAR
322 Battle of Abydos. Cleitus defeats Athenian fleet
322 Battle of Amorgos. Cleitus defeats Athens and blockades Athens
322 Battle of Crannon. Antipater invades Thessaly and defeats the Greeks
322 Perdiccas invades Cappadona and gives it to Craterus. Perdiccas is now regent of the whole empire, almost
322-319 WARS V. PERDICCAS
321 Battle of Lysimachia. Eumenes, for Perdiccas, defeats Craterus
321 Perdiccas invades Egypt. Army mutinies and kills him. Antipater is elected regent by the army in Syria; he gives Babylon to Seleucus
320 Antigonus invades Cappadocia and defeats Eumenes at the Battle of Oraynian Fields. Siege of Nova
319 Antipater dies. Macedonian army elects Polyperchon regent. Antigonus, Cassander and Ptolemy ally against him
WAR V. POLYPERCHON
Antigonus conquers Asia Minor, Ptolemy takes Syria
318 Cassander invades Greece
318 Battle of the Bosporus. Cleitus defeats Antigonus fleet. Eumenes takes Babylon
317 Antigonus fights Eumenes in Mesopotamia until Eumenes is betrayed. Antigonus now controls Asia and the East
317 Cassander conquers Athens and Macedon
317-16 Siege of Pydna. Death of Olympias, mother of Alexander

315-312 1ST ANTIGONID WAR **BC**
All ally against Antigonus and his son Demetrius. Much manoeuvring ensues
312 Battle of Gaza
Ptolemy defeats Demetrius, but Antigonus restores his position by 311 when peace is made. Antigonus has lost the East
311-308 Confused, futile campaigns on all sides
307-301 2ND ANTIGONID WAR
Antigonus mounts second attempt to reunite Alexander's empire: all ally against him and Demetrius
307 Demetius seizes Athens
306 Battle of Salamis. Demetrius defeats Ptolemy's fleet. Antigonus and Demetrius assume titles of Joint Kings of the Empire; Ptolemy declares himself king of Egypt
304 Battle of Thermopylae. Demetrius defeats Cassander and wins most of Greece and Thessaly
302-1 The allies invade Asia Minor and Syria, overwhelming Antigonus
301 Battle of Ipsus. Seleucus and Lysimachus defeat Antigonus, who is killed. They divide his kingdom and Cassander is recognised as king of Macedon. The war against Demetrius, with various re-alignments of alliance
294 Demetrius takes Athens and Macedonia
293 Demetrius expands into Thessaly etc.
292 Demetrius invades Thrace
288 Lysimachus and Pyrrhus of Epirus invade Macedonia
283 Death of Demetrius
281 Battle of Corupedium. Seleucus defeats Lysimachus
280 Death of Seleucus
279 Gauls raid Macedonia
277 Battle of Lysimachia. Antiochus, son of Seleucus defeats the Gauls
The rivals are now into a new generation, with established kingdoms: Antigonus II Tonatas (son of Demetrius) rules Macedon; Antiochus, son of Seleucid rules Asia Minor and Mesopotamia (Seleucid Empire), Ptolemy II rules Egypt
275 Battle of the Elephants. Antiochus defeats the Galatians

274-272 Pyrrhus wars of conquest in Greece/Macedon

274 Pyrrhus conquers Macedon

273 Antigonus Gonatas retakes Macedon

267-261 War of of Chremonides between Egypt and Macedon

265-261 Siege of Athens by Antigonus Eioriatas

263-261 War of Eumenes (Pergamine breakaway)

263 Battle near Sardis. Antiochus I defeated

258-255 '2nd Syrian War'. Macedonians and Seleucids v. Egypt

258 Battle of Cos. Macedon defeats Egyptian fleet. Seleucids take Syria

245-241 '3rd Syrian War'

245 Battle of Andros. Macedon and Rhodes defeat Egypt. Egypt fails to regain Syria

War of the Brothers (Seleucus II v. Antiochus Hierax)

Battle of Ancyra. Hierax defeats Selucus

239-229 Wars of Demetrius II of Macedon

233 Battle of Phylacia. Demetrius defeats Achaean League

229-222 War of Cleomenes

227 Battle of Megalopolis. Cleomenes of Sparta defeats Achaean League

222 Battle of Sellasia. Macedon and Achaeans defeat Cleomenes

219 '4th Syrian War'. Seleucid Antiochus III attacks Egypt in Syria

217 Battle of Raphia. Egyptians defeat Seleucus

220-217 Battle of the Allies (Macedon v. Aetolia/Sparta) and Philip V of Macedon begins encroachments on Roman theatre

207 Battle of Mantinea. Achaean League defeats Sparta

230-228 Roman campaign in Illyria

238-179 Wars of Philip V of Macedon

217-205 1st Rome-Macedonian War

203-200 Macedonian/Seleucid War against Egypt

201 Battle of Lade. Macedon defeats Rhodes' fleet

201 Battle of Chios. Macedon defeated by Pergamum

200-196 2nd Rome-Macedonian War

199-198 Flamininus defeats Philip

197 Battle of Cynoscephalae. Philip defeated

184, 183, 181 Philip's Balkan campaigns

Sicily

317 Agathocles wars of conquest

312 Agathocles begins conflict with Carthage

311 Carthage wins Battle of Himera and besieges Syracuse

310 Agathocles besieges Carthage to 307

302 Agathocles invades southern Italy

Rome

2nd Samnite Wars continued

316 Battle of Lantulae

315 Battle of Ciuna

309 Battle of Lake Vadimo

306 Battle of Mevania

305 Rome takes Bovanium

304 Peace. Rome annexes Campania

298-290 3RD SAMNITE WAR

298 Battle of Camerinum

295 Battle of Sentinum

293 Battle of Aquilonia

285-282 ROMAN CONQUEST OF CELTIC ITALY

285 Battle of Arretium

283 Battle of Lake Vadimo

282 Battle of Populonia ends Etruscan resistance

281-272 Pyrrhic Wars

280 Battle of Heraclea

279 Battle of Auschlum

275 Battle of Beneventum

272 Blockade and fall of Tarentum. Rome now dominates southern Italy too

269 Last Samnite uprising against Rome quashed

264-241 1st Punic War

262 Rome takes Agrigentum

260 Battle of Lipari Is

260 Battle of Mylae

259 Roman invasion of Corsica, Malta, Sardinia

256 Battle of Cape Ecnomus

256 Battle of Adys

255 Battle of Tunis

251 Battle of Panormus I

250 Battle of Panormus II

250/49 Battle of Drepanum

242 Rome takes Lilybaeum and Drepanum

241 Battle of Aegates Is

241 Peace. Carthage gives up Sicily

241-237 Mutiny of the Carthaginian army

238 Rome seizes Corsica and Sardinia

238-229 Carthage conquest of south-eastern Spain to Ebro frontier

219 Carthage captures Saguntum provoking full-scale war with Rome

218-202 2nd Punic war

219-203 HANNIBAL'S CAMPAIGN IN ITALY

218 Hannibal crosses Alps. Battle of Ticinus, Trebbia

217 Battle of Lake Trasimene

217 Battle of Gerunium

216 Battle of Cannae

215 Neapolis/Bruttium campaign

214 Battle of Beneventum

213 Hannibal takes Tarentum

212-11 Siege of Capua

212 Battle of Herdonea I

210 Battle of Herdonea II

207 Battle of the Metaurus

205 Mago takes Genoa

203 Hannibal returns to Africa

SPANISH THEATRE

218 Battle of Celsa

217 Battle of Ebro (naval) Battle of Ibera

213 Rome take Saguntum

211 Battle of Lorqui

209 Rome takes Nora Carthago

208 Battle of Baecula

206 Battle of Ilipa

SICILY AND OTHER THEATRES

218 Carthage attacks Lilybaeum but is repulsed

215 Sardinia revolts against Rome. Battle of Cavales

215-212 Sicily campaign. Romans storm Syracuse

210-9 Carthage incursion to Agrigentum

AFRICA

204 Scipio invades and besieges Utica

203 Battle near Utica

203 Battle of Great Plains

203 Hannibal returns to Africa

202 Battle of Zama. Final defeat of Hannibal by Scipio

200-191, 186, 181 Insubre, Boii uprisings in Cisalpine Gaul (sporadic)

China

Qin or Ch'in Dynasty

c.221 'The First Emperor' Qin Shi Huang-Ti unites 'civilised' China, improves the Great Wall and institutes great centralising reforms (uniform coinage, writing, canals, roads, etc). [His vast tomb and its

defending garrisons of terra-cotta warriors are only now being excavated]

206 Massive rebellions rock China after death of First Emperor

c.206 or 202 Liy-Bang again re-unites China and founds the Han Dynasty, which colonises southern and south-western China, Korea, Vietnam and Central Asia, opening the Silk Road to the West and sea routes to Burma and India

Wars of expansion of Han rulers, 206-113: campaigns eliminate Yuen Kingdoms of the south-east coast

Mid-2nd century offensive against the Hsiung-Nu

Mid-2nd century northern Vietnam occupied

117-115 Chiang tribes conquered

117-100 Western expansion

108 Invasions of China and Indochina

2nd half of 1st century sees beginning of Han decline

c.33 Peasant Revolts

Rome's Macedonian Wars

215-205 1ST MACEDONIAN-ROMAN WAR

214 Philip V seizes Oricum

213 Philip invades Illyria

212-11 Operations in central Greece

207 Battle of Mantinea (Sparta defeated by Achaean Leauge)

205 Peace

202 Philip campaigns in the Bosporus

201 Battle of Lade

200-106 2ND MACEDONIAN-ROMAN WAR

Rome invades Epirus

199 Battle of Ottalobus

197 Battle of Cynoscephalae ('Jena of Macedon')

195 Flamininus campaigns in Greece

216-196 Wars of Antiochus the Great (Seleucid King of Syria)

216-213 Antiochus' Sardis campaign

210 Antiochus regains Armenia

202 Antiochus invades Syria

200 Battle of Panion and siege of Sidon (-199)

199 Antiochus secures all Palestine

197 Antiochus conquers south-west coast of Asia Minor and Thrace

192-188 ROME'S WAR WITH ANTIOCHUS THE GREAT

192 Antiochus invades Greece

191 Battle of Thermopylae loses Greece for Antiochus.

191 Battle of Cape Corycus

190 Rome invades Asia Minor across Hellespont

140 Battle of Side

190 Battle of Myonnesus

189 Battle of Magnesia. L. Scipio defeats Antiochus. End of strong Seleucid kingdom

Rome in Spain

195-133 1st Celtiberian War. First phase to 179

153-151 Renewed war

134-133 Numantine War. Final siege and fall of Numantia

154-137 Lusitanian War

Cisalpine Gaul

197-6 Roman campaigns v. Insubre, Boii, etc

193 Roman campaigns v. Insubre, Boii, etc

183-177 Roman campaigns in Istria

181-177 Sardinian revolt and pacification

169 Egyptians invade Palestine v. Antioch IV (Seleucid). Antiochus' counter-invades Egypt

167 Antiochus temporarily controls Egypt and Cyprus

171-168 3rd Macedonian War

171 Battle of Callicinus

168 Battle of Pydna

186 Bithynia-Pergamum War

167-160 Revolt of the Maccabees (Palestine)

165 Battle of Emmaus

164 Battle of Beth-Sur

162 Battle of Beth-Zachariah

160 Battle of Adsa

160 Battle of Elasa

151 Carthage-Numidian War

149-146 3rd Punic War. Carthage city razed to the ground by Rome

154 Roman campaign v. Ligurians

152-145 Egyptian-Seleucid War in Palestine/Syria

145 Battle of Oenoparas

149-148 4th Macedonian War (pretender)

146 End of Achaean League

146 Battle of Scarpheia. Rome takes control of all Greece

133 King Attalus bequeaths Pergamum to Rome

132-130 Pergamine revolt quelled by Rome

BC

135-132 1st Servile War against Rome
129-118 Egyptian Civil War
129-76 Rome conquers Dalmatia
125-120 Rome conquest of southern Gaul (to Cevennes)

117-105 Jugurthine War
111 Roman intervention
110 Battle of Calama
109 Battle of 'Muthul'

113-101 Invasion of Gaul and Italy by Cimbri and Teutones
113 Battle of Noreia
109 Battle in Rhône valley
105 Battle of Arausio
102 Battle of Aquae Sextiae
101 Battle of Vercellae

2nd Servile War 104-101
103-76 Wars of Alexander Jannaeus

103 Judaean War -96-90
102 Roman campaign v. Cilician pirates

Spain
99, 98-93 Lusitanian revolts

91-98 The Social War against Rome (War of Rome's allied tribes)
90 Battle of Tolenos R
89 Battle of Fucine Lake
89 Battle of Asculu
89 Battle near Pompeii
89-88 Egyptian Civil War
88 Turmoil in Rome. Sulla marches on Rome
87 Counter-coup of Marius and Cinna in Rome

83-82 Sullan War
83 Sulla's return from the East. Battle of Mt Tifata. Sulla victorious
82 Battle of Sacriportus, Faventia, Clusium, Colline Gate. Sulla victorious over Marians

82-80 Pompey campaigns against rebels in Africa/Sicily
81-79 Sulla Dictator

88-85 1st Mithridatic War (Pontus v. Rome)
88 Mithridates invades Cappadocia
Battle of Amnias River
Athens rises against Rome
87 Sulla in command of operations in the East
87-85 Sulla campaigns in Greece
86 Battle of Mileopolis. Fimbria defeats Pontic army
86 Athens retaken by Sulla
86 Battle of Chaeronea. Sulla defeats Pontic army

86 Battle of Cyzicus. Lucullus victorious
85 Battle of Orchomenus. Sulla defeats Pontic army
85 Battle of Rhyndacus
85 Battle of Lectum, Battle of Tenedos
85 Sulla crosses to Asia Minor
83 Parthian conquest of Syria

83-72 Sertorian War (Spain) (Metellus)
77 Pompey joins Metellus in Spain
76 Battle of Lauro, Battle of Italica
75 Battle of Turia, Battle of Sucro, Battle of Turia
72/3 Sertorius assassinated

83-82 2nd Mithridatic War (Mithridates repulses Murena)

77 Revolt of Lepidus
Battle of Cosa (then Pompey transfers to Spain)
78-76 Roman campaign v. Cilician pirates
74 Marcus Antonius' campaign v. pirates (fails)

72-71 3rd Servile War (Revolt of Spartacus)
72 Battle of Mt Garganus
72 Battle in Picenum, Battle of Mutina
71 Crassus and Pompey march on Rome

74-62 3rd Mithridatic War
74 River battle of Rhyndacus. Mithridates invades Bithynia
73 Battle of Lemnos
69 Battle of Tigranocerta. Lucullus defeats Pontic army
68 Battle of Arsanias River
67 Battle of Zela. Mithridates defeats Romans
66 Pompey assumes command against Mithridates
64-62 Pompey campaigns in upper Mesopotamia and Syria and settles Roman affairs in the East

67 Pompey's campaign v. piracy in the Mediterranean
65 R intervenes in Judaea. Battle of Papyron
63-2 REVOLT OF CATILINA
62 Battle of Pistoria
60 1st Triumvirate rules Rome (Pompey, Crassus, Caesar)

58-50 Caesar's Conquest of Gaul
58 Campaigns against Helvetii and Suebi

58 Battle of Toulon-sur-Arroux
58 Battle near Cernay
57 Campaign against Belgae
57 Battle of Neuf-Mesnil
56 Campaign against maritime tribes of the west
56 Battle of Quiberon Bay
55 Campaigns on northern border of Gaul
55 1st invasion of Britain
54 2nd invasion of Britain
54 Rebellion of Ambiorix
53 Revolt of Ambiorix. Battle of Advatuca. Ambiorix defeats Sabinus. Campaigns against the Nervii, etc.
52 Rebellion of Vercingetorix
52 Battle of Gergovia
52 Battle of Lutetia
52 Siege and battle of Alesia
51 Siege of Uxellodunum

55 Gabinius intervenes in Egyptian succession crisis
55 Parthian succession crisis

54-53 Parthian campaign of Crassus
53 Battle of Carrhae. Romans defeated, Crassus killed

Roman Civil War
49 Bloodless conquest of Italy by Caesar
49 1ST SPANISH CAMPAIGN
49 Manoeuvres of Ilerda
49 Siege of Massilia
49 Curio defeated in Africa at Battle of the Bagradas
49 Mutiny of Caesar's army at Placentia
48 DYRRHACHIUM CAMPAIGN
48 Siege of Dyrrhachium
48 Campaign and battle of Pharsalia. Caesar defeats Pompey
48-47 CAESAR'S EGYPTIAN (ALEXANDRIAN) CAMPAIGN. Battle of Nile Delta. Battle of Canopus. Caesar sets Cleopatra on the throne of Egypt
47 Battle of Nicopolis. Pharnaces, son of Mithridates the Great, defeats Caesar's lieutenant Domitius
47 Caesar's Asian campaign. Battle of Zela. Caesar routs Pharnaces
47 Mutiny of troops in Rome
47-46 CAESAR'S AFRICAN CAMPAIGN
46 Battles of Ruspina and Thapsus. Caesar defeats Pompey's associates
46-45 CAESAR'S 2ND SPANISH CAMPAIGN
45 Battle of Munda

44 Assassination of Julius Caesar

Wars of the 2nd Triumvirate
43 Mutina war. Battle of Mutina
43 2nd Triumvirate rules Rome (Antony, Octavian, Lepidus)
42 Philippi Campaign
42 Battles of Philippi. Antony and Octavian defeat Brutus, Cassius and the other associates of Caesar
40 Parthia conquest of Syria, southern Asia Minor
41-40 War of Perusia. Siege of Perusia
43-35 SEXTUS POMPEY'S WAR
36 Battle of Mylae
36 Battle of Naulochus
39-33 ANTONY'S PARTHIAN WAR
38 Battle of Gindarus
36 Antony's Parthian invasion fails
34 Antony's Armenian campaign
35-33 Octavian's Illyrian Campaign
32-31 WAR BETWEEN ANTONY (WITH CLEOPATRA) AND OCTAVIAN
31 Battle of Actium. Antony and Egyptians defeated. Antony and Cleopatra commit suicide
25-24 Gallus's Arabian Expedition
26-24 Augustus' conquest of north-west Iberia
26 Battle of Vellica

30-28 Roman frontier operations in the Balkans
25-24 Gallus's Arabian expedition
17-14 Roman operations in Rhine-Danube area
14 Agrippa intervenes in Bosporan kingdom
12 German campaigns begin
12-9 Campaigns of Drusus
8 Tiberius takes command in Germany

BC
―――――――――
AD

China
AD 9-23 Wang Mang usurps throne; 23 restoration of the Han
Meanwhile the external menace of the Hsiung-nu begins to become major threat
Late 1st century Emperor Wu-ti launches a drive against the Hsiung-nu west into central Asia
25 Eastern Han
Court factionalism

weakens central authority by c.160; regional commanders become autonomous
184 Mass uprising - the 'Yellow Turbans'
220 Hsien-ti, the last Han emperor, abdicates and China splits into three kingdoms: Wei (North), which becomes Western Ch'in; Shu (West); Wu (South)
263 Wei conquer Shu
265 Ssuma coup in Wei

Middle East
4 Armenian succession crisis
5-6 Gaetrilian Revolt in Mauretania

Europe: Wars of Imperial Rome
6-9 Pannonian revolt put down by Tiberius
7 Battle of Volcaean Marsh. Tiberius, ambushed, defeats the rebels
9 Revolt in the newly won area of Germany by Arminius.
9 Battle of the Teutoburger Wald (or Clades Variana). A great disaster for Rome: P. Quintillius Varus is defeated with the loss of some 20,000 men. Effectively, this means the end of Roman plans to expand to the Elbe. Subsequent campaigns are raids rather than attempts at conquest
14-16 Revolt of German legions. Germanicus quells then campaigns into Germany
16 Battle of Idistaviso. Germanicus worsts Arminius. He is then deployed to the East, but dies, possibly poisoned, at Antioch
17-24 Revolt of Numidian chief Tacfarinus
22 Battle of Thala
21 Gallic Revolt of Julius Florus and Julius Sacrovir
25 Thracian Revolt
28-41 Frisian Revolt
35-52 Armenian succession operations
40-49 Conquest of Britain begun. After an aborted invasion in 40, Aulus Plautius leads a full-scale expedition in 43. By 49 the Romans have reached the Severn and the Wash. After the defeat of Caractacus, operations remain low-key until 61
35-52 Armenian succession operations

AD

AD

61 Revolt of the Iceni in Britain. Boudicca of the Iceni takes Camulodunum and Lincoln before Suetonius Paulinus defeats her near Lichfield

66-68 Judaean revolt

70-73 Siege of Massada

68 Revolt of Julius Vindex (suppressed), precursor to the major revolt against Emperor Nero, who kills himself when the Praetorian Guard support the usurper Galba

69-70 ROMAN WAR OF SUCCESSION

69 Year of the Four Emperors. A succession of coups raise Otho, then Vitellius to the throne

69 Battle of Locus Castorum. Otho's ally Caecina fails to defeat the Vitellians

69 First Battle of Bedriacum (Cremona). Vitellius vanquishes Otho

69 Second Battle of Bedriacum. Vespasian's legions defeat Vitellius

71-74 Brigantine War in Britain results in the advance of the Roman frontier farther north

72 Upper Euphrates campaign stabilises frontier for half a century

73-74 'Basel re-entrant' annexed in Germany

78-84 Cn Julius Agricola campaigns in Scotland, but the Romans are now over-extended

84 Battle of Mons Graupius. Agricola defeats Picts

89 Revolt of Saturninus in Germany

97-98 Suebian War

WARS OF HADRIAN

101-102 First Dacian War. Trajan invades and wins at Tapae (101), but severe losses and difficult terrain slow the Roman advance

102 First Battle of Sarmizegethusa (Dacian capital) defeats Dacian King Decebalus

105-106 Second Dacian War. Trajan's major offensive conquers Dacia completely

106 Second Battle of Sarmizegethusa. The Roman province of Dacia is established

113-116 Trajan's conquest of Parthia and Armenia

115-117 Revolts in Cyrenaica, Egypt and Palestine

116-117 Mesopotamian revolt

122/3-c.128 Hadrian's Wall built in Britain; it will become Rome's northern frontier

132-135 Bar Kochba revolt in Palestine

134 Recapture of Jerusalem

139-142 Brigantine Revolt in Britain and operations

155, 158. Lollius Urbicus builds the Antonine Wall between the Clyde and the Forth

145-152 Mauretanian disturbances

152-153 Egyptian rising

161 Parthian War

157-158 Dacian operations

167, 172-5 and after Danube security operations. Pressure from Germanic tribes including Chatti, Marcomanni, Quadi, Iazyges, Roxolani, etc., provoke Roman trans-Danube punitive raids. The scale of imperial commitment to the northern frontiers increases dramatically. After two centuries of relative stability and peace, the Roman Empire is approaching a period of crisis within and without

175-176 Revolt of Aridius Cassius in Syria

184 Antonine Wall overrun

184-186 Mutiny of legions in Britain

190 African revolt

192-197 Emperor Commodus assassinated. Rivals for the throne are eliminated by L. Septimius Severus

193 Battle of Cyzicus

194-195 197-199 Septimius Severus's Parthian campaigns

194 Battle of Issus

195-197 Revolt of Albinus

197 Battle of Lugdunum (Lyons); city destroyed, as Albinus is defeated by Severans

209 Major expedition to Moray Firth in Scotland led by Septimius Severus. Hadrian's Wall renovated to become new frontier in Britain

213-214 Alemanni campaign of Caracalla. Defensive *limes* completed in Rhine-Danube re-entrant

214 Theocritus's Armenian campaign

215 Caracalla's Alexandrian Massacres

216-217 Caracalla's Eastern Campaign

216 Battle of Nisibis

218 Battle of Antioch

Middle East

227 Ardashir Artaxerxes establishes Sassanid Empire

India

Yueh-chi Chief Kujula Kadphises conquers northern India

After 100, Zenith of Kusnana under Kanishka

2nd century, Satarahanas (Deccan)

Early 3rd century Pandya King Nedunjeliyan wins major victory over Ceras

By about 250 Kushans reduced to Gandhara and Kashmir and become vassals of Sassanid Persia

China

280 China reunified by Western Ch'in

'Wars of the Eight Princes' - internal dynastic conflicts wreck the authority of the central administration

'The Sixteen Kingdoms' or 'The Five Barbarians' disruption of China'. Some five barbarian groups conquer China

Near-permanent warfare exists between the states of northern China and many refugees flee south from the northern barbarian invaders

383 Chien Ch'in invades south but is repulsed

South China Dynasties Eastern Ch'in; Song; Qi; Liang; Chen

End of the 6th century Yang Chien conquers the south and reunites China, founding the Sui dynasty

Crisis of the Roman Empire

After the assassination of Caracalla (217), a succession of emperors are raised to the throne by their legions, only to be assassinated, overthrown by a rival or even by their own troops. Records of this period are poor but point to almost constant warfare within the empire and with the tribes north of the Rhine and Danube, together with continuing conflict in the East. Many battles are fought during this period, but they are rarely named, and details are few. Alemanni and Goths are the principal enemies in Europe. The strain on manpower and the economic resources of the empire is immense. And plague hits Rome in 262.

231-233 Severus Alexander's Eastern campaign

234-235 Alemanni War

236-237 Sarmatian/Dacian campaigns

238 War with Sassanias

240 Carthage rebellion

244 Balkan trans-Danube tribal invasions

251 Battle of Abritus. Emperor Decius perishes fighting the Goths

251 Battle of Forum Trebroni

253-260 Rome-Persian War

259 Battle of Edessa

260 Emperor Valentinian made prisoner by Persians

256 Saxons raid British coasts

258/9 Alemanni break into northern Italy where they are repulsed by Gallienus

269 Battle of Naissus. Claudius defeats the Goths

260-274/5 'Postumus's Gallic Empire'. C. Latinius Postumus proclaims himself emperor at Cologne. Gaul is recovered in 275 after Battle of Campi Catalaunii by Emperor Aurelian ('Restitutor Orbis', reuniting the Empire); but he is assassinated in 275. During his reign, construction begins on the walls of Rome, which has not been necessary since Republican times

262-267 Odaenathus of Palmyra's campaigns v. Persia

273 Palmyra destroyed

282-283 Carus invades Mesopotamia

Persians occupy much of the East during Roman strife

285 Battle of Margus (against rival Carinus) establishes Diocletian as emperor who will 're-found' the empire

286-293 Carausius declares independence in Britain and northern Gaul but is assassinated by Allectus

293 THE TETRARCHY - The Collegiate Emperors. Diocletian splits the running of the empire between two emperors with deputies/designated successors. The aim is continuity and increased efficiency in fighting off the incursions of barbarians from across the Rhine and Danube. The frontier is too long for one man to command it. And the capital, Rome, is no longer a strategic base for such operations

295-298 Crisis - Narses of Persia at war; Achillus in Egypt; Julianus and

Quinquegentanei in Africa; Carausius in Britain; plus warfare on Rhine and Danube fronts

296 Battle of Clausentum. Tetrarch Constantius recovers Britain for Rome

297 Battle of Carrhae - Persians defeat Galerius

297/8 Battle of Langres - great victory over Alemanni

306-323/4 Wars of the Tetrarchs

312 Constantine takes Italy from Maxentius

312 Battles of Turin, Verona, Saxa Rubra. Constantine defeats the troops of Maxentius

312 Battle of Milvian Bridge. Maxentius is killed. Constantine is converted to Christianity during the campaign and in future wears the sign of the labarum on his army's shields

313 Licinius defeats Maximin Daia

313 Constantine campaigns on Rhine

314 First War between Constantine and Licinius

315 Battle of Cibalis. Constantine defeats Licinius

315 Battle of Mardis is indecisive

323/324 War between Constantine and Licinius

323 Battle of Philippopolis-Adrianople. Constantine outmanoeuvres Licinius

323 Battle of Chrysopolis. Licinius is defeated, surrenders and is later executed

328 Constantine consecrates his new capital Constantinople (formerly Byzantium); the city has been under reconstruction as the imperial capital for four years. Strategically it will be better placed than Rome to meet the threats to the empire from the north and from the east. Gradually the Roman Empire will become more permanently divided into West and East, but while the West will succumb in a century and a half to the barbarians from across the Rhine and Danube, Constantinople, as capital of the 'Byzantine' Empire, will remain the bastion of the empire, now officially a Christian state, for more than 1100 years. Traditionally historians have seen this

AD

development as ushering in the Middle Ages

332 Constantine's son, Constantine, fights Goths on the Danube and inflicts a significant defeat on them

340 Constantine II invades Italy after disputes with his brothers

340 Battle of Aquileia. Constantine II defeated and killed by Constans

341, 342 Constans defeats Gauls

350-353 War against Magnetius. **351** Battle of Mursa. Constantius defeats barbarian usurper Magnetius, the first major triumph of cataphract armoured cavalry over infantry legions

354 Gallic crisis. Major incursions of barbarian tribes; from **364** constant operations on the Rhine-Danube frontier

356-361 Rhine-Danube operations

356-359 Julian (the Apostate)'s Rhineland campaigns

361 Julian's War with Constantius

358-361 Persian War

363 Julian's campaign in East. Jovian signs '30 Year Peace'

368/9-370 371-377 Valens' Armenian operations in Crisis East

370s Huns attack the Ostrogothic kingdom. Increasingly, the advance of the Huns from the steppe into eastern Europe is putting pressure on the tribes to their south and west; in turn, these tribes increase their attempts to cross the perimeter of the Roman Empire, seeking land in which to settle. And the frontier regions of the empire are becoming depopulated as a result of constant raids and depradations

376-382 GOTHIC WAR

378 Battle of Adrianople. One of the great decisive battles of history. The Huns defeat the Romans and the Emperor of the East, Valens, is killed. The Huns achieve their breakthrough into the empire. It is the beginning of the end of empire in the west. Fritigern leads the Goths into Thrace and Greece. That this disaster on the battlefield is not immediately fatal to the

empire is due to Theodosius the Great (379-395), who restores order in the empire. But the writing is on the wall

383-388 Revolt of Maximus

392-394 Revolt of Eugenius.

394 Battle of the Frigidus, near Aquileia. Theodosius defeats Eugenius, who is killed

395 Huns invade Cappadeonia, Armenia, Thrace and Syria

395 The division between Eastern and Western Empires becomes permanent. After the death of Theodosius, the decline of the empire becomes steeper. His heirs are not up to the task of maintaining the empire and increasingly delegate the running of affairs to their chief ministers while isolating themselves from the realities of the world in Ravenna. In the West, a succession of Masters of Horse (commanders-in-chief of the armies) are left to decide policy.

395-398 Alaric the Goth's campaign in Greece. Stilicho, Western Emperor Honorius's Master of Horse, cannot prevent the Goths, under Alaric, going where they please: Greece, Illyricum and then into Italy.

399 Revolt of Tribigild

400 Revolt of Gildo

400 Goth uprising

401-403 Alaric the Goth's first invasion of Italy

402 Battle of Pollentia. Stilicho defeats the Goths, but not decisively

405 Barbarian crossing of the Alps repulsed

406-7 Great barbarian breakthrough into Gaul. At the end of December **406** barbarian hordes cross the frozen Rhine at Mainz. There is no Imperial army to halt them. This is the second great break-in. From here, the tribes pour into Gaul

407 Revolt of Constantinus in Britain. He invades Gaul, which is meanwhile being devastated by Vandal tribes progressing south

407-10 Alaric's second invasion of Italy.

410 sack of Rome

408 Huns are active on the lower Danube

409-11 Revolt of Maximus

412-418 The Visigoths leave Italy and enter Gaul and the Iberian peninsula

413 Revolt of Heraclian The Goths establish themselves in southern Gaul with sporadic footholds in northern Spain. There is almost constant warfare with other barbarian tribes and the Romans

422 Huns raid Thrace

424-425 On the death of the Western Emperor Honorius in 423, Theodosius II of the Eastern Empire sends an army to place Valentinian III (aged 4) on the Western throne. Aetius (390-454) is meanwhile Master of Horse, making use of barbarian mercenaries (including Huns) to maintain some sort of Imperial authority in the West

430s Led by Clodion, the Franks advance to the Somme

434/5 The Huns, raiding into Thrace, demand payment with menace from Constantinople

435-7 Aetius repulses Burgundian invasion of Upper Belgica

441-443, 447-448 Attila leads the great confederation of Huns against Constantinople, laying waste the land and taking away vast booty. In the field they are all but invincible, but they lack the ability to assault or lay siege to major cities

451 The Huns invade Gaul. Battle of Catalaunian Plains, or Châlons. Aetius, with a mixed Roman army that includes a significant Visigoth element under their king, Theodoric defeats or holds the Huns, who retreat.

452 Attila invades Italy. With help, the Huns reduce and destroy the great city of Aquileia, but venture little farther south, ostensibly due to the intervention of the Pope, Leo, more plausibly because fodder for the Hun horses is in short supply and plague has broken out in Italy. This is the last great incursion by the Huns

453 Attila dies; his empire does not long survive him

429 Vandals enter Africa Vandals raid Mediterranean coasts

439 Persian invasion of Armenia

440-1 Great expedition v. Vandals fails

455 Vandal expedition sacks Rome

456 Vandal invasion of Sicily repulsed by Ricimer

468 Great expedition against the Vandals fails

454 Visigoths attack the Bagaudae in north-west Gaul on behalf of Rome

455 Battle of Nedao (location unknown). Breakup of the Hun empire

455-456 Usurpation of Avitus

456 Visigoths enter the Iberian peninsula in force

456 Battle of River Urbicus shatters the power of the Suebi tribes who have settled there

458-461 Emperor Majorian leads an expedition to Spain

By **464** The Visigoths (capital Toulouse) have advanced their domain north to Loire

466-484 Reign of Euric, founder of the Visigothic Kingdom in Spain (which will last

456-465 revolt of Aegidius in Gaul, which is a battleground between Franks moving south, Burgundians in the east, Visigoths in the south and Bretons in the north-west

Britain, meanwhile, cut off from Rome by these barbarian powers, is now deemed lost to the empire

468 and **472-3** The Visigoths conquer much of Spain

472-476 Anarchy in Italy, following the death of Ricimer (Master of Horse), who has made and unmade a series of unworthy emperors

475 Odovacar (Odoacer) leads an army revolt.

476 End of Western Empire with enforced abdication of the young Emperor Romulus Augustulus.

476-493 Odovacar rules Italy, nominally for the empire

475-477 Eastern Emperor Zeno deposed and returns to power

476 Euric's Italian expedition repulsed

481-511 Wars of Clovis expand the kingdom of the Franks

486 Battle of Soissons. Clovis defeats Syagrius

491 Frank campaign against the Thuringians

500 Campaign against the Burgundians

507 Battle of Vouillé. Clovis defeats Alaric and

conquers all southern Gaul except Provence

523 Campaign against the Burgundians

542 Expeditions to Saragossa

Ongoing campaigns for Septimania (Provence) between Franks, Burgundians and Ostrogoths

488 Ostrogoths. Led by Theodoric the Great, invade Italy 'on behalf of' the Eastern Empire to reclaim it from Odovacar. After much campaigning, the two leaders meet and Theodoric treacherously slays Odovacar. Theodoric (493-526) will be a major player in international diplomacy and rule nominally within the ambit of the Byzantine Empire

527-565 Justinian rules the Byzantine Empire and sets out to recover the West. His generals - especially Belisarius - are initially successful, but the enterprise places great strain on the empire's resources and cannot be sustained in the longer term

535-555 Byzantine conquest of Italy, bringing an end to the Ostrogothic Kingdom, but beginning a long period of turmoil and conflict in the peninsula

537 Battle of Rome

541 Battle of Faenza

546 Battle of Rome

549 Battle of Rome

552 Battle of Tagina

553 Battle of Mons Lactarius

554 Battle of Casilinum

520s-560s Sporadic conflicts between Slavs, Bulgars and Huns and Byzantium

533 Battle of Ad Decimum. Bellisarius destroys Vandal Kingdom in North Africa

India

Mid 4th century Samudragupta and son Chandragupta II campaign and found Gupta Empire

End of 5th century Hun incursions into northern India; after 500 the White Huns establish power in northenr India until they are gradually expelled durng the 6th century

510 Battle of Airikina. Hun victory

511 Huns sack Prayaya

3 major dynasties emerge. Pushyabhutis of Kanauj,

Chalukyas of Badami and Pallavas of Kanci

600-630 Establishment of Pallava power by Mahendravarman I

608-42 Establishment of Chalukya power by Pulakeshin II

620 Pulakeshin II defeats Harsha

After 647 breakup of Kanavj Empire into small Rajput states

China

Assassination of Emperor Uang-ti leads to establishment of T'ang dynasty and ten years of Civil War

626-640 Chinese expansion into Central Asia and (temporarily) Korea

660 destruction of Paekche state in Korea

Autonomous military districts established to protect China's frontiers

By 660s Chinese armies have penetrated India, the Tarim Basin, etc.

668 destruction of Korean state of Koguryo and occupation of northern Korea until 676 withdrawal leaving Silla state in control

751 Battle of Talas River. Muslims defeat Chinese

755 Mutiny of An Lu-shan leads to weakening of the T'ang state and eventual descent into turmoil with large-scale peasant uprisings

763-783 Tibet takes Tarim Basin after withdrawal of Chinese garrisons

c.790 Tufan Kingdom conquers China's Western provinces

By about 900, final collapse of central authority. China splits into ten states with five short-lived dynasties

'Five Dynasties and Ten Kingdoms' Period

Coup d'etat ends the last (later Chou) dynasty

960 Northern Sung Dynasty

963-979 Sung re-unite much of China

979-1004 China-Liao border War

982-1126 China and Hsi-Hsia border wars

c.1125-1127 Northern tribes conquer northern China and establish Ch'in Empire

By 1127 Sung control reduced to southern half of China: Southern Sung Empire

c.600 Unification and expansion of Tibet

Britain

Mid-6th century Angles, Saxons and Jutes invade Britain. Semi-legendary leaders Hengist and Horsa fight for the British king Vortigern against the Picts between 446 and 454; Hengis then establishes Jutish kingdom in Kent

491 Sack of Pevensey by Aelle (first bretwalda, or hegemon)

Resistance to invaders led by 'Aureius Ambrosius'

c.500 Battle of Mount Badon (Mons Badiconus) victory over the invaders by legendary Arthur

552 Battle of Old Sarum. Cynric of the Gewissae defeats Britons

577 Battle of Deorham. Ceawlin of the Gewissae defeats three British kings and extends nascent Wessex to the Severn

Kingdoms of Deira and Bernicia form Northumbria, which gains supremacy. Edwin of Northumbria is 5th bretwalda and adopts Christianity

633 Battle of Heathfield. Penda of Mercia and Cadwallon of Gwynedd defeat and kill Edwin

634 Battle of Heavenfield. Bretwalda Oswald of Northumbria defeats Cadwallon

642 Battle of Oswestry/Maserfield. Oswald defeated by Penda

655 Battle of Winwaedsfield. Christian Oswy of Northumbria defeats and kills heathen Penda and becomes bretwalda.

661 Mercia defeats West Saxons

675-704 Aethelred of Mercia defeats Northumbria decisively near the Trent. Northumbria declines

Mercia reaches zenith under Aethenbald (716-57) and Offa (757-96), latter styling himself King of all England. He builds defensive 'Offa's Dyke' from Dee to Wye, probably to prevent cattle raids. Mercia declines after Offa. Rise of Wessex

Byzantine Empire

602 Byzantine mutiny and anarchy - Civil War. Ongoing campaigns against Avar incursions

603 Revolt of Narsus. Persians involved in

Edessa-Dara operations

605-628 Byzantine-Sassanid War

608-610 Revolt of Heraclius; becomes emperor 610-641

613 Battle of Antioch

626 Constantinople besieged by Avars, Bulgars, Slavs, Gepids and Persians

627/8 Battle of Ctesiphon

Wars of the Franks

c.575 Inter-family strife among the Merovingians - a procession of minors (rois trainéants). These internecine conflicts in the Frankish kingdoms lead to the rise of the Mayors who come to hold effective power

c.670 Ebroin, Mayor of Neustria conquers Burgundians

687 Battle of Tertry. Pepin II, Mayor of Austrasia, defeats Berthar, Mayor of Neustria. He is assassinated in 681. Effective fall of Merovingians and beginning of the Carolingian rulers of the Franks. Pepin becomes undisputed master of all Gaul except Aquitaine. The Merovingians remain puppets

719-41 Charles Martel. He defeats Austrasians in two battles:

716 Battle of Amblève.

719 Battle of Vinay.

719 Battle of Soissons. He masters Burgundy

720-39 Arab invasion of France

720 Arabs seize Septimania

732 Tours or Poitiers (location unknown). Abd ar-Rahman defeated and killed by Charles

737 Charles takes Avignon from the Muslims

738 Charles's Saxon expedition

739 Charles repulses Muslim attack on Provence

Charles also campaigns against Aquitaine and Alemans

Wars of the Lombards

663 Byzantine expedition of Emperor Constans to Italy fails to expel the Lombards

678-81 Treaty and peace between Lombards and Byzantium

700-12 Lombard succession conflicts

712-44 Liutprand King of the Lombards consolidated Lombard power in Italy

751 Lombards take Ravenna, Byzantine capital in Italy

Middle East

630s-650s MUSLIM WARS OF CONQUEST

Muslim armies erupt from Arabia

636 Battle of Yarmouk

637 Battle of Qadisiya

640 Conquest of Egypt and Syria

642 Battle of Nahavend

650 Muslims take Persepolis

651 Battle of Merv: Muslim conquest of Persia; end of Sassanid Empire

Muslim Civil War

657 Battle of Camel

Battle of Basra

Battle of Siffiu

Muslim sea-borne campaigns against Byzantium

661-750 Umayyad Caliphate

674-8 Constantinople besieged by Muslims

690s-700s Muslim conquests

698 take Carthage

702 Muslims conquer Berbers

718-18 Constantinople besieged by Muslims

747-50 Muslim Civil War

750 Battle of the Zab. Abbasid Caliphate replaces Umayyads

755-72 Berber revolt in North Africa

763 construction of Baghdad

Byzantines recover Thrace from Slavs

776 to 843 Byzantium internal conflict over iconoclasm

798 Muslims take Ibiza

811-819 Abbasid Civil War

825 or 823 Crete captured

827-832 Muslim Aghlabids begin conquest of Sicily (achieved by 902)

830-8 Abbasid-Byzantine War

India

704-715 Muslims take Transoxania, Khwarzim and Tashkent

712-713 Muslim invasion of Sind

Arab conquest of Indus area to 745

740 Chalkyas defeat Pallavas

750 Gopal founds Pala dynasty. From 750s to c.950 Rashtrakutas constitute the main power in India

757 or 752-6 Rebellion of Rashtrakutas/defeat Chalukyas

c.840 Rise of Pratinaras (King Bhoja)

c.840 Collapse of central authority in Tibet

Wars of the Visigoths in Spain

610-12 King Witteric fights Vascons and Byzantines

629 last Byzantine possessions (Algarve) taken. Visigoths now rule almost all Iberian peninsula

631 Franks invade as far as Saragossa

653 rebellion of nobles quashed by King Receswinth (649-672)

672-80 King Wamba constantly at war against Vascons, rebels in Septimania and invasions from the Muslims

680 Wamba deposed. Erwig succeeds (to 678)

708 Muslim invasion of Iberian coast repulsed by King Witiza

709 Revolutions lead to reign of last Visigoth king: Roderick (Ruderico)

709, 710 Muslim invasions

711 Tarik of Mauretania leads Muslim invasion of Iberian peninsula; takes Gibraltar, Algeciras

19 July 711 Battle of La Jauda. Muslims defeat Roderick and take Seville, Ecija, Cordoba, Toledo. Musa brings Muslim reinforcements

Sept 713 Battle of Segoyuela. Final defeat of King Roderick. End of the Visigothic Kingdom. At Toledo, Musa proclaims the Caliph sovereign.

Balkans

Khazaks expand to Crimea, Ukraine and Caucasus

679-80 Bulgars conquer areas of Danube

Franks

751-68 Pepin ('the Short') King of the Franks

By early 750s Saracens driven out of France

753 Saxon campaigns

754 Pepin invades Italy to aid the Pope against the Lombards, the Byzantines failing him and he having to take refuge with the Franks. Pope annoints Pepin King of the Franks and 'Patrician of the Romans'

At Pavia, Aistulf of the Lombards surrenders but subsequently reneges on agreements. By 755/6 he is at the gates of Rome again

756 Pepin invades Italy again; same result

759 Saxon campaign

759 Franks take Narbonne

760-8 Conquest of Acquitaine, not fully absorbed into Frankia

768-814 Charlemagne

771 Charlemagne unites the Frankish realms. Begins wars of conquest in Italy, Pyrenees, Bavaria against the Avars, and into north/north-east Germany against Saxons, Slavs and Danes

Charlemagne's Italian campaigns

773-4 Charles invades Italy and besieges Pavia. 774 King Desiderius is made prisoner; thus Charlemagne destroys Lombard Kingdom. Subsequent operations in Italy and Istria (790)

805 Venetia and Dalmatia conquered

Charlemagne's Spanish campaigns

778 Franks cross into Spain and take Pamplona. A raid rather than conquest.

778 Roncesvalles reverse as the armies retire

785 Gerona voluntarily joins Frankish rule

793 Hisham I, Emir of Cordoba, invades, taking Gerona and penetrating to Narbonne and Carcassonne

Frank reponse leads to establishment of Spanish march by 795

799 Balearic Islands place themselves under Frankish rule

801 Franks take Barcelona

806 Franks take Pamplona and Novara

811 Franks take Tortosa

Charlemagne's Eastern campaigns

787-96 Franks conquer Bavaria and the Avars - destruction of Avar state 803 (main Avar ring taken 795). Practically annual campaigns. Depopulation results from the continual campaigning

772-85 Saxon campaigns. Annual campaigns, bitter and hard

779 Süntel Hill smashes Saxon rising (4500 Saxons beheaded in a day as punishment)

Subsequent risings, deportations, etc. over some thirty years

808-10 Confrontation with Danes

782 Sorbs attack Thuringia; 806 conquered

by Charlemagne's son Charles

800 Christmas Day, Charlemagne crowned 'Emperor of the Romans' in Rome

843 Empire divided. Temporarily reunited 885

887/8 Final disintegration of Carolingian Empire to become kingdoms of France, Italy and Germany

Balkans / Byzantium

803 Krum unites Bulgars

811 Krum defeats Nicephorus at Edirne (Adrianopolis)

Ongoing Bulgar Wars

805 Venetia, Dalmatia and Corsica conquered

Nicephorus I reconquers Greece

893-927 Tsar Symeon: zenith of Bulgarian Empire

Japan

740 Battle of Itabitsu

764 Battle of Miohosaki

989 Conflict between Kyoto and Nara

1051-63 Early Nine Years War

1086-9 Later Three Years War

1146 Battle of Kyoto

1156 and 1160 Japanese succession wars

1180-5 Gempei Wars

1185 Battle of Dan No Ura

1331-3 Jojo regency overthrown

1333-92 Nanbokucho Wars between northern and southern courts

Scandinavia

808-810 Danish War

c.895 Battle of Hafsfjord. Harald Finehair unites southern Norway

Spain: Emirate of Cordoba

755/6 Umayyad dynasty of Spain founded

Aghlabid Campaigns

Saracen pirates raid central Mediterranean coastlines, especially from bases at Bari (841-71) and Taranto (840-80)

846 or 850 Sack of Rome

847 Seize Bari

The Christian states of northern Iberia combine, fragment and intermittently fight one another and the Muslims

Middle East

852 Byzantine naval expedition against Egypt

867 Saffarids of Herat independent

867-886 Basil I emperor of Byzantium

868 Egypt independent

under Tulunid emirs

874 Sarmarids of Bukhava independent

905 Abbasids recover Egypt from Tulunids

909 Rise of Fatimids of North Africa; they ravage the coasts of Italy, Corsica, Sardinia and Liguria

914 and 919 Fatimid expeditions against Egypt fail

960 Fatimids conquer Egypt

961 Byzantines recover Crete

965 Byzantines recover Cyprus

966-8 Byzantine invasion of Syria

969 Byzantines retake Antioch

974-5 Byzantine invasion of Syria

976-1025 Basil II. Under his reign Byzantium attains the summit of its medieval greatness

Meanwhile Abbasid Caliphate continues in little but name until 1258

983-1055 Buwayhid Civil War in Iraq/Iran

989-1025 Wars of Basil II

997 or 999-1030 Wars of Mahmud of Ghazni in Transoxonia, Iran and Iraq

998 Collapse of Samarids

1032 Byzantines take Edessa

1039 Zendecan Turkish invasion of Afghanistan

1050 Hilali and Sullaym tribes from Upper Egypt invade Cyrenaica and Turkey

SELJUK WARS OF CONQUEST

1050s-1060s Almoravids conquer Morocco

1055 Seljuks take Baghdad

1060s Seljuks conquer northern Syria and the Hejaz

1060-1073 civil strife in Fatimid Egypt

1069 take Fez

1071 Battle of Manzikert: Seljuks take most of Asia Minor from the Byzantines

1073-7 Baar al-Jamah establishes military regime in Egypt

Three Seljuk Sultanates now exist: Rum, Hamadan and Merv

1096 The People's Crusade is massacred by the Turks

Americas

c.980 First European landing in N America

c.993, 995 battles between Vikings and native Americans

India

900 Samarids overthrow Saffavids

907 Parantaka I establishes Chola power in southern India

c.950 to c.1200 establishment of the Chola Empire

972 Paramara King Siyaka II sacks Rashtrakuta capital, Manyakheta

985-1014 Rajaraja I extends Chola power.

Major campaigns of the Cholas:

999, 1017 to Sri Lanka

1000 naval expedition to Maldives

1022 to Ganges

1022 or 1023 Northern campaign of Rajendra Chola

1025 Chola naval expeditions to SE Asia

997 or 999-1030 Wars of Mahmud of Ghazni in India. Conquest of Punjab

1001 Battle of Peshwar. Second Muslim invasion of India

1024 or 1025 Battle of Somnanth. Shiva temple destroyed

1040 Dandanquan Seljuks defeat Ghaznavids

1040 Seljuks break away from Ghazni. Decline of Ghaznis

1018 Turkic armies sack Kanauj, ending Pratihara

Mediterranean

870 Muslims conquer Malta

871 Conslingian Louis II retakes Bari for Pope

By 886 Venice independent

Vikings

793 Vikings raid Lindisfarne. Norse raids on British Isles and coasts of France, Spain - even into the Mediterranean - follow

834-45 Norse raids on Rhine, northern France and northern Germany

856-62 Norse raids reach their peak

862 Vikings seize Kiev

865-7 Viking 'Great Army' raids England

870 Norse capture Strathclyde

882-92 Viking 'Great Army' raids France

882 Oleg unites Novgorod and Kiev

885-6 Vikings besiege Paris

911 Establishment of County of Normandy by Viking Rollo

Britain

825 Battle of Ellendune. Egbert of Wessex decisively defeats

Beornwulf, King of Mercia

838 Battle of Hingston Down. Egbert defeats large Viking invasion

851 Viking incursion into the Thames to London

865 'Great Army' of Vikings invades East Anglia

869 Battle of Hoxne. Vikings defeat East Anglians

871 Battle of Reading. Aethelred I defeated by Vikings

871-99 Alfred the Great, King of Wessex

871 Battle of Wilton. Alfred defeated by Viking Guthrum

871 Battle of Chippenham. Guthrum defeats Alfred

871 Battle of Edington/Ethandun. Alfred decisively defeats Guthrum. Peace of Chippenham and Guthrum's conversion to Christianity

910 Battle of Tettenhall. Edward the Elder of Wessex defeats the Danes of York

937 Battle of Brunanburgh. Athelstan of Wessex defeats a coalition of Vikings, Scots and Britons and can claim to be King of all Britain

944 Edmund I of Wessex annexes York

954 Battle of Stainmore. Viking Eric Bloodaxe defeated and killed by Eadred of Wessex. Subsequent weakening of Wessex by succession of royal minors

991 Battle of Maldon. Olaf Triggvason defeats Earl of Essex

994 Expedition of Olaf Triggvason and Sweyn Forkbeard. Olaf returns to take kingdom of Norway, Sweyn to reclaim kingdom of Denmark

1002 Aethelred II the Unready massacres all Vikings in royal service including hostage sister of Sweyn

1013 Sweyn (now King of Denmark) lands at Humber and marches south, effectively conquering the country. Dies 1014

1015 Canute (Sweyn's son) masters most of the realm

1016 Battle of Pen Selwood. Canute defeated by pretender Edmund Ironside

1016 Battle of Ashingdon. Decisive victory of Canute over Edmund

1016-35 Canute rules

England and Denmark Succession to English throne subsequently disputed
1066 Harold II elected king; challenged by Duke William of Normandy

Magyars
895-900 Magyars conquer Hungarian Plain
First half of 10th century Magyars raid west and central Europe, inflicting major defeats on the Franks 899-910
906 Moravia destroyed
907 Battle of Pressburg
926, 933 North Italy, Germany and Swabia raided
929 Battle of Unstrut defeats Magyars
954 and 955 Northern France and Italy raided
955 Battle of Lechfeld. Defeat of Magyars by Otto the Great
977-1038 Stephen becomes Christian King of Hungary

939 Saracens sack Rome
941 Rus attack Constantinople

Umayyad Caliphate
920 Battle of Val de Junqueras. Emir of Cordoba defeats Navarre and León
962 Sancho I of Leon launches Reconquista
981 Battle of Rueda
985 Andalusians sack Barcelona
Decline of Umayyads - by 1031 era of 'taifas' (fragmentation)
1008-28 Muslim Civil War

Germany
Henry I (the Fowler) of Germany (919-36) extends eastwards against the Slavs and fortifies areas against Magyar invasions
938-72 WARS OF OTTO THE GREAT
Imperial control imposed on Germany and northern Italy
951 Otto invades Italy
962 Otto crowned in Rome as Holy Roman (German) Emperor
983 Great Slav revolt against German rule
995 Germans conquer Pomerania
1002-37 German conquest of northern Italy

965-972 Wars of Prince Sriatoslav of Rus

Balkans
986-1018 Wars of Basil II

against the Bulgars; end of Bulgar State by 1018
Byzantines conquer Serbs

Poland
992-1025 Wars of Boleslav I 'The Mighty' King of Poland

1047-1107 Wars of the Normans
1047-71 Norman Conquest of southern Italy by Robert Guiscard and brother Roger
1052 Muslims ejected from Sardinia
1050s-1070s Norman-French ongoing conflict
1054 Battle of Mortemer. William of Normandy defeats Angevin-French coalition
1061-1091 Norman conquest of Sicily
1066-72 NORMAN CONQUEST OF ENGLAND
1066 Battle of Stamford Bridge. Harold II of England defeats Harold Hardrada, King of Denmark
1066 Battle of Hastings. William of Normandy defeats Harold II and takes the crown of England
1066-71 William consolidates his conquest of England
1069 Danes invade Yorkshire
1071 Bari, last Byzantine city in southern Italy, falls to Normans
1072 Palermo taken by Normans
1079/80 Norman England at war with Scotland
1081 Norman invasion of Byzantium with Papal blessing. Robert and Bohemund take Corfu
1082 Durazzo captured by Normans
1083 Battle of Larissa. Bohemund's advance on Constantinople repulsed
1106 Battle of Tinchebray. Henry I defeats brother Robert Curthose and regains Normandy
1107 Bohemund's second invasion of Byzantium defeated by Alexis I

France
987-96 Hugh Capet King of France (Capetian dynasty to 1328)
1180-1223 Philip II Augustus ends the Angevin conflict, conquering English possessions north of the Loire
1209-29 Albigensian Crusade against heretics in the south of France

1223-6 Louis VIII
1224 Louis takes Poitou and Saintonge from England
1226 He takes Avignon and Languedoc
1226-70 Louis IX (St Louis) the Crusader (1248-54, 1270)

Crusades
1095-9 FIRST CRUSADE.
1097 Battle of Nicea. Christian victory
1098 Crusaders take Antioch
1099 Crusaders take Jerusalem and repulse counter-attack from Egypt at Battle of Ascalon
1147-9 SECOND CRUSADE.
1148 Failed siege of Damascus
1189-92 THIRD CRUSADE
1191 Acre retaken by Crusaders
1191 Battle of Arsuf. Richard I of England defeats Saladin
1189-92 Third Crusade perverted by Venetians
1202-4 FOURTH CRUSADE
1204 Crusaders take and sack Constantinople. Foundation of Latin Empire (to 1261)
1281-21 FIFTH CRUSADE (TO EGYPT)
1219 Damietta taken
1228-9 SIXTH CRUSADE Frederick II of Germany succeeds by negotiation into becoming crowned King of Jerusalem
1248-54 SEVENTH CRUSADE (to Egypt)
1250 Battle of Mansura indecisive
1250 Battle of Fariskur. Crusaders defeated and St Louis captured
1270 EIGHTH CRUSADE (to Tunis). St Louis dies in epidemic

Middle East
1129 Campaigns of Zangi and Nur al-Din
1144 takes Edessa
1154 takes Damascus
1141 Seljuks of Merv defeated by Qarakhitai Mongols
1140s Almohads replace Almoravids in Morocco
1152-60 Almohads take Maghreband Tripolitania
1146-1148 Second Crusade
1147 Normans attack Byzantium
1153 Seljuk Sultanate of Merv destroyed by Ghuzz tribes
1157 Death of last Seljuk Sultan
1163, 1167 Zangi attacks Egypt and conquers it in 1168-1169

1171 Saladin (1169-1193) establishes Ayyubid Sultanate
1176 Battle of Myriokephalon: Rum Seljuks defeat Byzantines
1184-1187 Saladin reconquers Mesopotamian empire from Zangids
1185 Normans attack Byzantium
1187 Battle of Hattin: fall of Jerusalem to Saladin

India
c.1149-1215 Wars of the Ghurids
1162-1206 Mohammed of Ghur
1175 Ghurids take Multan
1179 Ghurids take Peshawar
1186 Ghurids take Lahore
1187 Ghurids end Ghaznid State and rule to 1215
1192 Battle of Taraori: Mohammed of Ghur defeats Rajputs
1206 Mohammed assassinated. Ex-slave Qutbuddin Aibak revolts and establishes new dynasty
Sultanate of Delhi; 1206-1290 Slave Dynasty rules

German Empire
1024-1125 Salian Frankish Emperors of Germany
1033 Kingdom of Burgundy joined to the German Empire (Germany and Italy)
1026-7 Conrad II's 1st Italian campaign; he is crowned with the iron crown of Lombardy at Milan; 1027 Imperial coronation in Rome
1037-8 Conrad's 2nd Italian campaign, against Aribert of Milan
1041 Campaign to Prague; Bohemia becomes a German vassal
1044 Conrad's Hungarian campaign
Henry III: partition of Lorraine 1044, resulting in constant conflict between the Emperor and Duke Gottfried the Bearded
1056-1106 Henry IV
1075 Battle of Homburg on the Unstrut. Henry defeats Saxon uprising
1175 Beginning of Investiture conflict with the Papacy
1076-7 Henry IV excommunicated
1077-80 Civil War in the Empire.
1080 Battle of Hohenmölsen. Rival Rudolf of Swabia defeated and killed

1080 Henry is excommunicated again
1083 Henry conquers Rome in his 1st Italian campaign, defeating the Lombards
1084 Henry's Anti-Pope crowns him. Robert Guiscard relieves the Pope in Castel Sant'Angelo and Henry recoils. Normans sack Rome
1090-7 Henry IV's 2nd Italian campaign. But by 1106 he is forced to abdicate
1106-25 Henry V, last Salian emperor
1110-11 Henry V's 1st Italian campaign
1122 Concordat of Worms ends Investiture conflict

Iberian Peninsula
1085 Almoravids of Morocco invade Iberia: take Toledo
1086 Az-Sallaqg
1095 Take Badajoz
1087 Syracuse
By 1115 Almorovids conquer all Muslim Spain
1150-1172 Almohads conquer Iberia
1172 Almohads take Seville
PORTUGAL
1094 Portugal gains independence
1139 Portugal becomes a kingdom and expands to the south. Conflict with Castile ensues
1385 Battle of Aijubarrota or Aijbarrota. Portugal defeats Castile
CASTILE
1035-65 Ferdinand the Great
1037 He obtains Léon
1085 Castile conquers Toledo
1094 El Cid (Rodrigo Diaz) takes Valencia
1212 Battle of Navas de Tolosa. Alfonso VIII of Castile defeats Muslims, breaks Almohad power in Spain
ARAGON
1118 Aragon conquers Saragossa
1137 Aragon unites with Catalonoa
1229-35 Aragon seizes Balearic Islands
1238 Aragon takes Valencia
1118 Aragon conquers Saragossa
1125 Almohad rebellion in Morocco begins
1134 Battle of Fraga
1139 Portugal becomes a Kingdom
1147 Alfonso Henriques of Portugal takes Lisbon
1148-9 Aragon conquers Lower Ebro

Northern Europe
1099 Revolt of Sitvic Silken-beard, King of Dublin
1121 Boleslav III of Poland subdues Pomerania
c.1130 to 1240 Civil Wars over Norwegian Succession
1157-82 Waldemar the Great begins the rise of Denmark
1157 Battle of Viborg
1184-1201 Denmark conquers Pomerania, Schleswig, Holstein, Lübech and Hamburg
1202-41 Wars of Waldemar 'the Conqueror'. Denmark takes Norway, Estonia, Courland, etc., but loses all at Battle of Bornhöved 1227
1208-22 Dynastic struggles in Sweden
1226 Papal Golden Bull of Rimini tasks Teutonic Knights with conquest of heathen Prussia. By 1230 Livonia and Courland subjugated
c.1231-83 Teutonic Knights conquer Prussia
1236 Battle of Sante
1242 Battle of Lake Peipus
1261 Norwegians conquer Greenland and 1262-4 Iceland

Britain
1138 Battle of Standard. Scottish raid on northern England repulsed
1139-53 Anarchy. Civil War between King Stephen and Matilda and son Henry (to become Henry II)
1141 Battle of Lincoln. Stephen temporarily imprisoned
1154-89 Henry II's Angevin Empire
1158 Henry II invades Brittany
1167-71 English invasion of Ireland
1173-4 Revolt of the sons of Henry II
1190 Richard the Lion Heart takes Cyprus from Byzantines
1194-9 War between Richard the Lion Heart and Philip Augustus
1198 Battles of Courcelles and Vernon
1203-5 Philip Augustus of France conquers Normandy and Poitou
1203-4 Siege and capture of Château Gaillard
1204 France conquers Normandy
1213-17 English Civil War
1213 First Flemish campaign. John gathers a formidable alliance against Philip Augustus (inc Germany)

1213 Battle of Damme. William of Salisbury defeats Philip's fleet and frustrates his plan to invade England
1214 Campaign and Battle of Roch-au-Moine. Philip defeats John
27 July 1214 Battle of Bouvines. Philip defeats the Allies
1263-65 Barons War in England Simon de Montfort leads rebellion against Henry III
1264 Battle of Lewes. Simon captures Henry and his son Edward (future Edward I)
1265 Battle of Evesham. Edward decisively defeats the barons
1277-84 Edward I conquers Wales

German Empire
1152-90 Frederick I Barbarossa
1154-5 Frederick's 1st Italian campaign. He promises the Pope he will attack the Normans but does not
1158-62 Frederick's 2nd Italian campaign
1163-4 Frederick's 3rd Italian campaign. Veronese League formed
1166-8 Frederick's 4th Italian campaign
1174-8 Frederick's 5th Italian campaign
1160-4 Campaign against the Wends
1168 Conquest of Rügen Siege of Alessandria fails
1176 Battle of Legnano. Lombard League defeats Friedrich Barbarossa
1180-1 War of Henry the Lion
1184-6 Frederick's 6th Italian campaign
Henry VI crowned at Milan as King of Italy
1187 Frederick allies with Philip II Augustus of France against Guelphs and Anjous
1190-7 Henry VI
1191 Henry's 1st Italian campaign and coronation at Rome. Siege of Naples
1194-5 Henry's 2nd Italian campaign. 1194 Henry crowned King of Sicily at Palermo. He plans hereditary empire
1210-50 Frederick II
1214 Battle of Bouvines. Anglo-Guelphs defeated
1226 Golden Bull of Rimini. Pope tasks Teutonic Knights with conquest of heathen Prussia
1237 Battle of Cortenuova. Lombard League defeated

By the mid-13th century central authority of the German emperors has declined

Iberian Peninsula
1217-52 Ferdinand III conquers the south, taking Cordoba in 1236 to complete the Reconquista
c.1228-9 Almohads abandon Iberia
1229-35 Aragon seizes Balearic Islands
1236 Cordoba taken
1238 Aragon takes Valencia
1244 Treaty of Almiza agrees Portuguese reconquest on the Atlantic side of the peninsula; Aragonese on the Mediterranean side
1257 Only Granada left to Moors in Iberia

1206-1260 Mongol Empire
1206-1227 Genghis Khan
1218 Battle of Karaku
1220 Battle of Samarkand
1221 Forces of Genghis Khan penetrate as far as the Indus
1221 Battle of Kandahar
1231 Mongols estroy Khwarzim
1237-42 Mongol invasion of Europe
1241 Battle of Leignitz
1241 Death of Ogedei Khan
1243 Battle of Kösedag: Mongols defeat Seljuks
1256 Assassins of Alamut destroyed by Mongols and Baybars
1259 Death of Monghe Khan
After 1260 the Mongol Empire has no unified political direction it continues as Chagatai, Il-Khanate and the Golden Horde
1258-1365 Il-Khanate (begins break-up after 1335)
MONGOLS IN CHINA
1205-1209 Mongols conquer Hsi-Hsia as base for conquest of China
1211-1234 Mongol conquest of Ch'in. Mongols rule as the Yüan Dynasty
1215 Mongol capture of Peking
1227 Destruction of Hsi-Hsia
1260-79 Mongol conquest of Sung China
Mongol attacks on Burma and Java fail
Kublai Khan rules China as Shih-Tsu
1274 and 1281 Mongol invasions of Japan fail
1294 Death of Kublai Khan results in rivalry for the throne
1368-1398 Chu Yüan-Chang

drives Mongols back to the Steppe (1368 Yüen (Mongols) expelled from Peking) and estyablishes Ming Dynasty

1345 Great famine in China. 8,000,000 die. Uprising results
1346-1353 Black Death in Europe. Over 20 million die
1362-1363 Second Pandemic in Europe

Middle East
1250 Mameluke slave-soldiers kill last Ayyubid Sultan
1258 Sack of Baghdad; end of Abbasid Caliphate
1261 Byzantines retake Constantinople from the Latin Empire
1263 takes Antioch
1280-1324 Osman, founder of Ottoman State
1260-1277 CAMPAIGNS OF BAYBARS
1260 Battle of Ain Jalut: Mamelukes defeat Mongols
1289 Mamelukes take Tripoli
1291 Acre falls to the Mamelukes, last Crusader toe-hold in Palestine
By about 1400 the Mameluke Empire extends to Syria, Palestine and Hejaz

Sicily
1266 Battle of Benevento. Charles of Anjou defeats regent Manfred
1266-8 Charles of Anjou conquers Sicily
1268 Battle of Tagliacozzo. Charles defeats Conradin, son of Emperor Conrad IV
[1278 Charles of Anjou conquers Achaea]
1282-1302 Sicilian Vespers revolt against Charles of Anjou. Ongoing conflict
1302 Treaty splits Kingdom of Sicily in two

France
1285-1314 Philip IV the Fair
1297-1305 Philip IV's conquest of Flanders
1302 Battle of the Spurs (Courtrai). Flemish defeat French
1305 Flanders submits to France
1328-1498 House of Valois rules France

Germany
1273-91 Rudolf of Habsburg elected Holy Roman Emperor
1278 Battle of Marchfeld. Rudolf defeats and kills

rival Ottokar II of Bohemia
1282 Rudolf of Habsburg gains control of Austria
1298 Battle of Göllheim. Emperor Adolf of Nassau defeated and killed by Albrecht of Habsburg, son of Rudolf. He becomes emperor 1298-1308
1314-47 Louis the Bavarian. He defeats the Habsburgs at
1322 Battle of Mühldorf

India
1290-1320 Sultanate of Delhi: Khalji Dynasty
1296-1316 Wars of Alauddin Khali; he breaks resistance of Rajpurs and repulses Mongols in north-west India
1311 Alauddin Khali conquers India to its southern tip
1320-1414 Sultanate of Delhi: Tughluq Dynasty
1325-1351 Wars of Muhammed Ibn Tughluq. He conquers southern India but most is lost after his death
1336 Kingdom of Vijayanagara established
1347 Kingdom of Bahmani established
1358 Vijayanagara-Bahmani conflict begins (ongoing sporadic campaigns)
1370 Vijayanagara conquers Madurai
1382-1396 Khandesh, Malna, Jaunpur and Guerat break away from Delhi

Middle East
OTTOMAN WARS
1326 Ottomans take Bursa
1361 Ottomans take Ankara
1389-1403 Bayezid I Yildirim (The Thunderbolt)
1394-1403 Blockade of Constantinople by Ottomans

China
c.1390-1449 Wars of conquest by Ming Dynasty
Ongoing sporadic operations v. Mongols
1392 Korea becomes a vassal State
1405-1433 Cheng-Ho is sent on seven great naval expeditions as far as the Indian Ocean and East coast of Africa
1407-1422 Chinese occupation of Annam
1448 Huge rebellions in China
1449 Attack on Mongols fails; Emperor taken prisoner

After period of aggressive expansion, Ming fall back to the defensive
1450s Pirates infest Chinese sea and coastline; famines, plagues and floods afflict China

Campaigns of Timur (Tamerlane)
1380-1405 Annual 'raids' of destruction
1381-8 Iran
1391-5 Against the Golden Horde and Crimea
1384-9 Timur penetrates India and sacks Delhi in 1398
1400-2 against Ottomans
1402 Battle of Ankara. Timur defeats Bayezid

By 1430s Ottoman position fully restored
After Timurid Shah Rukh Empire splits

Switzerland
1291 Swiss Eternal Union for protection against Habsburgs, etc.
1315 Battle of Mortgarten. Swiss defeat Leopold I of Austria
1353 Swiss Confederation founded
Swiss War of the Cities
1386 Battle of Sempach. Swiss defeat Habsburgs.
1415 Swiss conquest of Habsburg Aargau
1422 Battle of Arbedo. Swiss defeated
1440-6 First 'Old War' of Zurich
1444 Battle of St Jacob
1474 'Perpetual Peace' signed

Germany and Northern Europe
1320 Battle of Rudau: Teutonic Knights defeat Lithuanians
1327 Poland loses Silesia and Bohemia
1327-8 Another German campaign in Italy
1330-55 Serbian Empire of Stefan Dushan
1340-75 Waldemar IV of Denmark Campaigns against Oland and Gotland
1346 Casimir II reunites Central Poland
1361 Casmir III conquers Galicia
1361-70 Danes conflict with the Hanseatic League
1373-1419 Wenceslaus, King of Bohemia, provokes uprising. 1394, 1402 he is taken prisoner after defeats
1381 Peasants' Revolt
1377-89 South German War of the Cities

1377 Battle of Ulm. Cities defeat Charles IV
1377 Battle of Reutlingen. Cities defeat Württemberg
1381 South German League of Cities formed; they ally with Swiss Confederation
1388 Battle of Döffingen. Allies defeated by the princes
1382 Teutonic Knights conquer Poland's Baltic provinces
1397 Union of Kalmar unites Norway, Sweden and Denmark
1390s-1402 Uprising of Wenceslaw of Bohemia
1398 Teutonic Knights drive Vitalian Brethren from Gotland
1402 Teutonic Knights seize Neumark
1419-36 Hussite Wars
1415 Execution and martyrdom of John Hus of Bohemia
1419 Bohemian uprising and first defenestration of Prague. Hussite people's army repulses five Imperial/Crusader attacks
1431 Battle of Taus. Indecisive
1434-6 Danish uprising of Englebrecht Engle-Brechtson
1471 Swedes defeat Danes
1466 Casimir IV of Poland/Lithuania takes much of Prussia from the Teutonic Knights

Mediterranean
1284 Battle of Meloria: Genoa defeats Pisa and takes Corsica
1298 Battle of Curzola: Genoese defeat Venetians
1309 Knights of St John establish base in Rhodes
1323-5 Pisa-Genoa war for Sardinia and Corsica
1340 Battle of Salano
1343 Aragon takes Majorca

1296-1346 Scottish War of Independence
1296 Edward I invades Scotland
1297 Battle of Stirling Bridge. Wallace defeats English force
1298 Battle of Falkirk. Wallace defeated by Edward
1303 Edward invades Scotland again
1305 Rebellion of Robert Bruce
1306 Battle of Methven
1307 Battle of Loudon Hill. Bruce defeats Pembroke
1314 Bruce takes Stirling Castle, stongest English fortress in Scotland

1314 Battle of Bannockburn. Bruce decisively defeats Edward II
1315-18 Bruce invades Ireland
1318 Bruce takes Berwick. Subsequent cross-border operations by both sides
1332 Battle of Dupplin. Edward Baliol usurps Scottish crown under suzerainty of Edward III of England
1333 Battle of Halidon Hill. Douglas defeated by Baliol

Iberian Peninsula
1311 Aragon takes Duchy of Athens
1323 Aragon takes Sardinia
1474-9 Castilian War of Succession against France and Portugal
1476 Battle of Toro. Defeat of Portugal
1479 Union of Aragon and Castile
1482 Aragon and Castile reduce Granada
1494 Spain takes Medilla
1509 Spain takes Oran

India
1414-1451 Sultanate of Delhi: Sayyid Dynasty
1451-1526 Sultanate of Delhi: Lodi Dynasty
1509-1530 Campaigns of Krishna Deva Raya bring Vijayanagara to zenith of power
1517-1526 Factions weaken Sultanate of Delhi

1338-1453 Hundred Years War
PHASE 1: PHILIP VI V. EDWARD III 1337-1347
1337-18 The French fleet attacks Portsmouth and Southampton.
1338 Edward III crosses to Flanders.
1340 Battle of Sluys. French fleet destroyed
1346 Battle of Crécy. Edward crushes French army of Philip VI
1346 Battle of Nevill's Cross. David II of Scotland defeated while raiding England
1346-7 Calais taken by Edward III in one of the first actions involving artillery
Oct 1350 Battle of Winchelsea/Sandwich. Edward III's fleet defeats Spanish fleet
1350 Death of Philip VI of Valois. John II succeeds him. Black Death ravages Europe. Estimated 25 million victims between 1347 and 1351.

PHASE 2: JOHN II V. EDWARD III 1351-1356
1355 Brief chevauchée of Edward III in Artois. Chevauchée of Black Prince in Languedoc.
1356 Battle of Poitiers. Black Prince defeats and captures King John of France
1358 Jacquerie peasant uprising in France
1360 Edward III seizes the suburbs of Paris. Peace of Brétigny
1364 Battle of Cocherel. Du Guesclin beats Jean de Grailly's Anglo-Gascon-Navarrese army
1364 Auray captured by the English
PHASE 3: CHARLES V V. EDWARD III 1357-1375
1367 Battle of Nájera. Black Prince and Pedro the Cruel of Castile defeat du Guesclin and the Count of Trasamara
1370 Battle of Pontvallain. Du Guesclin stops English chevauchée from Calais
1372 Du Guesclin and Clisson conquer Brittany.
1372 Battle of La Rochelle. English fleet destroyed by Castilian galleys (allies of the French).
Charles V reconquers Poitou and Saintonge.
1376 Death of the Black Prince.
1377 Death of Edward III.
PHASE 4: CHARLES V V. RICHARD II 1377-1380
1378 Naval victory of Jean de Vienne at Cherbourg over Lancaster. English take Cherbourg and Brest
1380 English offensive from Calais.
1380 Châteauneuf-de-Randon besieged and captured by du Guesclin, who dies in the process Franco-Castilian fleet destroyed by the English off the coast of Ireland. Death of Charles V
PHASE 5: CHARLES VI V. RICHARD II 1382-1396
1381 Truce between France and England. Peasants revolt (Wat Tyler) in England
Nov 1382 Battle of Roosbeke. Charles VI of France defeats Flemish
1387 Battle of Margate. Engish fleet defeats Franco-Castilian fleet, ending the threat of a French invasion of England
1388 Battle of Otterburn. Scots raiding force defeats defending troops of Henry Percy

1394 Revolt in Ireland repressed by Richard II
1395-6 Anglo-French conference in Paris. Truce providing for 28 years
1399 Richard II dethroned in favour of Henry IV
PHASE 6: CHARLES VI V. HENRY V 1414-1422
1405 French expeditionary force lands in Wales to help the Welsh uprising
1406 Welsh beaten by the English. French attempted offensives against Guyenne and Calais checked.
1407 Anglo-French truce. Beginning of Civil War in France.
1415 Henry V renounces the truce of 1396 and lands at Harfleur, which he besieges and takes
1415 Battle of Agincourt. Henry V defeats the French
1416 Battle of Harfleur. Franco-Genoese fleet defeated
1417 Henry V's second expedition to France.
1418 Conquest of Normandy by the English.
1418-19 Siege and capture of Rouen. Burgundians enter Paris
1419 Rouen taken by the English
1420 Treaty of Troyes. Henry V heir to the throne of France
1421 Henry V's third expedition to France.
1421 Battle of Beaugé. Franco-Scottish force defeated by Clarence's English
1422 Truce. Death of Henry V and of Charles VI in Paris
PHASE 7: CHARLES VII V. HENRY VI 1423-1453
1423 Battle of Cravant. Bedford defeats Franco-Scottish army
1424 Battle of Verneuil. Bedford defeats Franco-Scottish army
1427 Battle of Montargis. Dunois defeats Bedford and Warwick
1428 Salisbury besieges Orléans defended by Dunois.
1429 Rouvray ('The Herrings'). Falstolf repulses French attack on a convoy of supplies for the English besiegers of Orleans
1429 Siege of Orleans raised by Joan of Arc, leading to spirited counter-attack by the French, which rapidly gathers momentum. Coronation of the

101

dauphin at Reims as Charles VII

1429 English fortress of Jargeau taken by the French

1429 Battle of Patay. French surprise and defeat English army of Shrewsbury (Talbot)

1430 Joan of Arc checked before Paris and made prisoner

1431 Joan of Arc burnt at Rouen. Henry VI aged 10 is crowned king of France at Paris.

1436 English leave Paris. The French lay siege to Calais

1441 The French take Pontoise

1444-8 Successive truces of Tours

1448 Resumption of hostilities between France and England. French offensive in Normandy

1449 Rouen expels English garrison

1450 Battle of Formigny. Decisive French victory by Clermont over the English, leading to the fall of Caen and Cherbourg to the French

1450-1 French drive the English out of France, leaving only Calais in their hands

The people of Aquitaine revolt against the new French rulers and Shrewsbury takes an English expeditionary force to support them

1453 Battle of Castillon. Shrewsbury is defeated. Castillon, Bordeaux and all Aquitaine revert to French rule

1453 Battle of Castillon. French victory. French re-enter Bordeaux. End of the Hundred Years War. The English are left with only Calais, which they keep to 1558

Balkans

1360s-1390s Ottoman conquest of Thrace, Bosnia, Serbia, Greece and Bulgaria

1389 Kossovo Polje. Turks decisively defeat Serbs

1394-1403 Blockade of Constantinople by Ottomans

1396 Battle of Nicopolis: Christian Crusade defeated by Ottomans

1409-26 Venetian expansion in Dalmatia and Lombardy

1451-81 Mehmet 'The Conqueror' annexes Serbia, Bosnia, Greece, Crimea, etc.

1453 Siege and fall of Constantinople. End of Byzantine Empire. Constantinople becomes Istanbul

Britain: Wars of the Roses

22 May 1455 Battle of St Albans. York, Salisbury and Warwick defeat Royal army. Somerset and Northumberland are killed

23 Sept 1459 Battle of Blore Heath. Salisbury wins for York at Ludlow

10 July 1460 Battle of Northampton. Yorkists put Lancastrians to flight. Henry is captured

30 December 1460 Battle of Wakefield. Margaret defeats York and Salisbury who are killed

2 February 1461 Battle of Mortimer's Cross. Edward, new Duke of York, defeats Lancastrians and is proclaimed king

17 February 1461 Battle of St Albans. Margaret and Somerset defeat Warwick

29 March 1461 Battle of Towton. Lancastrians defeated with heavy loss of life. Edward controls England

1464 Battles of Hedgley Moor (25 April) and Hexham (15 May). Montagu (Warwick's brother) defeats Lancastrians

1465 Henry is captured

1468 Harlech, last Lancastrian stronghold, falls to the Yorkists. Warwick and Edward's brother Clarence change sides

26 July 1469 Battle of Edgecote Moor. Warwick defeats Pembroke.

12 March 1470 Battle of 'Lose-Coat Field' (Stamford). Rebels ambush Edward, but he defeats them

Sept 1470 Henry VI is restored to the throne

14 April 1471 Battle of Barnet. Warwick is defeated and killed

4 May 1471 Battle of Tewkesbury. Edward defeats Lancastrians and rules as Edward IV

1483 Edward IV dies. Richard of Gloucester usurps the throne as Richard III

7 August 1485 Lancastrian Henry Tudor lands in Wales

22 August 1485 Battle of Bosworth. Richard is killed. Henry VII is king

16 June 1487 Battle of

Stoke. Impostor 'Edward VI' defeated

21 July 1403 Battle of Shrewsbury. Henry VII defeats rebellion of Henry Percy (Hotspur)

Burgundy and Switzerland

1467-77 Charles the Bold Duke of Burgundy. He allies with England and Aragon against Louis XI of France, his bitter enemy; and with Sigmund of Austria against the Swiss

1474 Siege of Neuss

1476 Battle of Murten

1476 Battle of Grandson

1477 Battle of Nancy. Charles the Bold killed. His daughter has married Maximilian I of Austria who wins

1479 Battle of Guinegate. Treaty of Senlis divides the legacy

1477-99 Swabian War. Swiss establish independence and separation from the Empire

1513 Swiss Confederation of 13 cantons

1477-99 Swiss Swabian War

1477 Habsburgs inherit Burgundy

1471-80 Turkish attacks on Styria

1477 Hungarian attacks on Austria

1485 Seizure of Vienna, occupation of Lower Austria, Carinthia and Styria by Matthias I Corvinus, King of Hungary, who dies 1490; Habsburgs recover their territories including Vienna

Russia

1478 Ivan III annexes Novgorod

1480 Ivan III proclaims independence of Muscovy

Italy

1494-1559 Valois-Habsburg Wars for Italy [1499-1523 Italian wars involve Swiss mercenaries]

1494 Charles VIII of France begins wars for Naples, claiming Naples via the House of Anjou

1494 Charles conquers Naples

1495 Spanish and Habsburgs force him to retreat

1500 Louis XII of France takes Milan

1504 Treaty of Blois cedes Naples to Spain

By 1505 Habsburgs drive French from the south of Italy and take Naples

1511 Holy League to liberate Italy

1515 Battle of Marignano. Francis I of France defeats Swiss

1519-1556 Habsburg Empire of Charles V

1519-56 Charles V (1516 inherits Spanish Empire; 1519 Austria and the Holy Roman Empire)

1521-6 War against Francis I of France

1525 Battle of Pavia. Habsburgs drive French from Milan

1525 Peasant revolt in Germany

1526-9 2nd war against Francis I.

1527 Imperial army plunders Rome

1535 Habsburgs take Milan

1536-8 3rd war between Charles V and Francis I

1542-4 4th war between Charles V and Francis I

1546-7 Schmalkaldic War of south/central Germany

1547 Battle of Mühlberg. Habsburgs defeat German Protestants

1552-6 Charles V at war with France again. He abdicates 1556 splitting his empire into its Spanish and Austrian components

1559 Treaty of Câteau-Cambresis. French are excluded from Italy

Ottoman Empire in the Middle East

1516-1517 Ottomans conquer Syria, Palestine and Mameluke Egypt

1520-1566 Suleman I pushes the Ottoman Empire to its greatest extend

1529 Turks capture Algiers

1551 Turks take Tripoli

1565 Turks besiege Malta

1571 Turks take Cyprus

1574 Turks take Tunis

Mediterranean

1475-1546 Barbarossa raids Spanish and Italian coasts for Francis I of France

1529 Turks take Algiers

1535 Habsburg North African campaign against Barbarossa and seizure of Tunis

1541 Habsburg Algiers expedition fails

1551 Turks take Tripoli

1565 Turkish siege of Malta fails

1571 Battle of Lepanto. Don John of Austria leads Holy League fleet to victory over Turks

1571 Turks take Cyprus

1577 Ottoman-Habsburg

truce. The Turkish threat wanes. Habsburgs are busy in the north; Ottomans in conflict with Persia

Ottomans in Europe

1526 Battle of Mohacs. Turks take most of Hungary

1529 First Turkish siege of Vienna

Turks take Hungary

1577 Ottoman-Habsburg Truce

India

1504-1530 WARS OF BABUR

1526 Battle of Khanua: Babur defeats Rajput Confederation to conquer northern India

1526 Battle of Panipat: Babur defeats Sultan Ibrahim Lodi of Delhi and establishes the Moghul Empire, which becomes the dominant power in India

1535-1540 Campaigns of Humayan

1538 Bahmani State splits into 5 states

1539 Battle of Chaunsa: Defeated by usurper Sher-Shah

1540 Battle of Kanauj: Defeated by usurper Sher-Shah

1556-1605 Akbar, greatest of Mogul emperors

1556-1601 Campaigns of Akbar

1556 Second Battle of Panipat

1564 Five Deccan Kingdoms combine to destroy Vijayanagara

1610-29 Moghuls at war with Ahmadnagar

1623 Battle of Balochpur

Japan

1467-1615 'PERIOD OF THE WARRING STATES' as local warlords vie for supremacy

1467-77 Onin War

1561 Battle of Kawanakajima

1570-81 Siege of Ishiyama Honganji

1591 Siege of Kunoe

1592/3, 1597/8 Japanese invasions of Korea

1600 Battle of Sekigahara. Tokugawa decisively defeats his rivals, leading to the establishment of the Tokugawa shogunate

1637-8 Shimbara Revolt, the last uprising against the Togukawa shogunate. Peace in Japan. In 1639 Japan effectively cuts itself off from the outside world until the middle of the nineteenth century

Britain
1513-14 Anglo-Scottish War
1513 Battle of Flodden
Field. Earl of Surrey
defeats James IV of
Scotland.
1545 Battle of Ancram
Moor. Scots defeat
English raiding party
1547 Battle of Pinkie.
Somerset defeats Arran,
regent of Scotland
1594-1603 Irish Nine Years
War
1598-1603 Tyrone's
Rebellion in Ireland
1601 Spanish expeditionary
force invades Ireland
1601 Battle of Kinsale.
British defeat Tyrone

1531 Battle of Kappel.
Swiss Catholics defeat
Protestants of Zurich.
Zwingli killed

**Russia and Northern
Europe**
1552 Muscovy conquers
Kazan Khanate
1569 Union of Lublin.
Poland/Lithuania repulse.
Muscovite expansion
1604-6 The 'False
Demetrius' pretender
invades Russia to depose
Boris Godounov, the
murderer of Dmitri, the
last of the Rurik dynasty
in 1598
1605 He enters Moscow
1610 Boyars retake
Moscow and kill
Demetrius
A second false Dmitri is a
puppet of the Poles
1610-13 Time of Troubles -
anarchy in Russia
1600 Poland takes
Smolensk; Sweden
invades Russia
1609-13 Russo-Polish War
1610 Battle of Klondnot
1611 Battle of
Christianople
1612 Battle of Vringellen
1613 Battle of Wisby
1613 Michael Romanov
elected Tsar and restores
order
1617-18 Russian peace with
Poland and Sweden
1615 Battle of Plescow
1621 Battle of Riga
1621-2 Battle of Kotzim
1634 Poland invades Russia
1637 Don Cossacks
temporarily take Azov for
Russia
1672-1725 Peter I the Great
of Russia (sole ruler from
1689)
1695 Expedition against
Azov fails
1696 Expedition succeeds
in taking Azov
1698-9 Revolt of the
Streltsi. Mass executions
ensue

1703 Peter founds St
Petersburg

Anglo-Spanish conflict
1587, 1596 English raid
Cadiz
1558 Spanish Armada
defeated in English
Channel and off the Low
Countries

China
1516 Portuguese base at
Canton established
1563 Japanese pirates
eliminated
1627 Abortive Ch'ing
invasion of Korea
1628-44 Peasant rebellion
in China
1636-7 Ch'ing conquest of
Korea
1644-59 Ch'ing conquest of
China
Ch'Ing or Manchu Dynasty
1644 Manchu take Peking
1644 Citzu-Ch'eng ends
Ming Dynasty and is
immediately overthrown
by the Ch'ing Dynasty to
found the Manchu
Dynasty

1594-7 Peasant Wars in
Austria and Hungary
1605 Hungary invades
Austria

**Dutch War of
Independence (Eighty
Years War)**
During the Dutch War and
the Thirty Years War,
North Italy is vital to
Spain as the mustering-
point for the 'Spanish
Road' (Habsburg
possessions) via the
Valtellina, Alsace,
Rhineland to the Low
Countries, the English
Channel being dominated
by the Dutch and the
English
1587-1625 Campaigns of
Maurice of Nassau
1587-1609 Maurice secures
the Netherlands ('The
Closing of the Garden')
1600 Battle of Nieuport
1601-4 Siege and capture of
Ostend by Maurice
1604 Maurice takes Sluys
1604 Spanish take Ostend
1607 Battle of Gibraltar.
Dutch defeat Spanish at
sea
April 1609 Twelve Years
Truce
1621-48 Dutch War of
Independence resumed
and merges with Thirty
Years War
1625 Capture of Breda
1625-47 Campaigns of
Frederick Henry of
Orange
1626 Battle of Lütter
1626 Battle of Dessau

1636 Frederick Henry
captures Breda
1639 Battle of the Downs.
Tromp defeats second
Spanish Armada

France
1624-42 Richelieu First
Minister of France
1626-30 Anglo-French War
1627-9 Huguenot Rebellion
1628 Siege and capture of
La Rochelle
Buckingham attacks the
Île de Rhé
1629-31 War of the
Mantuan Succession.
France versus Spain
1635-59 France and Spain
at war, leaving Spain
militarily exhausted.
The Fronde - French civil
wars:
Jan-March 1649 First,
parliamentaire Fronde.
Condé besieges Paris
1650-2 Fronde of the
Princes.
8 Apr 1652 Battle of
Nemours
4 May 1652 Battle of
Etampes
14 June 1658 Battle of the
Dunes. Turenne captures
Dunkirk (to England)
1659 Treaty of the
Pyrenees

1618-48 Thirty Years War
Triggered by May 1618
Defenestration of Prague
1618-29 Phase I. Loss of
Palatinate and collapse
of German
Protestantism
1620 Battle of White
Mountain. Bohemian
rebellion ended and
conquest of Palatinate
enabled
[1624-42 Richelieu first
minister of France]
1626 Battle of Lütter
compels withdrawal of
Denmark. 1629 Peace of
Lübeck
1630-5 Phase II.
Restoration of
Protestantism by Sweden
1631 Battle of Breitenfeld
restores Protestant
fortunes and is the
turning-point of the war
1631 Sack of Magdeburg
1632 Battle of Lützen.
Victory, but death, of
Gustavus Adolphus.
Leads indirectly to
assassination of
Wallenstein in Feb 1634
1634 Battle of Nördlingen
undoes the work of
Sweden. War becomes
one of exhaustion
between France/Sweden
and Bavaria/Imperialists.
Disease and starvation
throughout Germany.
End of religious phases of

the war. 1635 Treaty of
Prague
1635-48 Phase III.
Intervention of France
[1634-8 Five years of
negotiations]
1635 French ally with
Dutch against Spain,
begins the Dutch War of
Independence with the
Thirty Years War
[1642-1661 Mazarin first
minister of France]
1643 Battle of Rocroi.
Condé destroys the
remnant of Spanish
military prestige
1648 Battle of
Süsmarshausen. Turenne
and Wrangel defeat
Imperialists and
Bavarians
1648 Battle of Lens. Condé
defeats the Spaniards
1648 Treaty of Westphalia
ends Thirty Years War
and Münster ends
Spanish-Dutch War

Poland
1609-13 Polish war against
Russia
1611 Poles capture
Smolensk
1617-29 Polish war against
Sweden
Ongoing Polish war against
Turkey
1625 Polish war against
Sweden; 1629 Six Years
Truce
1634 Poles invade Russia.
Leads to Treaty of
Viasma/Polyankova.
Ladislas IV renounces
claim to Russian throne
1648-68 Disastrous reign of
John Casimir
Raids of Dnieper Cossacks;
campaigns of Bogdan
Chmielnuski
1648 Battle of Zolte Wody.
Cossacks defeat Poles
and take Lemberg
1651 Battle of Beresteszko.
Poles defeated. Truce
c.1654 Bogdan and
Russians invade Poland
1655-7 Sweden invades
Poland. Civil War in
Poland
1667 Cossack uprising in
Poland
1672-6 Polish-Turkish War
1673 John Sobieski wins
Battle of Khoczoim in
Bessarabia
1674-96 John Sobieski King
of Poland

Middle East
1623 Abbarttu the Great of
Persia captures Baghdad
1638 Murad IV of Turkey
recaptures Baghdad

India
1632 Hooghey taken from
Portuguese

1649-53 Moghuls at war
with Persia
1664-1710 Moghul
persecution of non-
Muslims
1675 Rajput revolt

English Civil Wars
1642-6 First Civil War
22 Aug 1642 King Charles I
sets up standard at
Nottingham: beginning of
war
23 Sept 1642 Battle of
Powick Bridge. Rupert
routs Parliamentarians
23 October 1642 Battle of
Edgehill. King defeats
Earl of Essex
29 Oct King makes Oxford
his capital
13 November Battle of
Turnham Green.
Royalists repulsed from
London
19 Jan 1643 Battle of
Braddock Down. Hopton
clears Cornwall of
Parliamentarians
19 March Battle of Hopton
Heath. Royalist
Northampton defeats
Gell and Brereton
13 April 1643 Battle of
Ripple Field. Prince
Maurice defeats Waller
23 April 1643 Battle of
Launceston. Hopton
defeats Parliament army
of Chudleigh
25 April 1643 Battle of
Sourton Down.
Chudleigh defeats
Hopton
13 May 1643 Battle of
Grantham. Cromwell
defeats Cavendish
16 May 1643 Battle of
Stratton. Hopton defeats
Stamford and secures
south-west for the King
21 May 1643 Sir Thomas
Fairfax takes Wakefield
18 June 1643 Battle of
Chalgrove Field. Rupert
defeats Parliamentarians
29 June 1643 Battle of
Adwalton Moor. Fairfaxes
defeated by Newcastle's
Royalists
5 July Battle of Lansdown.
Hopton defeats Waller
13 July 1643 Battle of
Roundway Down. Hopton
and Prince Maurice
destroy Waller's army
26 July 1643 Bristol falls to
Rupert
27 July 1643 Battle of
Gainsborough. Cromwell
defeats Cavendish
20 Sept 1643 Battle of
Newbury I. King fails to
prevent Essex's return to
London
25 Sept 1643 Solemn
League and Covenant
signed between
Parliament and Scots

11 October Battle of Winceby. Eastern Association defeats Royalists advancing south

25 Jan 1644 Battle of Nantwich. Fairfax defeats Byron

21 March 1644 Rupert relieves besieged Newark

29 March 1644 Battle of Cheriton/Alresford. Waller defeats Forth and Hopton

25 May-11 June Rupert takes Stockport, Bolton and Liverpool and marches to relieve besieged York

29 June 1644 Battle of Cropredy Bridge. King defeats Waller

2 July 1644 Battle of Marston Moor. Scots (Leven), Manchester and Fairfax defeat Rupert and Newcastle. Turning-point: the North is effectively lost to the King (16 July York falls)

31 Aug 1644 Battle of Castle Dore. King destroys Essex's army

1 Sept 1644 Battle of Tippermuir. Montrose defeats Elgin's Covenanters

13 Sept 1644 Battle of Aberdeen. Montrose defeats Elgin's Covenanters

27 Oct 1644 Battle of Newbury II. King repulses Manchester and Waller

2 Feb 1645 Battle of Inverlochy. Montrose defeats Campbells

April 1645 Formation of Parliament's New Model Army, commanded by Sir Thomas Fairfax with Cromwell in command of the cavalry

9 May 1645 Battle of Auldearn. Montrose defeats Hurry's Covenanters

14 June 1645 Battle of Naseby. Fairfax and Cromwell decisively defeat King

2 July 1645 Battle of Alford. Montrose defeats Baillie's Covenanters

10 July 1645 Battle of Langport. Fairfax defeats Goring

1 Aug 1645 Battle of Colby Moor. Laugharne defeats Pembrokeshire Royalists

10 Sept 1645. Rupert surrenders Bristol

13 Sept 1645 Battle of Philiphaugh. Defeat of Montrose

24 Sept 1645 Battle of Rowton Heath. Royalists defeated at Chester

12 March 1646 Astley surrenders last Royalist army at Stow-in-the-Wold

8 Aug 1647 Battle of Dunganhill. Parliamentarian Jones defeats Irish

1648 SECOND CIVIL WAR

1648 Battle of Preston. Cromwell defeats Royalists and Scots

28 Aug 1648 Colchester surrenders to Fairfax

30 Jan 1649 King Charles I beheaded

1649 IRISH CAMPAIGN

2 Aug 1649 Battle of Rathmines. Ormonde's Royalists repulsed before Dublin

Sept-Dec 1649 Drogheda and Wexford beseiged and taken by Cromwell's army

1650-1 THIRD CIVIL WAR

27 April 1650 Battle of Carbisdale. Montrose's Royalists defeated

3 Sept 1650 Battle of Dunbar. Cromwell defeats Scots Covenanters

3 Sept 1651 Battle of Worcester. Cromwell defeats Charles II's Anglo-Scots army

CAMPAIGNS OF THE ENGLISH COMMONWEALTH

1650s England sends a fleet to the Mediterranean against Barbary pirates

May 1655 Britain captures Jamaica

1662-83 England holds Tangier

Anglo-Dutch Wars (naval)

1652-4 1st ANGLO-DUTCH WAR

1652 Battle of Kentish Knock. Blake defeats de With

1652 Battle of Dungeness. Tromp defeats Blake

1653 Battle of Portland/Beachy Head. Indecisive

1653 Battle of Gabbard/North Foreland/Nieuport. Monck and Deane defeat Tromp and de Ruyter

1653 Battle of Texel. Monck defeats Tromp, who is killed

1665-7 2nd ANGLO-DUTCH WAR

1665 Battle of Solebay/Lowestoft. Duke of York defeats Opdam

1666 Four Days Fight/Dover Strait. De Ruyter and Tromp Jr defeat Monck and Rupert

1666 Battle of North Foreland II. Monck defeats de Ruyter

1672-4 3rd ANGLO-DUTCH WAR

1672 Battle of Southwold.

De Ruyter defeats York and d'Estrées

1673 Battle of Schooneveld Bank. De Ruyter defeats Rupert and d'Estrées

1673 Battle of Texel II/Camperdown. De Ruyter defeats Rupert and d'Estrées

China

1674-81 Rebellion of the Three Feudatores

1683 Chinese conquest of Formosa

1696 Chinese conquest of Mongolia

1705 Chinese invasion of Tibet

1720 Chinese conquest of Tibet

1740-3 Chinese-Indonesian War

1758-9 Chinese conquest of Kashgaria

Wars of Louis XIV (King of France 1643-1715; regency 1643-51)

1659-1629 PHASE I

1668 Condé conquers Franche Comté

1672 France invades Holland, but Dutch flood the countryside forcing withdrawal next year

1674 Grand Alliance of the Hague against Louis XIV

1674 Battle of Sinzheim and Ladenburg. Turenne defeats Imperialists and devastates the Palatinate

1675 Battles of Mülhausen, Colmar, Türkheim. Again Turenne defeats the Imperialists and forces the evacuation of Alsace

1675 Battle of Sasbach. Turenne killed

1675 Battle of Fehrbellin. Brandenburg defeats Sweden

1678 Treaty of Nymegen

1667-8 War of Devolution against Spain

1679-97 PHASE II

French annexations (réunions) lead to 1681 Alliance of the Hague, of Dutch, Swedes, Spanish and the Empire

1681 France invades Luxembourg

1684 French fleet bombards Genoa

1689-97 War of the League of Augsburg (Nine Years War). Spain, Empire, Sweden and Bavaria ally against France over the Spanish succession

1688 Second French invasion of the Palatinate

1688-9 second devastation of the Palatinate unites Europe against Louis XIV

1689 English Revolution: William III usurps James II

May 1689 Alliance of Vienna: Empire, United Provinces, joined by England, Spain and Savoy against France

IRISH THEATRE:

Naval battles of Bantry Bay and Beachy Head: French defeat England and Holland. Louis XIV plans invasion of England with camp at Cherbourg.

1692 Battle of La Hogue. Tourville defeated by Russell

1689 France invades Low Countries

1692 Battle of Steinkirk. William III defeated

1693 Battle of Neerwinden (Landen) William III defeated

French campaign in Italy:
1690 Battle of Staffarde;
1693 Battle of Marsaglia

Jean Bart leads *guerre de course* in Channel

1696/7 Treaties of Turin and Ryswick

1697-1715 PHASE III

1700 death of Charles II of Spain; bequeaths Spanish Empire to Philip of Anjou

[1700 Brandenburg becomes Kingdom of Prussia]

French invade Netherlands

1701 Grand Alliance of the Hague against the French

1702-13 War of the Spanish Succession

1702 Battle of Friedlingen

1703 Battle of Höchstadt

1704 Battle of Blenheim, Marlborough's great victory. Allies conquer Bavaria

1704 Gibraltar taken by England

1706 Battle of Ramillies wins Belgium for the Allies

1706 Battle of Turin Philip V has to abandon Barcelona. France loses Belgium, Milanese, Spain in one summer

1707 Battle of Almanza

1708 Battle of Oudenarde. Allies invade France

1708-14 Sardinia is a British base

1708-83 Minorca is a British base

1709 Battle of Malplaquet, a Pyrrhic victory for Marlborough, which prevents the Allies invading France

1710 Battle of Lerida. Philip defeated

1710 Battles of Brihuega, Villviciosa. Allies defeated, effectively restoring Spain to the Bourbons

1711 French expedition takes Rio de Janeiro

1712 Battle of Denain. Villars wins France's only major victory and the Allies lose heart

1713/15 Treaty of Utrecht

Americas

1701-14 War of the Spanish Succession

1711-12 Tuscarora War

1702-13 Queen Anne's War (War of The Spanish Succession in Europe)

1715-28 Yamassee War

1718-20 Franco-Spanish War (War of the Quadruple Alliance)

1721-5 Paraguayan Revolution

1740-8 King George's War (War of the Austrian Succession in Europe)

Turkey

After Suleiman the Magnificent the Ottoman Empire suffers a series of weak rulers

1606 End of frontier war with the Habsburgs

1621 Turkish-Polish conflict over the Dniester

1623 Abbas the Great of Persia captures Baghdad

1638 Murad IV (1623-40) recaptured Baghdad

1645-69 Turkish War for Crete (Candian War)

c.1648 Ottoman Empire invaded by Cossacks and Venetians

1663 Turks invade Hungary, Moravia, Silesia with a large army; a Holy League is formed to oppose them

1664 Battle of St Gothard on Raab. Imperial army defeats Turks

1664 Truce

1669 Turks take Candia (Crete). They invade Poland; 1672 Treaty of Buczacs. Polish Ukraine ceded to Turkey

1683-99 AUSTRO-TURKISH WAR

1683 Turks march on Vienna

1683 Battle of Petronell. Kara Mustafa defeats Charles of Lorraine. Sixty-day siege of Vienna Battle of Vienna. John Sobieski defeats the Turks. Poland joins the Holy League, which already includes Austria, Venice, Malta and Russia

1686 They take Buda

1687 Battle of Mohacs. Austrian and Polish troops invade Moldavia, Wallachia and Croatia. Habsburgs obtain the crown of Hungary

1686 Venice takes the Morea, Athens and Dalmatia

1687 Battle of Mohacz. Turks defeated decisively and ejected from Hungary, which becomes a Habsburg kingdom
c.1689 Turks retake Nish and Belgrade
1691 Battle of Salankemen. Turks are defeated
1697 Battle of Zenta. Turks defeated in war against Poles, the Austrian Empire, Venice and Hungary; and are expelled from Serbia and Bosnia
1699 Treaty of Karlowitz

1703 Janissary revolt
1714-18 Turkish War with Austria and Venice

Middle East
1717 Afghan revolt
1722-3 Russo-Persian War
1726-7 Persian-Turkish War
1730-6 Turkish-Persian War
1737-8 Persian invasion of Afghanistan
1743-7 Turkish Persian War
1768-74 1st Turkish War with Catherine of Russia
1769-73 Egyptian revolt
1774 Rohilla War
1775 Failed Spanish invasion of Algeria
1779-94 Persian Civil War
1795-7 Persian invasion of Georgia
1798 Persian invasion of Afghanistan

India
1738-9 Persian invasion of India
1744-48 1st Carnatic War
1746 Battle of Madras
1748 Battle of Pondicherry
1749-54 2nd Carnatic War
1751 Battle of Arcot

South-East Asia
1704-5 1st Javanese war of Succession
1714-16 Cambodian Civil War and Vietnamese invasion
1717 Siamese invasion of Cambodia
1719-23 2nd Javanese war of Succession
1739-49 Cambodian-Vietnamese war
1740-52 Mon revolt in Burma
1749-57 3rd Javanese war of Succession
1755-60 Vietnam offensive in Cambodia
1760 Burmese invasion of Siam
1764-7 Burmese invasion of Siam
1765-9 Chinese-Burmese war
1769-73 Siamese-Vietnamese war
1773-1801 Vietnamese Civil War

1775-6 Burmese-Siamese war
1778 Siamese invasion of Laos
1780-2 Siamese invasion of Vietnam
1784-5 Burmese conquest of Arakan
1785-92 Burmese-Siamese war

1655-60 War of the North
1656 Secret Treaty of Marienburg. Brandenburg and Sweden agree partition of Poland
1655-7 Charles X of Sweden's invasion of Poland fails
1657-8 Swedish invasion of Denmark leads to treaty
1658-9 Second Swedish invasion of Denmark. Charles besieges Copenhagen but eventually surrenders to Dutch, Poles, Austrians and Danes. He dies 1660
1660 Treaties of Oliva and Copenhagen
Sweden becomes involved in wars against Louis XIV; Russo-Polish conflict continues to 1667
1675 Battle of Fehrbellin. Elector of Brandenburg defeats Sweden, this marking the beginning of Sweden's military decline. Denmark, Brandenburg and Austria are at war with Sweden

1700-21 Wars of Charles XII
1700-21 GREAT NORTHERN WAR
1700 Charles forces peace on the Danes
1700 Battle of Narva. Charles defeats Russia, occupies Courland and Riga
1702 Charles invades Poland and enters Warsaw
1702 Battle of Klissow. Charles defeats Augustus of Poland. By 1705 the Swedes have conquered Poland. Meanwhile Peter the Great of Russia conquers Livonia and Estonia
1706 Battle of Fraustadt. Sweden defeats Poles, Russians and Germans
1706 Charles invades Saxony
1707 Sweden signs treaty with Augustus of Poland and the Habsburgs
[April 1707 Marlborough visits Charles at Altranstadt]
1707-9 Charles invades Russia
1708 Battle of Holowczyn

1709 Battle of Poltava. Peter the Great decisively defeats Charles who languishes for five years in Turkey
1710 Turkey joins the war against Russia
1711 Peace of the Pruth
1712 Danes invade Bremen
1712 Battle of Gadebusch. Swedes are victorious but subsequently forced to surrender at Tönning to superior forces. Russia invades Finland. Sweden ceases to be a power in Germany
1709-13 Charles remains at Bender
1713 Charles besieged at Kalibalik and made prisoner
1713 Treaty of Adrianople ends Russo-Turkish war
1714 Charles returns clandestinely to Sweden
1715 Siege of Stralsund. Charles faces the armies of Russia, Prussia, Poland, Saxony, Hanover and Denmark
1719 Charles invades Norway and is killed at the siege of Frederickshald. During the wars of his reign, Sweden has lost nearly a third of its male population
1721 Treaty of Nystadt ends the Great Northern war. Sweden ceases to be a great power

Britain
1679 SCOTTISH COVENANTER UPRISING
1679 Battle of Dumclog. Scottish Covenanters defeated
1679 Battle of Bothwell Bridge. Covenanter rising suppressed
1685 MONMOUTH REBELLION
1685 Battle of Sedgemoor. Pretender Monmouth defeated and subsequently captured
1688-91 WAR OF THE ENGLISH REVOLUTION
1689 Londonderry besieged but not taken by James II
1689 Battle of Killiecrankie. Highlanders ambush government force
1689 Battle of Dunkeld
1690 Battle of The Boyne. William III defeats James II.
1691 Battle of Aughrim. Irish rebels dispersed
1691 Rebel Limerick taken by government troops
1692 Battle of Glencoe. Treacherous government attack on the Macdonalds massacres 38

1715 JACOBITE REBELLION
1715 Battle of Sheriffmuir. Indecisive
1715 Battle of Preston. Rebels destroyed
1745-6 JACOBITE REBELLION
1745 Prestonpans. Charles Edward Stuart destroys government force then sorties into England
1746 Battle of Falkirk. Murray leads Jacobites to their last victory
1746 Battle of Culloden: Pretender 'Bonnie Prince Charlie' decisively defeated by Duke of Cumberland

Russia
1695-6 Russian conquest of Azov
1698-9 Revolt of the Streltsi in Russia
See Great Northern War above
1710-11 Russo-Turkish War

1703-11 Hungarian Revolt

1716-18 AUSTRO-TURKISH WAR
1717 Battle of Belgrade. Prince Eugene of Savoy's Austrian army defeats Turks

1727-9 Spanish War with Britain and France
1735-7 Spanish-Portuguese War
1736-9 Russo-Turkish War
1737-9 Austro-Turkish War
1739-43 Anglo-Spanish War of Captain Jenkins' Ear

War of the Polish Succession 1733-9

1740-8 WAR OF THE AUSTRIAN SUCCESSION
1741 Battle of Mollwitz. Prussians defeat Austrians
1743 Battle of Dettingen. King George II of Britain defeats the French; the last battle to be commanded by a British monarch
1745 Battle of Hohenfriedburg. Frederick the Great of Prussia defeats Austro-Saxons
1745 Battle of Sohr. Frederick the Great of Prussia defeats Austrians
1747 Battle of Laffeldt. Count Maurice de Saxe of France defeats Allies

1741-3 Russo-Swedish War

1756-63 Seven Years War
1756 Battle of Lobositz. Frederick the Great of Prussia defeats Austrians
1757 Battle of Prague.

Frederick the Great of Prussia defeats Austrians
1757 Battle of Kolin. Marshal Leopold von Daun of Austria defeats Frederick the Great's Prussians
1757 Battle of Rossbach. Frederick the Great of Prussia defeats Franco-Austrians
1757 Battle of Leuthen. Frederick the Great of Prussia defeats Austrians
1758 Battle of Zorndorf. Frederick the Great of Prussia defeats Russians
1758 Battle of Hochkirch. Marshal Leopold von Daun of Austria defeats Frederick the Great
1759 Battle of Minden. Duke Ferdinand of Brunswick led the Allies to defeat the French
1759 Battle of Kunersdorf. Lieutenant-General Gideon von Laudon of Austria and Count Peter Soltikov of Russia defeat the Prussians
1760 Battle of Warburg. Anglo-Prussians under Duke Ferdinand of Brunswick defeat the French
1760 Battle of Liegnitz. Frederick the Great of Prussia escapes Austro-Russian encirclement
1760 Battle of Torgau. Frederick the Great of Prussia defeats Austrians
SEVEN YEARS WAR IN INDIA
1756 Back Hole of Calcutta
1757 Clive captures Calcutta and wins Battle of Plassey, imposing British control over Bengal

Americas
FRENCH AND INDIAN WAR IN NORTH AMERICA, 1754-1763 (corresponds to Seven Years War in Europe)
9 Aug 1757 Fort William Henry
3 June-20 July 1758 Louisburg
8 July 1758 Fort Ticonderoga
24 Nov 1758 Fort Duquesne
13 Sept 1759 Wolfe captures Quebec
1763 Pontiac Rebellion

1768-72 Polish Civil War, Russian invasion and 1st partition of Poland
1768-74 Russo-Turkish War
1776-7 Spanish-Portuguese War
1777-9 War of the Bavarian Succession
1787-91 Austro-Turkish War
1788-90 Swedish War with Russia and Denmark

1792-5 Russo-Prussian invasion and 2nd partition of Poland

India
1766-9 1st Mysore War
1771 Mysore-Maratha War
1779-82 1st Maratha War
1780-3 2nd Mysore War
1789-92 3rd Mysore War
1790 Battle of Calicut
1791 Battle of Bangalore
1792 Battle of Seringapatam
1795-6 British expedition to Ceylon
1799 4th Mysore War
6 April-3 May 1799. Wellesley captures Seringapatam, ending third conflict with Tippo Sahib
1803-1805 Second Maratha War
23 Sept 1803 Assaye. Wellesley defeats Marathas in a bloody fight against enormous odds
1803-5 British 2nd Maratha War
1817-18 British 3rd Maratha War

Americas
1769-1807 Yankee-Pennamite War
1775-86 AMERICAN WAR OF INDEPENDENCE
1775 Battle of Lexington. British survive American militia attacks
1775 Battle of Bunker Hill. Gage/ Howe of Britain defeat Americans
1775 Battle of Quebec. Carleton of Britain defeats Americans
1776 Battle of Long island. Howe defeats Americans
1776 Battle of White Plains. Howe defeats Americans
1776 Battle of Trenton. George Washington defeats British
1777 Battle of Princeton. Washington defeats British
1777 Battle of Brandywine. Howe defeats Americans
1777 Battle of Germantown. Howe defeats Americans
1777 Battle of Saratoga - Freeman's Farm and Bemis Heights. Gates of America defeats British; the turning-point of the war
1778 Battle of Monmouth. Clinton of Britain holds off Americans
1781 Battle of Guildford Court House. Cornwallis of Britain defeats Americans
1779-83 Siege of Gibraltar. Eliott of Britain defeats French/Spanish

1779 Battle of Savannah. Prevost of Britain defeats Americans
1780 Battle of Charleston. Clinton defeats Americans
1780 Battle of Waxaws. Tarleton leading British and Loyalists defeats Americans
1780 Battle of Camden. Cornwallis defeats Americans
1789 Battle of King's Mountain. Colonels John Sevier, Isaac Shelby and Richard Campbell defeat British loyalists
1781 Battle of Cowpens. Morgan of America defeats British
1781 Battle of Yorktown. Washington and Jean-Baptiste de Rochambeau of France defeat British. The British surrender. Was the coup de grace to British rule
1781 Battle of Eutaw Springs. Lieutenant-Colonel Alexander Stewart defeats Americans

1792-9 French Revolutionary and Napoleonic Wars
1792-1798 WAR OF THE FIRST COALITION
20 Sept 1792 Valmy. Indecisive, but Prussians retreat and the French Republic survives
1792 Battle of Jemappes: the first French offensive victory of the war
27 Aug-19 Dec 1793 Toulon besieged by French, garrison having been taken over by Royalists with British naval support. Significant for Bonaparte's command of the French artillery
26 June 1794 Fleurus. Jurdan's French defeat Austrians, leadng to French capture of Netherlands
1796-7 Bonaparte's First Italian Campaign
10 May 1796 Lodi. Bonaparte defeats and outmanoeuvres Austrians, leading to capture of Mantua
15-17 Nov 1796 Arcola. Bonaparte defeats the Austrians
14 Jan 1797 Rivoli. Bonaparte defeats the Austrians' last attempt to relieve besieged Mantua
12 June 1798 Battle of Vinegar Hill. Rebellion in Ireland ended
1798-1801 FRENCH EXPEDITION TO EGYPT
21 July 1798 Pyramids.

Bonaparte defeats Mameluke rulers of Egypt
25 July 1799 The Nile/Aboukir Bay. Nelson destroys Bonaparte's fleet
March-May 1799 Unsuccessful siege of Acre by Bonaparte
21 March 1801 Alexandria. French garrison of Egypt defeated by British expeditionary force under Abercromby
1798-1800 WAR OF THE SECOND COALITION
14 June 1800 Marengo. Bonaparte's narrow victory over Austrians after epic trans-Alpine march into Italy
3 Dec 1800 Hohenlinden. French victory over Austria in Germany
1805-6 WAR OF THE 3rd COALITION
1800 Battle of Marengo. Bonaparte defeats Austrians in Italy after transalpine march
1805 Battle of Trafalgar. Nelson defeats combined fleets of France and Spain
1804 Napoleon crowns himself Emperor of the French
1805 Capitulation of Ulm. Mack, outmanoeuvred and surrounded, surrenders an Austrian army to Napoleon
1805 Battle of Trafalgar. Nelson defeats the combined fleets of France and Spain. Britain attains undisputed mastery of the seas
1805 Battle of Austerlitz. Napoleon defeats Austro-Russian army
1806 Battles of Jena and Auerstadt. Napoleon defeats Prussia
1807 Battles of Eylau and Friedland. Napoleon defeats Russia
1807 Treaty of Tilsit confirms Napoleon's mastery of north-western Europe
WAR OF THE FIFTH COALITION, 1809
1809 Battles of Aspern-Essling and Wagram. Napoleon defeats Archduke Charles of Austria after initial repulse
WAR OF THE SIXTH COALITION, 1812-1814
1812 Napoleon invades Russia to enforce Continental System measures against Britain. Battle of Borodino. Napoleon defeats Russians and occupies Moscow. Tsar will not

make peace. Napoleon forced into disastrous retreat made worse by winter. Most of his army wiped out.
1813 Battle of Leipzig - 'Battle of the Nations'. Napoleon is defeated by armies of Austria, Russia, Prussia and Sweden
1814 Campaign of France. Brilliant defensive campaign fails to prevent Allies converging on Paris. Napoleon abdicates and is banished to Elba.
1807-1814 PENINSULAR WAR
19 July 1808 Baylen. Shocking surrender of 28,000 French to Spanish, which destroys the 'myth' of French invincibility
21 Aug 1808 Vimeiro. British expeditionary force under Wellesley defeats Junot. Scandalous Convention of Cintra by Wellesley's superiors wastes the victory. Next year Napoleon personally leads French army into the peninsula
16 Jan 1809 Corunna. Moore's reargard action enables evacuation of British expeditionary force by sea
27-28 July 1809 Talavera. Wellesley defeats French army of Victor
27 Sept 1809 Busaco. Wellesley (now Wellington) repulses Masséna
Winter 1809/10 Wellington builds defensive Lines of Torres Vedras north of Lisbon as safe-haven for Allied army
3-5 May 1811 Fuentes de Onoro. Wellington repulses Masséna
16 May 1811 Albuera
7-19 Jan 1812 Cuidad Rodrigo besieged and captured by Wellington
16 March-6 April 1812 Badajoz besieged and captured by Wellington
22 July 1812 Salamanca, Wellington defeats Marmont, opening the road to Madrid
21 June 1813 Vittoria. Wellington defeats Jurdan, ending French control of Spain
10 April 1814 Toulouse. After crossing the Pyrenees, Wellingotn defeats Soult, ending the Peninsular War. Napoleon abdicates the following day
1815 THE HUNDRED DAYS
1815 Napoleon returns to France. Battles of Quatre

Bras and Ligny against Britain and Prussia are not decisive. Battle of Waterloo. Wellington and Blücher decisively defeat Napoleon, who abdicates again and is banished to St Helena

Anglo-American War, 1812-1814 (War of 1812)
11 Nov 1813 Chrysler's Farm. Second US invasion of Canada reulsed
5 July 1814 Chippewa. US victory on Canadian border
25 July 1814 Lundy's Lane. US invasion of Ontario repulsed
24 Aug 1814 Bladensburg. US fail to halt British entering Washington
8 Jan 1815 New Orleans. Jackson repulses Packenham's British after peace has been agreed between Britain and the USA

Europe
1808 Russo-Finnish War
1804-13 Serbian insurrection
1815-17 Serbian insurrection
1806-12 Russo-Turkish War
1820 Neapolitan Revolution
1821 Sardinian Revolution
1821-3 Russo-Persian War
1821-8 Greek War of Independence
1821 Battle of Navarino
1823 French intervention in Spain
1825-8 Russo-Persian War
1828-9 Russo-Persian War
1830 French 'July' Revolution
1830-2 Polish insurrection
1831 Russo-Turkish War
1848 Revolutions and turmoil across Europe including French Revolution and revolts in Austria-Hungary
1848-9 Hungarian War of Independence
ITALIAN WARS OF INDEPENDENCE
4 June 1859 Battle of Magenta. MacMahan's Franco-Piedmontese army defeats Austrians
24 June 1859 Battle of Solferino. Napoleon III and Victor Emmanuel II (Franco-Piedmontese) defeat Austrians at a cost. The carnage led Napoleon to conclude a peace deal, and inspired the founding of the Red Cross

Americas
1806-7 British unofficial expeditions to Buenos

Aires and Montevideo fail
1810-14 Chilean rebellion
1811 US Indian War
1811-25 Latin-American wars of Independence
1812-15 US-British War of 1812
1818 US 1st Seminole War
1818 US invades Florida
1823 US Monroe doctrine declines European involvement in American political affairs
1835-6 Texan War of Independence
1836 Siege of the Alamo and Battle of San Jacinto
1825-8 Brazil-Argentine War
Mackenzie's Rebellion in Canada
1827-9 Peruvian War
1829 Spanish involvement in Mexico
1832 US Black Hawk Indian War
1835-43 US 2nd Seminole Indian War
1836-9 Peru-Bolivian War
1838-9 French expedition to Mexico
1841 Peruvian invasion of Bolivia
1843-52 Argentine-Uruguayan War
1846-1848 US-MEXICAN WAR
10-24 Sept 1846 Battle of Monterrey. Taylor defeats Mexicans and captures the city
22-23 Feb 1847 Battle of Buena Vista. Taylor defeats Mexicans
8 Sept 1847 Battle of Molino del Rey. Scott defeats Mexicans
13 Sept 1847 Battle of Chapultepec. Scott captures the fortress and advances to Mexico City. Final major action of the war
1849-51 Lopez's invasion of Cuba
1850-98 Series of US-Indian Wars
1856 US Kansas Civil War
1857-60 Mexican Civil War
1860-1 Colombian Civil War
1861-2 Spanish expedition to Mexico
1861-7 French expedition to Mexico
4-17 May 1863 Battle of La Puebla. Forey of France captures city and advances on Mexico City to create a puppet government

1861-5 American Civil War
12-14 April 1861 Battle of Fort Sumter. Bombardment and capture of the fort by Beauregard's Confederates made war between North and South inevitable

21 July 1861 Battle of Bull Run, First. The first major battle of the war and the first use of rail transport for troops. Johnston's and Beauregard's Confederates fail to exploit victory. Confed General Jackson's stubborn defence earns him the nickname 'Stonewall'
6-16 Feb 1862 Battle of Fort Donelson. Grant wins first major Federal victory
6-7 April 1862 Battle of Shiloh (Pittsburg Landing0. Grant eventually defeats Confeds and gives Federals strategic initiative in the west
31 May-1 June 1862 Battle of Seven Pines (Fair Oaks).
9 June 1862 Battle of Port Republic. Jackson defeats Union and joins Lee's army
25 June-1 July 1862 Seven Days Battles. Lee forces Confed retreat
9 Aug 1862 Battle of Cedar Mountain. Inconclusive, but allowed Confeds to advance north
28-30 Aug 1862 Battle of Bull Run, Second. Lee defeats Union army
13-15 Sept 1862 Battle of Harper's Ferry. Jackson defeats Union garrison
17 Sept 1862 Battle of Antietam (Sharpsburg). Politically and strategically crucial for the Union. Although Lee of the Confederacy wins a tactical victory, his losses force him to abandon his invasion of the north.
3-4 Oct 1862 Battle of Corinth. Rosecrans of the Union repulses Confeds
8 Oct 1862 Battle of Perryville.
13 Dec 1862 Battle of Fredericksburg. Lee defeats Union
31 Dec 1862-2 Jan 1863 Battle of Stones River (Murfreesboro).
1-5 May 1863 Battle of Chancellorsville. Lee defeats Union and prepares the second invasion of the north
19 May-4 July 1863 Battle of Vicksburg. Grant of the Union takes the fortress and splits the Confederacy in two in a crucial action
9 June 1863 Battle of Brandy Station. Lee defeats Union but not decisively

1-3 July 1863 Battle of Gettysburg. Meade of the Union defeats Lee's invasion force, inflicting unsustainable casualties
18-20 Sept 1863 Battle of Chickamauga. Bragg wins tactical victory over Union
24-25 Nov 1863 Battle of Chattanooga. Union breaks Confed siege
5-6 May 1864 Battle of Wilderness. Grant of the Union holds off Confeds and advances towards Richmond
8-18 May 1864 Battle of Spotsylvania Court House. Grant defeats Confeds
31 May-3 June 1864 Battle of Cold Harbor. Lee repulses Federal attack
15-18 June 1864 Battle of Petersburg. Confeds prevent capture of city
20 July-31 Aug 1864 Battle of Atlanta. Sherman captures the city
9-21 Dec 1864 Battle of Savannah. Sherman of the Union takes the city
15-16 Dec 1864 Battle of Nashville. Thomas conclusively defeats Confeds
I April 1865 Battle of Five Forks. Grant's Union cavalry under Sheridan defeat Confeds and force Lee to retreat
9 April 1865 Battle of Appomattox Court House. Grant traps Confeds. Lee surrenders, effectively ending the war

AMERICAN INDIAN WARS
21 Dec 1866 Battle of Fetterman Massacre, The. Red Cloud's Sioux and Cheyenne kill garrison unit but fail to press their advantage
25-26 June 1876 Battle of Little Big Horn. Sitting Bull and Crazy Horse defeat US 7th Cavalry, killing Gen. Custer and temporarily winning respite

Middle East
1801-5 US-Tripolitanian War
1804-13 Russo-Persian War
1806-12 Russo-Turkish War
1807 Failed British invasion of Egypt
1807 Battle of Rosetta
1811-18 Egyptian war with Wahhabis
1815-16 US-Dutch war with Algiers
1816 Persian invasion of Afghanistan
1820-3 Russo-Persian War
1825-8 Russo-Persian War

1828-9 Russo-Turkish War
FRENCH CONQUEST OF ALGERIA
14 Aug 1844 Battle of Isly. Using a 'Boar's Head' formation, Bugeaud's French decisively defeat Algerians
1831 Russo-Turkish War
1832 -3 1st Turkish-Egyptian war
1836-8 Persian invasion of Afghanistan
1839-42 1st British-Afghan War
FIRST AFGHAN WAR, 1839-1842
14 Nov 1841-16 April 1842 Battle of Jellalabad. Sale of Britain defends garrison town
1839 Battle of Ghanzi
1839-47 Russian conquest of Khiva
1839-42 2nd Turkish-Egyptian War
1855 Persian invasion of Afghanistan
1856 British-Persian War
1859-60 Spanish-Moroccan War
1878-80 2ND BRITISH-AFGHAN WAR
27 July 1880 Battle of Maiwand. Ayub Khan destroys British brigade. Survivors retreat to Kandahar
I Sept 1880 Battle of Kandahar. Roberts relieves besieged British garrison and defeats Ayub Khan, replacing him on the throne with Abdur Rahman Khan
1882 British-Egyptian War Bombardment of Alexandria
13 Sept 1882 Battle of Tel-el-Kebir. Wolseley (Britain) defeats rebels and imposes British control over Egypt

China/Japan
1839-42 1st British-Chinese 'Opium War'
1850-64 China: Taiping rebellion
1856-60 2nd British-Chinese 'Opium War'
21 Aug 1860 Battle of Taku Forts. Anglo-French forces, including Indians, under Grant and Cousin-Montauban storm forts and advance towards Beijing
1863-4 European bombardments of Kagoshima and Shimonoseki
1863-8 Civil War in Japan
1866 French expedition to Korea
1875-6 Japanese expedition to Korea
1877 Satsuma rebellion in Japan

1882-5 Chinese and Japanese expeditions to Korea
1883-1885 FRANCO-CHINESE WAR
14-16 Dec 1883 Battle of Son-Tai. French capture Chinese-occupied fort
1894-5 Sino-Japanese War
1900 Boxer rebellion in China
20 June-14 Aug 1900 Battle of Peking. International relief force breaks siege of Foreign Legations
1904-5 RUSSO-JAPANESE WAR
30 April-1 May 1904 Battle of Yalu River. Oyama defeats Russians and leads Japanese invasion of Manchuria
25 May 1904 Battle of Nanshan. Oyama breaks through Russian defence line and aproaches Port Arthur
1 June 1904-2 Jan 1905 Siege of Port Arthur. Nogi's Japanese army eventually captures the naval base
25 Aug-3 Sept 1904 Battle of Liaoyang. Both sides seek a major victory, but Oyama forces Russians to retreat
21 Feb-10 March 1905 Battle of Mukden. Coming to the end of his manpower resources, Oyama attempts to crush Russians, and succeeds in forcing a withdrawal. Russians eventually evacuate Manchuria and Japan emerges as a major world power
27 May 1905 Battle of Tsushima. In the last of the 'Trafalgar-style' sea battles of annihilation, Togo destroys the Russian fleet. This had sailed half way round the world from the Baltic. In the North Sea it panicked and attacked UK fishing boats, thinking they were Japanese torpedo boats
1911 Chinese Civil War

South-East Asia
1810-11 British expedition to Indonesia
1812 Siamese invasion of Cambodia
1819 Burmese conquest of Assam
1823-6 1st British-Burmese war
1825-30 Great Java war
1826-7 Siamese-Laotian war
1831-4 Siamese invasion of Cambodia
1841-5 Siamese-Vietnamese war

1852-3 2nd British-Burmese war
1858-61 French conquest of Indo-China
1882-3 French-Vietnamese war
1873-7 Siamese-Laotian war
1873-95 continuing French expansion in Indo-China
1885 3rd British-Burmese war

Australasia
1804, 1806, 1808 Mutinies in Australia
1843-8 New Zealand: 1st Maori war
1860-79 New Zealand: 2nd Maori war

India
1843 British conquest of Sind
17 Feb 1843 Battle of Meeanee. Napier of Britain defeats the Amirs of Sind
1845-6 1ST BRITISH-SIKH WAR
18 Dec 1845 Battle of Mudki. Gough of Britain defeats Sikhs
21-22 Dec 1845 Battle of Ferozeshah. In the most bitterly contested battle the British fought in India, Gough defeats Sikhs
28 Jan 1846 Battle of Aliwal. Smith destroys Sikh army
10 Feb 1846 Battle of Sobraon. Gough defeats Sikhs
1848-1849 SECOND SIKH WAR
13 Jan 1849 Battle of Chilianwallah. Sikhs hold off British
21 Feb 1849 Battle of Gujerat. Gough defeats Skikhs/Afghans and Britain annexes the Punjab
1857-8 INDIAN MUTINY AGAINST BRITISH RULE
8 June-20 Sept 1857 Battle of Delhi. Wilson's British/Indian troops re-capture the city
I July-19 Nov 1857 Battle of Lucknow. British/Indians break rebel siege of garrison
6 Dec 1857 Battle of Cawnpore. At a turning-point for the mutiny, Campbell routes the rebels
17-20 June 1858 Battle of Gwalior. Rose defeats Indian rebels in last major battle of the mutiny
NORTH-WEST FRONTIER OF INDIA CAMPAIGNS
1897 Tirah
20 Oct 1897 Battle of

Dargai. Lockhart of Britain defeats Afridis and Orakzais
1888-98 Further British North-West India frontier campaigns and expeditions

1853-5 Crimean War
20 Sept 1854 Battle of Alma. British/French/Turkish Allies defeat Russians and advance to besiege Sevastopol
1854-5 Siege of Sevastopol
25 Oct 1854 Battle of Balaklava. Raglan of Britain defeats Russians. Heroic failure of the Charge of the Light Brigade along the 'Valley of Death'
5 Nov 1854 Battle of Inkerman. Raglan's British and French troops repulse Russians
28 Sept 1854-8 Sept 1855 Battle of Sevastopol. Raglan of Britain and Canrobert of France eventually force Russians to abandon the fortress

Europe
1863-4 Polish insurrection
1864 Schleswig-Holstein War. The first phase of Bismarck's campaign to unify Germany, which results in 1870 in the formation of the German Empire
1866 AUSTRO-PRUSSIAN (SEVEN WEEKS') WAR
24 June 1866 Custozza, Second Battle of. Archduke Albert defeats Italians, allied with Prussia
3 July 1866 Battle of Königgrätz. von Moltke of Prussia defeats Austrians and gives Prussia dominance in Central Europe
1866 Austro-Italian War

1870-1 Franco-Prussian War
1870 Battle of Gravelotte-St Privat
1870 Battle of Sedan
1870-1 Siege of Paris
1870-1871 FRANCO-PRUSSIAN WAR
6 Aug 1870 Battle of Worth. Crown Prince Friedrich Wilhelm (Prussia) defeats French
16 Aug 1870 Battle of Mars-la-Tour.
18 Aug 1870 Battle of Gravelotte-St Privat. Von Moltke of Prussia eventually forces French to withdraw
1 Sept 1870 Battle of Sedan. von Moltke of

Prussia captures the town. Napoleon III of France goes into captivity and the Third Republic replaces the Second French Empire.
20 Sept 1870-28 Jan 1871 Siege of Paris. Von Moltke starves the city into capitulation and ends the Franco-Prussian War
1873-6 Spanish Carlist War
1877-8 RUSSO-TURKISH WAR
1877 Battle of Plevna
19 July-10 Dec 1877 Battle of Plevna. Krudener of Russia eventually defeats Turks
17-18 Nov 1877 Battle of Kars. Melikoff takes the fortress for Russia in a surprise night attack
1885-6 Serbo-Bulgarian War
1896-7 Greco-Turkish War

Africa
1800-1 British reconquest of Egypt
1801-5 US-Tripolitanian war
1806 British take Cape Town
1806-7 Ashanti conquest of the Gold Coast
1807 British occupy Alexandria
1807 British take St Louis (Senegal) from French
1811-18 Egyptian war with Wahhabis
1818-19 Zulu Civil War
1820-39 Egypt conquers Sudan
1824-31 1st British-Ashanti war
1830-48 French conquest of Algeria
1832-3 Turkish-Egyptian war
1838 Boer-Zulu Battle of Blood River
1839-41 Turkish-Egyptian war
1856 Zulu Civil War
1858-68 Cape Wars
1859-60 Spanish-Moroccan war
1862-4 Transvaal-Orange Free State War
1867-1868 ANGLO-ABYSSINIAN WAR
31 April 1868 Battle of Aroghee. Napier's British/Indian troops, using breech-loading rifles for the first time, defeat Abyssinians
1868-72 Abyssinian Civil War
1873-4 2nd British-Ashanti war
1873-9 Egypt-Abyssinian war
1879 ANGLO-ZULU WAR
22 Jan 1879 Battle of Isandhlwana. Tshingwayo and Mavumengwana

overun British camp but suffer heavy casualties
22-23 Jan 1879 Battle of Rorke's Drift. Chard leads a small band of British defenders in beating off repeated attacks, and is relieved by Chelmsford the next day
29 March 1879 Battle of Kambula. Wood (Britain) repulses Zulu attack
4 July 1879 Battle of Ulundi. Chelmsford destroys a much larger Zulu army
1880-1 1st Anglo-Boer war
28 Jan 1881 Battle of Laing's Nek. Joubert's Boers defeat British infantry
27 Feb 1881 Battle of Majuba Hill. Joubert's Boer commandos defeat British, leading to armistice
1881 French occupy Tunis
1883-4 Zulu Civil War
1883-9 Mahdist uprising and war with Abyssinia
1ST BRITISH SUDAN CAMPAIGN
29 Feb 1884 Battle of El Teb, Second. Graham defeats Mahdist army
12 March 1884-26 Jan 1885 Siege of Khartoum and death of General Gordon. Mahdi Mohammed Ahmed's rebels take the town, kill the garrison, and force most Anglo-Egyptian forces to withdraw from the Sudan
13 March 1884 Battle of Tamai. Graham defeats Mahdists but fails to destroy their army
17 Jan 1885 Battle of Abu Klea. British column flying to the relief of Khartoum beats off dervish attack
19 Jan 1885 Battle of Abu Kru. British flying column defeats renewed dervish attacks
1888-90 German East Africa uprising
21 Dec 1893 Battle of Agordat. Arimondi leads Italian defeat of Mahdists
1893 Spanish Riff war in Morocco
1893 Mashona-Matabele war
1893-4 3rd British-Ashanti war
1895-6 4th British-Ashanti war
1895-6 French conquer Madagascar
1895-6 Italian-Abyssinian war
ITALO-ABYSSINIAN WAR, 1895-1896
1 March 1896 Battle of Adowa. Emperor Menelek of Abyssinia wins

independence by defeating Italian forces. At that time the biggest victory of irregulars over regular, well-equipped colonial troops
1896 Battle of Adowa
1896-8 BRITISH-EGYPTIAN RECONQUEST OF SUDAN
8 April 1898 Battle of Atbara River. Kitchener leads Anglo-Egyptian destruction of Mahdist army, and continues to advance towards Mahdist capital, Omdurman
2 Sept 1898 Battle of Omdurman. Kitchener's Anglo-Egyptian forces destroy dervish army and end Mahdist rebellion
1897 British conquer Nigeria
1897-1901 Uganda uprising
1899-1902 SECOND ANGLO-BOER WAR
13 Oct 1899-17 May 1900 Battle of Mafeking. Badon-Powell withstands Boer siege
15 Oct 1899-15 Feb 1900 Battle of Kimberley. British break Boer siege
2 Nov 1899-28 Feb 1900 Siege of Ladysmith
28 Nov 1899 Battle of Modder River. Methuen defeats Boers with heavy losses
10 Dec 1899 Battle of Stormberg. Olivier defeats British
10-11 Dec 1899 Battle of Magersfontein. Cronje/De La Rey defeat British
15 Dec 1899 Battle of Colenso. Botha defeats British
19-24 Jan 1900 Battle of Spion Kop. Botha repulses British
18-27 Feb 1900 Battle of Paardeberg. Roberts defeats Boers
1904 South-West African Hottentot uprising
1907 South Africa Zulu uprising
1911 Italy annexes Libya, Tripolitania, Cyrenaica
1911-12 war with Turkey

Americas
1863 Colombia-Ecuador War
1864-6 Spanish war with Peru then Chile
1864-70 Lopez's war
1869-70 Canada: 1st Riel rebellion
1876-7 US Sioux and N Cheyenne War
1876 Battle of the Little Big Horn
1885 Canada: 2nd Riel rebellion
1890-1 US S Dakota war
1895-8 Cuban revolution

1898 SPANISH-AMERICAN WAR
1 July 1898 Battle of San Juan. Americans under Shafter capture hill positions near Santiago
1901 Colombian Civil War
1903 Panamanian revolution
1906-9 US intervention in Cuba
1907 Nicaraguan-Honduran war
1909-11 Honduran Civil War
1911-14 Mexican revolution
1912 Nicaraguan Civil War
1912 US intervention

Pacific
1879-83 War of the Pacific
1898 USA conquers Philippines (Spanish-American war)
1899-1902 Philippine uprising

Wars of Turkish Dissolution
1911-12 Italian war with Turkey. Italy annexes Libya, Tripolitania, Cyrenaica and occupies the Dodecanese
1912-13 First Balkan War
1913 Second Balkan War

1914-1918 First World War
WORLD WAR I: WESTERN FRONT
Aug 1914 Battle of the Frontiers. German armies sweep forward in modification of the Schlieffen Plan
5-10 Sept 1914 Battle of Marne. Anglo-French armies repulse over-extended Germans
13-27 Sept 1914 1st Battle of the Aisne
Sept-Oct 1914 'Race to the Sea'. Closure of the 'open flank' and establishment of stabilised Western Front (trench-lines from the English Channel to Switzerland)
18 Oct-30 Nov 1914 1st Battle of Ypres
22 April-25 May 1915 2nd Battle of Ypres
21 Feb-18 Dec 1916 Battle of Verdun. Massive, repeated German assults fail to capture Verdun but cause huge casualties on each side
1 July-18 Nov 1916 Battle of the Somme. Major British offensive results in massive casualties for the attackers
9-15 April 1917 Battle of Arras
9-15 April 1917 2nd Battle of the Aisne
7-14 June 1917 Battle of Messines

Aug-Nov 1917 3rd Battle of Ypres
20 Nov-3 Dec 1917 Battle of Cambrai. First use of tanks
Ludendorff's Final Offensives on the Western Front:
21 March-5 April 1918 Somme German Offensive almost breaks British lines
April 1918 Lys German Offensive
27 May-6 June 1918 Aisne German Offensive
June 1918 Noyon-Montdidier German Offensive
July 1918 Champagne-Marne German Offensive
July-Aug 1918 Reduction of the Marne Salient
Aug-Sept 1918 Reduction of the Amiens Salient
Aug-Sept 1918 Evacuation of Lys Salient
12-16 Sept 1918 St Mihiel Offensive
Sept-Nov 1918 General Allied Offensives
WORLD WAR I: EASTERN (RUSSIAN) FRONT
26-30 Aug 1914 Battle of Tannenberg. Hindenburg-Ludendorff victory prevents Russian capture of East Prussia
23-Aug-26 Sept 1914 Galician battles
9-14 Sept 1914 Masurian Lakes I
Sept-Oct 1914 S.W. Poland
11-25 Nov 1914 Battle of Lodz
7-22 Feb 1915 Battle of Masurian Lakes II
2 May-27 June 1915 Gorlice-Tarnow
July-Sept 1915 Russian withdrawal
March 1916 Lake Narotch Operations
June-Aug 1916 Brusilov Offensive
Aug-Sept 1916 Roumanian Offensive
Sept-Dec 1916 Roumania eliminated
March 1917 Russian Revolution
July 1917 Kerensky (2nd Brusilov) Offensive
1-5 Sept 1917 Riga Operation
Dec 1917 Russian armistice
WORLD WAR I: ITALIAN FRONT
June-July 1915 1st Battle of Isonzo
July-Sept 1915 2nd Battle of Isonzo
Oct-Nov 1915 3rd Battle of Isonzo
Nov 1915 4th Battle of Isonzo
March 1916 5th Battle of Isonzo
15 May-17 June 1916

Asiago Offensive
Aug 1916 6th Battle of Isonzo
Sept 1916 7th Battle of Isonzo
Oct 1916 8th Battle of Isonzo
Nov 1916 9th Battle of Isonzo
May-June 1917 10th Battle of Isonzo
Aug-Sept 1917 11th Battle of Isonzo
24 Oct-7 Nov 1917 Battle of Caporetto
15-22 June 1918 Battle of the Piave
24 Oct-4 Nov 1918 Battle of Vittorio Veneto
WORLD WAR I: SERBIA / SALONIKA FRONTS
Aug 1914 1st Austrian invasion of Serbia
Sept 1914 2nd invasion of Serbia
Nov-Dec 1914 3rd invasion of Serbia
Oct-Nov 1915 4th invasion of Serbia
Oct 1915 Salonika Front established
Nov 1916 Fall of Monastir
Sept 1918 Final Allied Offensive

WORLD WAR I: GALLIPOLI FRONT
Nov 1914 Dardanelles bombarded
Feb-March 1915 Naval attempt to force passage of the Dardanelles fails
April-May 1915 Landings at Gallipoli
August Landings at Suvla Bay
Dec 1915-Jan 1916 Evacuation of Gallipoli expeditionary force
WORLD WAR I: MESOPOTAMIA FRONT
Nov-Dec 1914 Allied landing in Mesopotamia
Jan-July 1915 Allied advance in Mesopotamia
Sept 1915 1st Battle of Kut
22-25 Nov 1915 Battle of Ctesiphon
8 Dec 1915-29 April 1916 Siege and fall of Kut
Sept 1916-Feb 1917 2nd British advance in Mesopotamia
Feb 1917 2nd Battle of Kut
March 1917 British capture Baghdad
WORLD WAR I: PALESTINE FRONT
Jan 1915 1st Turkish attack on Suez Canal
March 1917 1st Battle of Gaza
April 1917 2nd Battle of Gaza
Oct-Nov 1917 3rd Battle of Gaza
Nov-Dec Battles of Junction Station and Jerusalem

18 Sept-31 Oct 1918 Battle of Megiddo. Allenby's decisive victory leads to fall of Damascus and Aleppo
WORLD WAR I: NAVAL BATTLES
1 Nov 1914 Battle of Coronel. British squadron defeated
28 Aug 1914 1st Battle of Heligoland Bight
8 Dec 1914 Battle of Falkland Islands. British battlecruisers avenge Coronel
24 Jan 1915 Battle of Dogger Bank
31 May-1 June 1916 Battle of Jutland. Epic battle between British and German main fleets. Germans escape defeat
1917 2nd Battle of Heligoland Bight
WORLD WAR I: AFRICAN THEATRE
June 1915-Jan 1916 Allied operations *v.* Germans in Cameroon
August 1915 Anglo-French capture German Togoland
Sept 1916 Allies take Dar-es-Salaam in German East Africa

1916 Easter Uprising in Ireland
1917-20 Russian Civil War
1919-22 Greco-Turkish War
1919-22 Russo-Polish War
16-25 Aug 1920 Battle of Warsaw. Pilsudski of Poland, advised by French General Weygand, smashes invading Russian Bolshevik army

Americas
1914 Veracruz US intervention
1915 US intervention in Haiti
1916 Villa raids US
1916 US intervention in dominican Republic
1917 Cuban revolution
1918-19 Haitian revolt against USA
1920 Mexican Civil War
1921 Panama-Costa Rica conflict
1921-29 Chile-Peru Tacha-Arica dispute
1925 Nicaraguan Civil War. US intervention (to 1933)
1929 Bolivia-Paraguayan border dispute
1932-35 Chaco War between Bolivia and Paraguay
1937 Haiti-Dominican Republic border dispute

Far East
1921 Chinese Civil War
1924 British troops intervene in Shanghai

1931 Japan invades Manchuria
1931-32 Sino-Japanese war over Manchuria
1937-1945 SINO-JAPANESE WAR
April 1938 Battle of Taierchwang. General Li Tsung-jen defeats Japanese
1939 Noonahan War between the Soviet Union and Japan

Middle East
1919 3rd British-Afghan War
1920 USSR invades Persia
1928 Mutiny of Afghan Army
1934 Saudi attacks Yemen
1920-22 Irish War for Independence. 2nd Civil War

1936-39 Spanish Civil War
1938 Germany annexes Czechoslovakia and Austria
1939-40, 1941-45 Russo-Finnish War

1939-1945 Second World War
1 SEPT-6 OCT 1939 WORLD WAR II: POLISH CAMPAIGN. First German blitzkrieg overwhelms Poland and triggers war against Britain and France
13 Nov 1939-12 MARCH 1940 WORLD WAR II: RUSSO-FINNISH WAR
30 Nov 1939-8 Jan 1940 Battle of Suomussalmi. Finns trapped and destroy two Soviet divisions
30 Nov 1939-13 Feb 1940 Mannerheim Line. Russia forces a way up the Karelian Isthmus
9 APRIL-8 JUNE 1940 WORLD WAR II: SCANDINAVIAN CAMPAIGN. German invasion of Denmark and Norway. British and French counter-invasion of Norway defeated (Narvik, Namsos, Aandalesnes)
WORLD WAR II: CAMPAIGN IN THE WEST, 1940
10 May-25 June 1940 France, Belgium and Holland. German blitzkrieg drives Britain out of the continent, overwhelms Holland, Belgium and France
21 May 1949 Arras. British counterattack
26 May-4 June 1940 Dunkirk evacuation of British Expeditionary Force
19 Aug 1942 Dieppe. Prototype amphibious

landing by predominantly Canadian force

WORLD WAR II: AIR OPERATIONS, EUROPE

15 Aug-15 Sept 1940 Battle of Britain. German Luftwaffe fails to attain air superiority over British Isles

7 Sept 1940-10/11 May 1941 The Blitz. Luftwaffe attempt to bomb Britain into submission fails

c.7/8 Nov 1941 onwards Strategic Bombing of Germany. RAF and (later) USAAF strategic strikes against enemy cities and installation; 30/31 May 1942 Cologne 1st 1000-bomber raid; 5/6 March-9/10 July 1943 Battle of the Ruhr; 16/17 May 1943 Dambuster raid; 24 July-3 Aug 1943 Hamburg; 17 Aug USAAF Schweinfurt/Regensburg; 18/19 Nov 1943-24/25 March 1944 Berlin; 13/14 Feb 1945 Dresden

WORLD WAR II: NORTH AFRICAN / MEDITERRANEAN / MIDDLE EASTERN CAMPAIGN

9 Dec 1940-7 Feb 1941 O'Connor's blitzkrieg destroys most of Italian forces in North Africa

6-8 April 1941 German/Italian invasion of Yugoslavia and Greece, completed by 20 April

20 May-1 June 1941 Crete. German airborne conquest

24 March-25 April 1941 Rommel's first offensive

18 Nov-7 Dec 1941 Operation 'Crusader'. British eject Rommel from Cyrenaica and relieve Tobruk

26 May-21 June 1942 Gazala. Rommel defeats British Eighth Army and captures Tobruk

1-27 July 1942 First Battle of Alamein. Rommel repulsed by Eighth Army

30 Aug-2 Sept 1942 Alam Halfa. Indecisive attacks and counterattacks by Rommel and Auchinlech/Montgomery

23 Oct-4 Nov 1942 Second Battle of Alamein. Montgomery decisively defeats Rommel

14-22 Feb 1943 Kasserine Pass. Rommel inflicts sharp reverse on US II Corps in Tunisia

6 March 1943 Medenine. Rommel repulsed

20-27 March 1943 Mareth Line. Montgomery forces Rommel's retreat

June 1940-May 1943 Siege of Malta. The island is

attacked from the air and supplied perilously by sea

WORLD WAR II: SICILY/ITALIAN CAMPAIGN

9-18 Sept 1943 Salerno. Allies land in southern Italy

12 Oct-14 Nov 1943 Volturno River. Major conflict for German defence line south of Rome

17 Jan-22 May 1944 Monte Cassino. Major obstacle to Allied advance south of Rome

22 Jan-23 May 1944 Anzio landing to turn the Gustav Line. In desperate fighting, Allies almost defeated

30 Aug-28 Oct 1944 Gothic Line. Allied struggle to breach last major German defence line in Italy

WORLD WAR II: EASTERN FRONT

22 June 1941 Operation 'Barbarossa' launched. Germany invades USSR

17 July-5 Aug 1941 Smolensk. Major encirclement of Soviet forces

1 Sept 1941-27 Jan 1944 Siege of Leningrad

9-26 Sept 1941 Kiev. Major encirclement of Soviet forces

5-20 October 1941 Vyazma-Bryansk. Major encirclement of Soviet forces

8 Oct 1941-30 April 1942 Battle for Moscow. Hitler fails to capture Moscow. Central front stabilises while German main thrust moves south

29 Oct 1941-3 July 1942 Sevastopol. Manstein secures the Crimea

19 Aug 1942-2 Feb 1943 Stalingrad. German Sixth Army trapped and, after epic battle, forced to capitulate. A turning-point battle

16 Feb-15 March 1943 Kharkov. Manstein inflicts sharp reverse on Soviets

5-17 July 1943 Kursk. Last major German offensive on the Eastern Front and probably the largest tank battle ever fought

22 June-27 Aug 1944 Operation 'Bagration'. Soviet 'steamroller' liberates Byelorussia

1 Aug-2 Oct 1944 Warsaw. Failed Polish uprising significantly unsupported by Soviet offensive

16 April-2 May 1945 Berlin. Zhukov/Konev force Soviet conquest of Berlin.

Hitler commits suicide amid the rubble

World War II: Campaign in the West, 1944-5

6 June 1944 D-Day. Montgomery directs successful Allied landing in Normandy

6 June-25 July 1944 Caen. Hard-fought battle to break out from the beachhead

13-21 Aug 1944 Falaise Gap. Significant trapping of German forces in Normandy after 'Cobra' breakout on Allied right flank

17-25 Sept 1944 Arnhem. Failed Allied airborne attempt to breach German riverine defence lines in Netherlands

16 Dec 1944-16 Jan 1945 Battle of the Bulge (Ardennes). 'Last-throw' German counterattack fails

7-31 March 1945 Rhine Crossings. Allies enter Germany

WORLD WAR II: PACIFIC THEATRE

7 Dec 1941 Pearl Harbor raid by Japanese devastates US fleet

22 Dec 1941-10 May 1942 Japanese conquest of Philippines

27-8 Feb 1942 Battle of the Java Sea. Japanese destroy Allied cruiser/destroyer squadron in Dutch East Indies

4-8 May 1942 Battle of the Coral Sea. Tactical Japanese victory

4-7 June 1942 Battle of Midway. Major turning-point defeat for Japanese, crippling their carrier fleet

7 Aug 1942-7 Feb 1943 Guadalcanal. Air, land and sea battle is major turning-point in Pacific theatre

US amphibious landings and capture of stepping-stone islands across the Pacific:

20-23 Nov 1943 Tarawa
1-4 Feb 1944 Kwajalein
17-23 Feb 1944 Eniwetok
15 June-9 July 1944 Saipan
21 July-10 Aug 1944 Guam
24-31 July 1944 Tinian
15 Sept-25 Nov 1944 Peleliu
19 Feb-16 March 1945 Iwo Jima
1 April-22 June 1945 Okinawa

19-20 June 1944 Battle of the Philippine Sea ('Great Marianas Turkey Shoot') breaks back of Japanese naval air power

20 Oct-25 Dec 1944 Leyte. Largest battle in naval history. US defeats last major offensive by Japanese fleet and secures landings in Philippines

3 Feb-4 March 1945 Manila

9-17 Aug 1945 Soviet invasion and conquest of Manchuria from Japanese

6 and 9 Aug 1945 Atomic bombing of Hiroshima and Nagasaki

WORLD WAR II: SOUTH-EAST ASIA CAMPAIGN

8 Dec 1941-15 Feb 1941 Japanese conquest of Malaya

10 Dec 1941 Japanese sink British Force Z (battleship *Prince of Wales* and battlecruiser *Repulse*)

8-15 Feb 1942 Singapore surrenders, the worst British defeat since the 18th century

29 March-22 June 1944 Battle of Imphal/Kohima. Slim's Fourteenth Army repulses attempted Japanese invasion of India

WORLD WAR II: NAVAL EVENTS (not covered in major theatres)

13 Dec 1939 Battle of the River Plate. British cruiser squadron encounters German 'pocket battleship' *Graf Spee*, subsequently scuttled

9, 13 April 1940 Battle of Narvik. German destroyer force devastated by Royal Navy

Battle of of the Atlantic. German U-boat campaign against Allied convoys to Britain, defeated by ULTRA code-breaking and Allied air and technical advances

21-27 May 1940 *Bismarck* action. German battleship sinks British battlecruiser *Hood* (24 May) before being sunk by Royal Navy forces

11/12 Nov 1940 Taranto raid by Royal Navy cripples part of Italian fleet

28 March 1941 Battle of Cape Matapan. Cunningham's fleet defeats Italians

1-5 July 1942 Destruction of Arctic Convoy PQ17

1946 Greek Civil War
1954-9 Cyprus Emergency
1956 Hungarian Uprising
1968 Czechoslovakia Spring uprising and Warsaw Pact intervention

Far East

1945-9 Chinese Civil War
1950-3 KOREAN WAR

5 Aug-15 Sept 1950 Battle of Pusan Perimeter. MacArthur (UN)/Walker (US) destroy North Korean army

15-25 Sept 1950 Battle of Inchon. Succeeding with a difficult amphibious landing, MacArthur's UN forces capture Seoul and contribute to disintegration of North Korean army

16-18 April 1953 Battle of Pork Chop Hill. Trudeau (US/UN) drives off Chinese

22-30 April 1951 Battle of Imjin River. British, Belgian and American troops force Chinese army to withdraw, inflicting 40 per cent casualties

Americas

1945-65 Colombian Civil War
1947-49 Paraguayan Civil War and turmoil
1948 Nicaraguan invasion of Costa Rica (Costa Rica Civil War)
1951-55 Ecuador-Peru border dispute
1952-59 Cuban revolution
1953 British intervention in Guiana
1955 Nicaraguan invasion of Costa Rica
1956-58 Haiti unrest
1959 Cuban invasion repelled
1960-65 Brazil: Communist insurgency
1961 Cuba: US Bay of Pigs invasion repelled
1964 British Guiana state of emergency
1965 Dominican Republic Civil War US intervention
1979-91 El Salvador Civil War
1982 British-Argentinian Falklands war
FALKLANDS/MALVINAS WAR, 1982
27-28 May 1982 Battle of Goose Green. Jones/Keeble of Britain capture Argentinian garrisons
11-14 June 1982 Battle of Port Stanley. Moore's British forces defeat Argentinians and liberate the port
1983 US intervention in Grenada
25-27 Oct 1983 Grenada. Metcalf's US task force, with token Caribbean units, defeat Granadians/Cubans
1979-89 Nicaragua Civil War

1989 US invades Panama
1994 US intervention in Haiti
1995 Oklahoma City terrorist bombing

Middle East
1948-49 War of Israeli Independence
1956 SUEZ CANAL CRISIS AND ARAB/ISRAELI WAR
29 Oct-5 Nov 1956 Battle of Sinai. Dayan fulfils all Israeli objectives, defeating Egyptian army and overrunning the Sinai
5-7 Nov 1956 Battle of Suez Landings. UK/French Allies under Stockwell try to regain control of the nationalised Suez Canal, and advance along the canal until the UN demands a ceasefire
1958-67 Aden emergency
ARAB/ISRAELI WAR OF 1967 ('THE SIX DAY WAR')
5-8 June 1967 Battle of Sinai. Israelis under Gavish destroy Egyptian army and set up defence line along Suez Canal
9-10 June 1967 Battle of Golan Heights. Elazar of Israel defeats Syrians and captures the plateau
1970 Jordanian conflict with Palestinians
1973 ARAB-ISRAELI OCTOBER (YOM KIPPUR) WAR
6-8 Oct 1973 Battle of Suez Canal Crossing. Under Ali and Shazli, Egypt crosses the canal to regain the Sinai and its honour. Israelis push back until US and USSR force a UN ceasefire resolution
6-10 Oct 1973 Battle of Golan Heights. Hofi leads Israeli repulse of Syrians
1975/6 Lebanese Civil War
1974 Turkish invasion of northern Cyprus
1978 Israeli invasion of Southern Lebanon
1978 Iranian Revolution
1979-89 Russo-Afghan War
1980-9 Iran-Iraq War
1982 Israeli invasion of Lebanon (Operation 'Peace for Galilee')
1983-4 Israeli intervention in Lebanon
1986 Yemeni Civil War
1986 US bombs Libya (Operation 'Eldorado Canyon')
1987 Arab intifada against Israel begins
1990-1991 GULF WAR
1990 Iraqi invasion of Kuwait
24-28 Feb 1991 Operation 'Desert Storm'. Schwarzkopf's Coalition forces destroy the Iraqi

army and liberate Kuwait
1992-94 Armenia-Azerbaijan war over Nagorno-Karabakh
1993 Tadjikistan State of Emergency
1994 Jordan-Israel formal peace (having been technically at war since 1948)
1995-6 Russian intervention in Chechnya

India
1947-8 Indian War of Separation
1961 Ceylon state of emergency
1965 Second Indo-Pakistan War
1969 Indo-Pakistan War
1984-89 Sri Lankan emergency
1984 Indian offensive in Punjab
1999 Kashmir: Indo/Pakistan border conflict

South-East Asia
1946-1954 FRENCH INDOCHINA WAR
1948-60 Malayan emergency
20 Nov 1952-7 May 1954 Battle of Dien Bien Phu. Giap's Viet Minh capture French base, forcing French to agree to independence for Vietnam
1953 Vietnamese invasion of Laos
1955 Vietnamese Civil War
1959-76 Laos state of emergency
1961-1975 VIETNAM WAR (US involvement 1961-73)
1964 Gulf of Tonkin incident
19 Oct-26 Nov 1965 Battle of Ia Drang Valley. Kinnard's US 1st Cavalry inflicts crippling losses on the North Vietnamese and Viet Cong
18 Aug 1966 Battle of Long Tan. Australians under Jackson soundly defeated Viet Cong
22 Feb-14 May 1967 'Junction City', Operation. Under Westmoreland, US/South Vietnamese inflicted heavy defeat on Communists, who retreated to Cambodia, but claimed to have devastated American troops. This inspired Communist leaders to launch the disastrous Tet Offensive against South Vietnamese towns
19-23 Nov 1967 Battle of Dak To (Hill 875). North Vietnamese distracted American attention from

South Vietnam by laying an ambush and fighting for the hill.
21 Jan-14 April 1968 Khe Sanh, Siege of. As part of Tet Offensive, North Vietnamese try to take American base. Lownds succeeds in holding on until relieved
31 Jan-25 Feb 1968 Battle of Hue. Truong (South Vietnamese)/LaHue (USA) recapture city from North Vietnamese, who had seized it in a surprise attack on 30-31 January
1964-66 Indonesian-Malaysian emergency
1970 Vietcong-Cambodian fighting
1973 Cambodian uprising in Cambodia
1975 Indonesia invades East Timor
1975 Khmer Rouge control Cambodia
1979 Sino-Vietnamese war
1979-89 Vietnamese intervention in Cambodia
1985 Major Vietnamese offensive

1947/8 to 1989/90 The Cold War
At the close of World War II, Germany and Austria are occupied by the victors. Eastern Europe, 'liberated' from the Nazis, falls into Soviet sphere. Communist regimes are installed and in Churchill's words, an 'iron curtain' divides Europe. Tension grows between the USSR and the West. Berlin is divided and West Berlin forms an enclave of democracy within the Eastern bloc
1948-53 Height of the Cold War.
1949 Formation of North Atlantic Treaty Organisation, between most of the European democracies and the North American powers
1949 USSR becomes an atomic power
1949 Berlin Airlift. USSR interdicts access to West Berlin, and the city is supplied by air from the West
1955 USSR forms Warsaw Pact
Intercontinental ballistic missiles increasingly form the principal deterrent between the superpowers, based on Mutual Assured Destruction, with fleets of bombers on constant stand-by and nuclear-

powered submarines deployed with targeted missiles aboard
1962 Cuban missile crisis. US spyplanes discover Soviet missiles deployed in Cuba. The world teeters on the brnk of nuclear war, with Cuba blockaded by the US Navy, before the USSR backs down
With the stalemate nuclear confrontation, and armies stationed on either side of the 'Iron Curtain', the ideological and political conflict between East and West is played out by surrogate means in the Third World
1980s Attempts by Mikhail Gorbachev to democratise USSR. During the 1980s the USSR finds it increasingly difficult to maintain the 'arms race', the US constantly outspending its rival and developing new technologies such as Stealth aircraft and the so-called 'Star Wars' anti-missile system. Soviet involvement in Afghanistan exacerbates the situation
1989/90 Collapse of Communist regimes in Soviet-bloc Europe and reunification of Germany

Africa
1952 Kenya: Mau-Mau emergency
1954-62 Algerian-French war of Independence
1959 Rhodesian emergency
1960 South Africa: Sharpeville massacre
1960-63 Congo
1961-75 Angolan war of Independence
1964 Rwanda: Tutsi massacres
1966-79 Rhodesian Civil War
1967-70 Nigerian Civil War
1975-7 Chad Civil War
1975-89 Angolan Civil War
1975-91 1st Angolan Civil War
1976 Morocco invades West Sahara
July 1976 Entebbe raid by Israelis frees hostages
1977 Mogadisho incident
1977 Egyptian-Libyan conflict
1977 Ethiopia: Ogaden war
1977-8 Liberian Civil War
1979 Tanzania invades Uganda
1981 Zimbabwe uprising quashed
1983 Polisario attack Moroccans in West Sahara

1984-87 Chad war
1991 Ethiopian Civil War
1991 Somali Civil War / US intervention
1992-5 2nd Angolan Civil War
1993 Burundi Civil War
1994 Rwandan Civil War
1996-7 War of African Great Lakes

Europe
1969-98 NORTHERN IRELAND TERROR CAMPAIGN
1972 Bloody Sunday.
1979 Mountbatten murdered by IRA
1984 Brighton Bomb fails to kill British Prime Minister Margaret Thatcher
1980 Iranian Embassy Siege, London. British élite SAS unit rescues hostages
1991-9 WAR OF YUGOSLAVIAN DISSOLUTION
1991-5 Serbia/Croatia/Slovenia/Bosnia phase
1999 Serbia/Kosovo phase

BATTLE MAPS

SELECTED MAPS AND STATISTICS

Battle of MARATHON

Context Greek-Persian Wars

Date September 490 BC

Location 26 miles north-east of Athens, Greece

Commanders/Forces Datis commanding 15,000 to 20,000 Persians. Miltiades and Callimachus commanding 10,000 Athenians and 1,000 Plataean hoplites

Objectives Greeks aimed to eject Persian expeditionary force from the Greek mainland

Casualties Said to be 192 Greeks, unknown number of Plataeans; 6,400 Persians

Victor Greeks

Consequences Seen as one of the decisive battles of history, demonstrating the superiority of the Greek infantry and encouraging resistance to the Persians among the Greek city-states. It broke the spell of Persian invincibility. The battle saved the Greeks from the Persian invasion and was long celebrated

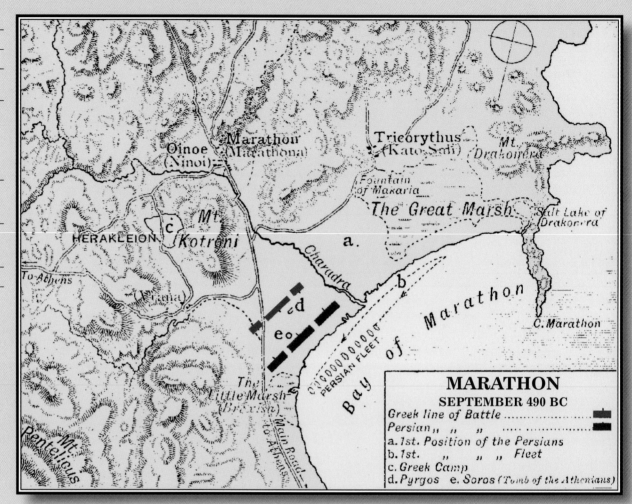

MARATHON
SEPTEMBER 490 BC
Greek line of Battle ....
Persian „   „   „
a. 1st. Position of the Persians
b. 1st.   „   „ „ Fleet
c. Greek Camp
d. Pyrgos   e. Soros (Tomb of the Athenians)

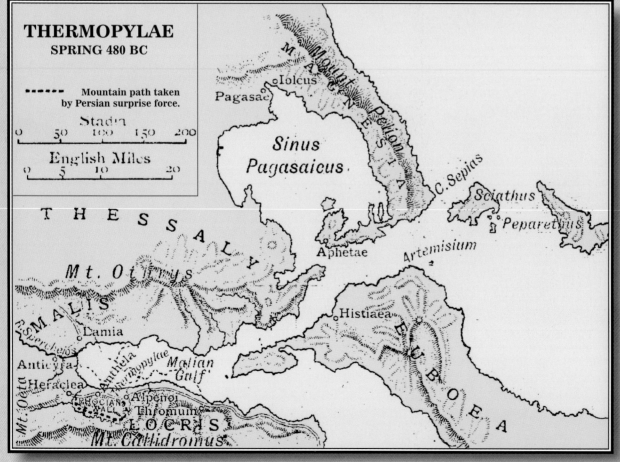

THERMOPYLAE
SPRING 480 BC

- - - - - Mountain path taken by Persian surprise force.

Stadia
0   50   100   150   200

English Miles
0   5   10   20

Battle of THERMOPYLAE

Context Greek-Persian Wars

Date Spring 480 BC

Location Narrow mountain pass south of Lamia on northern shore of Lamian Gulf, east-central Greece

Commanders/Forces Leonidas, King of Sparta, commanding 300 Spartans and 5-7,000 Greek allies. Mardonius commanding (for King Xerxes) Persians said to number 100,000 but probably a fraction of that

Objectives Greeks sought to delay the advance of the invading Persians and give time for the withdrawal and concentration of their Greek allies

Casualties Greeks overall unknown, but the Spartan element fought to the death after a traitor showed the Persians a route bypassing their defensive position. Persians unknown

Victor Persians

Consequences An epic of heroic resistance to overwhelming force, and an inspiration to the Greeks who were thereby given time to withdraw to the Corinth isthmus defence line

Battle of SALAMIS

Context Greek-Persian Wars

Date September 480 BC

Location Saronic Gulf off Piraeus, the port of Athens

Commanders/Forces Themistocles and Eurybiades commanding 366 Greek triremes from Athens and Aegina. Persians 600 galleys

Objectives Persians aimed to capture Athens and conquer Greece. Greeks aimed to defeat and eject the Persian invaders

Casualties 2-300 Persian ships. 40 Greek triremes

Victor Greeks

Consequences The first decisive naval battle of history. Persian fleet driven out of Greek waters, delaying the attack of the Persian army. The battle secured the Peloponnese, but central Greece remained in the hands of the Persians until the Battle of Plataea.

Battle of PLATAEA

Context Greek-Persian Wars

Date 479 BC

Location Southern Boeotia 12 km south of Thebes

Commanders/Forces Pausianius commanding the forces of the Peloponnesian League; 26,500 hoplites and 11,500 Athenians, Aeginetans, Plataeans and Megarians. Mardonius commanding an unknown, but large, number of Persians

Objectives Persians aimed to conquer Greece. Greeks sought a decisive battle to eject them

Casualties 1,360 Greeks and over 50,000 Persians according to Plutarch; evidently much exaggerated

Victor Greeks

Consequences Decisive end to the Persian attempt to conquer Greece and another demonstration of the superiority of Greek formations and discipline

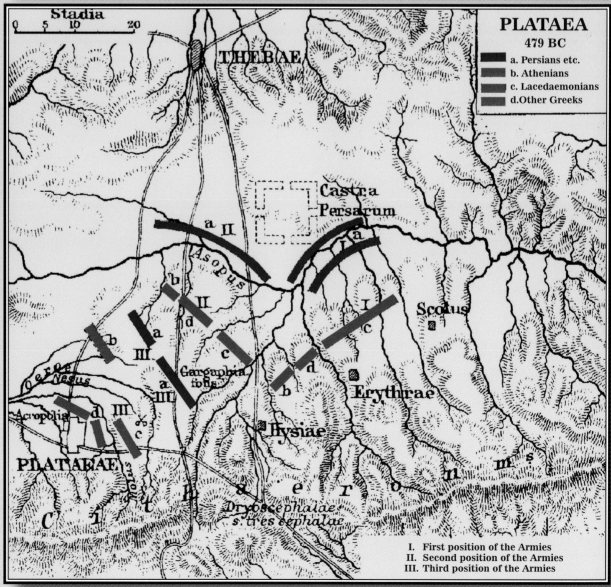

113

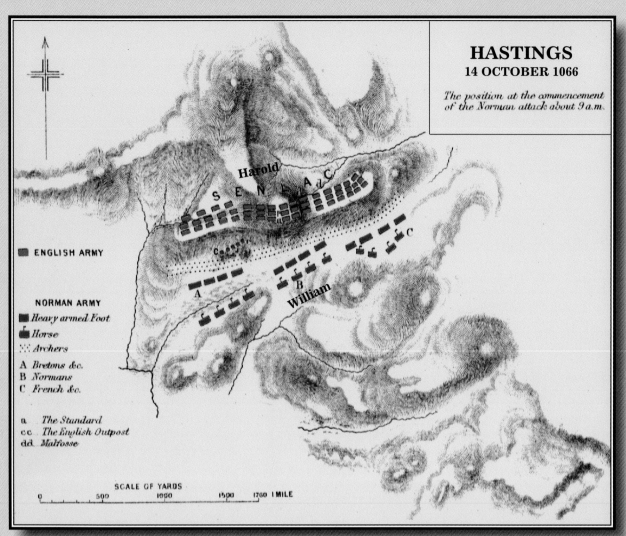

HASTINGS
14 OCTOBER 1066

The position at the commencement of the Norman attack about 9 a.m.

■ ENGLISH ARMY

NORMAN ARMY
■ *Heavy armed Foot*
▌ *Horse*
∴ *Archers*

A *Bretons &c.*
B *Normans*
C *French &c.*

a   *The Standard*
cc *The English Outpost*
dd *Malfosse*

SCALE OF YARDS
0   500   1000   1500   1760 1 MILE

Battle of HASTINGS (SENLAC)

Context Norman invasion of England

Date 14 October 1066

Location Near town of Hastings, East Sussex, south coast of England

Commanders/Forces King Harold of England commanding c.7,500 men. Duke William of Normandy commanding c.7,000

Objectives William had invaded England in pursuit of his claim to the English crown

Casualties English c.2,000 including the King and two of his brothers. Normans c.2,000

Victor Normans

Consequences William went on to conquer England and be crowned King of England

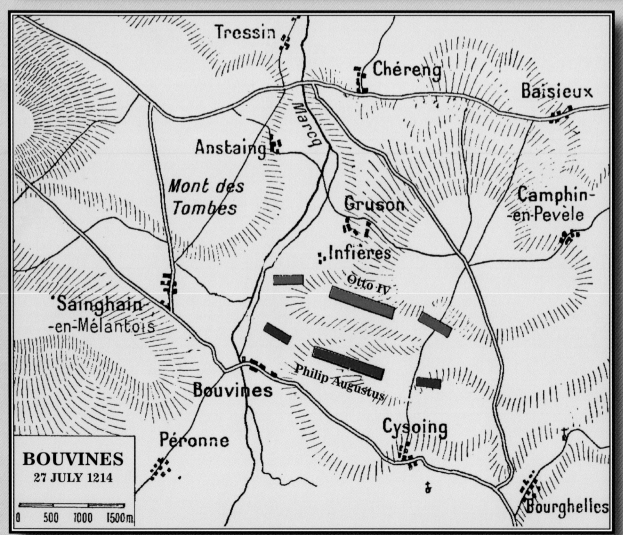

BOUVINES
27 JULY 1214

0   500   1000   1500m

Battle of BOUVINES

Context French-Angevin Wars of Philip II Augustus of France and King John of England

Date 27 July 1214

Location South-east of Lille, France

Commanders/Forces Otto IV, Holy Roman Emperor, commanding between 15,000 and 24,000 men. Philip Augustus commanding between 10,000 and 22,000 French

Objectives English attempt to regain lands in France already conquered by the French king. John was invading south-central France; John's allies, including Otto (with a force under the Earl of Salisbury), invading the north

Casualties Allies 170 knights and unknown number of infantry; Count of Flanders captured. French losses light

Victor French

Consequences Philip destroyed the coalition ranged against him and ended England's hope of recovering lands north of the Loire

Battle of CRÉCY

Context Hundred Years War

Date 26 August 1346

Location 10 miles north of Abbeville, northern France

Commanders/Forces King Edward III of England commanding c.9,000 men. King Philip IV of France commanding c.30,000

Objectives Edward was brought to battle during a chevauchée across northern France; the French sought his destruction

Casualties English c.100. French more than 1,500 nobles and knights and c.10,000 infantry

Victor English

Consequences The French army was devastated, and Edward was free to march on to Calais, which he captured

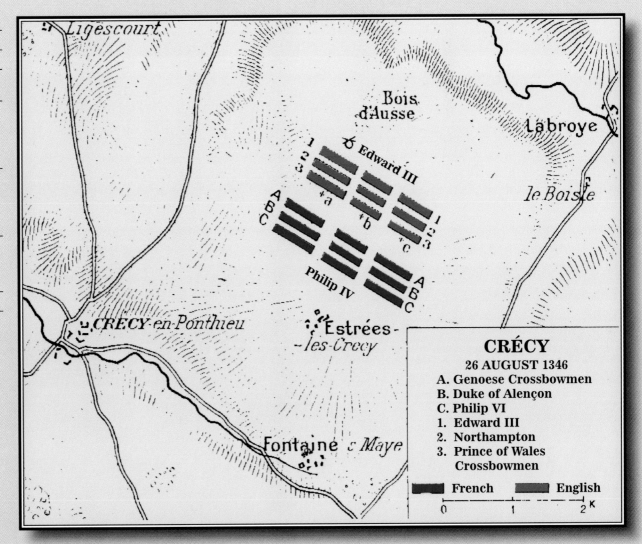

CRÉCY
26 AUGUST 1346
A. Genoese Crossbowmen
B. Duke of Alençon
C. Philip VI
1. Edward III
2. Northampton
3. Prince of Wales Crossbowmen

French   English

0   1   2 K

Battle of AGINCOURT

Context Hundred Years War

Date 25 October 1415

Location Midway between Abbeville and Calais in northern France

Commanders/Forces King Henry V of England commanding c.5,700 English. King Philip VI of France commanding c.25,000 French

Objectives French attempt to intercept and destroy the invading English who were en route to Calais

Casualties English c.400 including the Duke of York. French c.8,000 including the Constable of France, 3 dukes, 90 nobles and more than 1,500 knights

Victor English

Consequences The cream of the French army was shattered. Henry continued to Calais rather than exploiting this spectacular success by a march on Paris

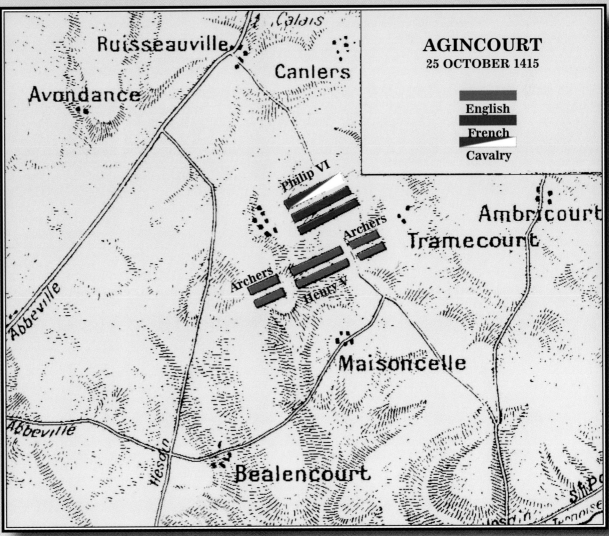

AGINCOURT
25 OCTOBER 1415

English
French
Cavalry

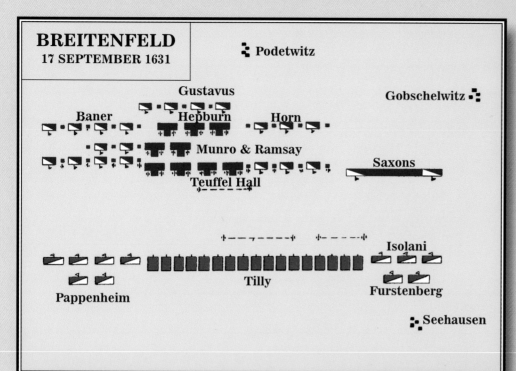

BREITENFELD
17 SEPTEMBER 1631

Podetwitz

Gustavus

Gobschelwitz

Baner
Hepburn
Horn

Munro & Ramsay

Teuffel Hall

Saxons

Isolani

Pappenheim
Tilly
Furstenberg

Seehausen

Battle of BREITENFELD

Context Thirty Years War, Swedish Phase

Date 17 September 1631

Location 5 miles north of Leipzig, Germany

Commanders/Forces Protestant army: King Gustavus Adolphus of Sweden and the Elector of Saxony commanding 36-40,000 Swedes and Saxons with 60-70 guns. Imperial/Catholic army: Count John de Tilly commanding 32,000 and 30 guns

Objectives Protestants aimed to capture Leipzig

Casualties Protestants 4,000 killed/wounded. Imperialists 7,000 killed/wounded and 6,000 taken prisoner

Victor Protestants

Consequences The Protestants captured Leipzig. Breitenfeld marked the emergence of Sweden as a major military power

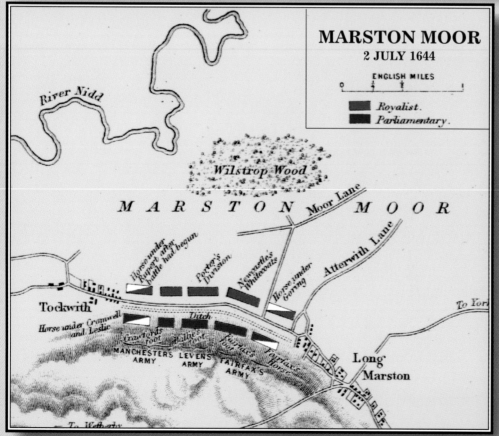

MARSTON MOOR
2 JULY 1644

ENGLISH MILES

Royalist.
Parliamentary.

River Nidd

Wilstrop Wood

MARSTON MOOR

Moor Lane

Atterwith Lane

Tockwith

Porter's Division

Newcastles Whitecoats

Horse under Goring

To York

Long Marston

Battle of MARSTON MOOR

Context English Civil War

Date 2 July 1644

Location 6 miles west of York, England

Commanders/Forces Royalists: Prince Rupert of the Rhine and the Marquis of Newcastle commanding c.11,000 foot and 6,000 cavalry.
Parliament/Scots: Fairfax, Manchester and Leven commanding the forces of Yorkshire, the Eastern Association and Scotland, consisting of 12,200 infantry, 1,000 dragoons and 8,000 cavalry

Objectives Prince Rupert, having relieved the siege of York, sought a decisive battle

Casualties Unknown, but thought to be c.3,000 Royalists and c.2,000 Allied

Victor Parliament/Scots

Consequences The north was effectively lost to the King, and York surrendered 16 July. Prince Rupert had squandered his brilliant success in relieving York by venturing upon an unnecessary battle, it being probable that the Allied army would have broken up in face of the prolongation of the siege

Battle of LÜTZEN

Context Thirty Years War, Swedish Phase

Date 16 November 1632

Location 15 miles south-west of Leipzig

Commanders/Forces Protestant army: Gustavus Adolphus commanding 16-19,000. Imperial army: Albrecht von Wallenstein commanding 15-20,000 infantry and 8-10,000 cavalry

Objectives Imperial army sought to cut the Swedish army's lines of communication from the Baltic and force the Elector of Saxony to leave the alliance with Sweden

Casualties Protestants c.5,000 killed/wounded; Gustavus Adolphus mortally wounded. Imperialists 6,000 killed/wounded

Victor Swedes

Consequences The Imperial army was frustrated in its aim; but the death of Gustavus Adolphus deprived the Protestants of the greatest general of his time

Left: The Battle of Lützen, showing the dense formations of mutually supporting pike and musket tercios in action.

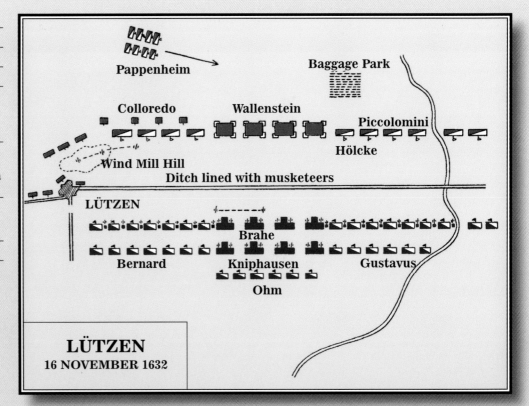

The 'gunpowder revolution' in warfare had, by the mid-seventeenth century, reached the point where artillery was becoming a major factor on the battlefield and hand-held muskets were the principal weapons of the infantry. Artillery could still be cumbersome, but one of the innovations of Gustavus Adolphus was the introduction of tactical artillery, making use of lighter, smaller-calibre guns. The musket, however, was still a relatively crude and heavy weapon, fired by matchlock. Volleys of musket fire poured into dense enemy formations at close range could be devastating, but the loading process was long and the rate of fire correspondingly slow, so that the musketeers needed protection from cavalry. Later, with lighter and easier-to-load muskets, the defence against cavalry would be to form square, with the bayonets of the infantry outward-facing, an effective hedge of sharp points. During the seventeenth century, this protection was still provided by pikes. The pike was often as long as 16 feet and en masse could present a dense hedgehog front to the enemy cavalry. Pike and musket, in square mutually supporting tercio formations, were slow to manoeuvre. Thus the decisive arm in these battles was more often than not the cavalry – in the case of the English Civil War, epitomised by Cromwell's well disciplined 'Ironsides'.

Battle of NASEBY

Context English Civil War

Date 14 June 1645

Location 8 miles south-west of Market Harborough, Midlands of England

Commanders/Forces King Charles I commanding 4,000 infantry and 5,000 cavalry. Sir Thomas Fairfax commanding Parliament's New Model Army, consisting of 7,000 infantry and 6,000 cavalry

Objectives Parliament sought a decisive victory and the speedy end of the war

Casualties Royalists 6,000 killed/wounded/taken prisoner. Parliament less than 1,000 killed/wounded

Victor Parliament

Consequences The Royalist cause was lost in the Midlands with this defeat of the King's last major army. It was the decisive battle of the English Civil War

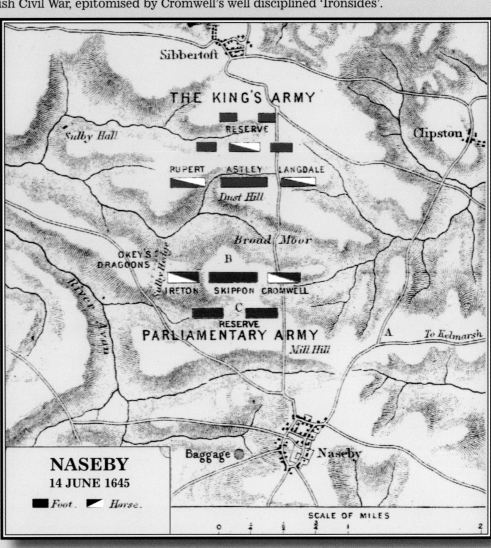

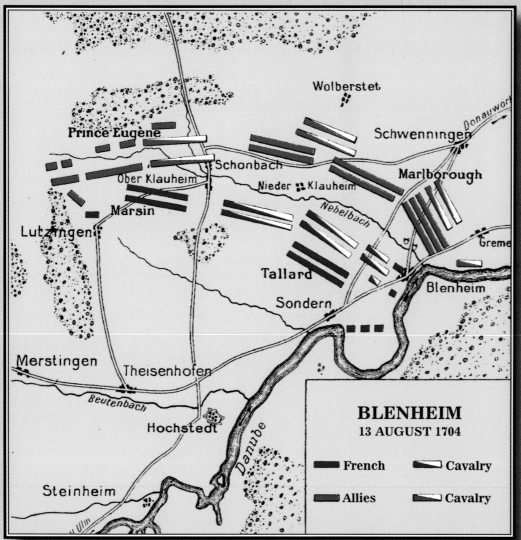

BLENHEIM
13 AUGUST 1704

▬ French	◣ Cavalry		
▬ Allies	◣ Cavalry		

MALPLAQUET
11 SEPTEMBER 1709

French	◣	▬
Allies	◣	▬

Battle of BLENHEIM

Context War of the Spanish Succession

Date 13 August 1704

Location Blindheim, 10 miles west of Donauworth, south Germany

Commanders/Forces Duke of Marlborough and Prince Eugene of Savoy commanding 52,000 men with 60 guns. Count Camille de Tallard commanding a French army of 56,000 men and 90 guns

Objectives The Allies aimed to break the deadlock in the Danube theatre of operations and remove the French threat to Vienna

Casualties Allies 12,000 killed/wounded. French 20,000 killed/wounded and 14,000 taken prisoner

Victor Allies

Consequences Vienna was saved. The battle followed a brilliant march by the Allies which completely deceived the French. The Allies now had the initiative

Battle of MALPLAQUET

Context War of the Spanish Succession

Date 11 September 1709

Location 10 miles south of Mons,

Commanders/Forces Duke of Marlborough and Prince Eugene of Savoy commanding Allied army of 110,000 men and 100 guns. Duke Claude de Villars and Louis de Boufflers commanding a French army of 80,000 men and 60 guns

Objectives The Allies aimed to take Mons, destroy the last French army and advance on Paris, thus ending the war

Casualties Allies 6,500 killed, 14,000 wounded. French 4,500 killed and 8,000 wounded

Victor Allies

Consequences The French were forced to quit the field, but the Allied victory was Pyrrhic. The bloodiest battle of the century, Malplaquet precluded any further Allied advance that year and turned British opinion against the war. It also speeded Marlborough's political downfall

Battle of POLTAVA

Context Great Northern War

Date 28 June 1709

Location Ukraine 85 miles south-west of Kharkov

Commanders/Forces Peter the Great of Russia commanding 42,000 regular troops and 35,000 irregulars. Charles XII of Sweden commanding 16,000 men

Objectives At the end of lines of communication that were tenuous at best, Charles was besieging Poltava but was forced to turn and fight Peter's approaching army

Casualties Russians 1,300 killed/wounded. Swedes 7,000 killed, 2,600 captured

Victor Russians

Consequences The remainder of the Swedish army surrendered several days later. The battle marked the end of Sweden as a great power and the appearance on the European stage of Russia as a military force

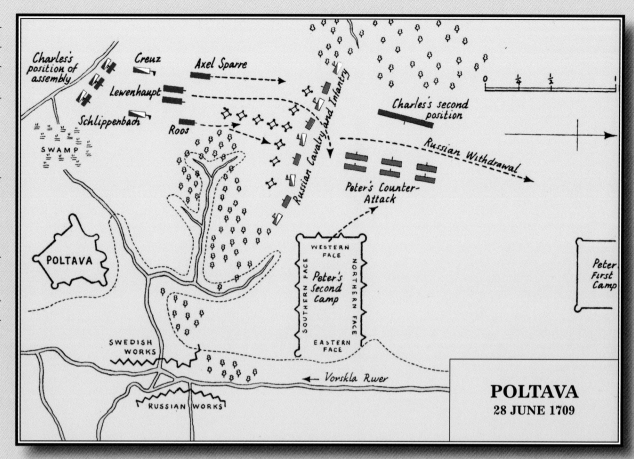

POLTAVA
28 JUNE 1709

Battle of FONTENOY

Context War of the Austrian Succession

Date 11 May 1745

Location 5 miles east of Tournai, Belgium

Commanders/Forces Duke of Cumberland commanding British army of 53,000 men and 80 guns. Maurice de Saxe commanding a French army of 52,000 and 70 guns

Objectives Cumberland planned to break the French siege of Tournai, seen as the gateway to western Flanders

Casualties British 7,500. French 7,200

Victor French

Consequences The French took Tournai and most of the Austrian Netherlands

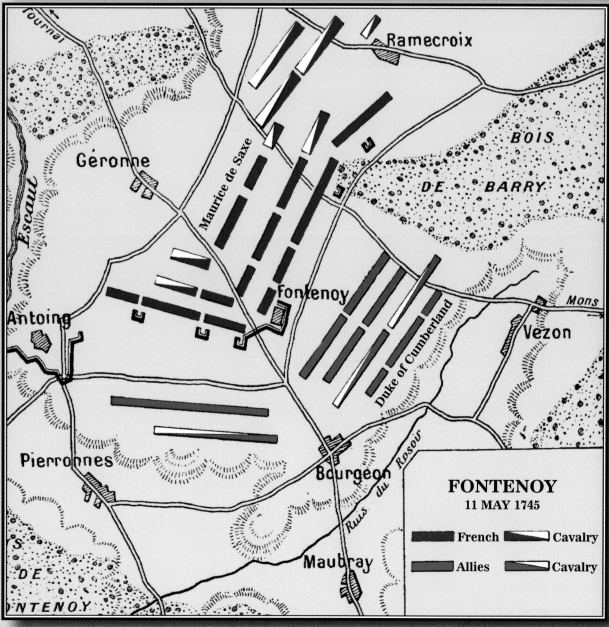

FONTENOY
11 MAY 1745

French — Cavalry
Allies — Cavalry

Battle of PLASSEY

Context Seven Years War

Date 23 June 1757

Location On the banks of the River Baggiruttee, central Bengal

Commanders/Forces Colonel Robert Clive leading about 3,000 British and Indian troops, with 8 cannon and 1 or 2 howitzers. The Nawab Suraj-ud-Daula leading 35-40,000 Bengali infantry, 18,000 mounted Pathans, plus 50 cannon and armoured elephants.

Objectives Wanting to remove British influence in Bengal, the Nawab tried to overrun the Anglo-Indian entrenchments

Casualties Light. Anglo-Indian c.22 killed, 50 wounded. Bengalis c.500 killed

Victor British.

Consequences Clive's victory put Bengal firmly in British hands and helped establish the British Empire in India

Clive on the roof of the Nawab's hunting lodge, the only building on the battlefield, at Plassey surveying the enemy's position.

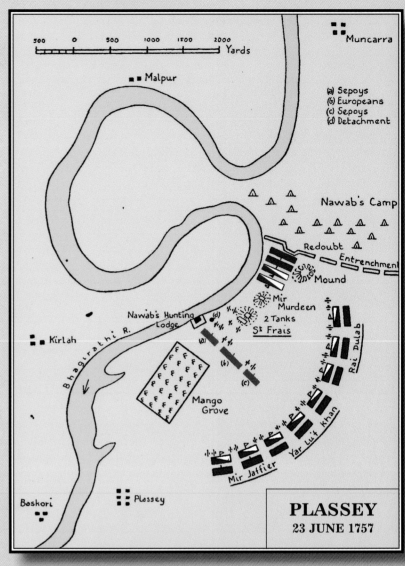

PLASSEY
23 JUNE 1757

Battle of ROSSBACH

Context Seven Years War

Date 5 November 1757

Location 26 miles south-west of Leipzig, Germany

Commanders/Forces Frederick the Great commanding 21-22,000 Prussians. Prince Charles de Soubise and Prince Joseph of Saxe-Hildburghausen commanding a Franco-Austrian army of 41,000

Objectives The Allied army was one of several major thrusts being propelled at beleaguered Prussia

Casualties Prussians 550 killed. Allies 3,000 killed, 5,000 taken prisoner

Victor Prussians

Consequences This brilliant victory enabled Frederick to meet the other armies invading Prussia. It also renewed the support of his ally, England

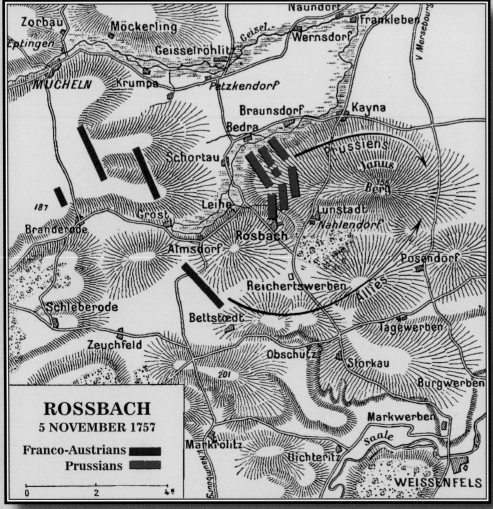

ROSSBACH
5 NOVEMBER 1757

Franco-Austrians ▬▬▬
Prussians ▬▬▬

Battle of Saratoga

Context American War of Independence

Date 7 October 1777

Location New York State

Commanders/Forces General Horatio Gates commanding 11,000 Americans. General John Burgoyne commanding 6,000 British troops

Objectives Burgoyne attempted to break free from the well-supplied American armies

Casualties British c.1,000 Americans c.150

Victor Americans

Consequences The turning-point of the war. British operations in the north were halted, and American independence began to be recognised internationally

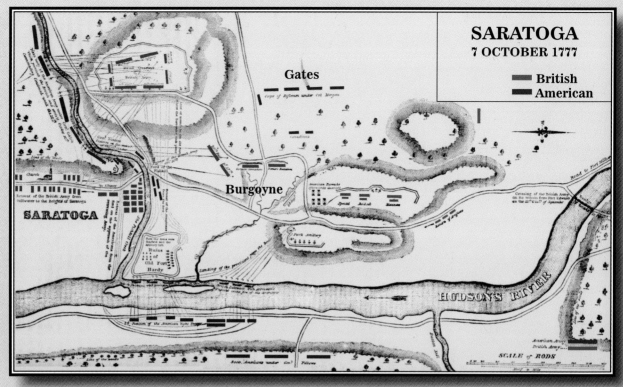

SARATOGA
7 OCTOBER 1777

▬ British
▬ American

Gates

Burgoyne

SARATOGA

HUDSON'S RIVER

SCALE of RODS

SIEGE OF YORKTOWN

Context American War of Independence

Date 28 Sept to 19 Oct 1781

Location East Virginia, 12 miles south-east of Williamsburg, overlooking the York River

Commanders/Forces General George Washington with 16,000 Americans, including militia and the French troops of General Jean-Baptiste, Comte de Rochambeau. General Charles, Earl Cornwallis, commanding 7,500 British, German and American Loyalist troops

Objectives Washington had marched through Virginia determined to find and exploit British weak points. Cornwallis intended to fortify a port position where he could be supplied by sea, but the Royal Navy temorarily lost control of the sea to the French

Casualties Light

Victor Americans

Consequences The loss of Yorktown was the *coup de grâce* to British rule in America. No further major military operations took place, and, with mounting costs, the British people lost the will to continue the war

YORKTOWN
28 SEPT TO 19 OCT 1781

▬ British
▬ American
▬ French

Choisy's H.Q.

Va. Militia

Lauzuns Legion Marines

Glouester Point

YORK RIVER

Gatinais

Touraine

Agénais

Fusiliers

FRENCH BATTERIES

YORKTOWN

Cornwallis's H.Q

Saintonge

Soissonnais

Royal Deux-Ponts

Stormed by British on Oct.15

BRITISH REDOUBTS stormed on Oct.14

2nd PARALLEL

1st PARALLEL

MOORE'S HOUSE

FRENCH

Bourbonnais

British works abandoned on Sept. 29

Field where British laid down their arms

Wormley Cr.

Fr. Park Arty.

SWAMP

Md. Va. Pa.

Steuben's H.Q.

Light Infty.

Va. Militia

Lafayette's H.Q.

Rochambeau's H.Q.

N.Y.

R.I. N.J.

TO HAMPTON

Washington's H.Q.

Am. Park Arty.

AMERICANS

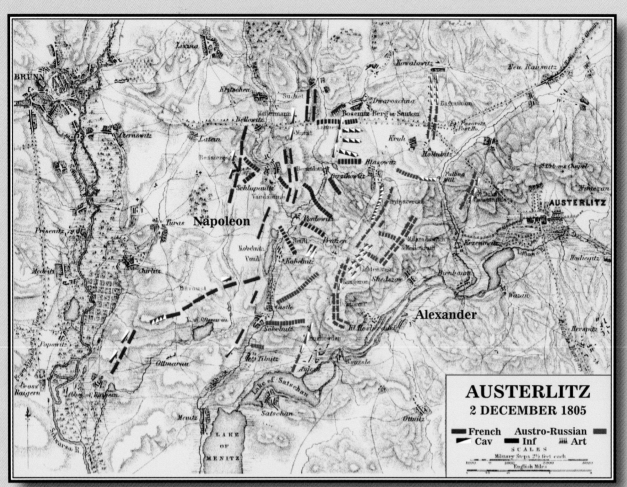

Battle of AUSTERLITZ

Context War of the Third Coalition against Napoleon

Date 2 December 1805

Location South-east Czecho-slovakia, 16 km east of Brno

Commanders/Forces Emperor Napoleon of the French commanding 50,000 infantry, 15,000 cavalry and 282 guns. Tsar Alexander of Russia commanding an Austro-Russian army of 70,000 infantry, 16,500 cavalry and 252 guns

Objectives Both sides sought a decisive battle

Casualties French c.10,000 killed/wounded. Allies 16,000 killed/wounded, 20,000 taken prisoner and 186 guns lost

Victor French

Consequences Seen by many as Napoleon's finest battle, Austerlitz eliminated Austria from the ranks of Napoleon's opponents, ended the Third Coalition and led to the establishment of the Confederation of the Rhine. (Battle also known as the Battle of the Three Emperors)

The Duke of Wellington's reputation as a general rests very largely upon his success in defensive battles, such as Talavera. During the Peninsular War he time and again demonstrated that the French column of attack could be defeated by steady troops formed in two-deep line. Wellington had an exceptional eye for terrain and would make his troops lie down, often on the reverse slope of the ridge they were defending, to protect themselves from enemy fire. As the French columns neared, his men would stand up in line and pour disciplined and devastating volleys of fire at the head of the approaching columns. European armies, often less disciplined, eventually followed the French column system, dispensing with linear tactics that harked back to the days of Frederick the Great.

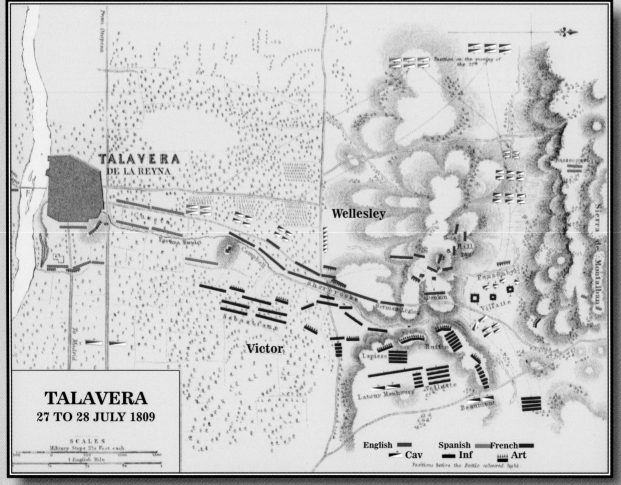

Battle of TALAVERA (DE LA REINE)

Context Peninsular War

Date 27-28 July 1809

Location 70 miles south-west of Madrid

Commanders/Forces Sir Arthur Wellesley commanding 17,600 British infantry, 2,900 cavalry and 30 guns; plus 28,000 Spanish infantry, 6,000 cavalry and 30 guns. Marshal Victor commanding (for King Joseph of Spain) a French army of 38,300 infantry, 8,400 cavalry and 80 guns

Objectives The French aimed to trap and destroy the British expeditionary force

Casualties British 5,400. French 7,300

Victor Allies

Consequences Both sides drew back after a hard fight. The French had failed to trap the British, despite heavily outnumbering them, with Wellesley's Spanish allies notable for their lack of support

Battle of SALAMANCA

Context Peninsular War

Date 22 July 1812

Location 100 miles north-west of Madrid

Commanders/Forces The Earl of Wellington commanding 48,500 infantry, 3,360 cavalry and 54 guns. Marshal Marmont commanding the French Army of Portugal with 43,000 infantry, 3,500 cavalry and 78 guns

Objectives Wellington sought a decisive battle with the French

Casualties British 4,760. French 10,000 killed/wounded and 4,000 taken prisoner

Victor British

Consequences Wellington was able briefly to enter Madrid, but he failed to destroy Marmont's army completely

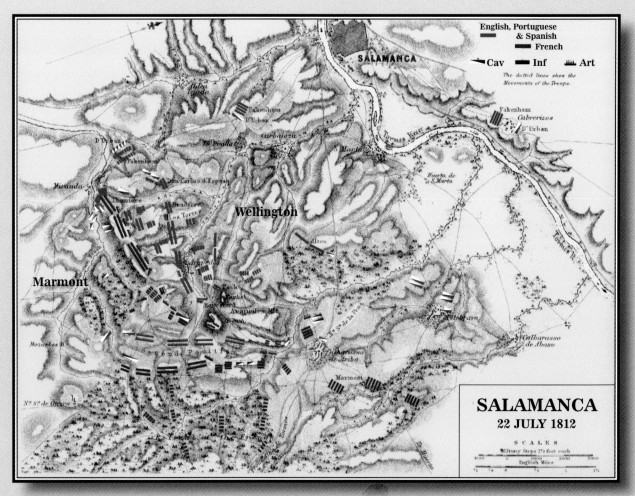

Wellington could also fight offensive battles, such as Salamanca, with consummate skill. A striking aspect of his generalship was the ability always to be at the right place at the right time, which he demonstrated for the last time at Waterloo. As at Salamanca, he personally directed every movement and manoeuvre. For Napoleon, the battles of Austerlitz and Waterloo provide a dramatic contrast. Austerlitz is generally seen as his masterpiece, an audacious, dynamic battle of manoeuvre that surprised and smashed the Allied army. Ten years later, at Waterloo, Napoleon was content to delegate the tactical handling of the battle to Marshal Ney, who proceeded to throw in a series of ill-coordinated attacks, which Wellington, by careful deployment and shifting of units, matched and repulsed.

Battle of WATERLOO

Context Napoleon's 100 Days

Date 18 June 1815

Location 15 miles S of Brussels

Commanders/Forces Emperor Napoleon I commanding French Army of the North (c.72,000 men, 236 guns). Duke of Wellington commanding Allied (Anglo-Netherlands) Army (c.82,000 infantry, 14,500 cavalry, 204 guns), reinforced later in the battle by the Prussian Army (50,000) under Marshal Blücher

Objectives Napoleon aimed to defeat Wellington's army, open the road to Brussels and destroy the coalition ranged against him

Casualties French 42,000 killed, wounded, missing; Allied Army 15,000 killed, wounded, missing; Prussians 7,000

Victor Allies.

Consequences The final, decisive defeat of Napoleon I, who abdicated four days later

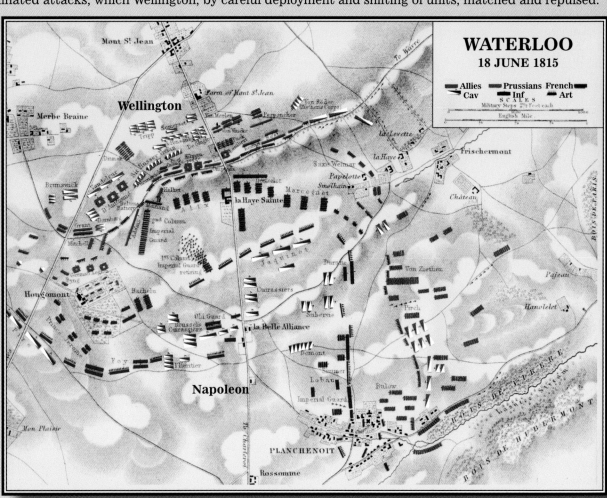

GETTYSBURG
1 TO 3 JULY 1863

SCALE OF MILES

Confederate Infantry
Confederate Artillery
Federal Infantry
Federal Artillery
Federal Cavalry

Battle of GETTYSBURG

Context American Civil War

Date 1-3 July 1863

Location junction town in southern Pennsylvania

Commanders/Forces George Meade commanding the Union Army of the Potomac (c.95,000). Robert E. Lee commanding the Confederate Army of Northern Virginia (c.75,000)

Objectives Taking the war north, Lee aimed to inflict a decisive defeat on the Army of the Potomac, which was trying to intercept him

Casualties Union c. 3,000 killed, c.15,000 wounded, c.5,000 missing. Confederates c.4,000 killed, c.19,000 wounded, c.5,000 missing

Victor Union

Consequences Lee was halted with unsustainable casualties. The climax of the battle, Pickett's charge, has been called 'the high tide of the Confederacy'; from now on the South would be entirely on the defensive, making this, with the fall of Vicksburg the following day, the turning-point in the war

Battle of THE SOMME

Context World War I, Western Front

Date 1 July to 18 November 1916

Location Area between Amiens, Bapaume and Peronne

Commanders/Forces Haig commanding BEF: c.500,000 men and 1,637 guns; Third and Fourth Armies involved (18 divisions); with French Sixth Army (13 divisions). Hindenburg/ Ludendorff commanding the Germans: sector of Second Army (11 divisions)

Objectives Joffre had planned a coordinated Anglo-French attack, the British attack being secondary, but this was modified so that the British attacked on a 15-mile front with much weaker French support

Casualties British 95,675 killed; French 50,729 killed. Germans 164,055 killed or made prisoner

Victor The British front was advanced by 6 miles

Consequences One of the controversial battles of World War. Nearly 20,000 British were killed on the first day alone

Battle of ISLY RIVER

Context French conquest of Algeria

Date 14 August 1844

Location Eastern Morocco

Commanders/Forces Marshal Bugeaud commanding 8,000 French infantry and cavalry. Algerian leader Abd el-Kader with up to 40,000 Algerians and Moroccans

Objectives French conquest of the interior of Algeria. The Algerian leader was driven across the border into Morocco, where he was joined by Sultan Abd er-Rahman

Casualties French unknown. Algerians and Moroccans 1,500

Victor French

Consequences France gained complete control of Algeria, Abd el-Kader surrendering three years later

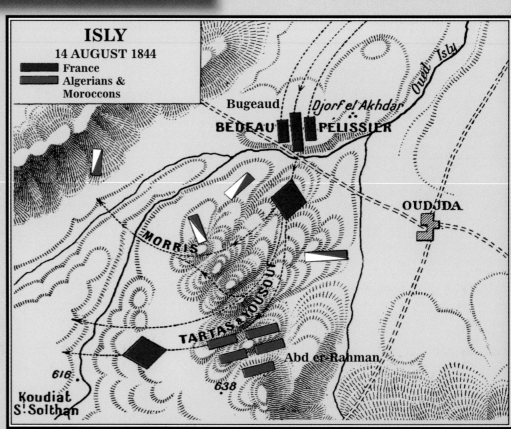

ISLY
14 AUGUST 1844

France
Algerians & Moroccans

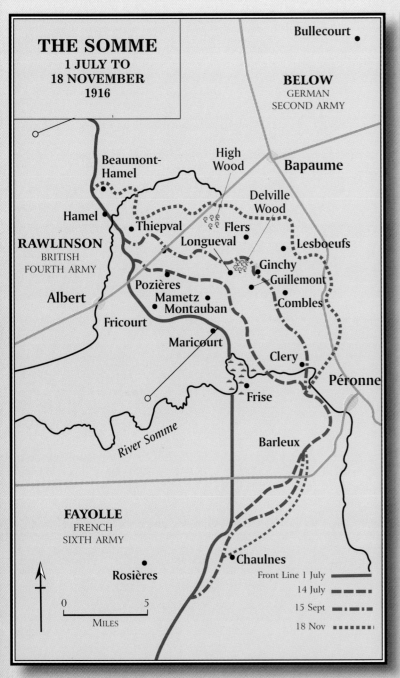

THE SOMME
1 JULY TO 18 NOVEMBER 1916

Bullecourt

BELOW
GERMAN SECOND ARMY

Beaumont-Hamel

High Wood

Bapaume

Delville Wood

Hamel

Thiepval

Flers

Longueval

Lesboeufs

RAWLINSON
BRITISH FOURTH ARMY

Ginchy

Guillemont

Albert

Pozières

Mametz

Montauban

Combles

Fricourt

Maricourt

Clery

Péronne

Frise

Barleux

FAYOLLE
FRENCH SIXTH ARMY

River Somme

Rosières

Chaulnes

Front Line 1 July
14 July
15 Sept
18 Nov

0   5
MILES

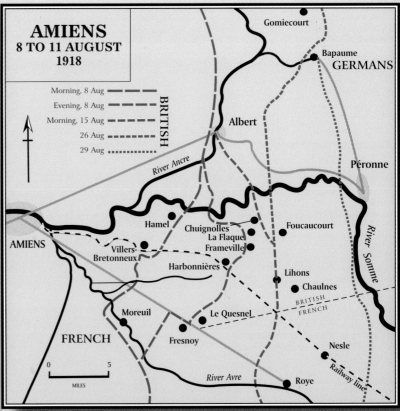

AMIENS
8 TO 11 AUGUST 1918

Gomiecourt

Bapaume

GERMANS

Morning, 8 Aug
Evening, 8 Aug
Morning, 15 Aug
26 Aug
29 Aug

BRITISH

Albert

Péronne

River Ancre

AMIENS

Hamel

Chuignolles

La Flaque

Foucaucourt

Villers-Bretonneux

Frameville

River Somme

Harbonnières

Lihons

Chaulnes

Moreuil

Le Quesnel

BRITISH
FRENCH

FRENCH

Fresnoy

Nesle

0   5
MILES

River Avre

Roye

Railway line

Battle of AMIENS

Context World War I, Western Front

Date 8-11 August 1918

Location River Somme, in Northern France, east of Amiens

Commanders/Forces Haig commanding the British Expeditionary Force; Fourth Army (Rawlinson) most directly involved (17 divisions); with French First Army (7 divisions). Ludendorff commanding the German Army; Second Army (Marwitz, 14 divisions) directly involved

Objectives The British aimed to eliminate the German salient that enabled their artillery to strike the Paris-Amiens railway

Casualties British 22,000, 480 tanks, over 148 aircraft; French 24,000. Germans 75,000 men, 500 guns, over 48 aircraft

Victor Allies

Consequences Seen as a turning-point on the Western Front. Ludendorff described 8 August, when he lost 16,000 men made prisoner in two hours, as 'the black day of the German Army'.

Battle of MEGIDDO

Context World War I, Turkish Palestine Front

Date 19-21 September 1918

Location Palestine

Commanders/Forces General Sir Edmund Allenby commanding 57,000 infantry, 12,000 cavalry and 400 guns. Liman von Sanders commanding 28,000 Turkish troops

Objectives Allenby planned a decisive blow to finish the campaign and eject the Turks from Palestine

Casualties British 5,600. Turks unknown but 75,000 taken prisoner

Victor British

Consequences Three Turkish armies were destroyed. Damascus and Aleppo fell to the British, leading to an armistice

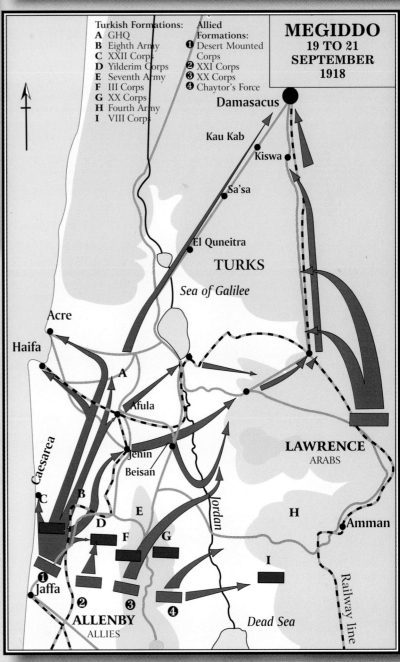

Turkish Formations:
A GHQ
B Eighth Army
C XXII Corps
D Yilderim Corps
E Seventh Army
F III Corps
G XX Corps
H Fourth Army
I VIII Corps

Allied Formations:
❶ Desert Mounted Corps
❷ XXI Corps
❸ XX Corps
❹ Chaytor's Force

MEGIDDO
19 TO 21 SEPTEMBER 1918

Damasacus

Kau Kab

Kiswa

Sa'sa

El Quneitra

TURKS

Sea of Galilee

Acre

Haifa

Caesarea

Afula

Jenin

Beisan

Jordan

LAWRENCE
ARABS

Amman

ALLENBY
ALLIES

Jaffa

Dead Sea

Railway line

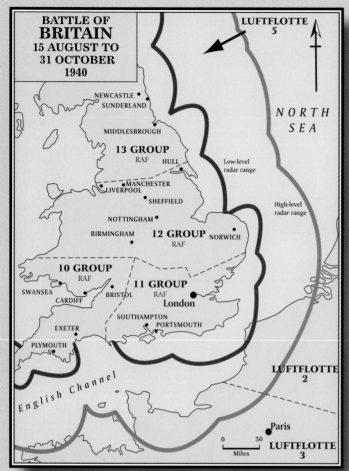

BATTLE OF BRITAIN
15 AUGUST TO 31 OCTOBER 1940

LUFTFLOTTE 5

NORTH SEA

NEWCASTLE
SUNDERLAND
MIDDLESBROUGH

13 GROUP RAF

HULL

MANCHESTER
LIVERPOOL
SHEFFIELD

Low-level radar range

NOTTINGHAM

High-level radar range

BIRMINGHAM

12 GROUP RAF

NORWICH

10 GROUP RAF

SWANSEA
CARDIFF
BRISTOL

11 GROUP RAF

London

EXETER
SOUTHAMPTON
PORTSMOUTH

PLYMOUTH

English Channel

LUFTFLOTTE 2

Paris

0   50   Miles

LUFTFLOTTE 3

STALINGRAD
19 AUGUST 1942 TO 2 FEBRUARY 1943

Axis Forces
Russian Thrusts

SOUTH-WEST FRONT
VATUTIN

5th Tank Army

1st Guards Army

21st Army

DON FRONT
ROKOSSOVSKY

65th Army

24th Army

66th Army

Romanian 3rd Army

XXVI Tank Corps

IV Tank Corps

Front Line 19 Nov

CHIR

I Tank Corps

River Volga

62nd Army

Gumrak ❷

Stalingrad

STALINGRAD FRONT
YEREMENKO

Front Line 30 Nov

Kalach

Front Line 23 Nov

XIII Mech Corps

IV Mech Corps

64th Army

57th Army

Part 4th Panzer Army

MYSHKOVA

51st Army

❶ Five Romanian Divs trapped

❷ German Sixth Army and part 4th Panzer Army

ARMY GROUP B
WEICHS

IV Cav Corps

Front Line 22 Nov

Romanian 4th Army

River Don

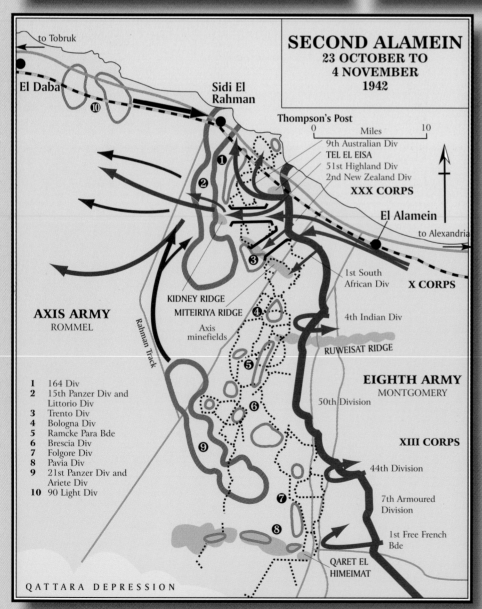

SECOND ALAMEIN
23 OCTOBER TO 4 NOVEMBER 1942

to Tobruk

El Daba ⑩

Sidi El Rahman

Thompson's Post

0   Miles   10

9th Australian Div
TEL EL EISA
51st Highland Div
2nd New Zealand Div

XXX CORPS

El Alamein

to Alexandria

1st South African Div

X CORPS

KIDNEY RIDGE
MITEIRIYA RIDGE

4th Indian Div

Axis minefields

RUWEISAT RIDGE

EIGHTH ARMY
MONTGOMERY

50th Division

AXIS ARMY
ROMMEL

Rahman Track

1   164 Div
2   15th Panzer Div and Littorio Div
3   Trento Div
4   Bologna Div
5   Ramcke Para Bde
6   Brescia Div
7   Folgore Div
8   Pavia Div
9   21st Panzer Div and Ariete Div
10   90 Light Div

XIII CORPS

44th Division

7th Armoured Division

1st Free French Bde

QARET EL HIMEIMAT

QATTARA DEPRESSION

Battle of BRITAIN

Context World War II

Date 15 August to 31 October 1940 (Blitz phase continuing into spring 1941)

Location British Isles

Commanders/Forces Reichsmarschall Hermann Göring's Luftwaffe deployed 2,784 aircraft, including 844 Messerschmitt 109s, 250 Messerschmitt 110s and 1,690 bombers. RAF Fighter Command, under the leadership of Air Chief Marshal Sir Hugh Dowding, could call on 900 fighters, including 286 Spitfires and 463 Hurricanes

Objectives The Germans needed control of the skies above England in order to mount an invasion

Casualties RAF 902 fighters. Luftwaffe 1,598 aircraft

Victor British

Consequences Hitler postponed the planned invasion on 17 September and turned his attention to the east

Second Battle of EL ALAMEIN

Context World War II: North African Campaign

Date 23 October to 4 November 1942

Location Coast of Egypt 65 miles west of Alexandria

Commanders/Forces General Sir Bernard Montgomery commanding British Eighth Army with 195,000 men, 1,029 tanks and 2,311 guns. Field Marshal Erwin Rommel commanding Panzer Army Africa with 104,000 men (50,000 Germans, 54,000 Italians), 520 tanks and 1,219 guns.

Objectives Having held Rommel's advance into Egypt, and having built up a considerable superiority in forces, Montgomery planned to break Rommel's army and eject him from North Africa

Casualties British 2,350 killed, 8,950 wounded. Axis 10,000 killed, 15,000 wounded, 30,000 made prisoner; most tanks lost

Victor British

Consequences Decisive end to the Western Desert campaign; Rommel retreated to Tunisia, where, reinforced from Europe, he fought a losing campaign against Allied forces from east and west

Battle of STALINGRAD

Context World War II: Eastern Front

Date 19 August 1942 to 2 February 1943

Location Russian city on the western bank of the lower Volga

Commanders/Forces Von Paulus commanding German Sixth Army with c.300,000 troops. Soviet General Yeremenko commanding the Stalingrad Front, with General Chuikov commanding 62nd Army with over 300,000 men

Objectives Germans aimed to capture Stalingrad and the line of the Volga to protect the flank of the offensive into the Caucasus.

Casualties Germans 110,000 killed, 90,000 taken prisoner. Russians unknown

Victor Russians

Consequences The turning-point on the Eastern Front. The German twin offensives to Stalingrad and the Caucasus gave the Soviets the chance to isolate and destroy Sixth Army, which they did, despite Manstein's attempts to break through to the beleaguered Paulus. The battle for the city was an epic house-to-house struggle, and Luftwaffe attempts to replenish Sixth Army by air alone proved hopelessly inadequate

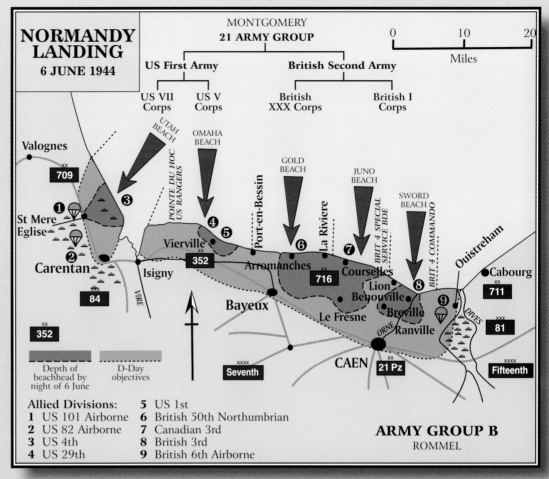

NORMANDY (D-DAY) LANDING

Context World War II: North-West Europe Campaign

Date 6 June 1944

Location Coast of Normandy between the River Orne and the Cotentin Peninsula, northern France

Commanders/Forces General Eisenhower (Supreme Allied Commander) with General Sir Bernard Montgomery's 21st Army Group commanding the landings; 175,000 men (150,000 to land on the first day). Field Marshal Erwin Rommel commanding German Army Group B (80,000 in the beachhead sector)

Objectives The opening of the third front against the Germans on the mainland of Europe

Casualties Allies 2,500 killed, 8,500 wounded. German losses unknown

Victor Allies

Consequences Though they did not attain their planned objec-tives, the Allies were firmly ashore. It would take the rest of June and most of July to achieve a breakout from the beachhead

Battle of KUWAIT (OPERATION 'DESERT SABRE')

Context Gulf War

Date 24-28 February 1991

Location Kuwait and southern Iraq at the head of the Persian Gulf

Commanders/Forces General Norman Schwarzkopf commanding multi-national coalition forces comprising 665,000 troops. Possibly 500,000 Iraqi troops nominally commanded by President Saddam Hussein

Objectives Liberation of Kuwait from Iraqi occupation

Casualties Coalition c.500 killed or wounded. Iraq esti-mated 60,000 killed and 175,000 made prisoner

Victor Allies

Consequences Kuwait was freed and another Middle East crisis ended. But Saddam Hussein's despotic régime continued to make mischief in the region

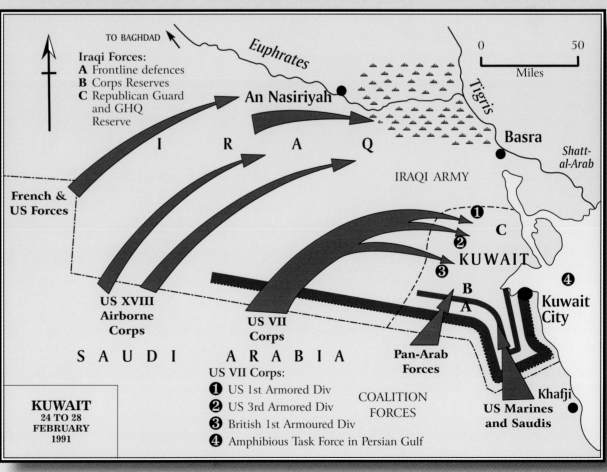

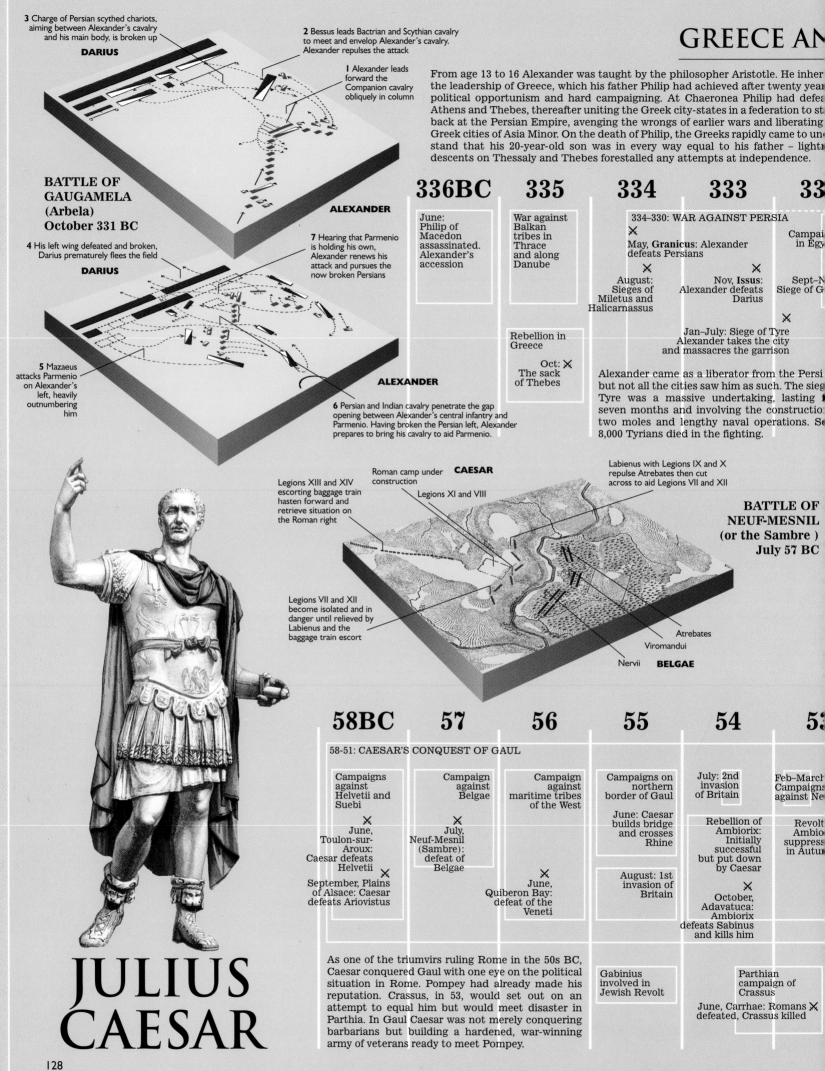

3 Charge of Persian scythed chariots, aiming between Alexander's cavalry and his main body, is broken up

DARIUS

2 Bessus leads Bactrian and Scythian cavalry to meet and envelop Alexander's cavalry. Alexander repulses the attack

1 Alexander leads forward the Companion cavalry obliquely in column

ALEXANDER

BATTLE OF GAUGAMELA (Arbela) October 331 BC

4 His left wing defeated and broken, Darius prematurely flees the field

DARIUS

7 Hearing that Parmenio is holding his own, Alexander renews his attack and pursues the now broken Persians

5 Mazaeus attacks Parmenio on Alexander's left, heavily outnumbering him

ALEXANDER

6 Persian and Indian cavalry penetrate the gap opening between Alexander's central infantry and Parmenio. Having broken the Persian left, Alexander prepares to bring his cavalry to aid Parmenio.

GREECE AN

From age 13 to 16 Alexander was taught by the philosopher Aristotle. He inher the leadership of Greece, which his father Philip had achieved after twenty year political opportunism and hard campaigning. At Chaeronea Philip had defea Athens and Thebes, thereafter uniting the Greek city-states in a federation to st back at the Persian Empire, avenging the wrongs of earlier wars and liberating Greek cities of Asia Minor. On the death of Philip, the Greeks rapidly came to un stand that his 20-year-old son was in every way equal to his father – lightn descents on Thessaly and Thebes forestalled any attempts at independence.

336BC	**335**	**334**	**333**	**33**
June: Philip of Macedon assassinated. Alexander's accession	War against Balkan tribes in Thrace and along Danube	334–330: WAR AGAINST PERSIA ✕ May, **Granicus**: Alexander defeats Persians ✕ August: Sieges of Miletus and Halicarnassus	✕ Nov, **Issus**: Alexander defeats Darius	Campai in Egy Sept–N Siege of G
	Rebellion in Greece Oct: ✕ The sack of Thebes		Jan–July: Siege of Tyre Alexander takes the city and massacres the garrison ✕	

Alexander came as a liberator from the Persi but not all the cities saw him as such. The sieg Tyre was a massive undertaking, lasting seven months and involving the constructio two moles and lengthy naval operations. Se 8,000 Tyrians died in the fighting.

Roman camp under construction

CAESAR

Legions XIII and XIV escorting baggage train hasten forward and retrieve situation on the Roman right

Legions XI and VIII

Labienus with Legions IX and X repulse Atrebates then cut across to aid Legions VII and XII

BATTLE OF NEUF-MESNIL (or the Sambre) July 57 BC

Legions VII and XII become isolated and in danger until relieved by Labienus and the baggage train escort

Atrebates

Viromandui

Nervii

BELGAE

JULIUS CAESAR

58BC	**57**	**56**	**55**	**54**	**53**
58-51: CAESAR'S CONQUEST OF GAUL					
Campaigns against Helvetii and Suebi ✕ June, Toulon-sur-Aroux: Caesar defeats Helvetii ✕ September, Plains of Alsace: Caesar defeats Ariovistus	Campaign against Belgae ✕ July, Neuf-Mesnil (Sambre): defeat of Belgae	Campaign against maritime tribes of the West ✕ June, Quiberon Bay: defeat of the Veneti	Campaigns on northern border of Gaul June: Caesar builds bridge and crosses Rhine August: 1st invasion of Britain	July: 2nd invasion of Britain Rebellion of Ambiorix: Initially successful but put down by Caesar ✕ October, Adavatuca: Ambiorix defeats Sabinus and kills him	Feb–March Campaigns against Ne Revolt Ambio suppress in Autun
			Gabinius involved in Jewish Revolt	Parthian campaign of Crassus June, Carrhae: Romans ✕ defeated, Crassus killed	

As one of the triumvirs ruling Rome in the 50s BC, Caesar conquered Gaul with one eye on the political situation in Rome. Pompey had already made his reputation. Crassus, in 53, would set out on an attempt to equal him but would meet disaster in Parthia. In Gaul Caesar was not merely conquering barbarians but building a hardened, war-winning army of veterans ready to meet Pompey.

contrast to the seasonal, limited warfare of the Greek cities, the acedonians waged a new type of warfare, with a professional nding army able take the field at all times of the year and to ow up victory on the battlefield, exploiting success to make ting gains. Alexander fully understood the importance of a entless pursuit, so that the set-piece battle was but the first step total victory. Only thus could he contemplate the conquest of a at empire. His exploits were achieved in just a dozen years.

ALEXANDER THE GREAT

Alexander, wrote Delbrück, 'occupies a unique position in that he combined in one person the world-conquering strategist and the unexcelled courageous knightly combatant'.

331	330	329	328	327	326	325	324	323

exander sses the gris to tinue the r with rius

✕ Oct, uagamela: Alexander again routs us' army of ersians and Greek ercenaries

July: Death of Darius

Jan–May: The occupation of Mesopotamia and Babylon

✕ March: Siege of Persepolis. Alexander massacres Persian garrison

Spartan uprising

May, Megalopolis: ✕ tipater defeats Agis

Summer: Campaign against Bactrians

327–326: Campaign in NW India in alliance with Taxila against Porus

✕ May, **Hydaspes**: Alexander defeats Porus's Indian army

326–325: War against the Malli and campaigns in the Indus valley

324: Return to Babylon followed by Alexander's death from fever in June 323

Summer: Mutiny at Opis

At Issus, Darius fled. After an interlude in Egypt, Alexander set off in pursuit of the Persian king in 331, defeating him again at Gaugamela. Again Alexander pursued Darius, but was to find him dying, betrayed by his officers led by Bessus, Satrap of Bactria. By 330 the Persian Empire was Alexander's. Four years of guerrilla fighting and mountain warfare ensued in the north-east of the empire, subduing the tribes at the very edges of the great empire. In 327 a new enterprise drew the Greeks towards the Indus, and on the banks of the Hydaspes Alexander defeated an Indian army. Further conquests beckoned, but the army had had enough. Having followed him for more than 2,000 miles from Greece; now they would go no farther; their king had turned explorer. The Greeks returned to Babylon, by land and by sea, Alexander's new fleet braving the Indian Ocean, the army marching across the Gedrosian desert.

etonius relates that, some and a half centuries after e death of Alexander, the 32- ar-old Caesar, while quaestor Rome's province of Farther ain, saw a statue of exander and was heard to h, vexed that at an age when e Macedonian had conquer- practically all the known rld he himself had done thing in the least epoch- king. But circumstances re very different. Caesar ws a king, but a noble in a rcely competitive political vironment. He was to fight l win two major wars and ve an indelible impression the history of the world.

BATTLE OF PHARSALUS 29 June 48 BC

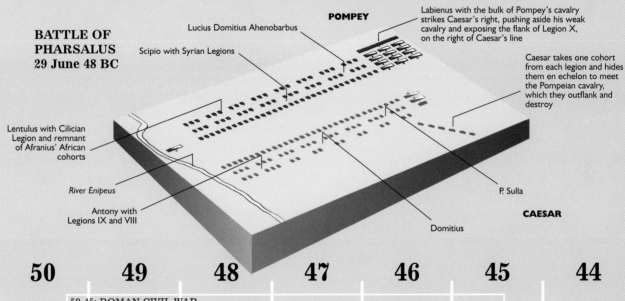

Scipio with Syrian Legions

Lucius Domitius Ahenobarbus

POMPEY

Labienus with the bulk of Pompey's cavalry strikes Caesar's right, pushing aside his weak cavalry and exposing the flank of Legion X, on the right of Caesar's line

Caesar takes one cohort from each legion and hides them en echelon to meet the Pompeian cavalry, which they outflank and destroy

Lentulus with Cilician Legion and remnant of Afranius' African cohorts

River Enipeus

Antony with Legions IX and VIII

Domitius

P. Sulla

CAESAR

52	51	50	49	48	47	46	45	44

50-45: ROMAN CIVIL WAR

c 53 – y 52: ellion of rcingetorix Gaul

March, Noviodunum: aesar defeats Vercingetorix

May, Lutetia: Labienus defeats Gauls

May, Gergovia: Vercingetorix repulses Caesar

✕ Siege and battle of Alesia: Vercingetorix surrenders after costly battle

Spring: Siege of Uxellodunum: Rebilus defeats Gauls

2nd Civil War begins: Caesar crosses the Rubicon on 17 Dec

July: Manoeuvres and two battles of Ilerda

✕ Apr to Sept: Siege of Massilia

2 March: Caesar enters Rome after taking Corfinium

April–Sept: 1st Spanish campaign

Oct 49–Aug 48: Dyrrhachium campaign against Pompey

Campaign and battle (29 June) of Pharsalus. Caesar defeats Pompey, who flees to Egypt

March–May: ✕ Siege of July, Bagradas: Dyrrhachium Curio defeated in Africa

October: Mutiny of Caesar's army at Placentia

27 Sept: ✕ Destruction of the Egyptian fleet

✕3 Feb, Nile: Caesar defeats Ptolemy XIII

Oct 47–April 46: Campaign in Africa against Pompeians

✕ ✕ 8 Nov, Ruspina: 6 Feb, Thapsus: Pompeians Caesar defeats defeat Caesar Pompeians

May–June: Revolt of Phanaces, son of Mithridates

Nicopolis: ✕✕ June, Zela: Pharnaces Caesar destroys defeats Pharnaces Calvinus

August 48–May 47, Egyptian campaign. Caesar sets Cleopatra on the throne of Egypt

Nov 46–June 45: 2nd Spanish Campaign

✕ March, Munda: Caesar defeats Gnaeus Pompeius

After being made dictator for life in February, Caesar is assassinated on 15 March

e conquest of Gaul and the expeditions to tain were followed by revolt in Gaul. numbered and surrounded once more by tile tribes, Caesar marched and fought l the rebel leader, Vercingetorix, was ieged at Alesia. By dint of herculean efforts ge lines a dozen miles long were dug and a t relieving army defeated, one of the atest feats of arms in ancient times

With Caesar, the art of war in the ancient world reaches its peak. He was not an innovator but a supreme exponent of Roman warfare. The Roman cohort was a much finer instrument of war than the old phalanx, enabling him to move and manoeuvre with speed. He took risks, and sometimes these failed, condemning him to a long, hard campaign where the spade was as important as the shovel. Always, however, his indomitable will- power – and the endurance of his veterans – brought victory.

THE HUNDRED YEARS WAR, 1337

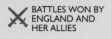 BATTLES WON BY ENGLAND AND HER ALLIES

 SIEGES WON BY ENGLAND AND HER ALLIES

 BATTLES WON BY FRANCE AND HER ALLIES

 SIEGES WON BY FRANCE AND HER ALLIES

| | 1335 | 1340 | 1345 | 1350 | 1355 | 1360 | 1365 | 1370 | 1375 | 1380 | 1385 |

KINGS OF FRANCE: PHILIP VI: REIGN 1328-50 | JOHN II: REIGN 1350-64 | CHARLES V: REIGN 1364-80

KINGS OF ENGLAND: EDWARD III: REIGN 1327-77 | RIC...

POLITICS

1337: EDWARD III LAYS CLAIM TO FRENCH CROWN

1343: TRUCE OF MALSTROIT

1340-41: TRUCE OF ESPLECHIN

1347: OUT BREAK OF BLACK DEATH

1357: TREATY OF BORDEAUX

1359: 1ST & 2ND TREATIES OF LONDON

1360: TREATY OF BRETIGNY

1364: PEACE OF GUÉRANDE

1368: CHARLES V BREAKS TREATY OF BRETIGNY

1369-96: BERTRAND DU GUESCLIN PROMINANT IN THE FIGHT AGAINST THE ENGLISH

1376: DEATH OF BLACK PRINCE

1376: TRUCE BETWEEN FRANCE & ENGLAND

LOW COUNTRIES PICARDY ISLE DE FRANCE

1338: EDWARD III CROSSES TO FLANDERS, JOINED BY FLEMINGS

26 AUGUST 1346: CRÉCY

20-26 SEPT 1339: EDWARD'S SEIGE OF CAMBRAI FAILS

4 SEPT 1346-4 AUG 1347: CALAIS

6 JUNE 1351: ARDES

1359: EDWARD III CONDUCTS A CHEVAUCHÉE FROM CALAIS TO PARIS VIA RHEIMS, WHERE HE IS CHECKED. HE TAKES PARIS SUBURBS

4 DEC 1359-11 JAN 1360: ENGLISH SIEGE OF RHEIMS FAILS

AUG 1373: TALBOT BEGINS HIS GRANDE CHEVAUCHÉE THROUGH FRANCE

1371: BOURGNEUF. ENGLISH CRUSH FLEMISH

1370: SIR ROBERT KNOWLES CONDUCTS A CHEVAUCHÉE FROM CALAIS VIA THE ISLE DE FRANCE, STOPPPED AT PONTVALLION BY DU GUESCLIN

1382: ROOSBEK... FRENCH VICTO... OVER FLEMISH

NORMANDY MAINE ANJOU

22 JUNE-12 JULY 1355: LANCASTER'S CHEVAUCHÉE

26 JULY 1346: CAEN

JOHN II

4 DEC 1370: PONTVALLION

16 MAY 1364: COCHEREL

1380: THE EARL OF BUCKINGHAM CONDUCTS A CHEVAUCHÉE FROM CALAIS TO MAINE A... THEN ON TO RENNE... CAPITAL OF BRITTA...

BRITTANY

30 SEPT 1342: MORLAIX

9 JUNE 1346: ST POL DE LÉON

20 JUNE 1347: ROCHE-DERRIEN

27 MARCH 1351: BATTLE OF THE THIRTY

14 AUG 1352: MAURON

29 AUG 1364: AURAY. DU GUESCLIN IS CAPTURED BUT RANSOMED

1372: BRITTANY IS CONQUERED BY DU GUESCLIN AND CLISSON

1380: CHATEAUNEUF-DE-RONDON. DU GUESCLIN KILLED

GASCONY AQUITAINE

21 OCT 1345: AUBEROCHE

SUMMER 1349: LUNALONGE

7 APRIL 1352: SAINTES

5 OCT-9 DEC 1355: THE BLACK PRINCE'S GRANDE CHEVAUCHÉE

BLACK PRINCE CONDUCTS ANOTHER CHEVAUCHÉE.

19 SEPT 1356: POITIERS. KING JOHN OF FRANCE CAPTURED

25 SEPT 1370: SACK OF LIMOGES

JULY 1372: CHIZE

AUG 1372: SOUBISE

1374: DU GUESCLIN CONQUERS GUYENNE

DEC 1373: THE ARRIVAL IN BORDEAUX OF JOHN OF GAUNT'S DISASTROUS CHEVAUCHÉE FROM CALAIS

BURGUNDY

1359: PARTS OF BURGUNDY PILLAGED BY ENGLISH DURING THE CHEVAUCHÉE OF EDWARD III

CHARLES V

HENRY IV

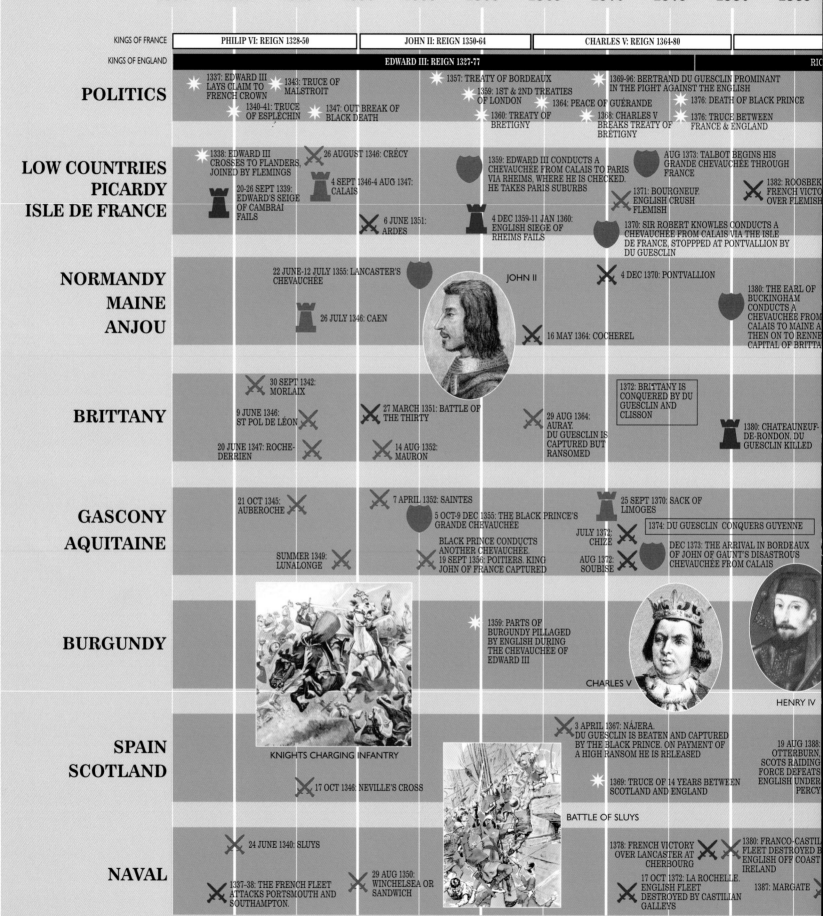

KNIGHTS CHARGING INFANTRY

SPAIN SCOTLAND

3 APRIL 1367: NÁJERA. DU GUESCLIN IS BEATEN AND CAPTURED BY THE BLACK PRINCE. ON PAYMENT OF A HIGH RANSOM HE IS RELEASED

1369: TRUCE OF 14 YEARS BETWEEN SCOTLAND AND ENGLAND

17 OCT 1346: NEVILLE'S CROSS

19 AUG 1388: OTTERBURN, SCOTS RAIDING FORCE DEFEATS ENGLISH UNDER PERCY

BATTLE OF SLUYS

NAVAL

24 JUNE 1340: SLUYS

1337-38: THE FRENCH FLEET ATTACKS PORTSMOUTH AND SOUTHAMPTON.

29 AUG 1350: WINCHELSEA OR SANDWICH

1378: FRENCH VICTORY OVER LANCASTER AT CHERBOURG

17 OCT 1372: LA ROCHELLE. ENGLISH FLEET DESTROYED BY CASTILIAN GALLEYS

1380: FRANCO-CASTIL... FLEET DESTROYED B... ENGLISH OFF COAST... IRELAND

1387: MARGATE

453

More properly a series of wars, the Hundred Years War was fought essentially between the kings of England and France, with the Duke of Burgundy as a third major player in the game. The first phase, 1337–60 was fought over the Duchy of Guyenne. Only in 1340 did Edward III make claim to the throne of France. 1360–1413 was a period of confused conflict with no decisive outcome. 1413–53 saw Henry V's revival of the claim to the French throne, but his early death threw all into the melting pot once again. Thereafter the intervention of Joan of Arc was decisive, coupled with the return of Burgundy to alliance with the French and the weakness of the English monarchy during the reign of Henry VI.

1395	1400	1405	1410	1415	1420	1425	1430	1435	1440	1445	1450	1455

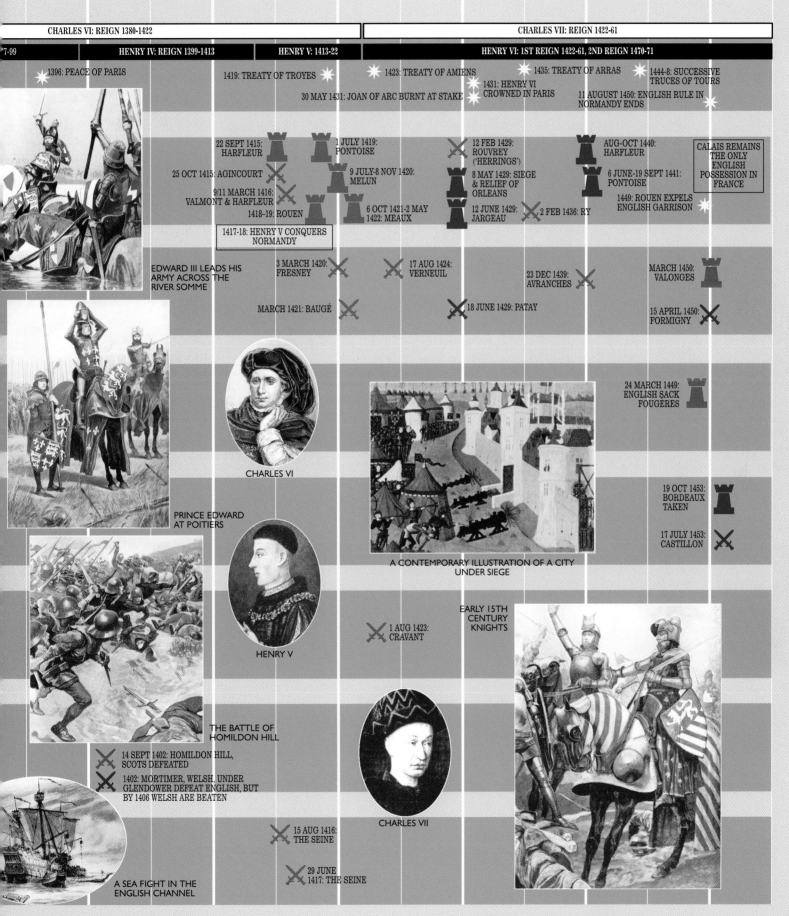

CHARLES VI: REIGN 1380-1422

CHARLES VII: REIGN 1422-61

77-99

HENRY IV: REIGN 1399-1413

HENRY V: 1413-22

HENRY VI: 1ST REIGN 1422-61, 2ND REIGN 1470-71

1396: PEACE OF PARIS

1419: TREATY OF TROYES

1423: TREATY OF AMIENS

1435: TREATY OF ARRAS

1444-8: SUCCESSIVE TRUCES OF TOURS

1431: HENRY VI CROWNED IN PARIS

30 MAY 1431: JOAN OF ARC BURNT AT STAKE

11 AUGUST 1450: ENGLISH RULE IN NORMANDY ENDS

22 SEPT 1415: HARFLEUR

1 JULY 1419: PONTOISE

12 FEB 1429: ROUVREY ('HERRINGS')

AUG-OCT 1440: HARFLEUR

CALAIS REMAINS THE ONLY ENGLISH POSSESSION IN FRANCE

25 OCT 1415: AGINCOURT

9 JULY-8 NOV 1420: MELUN

8 MAY 1429: SIEGE & RELIEF OF ORLEANS

6 JUNE-19 SEPT 1441: PONTOISE

9/11 MARCH 1416: VALMONT & HARFLEUR

1449: ROUEN EXPELS ENGLISH GARRISON

1418-19: ROUEN

6 OCT 1421-2 MAY 1422: MEAUX

12 JUNE 1429: JARGEAU

2 FEB 1436: RY

1417-18: HENRY V CONQUERS NORMANDY

EDWARD III LEADS HIS ARMY ACROSS THE RIVER SOMME

3 MARCH 1420: FRESNEY

17 AUG 1424: VERNEUIL

23 DEC 1439: AVRANCHES

MARCH 1450: VALONGES

MARCH 1421: BAUGÉ

18 JUNE 1429: PATAY

15 APRIL 1450: FORMIGNY

CHARLES VI

PRINCE EDWARD AT POITIERS

24 MARCH 1449: ENGLISH SACK FOUGERES

A CONTEMPORARY ILLUSTRATION OF A CITY UNDER SIEGE

19 OCT 1453: BORDEAUX TAKEN

17 JULY 1453: CASTILLON

HENRY V

EARLY 15TH CENTURY KNIGHTS

1 AUG 1423: CRAVANT

THE BATTLE OF HOMILDON HILL

14 SEPT 1402: HOMILDON HILL, SCOTS DEFEATED

1402: MORTIMER, WELSH, UNDER GLENDOWER DEFEAT ENGLISH, BUT BY 1406 WELSH ARE BEATEN

CHARLES VII

15 AUG 1416: THE SEINE

29 JUNE 1417: THE SEINE

A SEA FIGHT IN THE ENGLISH CHANNEL

131

THE WARS OF JAPAN

794 Capital transferred to Heian (Kyoto)
940 Battle of Kojima End of rebellion of Taira Masakado
989 First armed conflict between the warrior monks of Kyoto and Nara

Japanese swordsmen in Action

1050 .... **1100** **1150**

1051-63 Early Nine Years War earns great glory for the Minamoto family

Toyotomi Hideyoshi, d.1598, leading 2nd Korean Invasion

1086-9 Later Three Years War consolidates the Minamoto as one of Japan's two leading warrior families serving the Emperor

Minamoto Yoritomo, the first shogun (or 'C-in-C for suppressing barbarians'), 1192

1146 Taira Kiyomori frustrates a warrior monk assault on Kyoto ✕

1156 Hogen Insurrection sees samurai families fighting for the first time over the Imperial succession

1160 Heiji Incident the first direct clash between the Taira and Minamoto. The Taira are victorious

118[0] Battle The ve[rry] Mina[moto] Yorim[oto] defeat[s] the

1180 Siege of Taira burn th[e] in revenge f[or] monks' supp[ort] Mina[moto]

1300 .... **1350** **1400**

1331 Emperor Go-Daigo begins a war to overthrow the Hojo Regency

14th century Samurai

1333-1392 Nanbokucho Wars (Between Southern and Northern Court)

1419 Korean force lands on Tsushima in revenge for pirate raids from Japan

✕ **1331 Go-Daigo besieged at Kasagi**
1331 Kusunoki Masashige fortifies Akasaka in support of Go-Daigo
✕ **1333 Siege of Chihaya.** Driven from Akasaka, Masashige defends at a long and celebrated siege
✕ **1333** Nitta Yoshisada captures **Kamakura**, and the last of the Hojo Regents commit suicide

Dissatisfied by his rewards, Ashikaga Takauji sets up a rival Emperor (the Northern Court) and a capital in Kyoto. Go-Daigo (the Southern Court) flees to Yoshino

✕ **1336 Tatarahama** Driven from Kyoto, Ashikaga raises an army in Kyushu and defeats rivals
✕ **1336 Minatogawa** Ashikaga defeats Kusunoki Masashige and re-enters Kyoto in triumph
✕ **1338 Fujishima** Death of Nitta Yoshisada

✕ **1348 Shijo Nawate** Kusunoki Masatsura (son of Masashige) is defeated
✕ **1352** Southern Court supporters capture **Kyoto** but are soon driven out

For 50 years, the camp[aign] continues with skirmishes [and] raids from the Southern C[ourt]

1392 Ashikaga Yoshimitsu ne[goti]ates an end to the division[.] Southern Court parti[sans] continue resistance up till[...]

1550 .... **1555** .... **1560** .... **1565** .... **1570** .... 1[...]

1467-1615 Period of Warring States →

1560-1591 Age of Unification

1408-1589 Slide into Anarchy and Growth of Daimyo Territories

✕ **1560 Okehazama** Oda Nobunaga defeats Imagawa Yoshimoto

1564 Inabayama (Gifu) ✕ Oda Nobunaga makes the captured city his capital

1570 Anegawa Oda and ✕ Tokugawa defeat the Asai and Asakura

1570 Ishiyama Honganji ✕ Beginning of ten-year siege of the main base of the Ikko-ikki

✕ **1572 Mikata[ga]hara** Takeda Shingen fails to [...] exploit defeat of Tokuga[wa]

✕
1574 Nagashima Oda Nobuna[ga] defeats the Ikko-ik[ki]

✕ **1553 Kawanakajima** First of five battles between Uesugi Kenshin and Takeda Shingen

✕ **1555 Miyajima** Mori family gain supremacy in Inland Sea area

✕ **1561 Kawanakajima (4th)** largest percentage of casualties in Japanese warfare

Uesugi Kenshin defeats Oda Nobu[naga]

1573 Death of Takeda Shingen

Shimazu defeat the Otomo, the m[ost] powerful clan on Kyu[shu]

1600 .... **1610** .... **1620** .... **1630** **1640**

1467-1615 Period of Warring States

1603-1615 Establishment of the Tokugawa Shogunate

1632 Yagyu Munenori publishes *Heiho kadensho*, a classic work on swordsmanship

1637 Shimabara Rebellion

✕ **1702 Reve[nge]** of the 47 R[onin]

✕ **1600 Fushimi** A classic of samurai loyalty as Torii Mototada defends the castle
✕ **1600 Siege of Ueda** Sanada Masayuki's defence keeps Tokugawa Hidetada from fighting at Sekigahara
✕ **21 Oct 1600 Sekigahara** Tokugawa Ieyasu defeats a coalition of rivals at a crucial battle in Japanese history

1603 Tokugawa Shogunate Founded

✕ **1614 Winter Campaign of Osaka** Tokugawa confronts the last of the Hideyoshi loyalists. Castle defences weakened

✕ **1615 Summer Campaign of Osaka** The last samurai field battle at **Tennoji** Tokugawa triumphs

Peasants and Christians fortify Hara castle

1638 Siege of Hara castle ✕ Castle captured and rebels executed. Last major defiance of Tokugawa squashed

1639 Final Sakoku Edict Japan isolates itself, banning contact with Catholic Europe and restricting all trade

1837 Os[aka] ✕ Rebel[lion]

1863 Kagosh[ima] bombarde[d by] ✕ Royal N[avy]

1867 Shogu[nate] abolis[hed]

THE INTRODUCTION AND DEVELOPMENT OF FIREARMS IN JAPAN (1468-1575)

1468	Chinese catapult firebombs used during the Onin War	1550	Ashikaga Yoshiharu uses arquebuses at Nakanao
1510	Primitive handguns introduced from China	1554	First use of volley firing at siege of Muraki by Oda Nobunaga
1543	Portuguese arquebuses introduced on Tanegashima	1560	First Japanese general to be killed by gunfire dies at Marune
1544	Gunmaking begins at Kunitomo	1570	Large scale use of arquebuses by Ikko-ikki at Nagashima
1548	Chinese guns used at battle of Uedahara. Portuguese guns used by Japanese pirates in China	1575	Battle of Nagashino is won by large scale use of controlled volley firing
1549	First use of Portuguese-derived firearms in battle at Kajiki		

A Japanese warrior fires a hefty looking firearm

A Warrior Monk, one of the formidable fighters who played a major part in 11th and 12th century warfare in Japan

1200 | **1250** | **1300**

1180 - 1185 Gempei Wars

1192 Minamoto Yoritomo becomes first Minamoto Shogun.

1219 The third Shogun, Sanetomo, is assassinated, leading to the establishment of the Hojo Regency

✕ **1221 Third Battle of Uji** Emperor Go-Toba fails to overthrow Hojo regency

1274 1st Mongol Invasion A brief, intense raid involving exploding bombs and mass infantry

1281 2nd Mongol Invasion Mongols are held at bay. Their ships are then destroyed in a 'kami-kaze' typhoon

✕ **1180 Ishibashiyama** Minamoto Yoritomo rebels against the Taira but is defeated

✕ **1180 Fujikawa** Taira are surprised at night by waterfowl. Thinking the noise to be a Minamoto attack they withdraw

✕ **1181 Sunomata, Yahagigawa,** M. Yukiie defeated by the Taira

✕ **1183 Minamoto Yoshinaka** raises a rebellion in north central Japan. The Taira send an expeditionary army which captures Hiuchi

✕ **1183 Kurikara Pass (Tonamiyama)** Using dummy troops and causing a stampede of oxen, Yoshinaka defeats the Taira army

✕ **1183 Muroyama** M. Yukiie again defeated

✕ **1184 Uji (2nd)** M. Yoshinaka enters Kyoto in triumph, but his behaviour leads to him being challenged by his cousins Yoritomo and Yoshitsune

1184 Awazu Yoshinaka and his wife Tomoe Gozen, the only woman warrior, killed

✕ **1184 Ichinotani** M. Yoshitsune leads his men down a precipitous cliff to defeat the Taira from behind, but most escape.

✕ **1184 Yashima** M. Yoshitsune pursues and defeats Taira in a sea and land battle famous for archery feats

✕ **1185 Dan no Ura** Taira defeated in decisive sea battle. The child Emperor is drowned, and the Taira leaders commit suicide

✕ **1189 Koromogawa** Outlawed by his brother Yoritomo, Yoshitsune is pursued and defeated

1450 | **1500** | **1550**

... bat the ... ring ... tes ...riod

─── **1467-1615 Period of Warring States** ───

1408 -1589 Slide into Anarchy and | Growth of the | Daimyo Territories

1467-77 Onin War Kyoto reduced to a wasteland. Fighting spreads to the provinces. Small-scale warlords begin to fight for territory

1488 Ikko-ikki sectarians take control of Kaga province from samurai

1494 Hojo Soun takes possession of Odawara by murder

✕ **1524 Siege of Edo** Hojo capture the city (now Tokyo)

✕ **1528 Kyoto** Ikko-ikki attack Kyoto but are repulsed by the Nichiren sect

✕ **1545 Kawagoe** Fought in darkness. Hojo victorious, confirming their superiority in the Kanto area

1580 | **1585** | **1590** | **1595** | **1600**

✕ **1582 Honnoji** Oda Nobunaga killed

1582 Yamazaki Toyotomi Hideyoshi avenges Nobunaga

1581 Surrender of Ishiyama Honganji

1581 Oda Nobunaga pacifies Iga province

✕ **1583 Shizugatake** Hideyoshi secures his position by victory

✕ **1584 Nagakute** Stalemate between Hideyoshi and Tokugawa Ieyasu

1585 Hideyoshi conquers Shikoku island and the Chosokabe family, defeats the warrior monks of **Negoroji**

1588 Sword Hunt Edict Peasants disarmed

1590 Siege of Odawara Hojo family collapses

✕ **1587 Kyushu** Hideyoshi defeats the Shimazu family

✕ **1591 Siege of Kunoe** Last resistance to Hideyoshi

✕ **1590 Date & other** N. families submit

1592-3 1st Invasion of Korea

1597-8 2nd Invasion of Korea

Odani ...oyed

...shino

─── **1577** ...rigawa

✕ **1578 Mimigawa**

✕ **1578 Death of Uesugi Kenshin,** possibly by a ninja

1582 Final defeat of Takeda Katsuyori

1583 Chosokabe complete conquest of Shikoku island

1584 Okita Nawate ✕ Shimazu defeat Ryuzoji

1585 Hitotoribashi Important victory for Date Masamune

✕ **1586 Shimazu family completes** conquest of Kyushu

1589 Date Masamune completes conquest of N. Japan

✕ **1592 Pusan, Ch'ungju, Seoul** and **P'yongyang** captured in a rapid advance. Kato Kiyomasa reaches Manchuria.

✕ **1592 Okp'o Tangp'o, Tanghangp'o, Hansando** Japanese navy beaten. Army harassed by Korean guerillas

✕ **1593 P'yong-yang** Ming army, helping Korea, retakes the city but defeated at Pyokje. Japanese attack **Haengju,** capture **Chinju,** evacuate **Seoul**

✕ **1597 Japanese win naval battle Chilchonnyang**

✕ **1597 Japanese capture Namwon,** but stopped at **Chiksan**

✕ **1597 Myongyang** Japanese navy defeated. Retreat

✕ **1598 Siege of Ulsan**

1598 Sach'on Over 37000 Chinese killed

✕ **Siege of Sunch'on.** Japanese withdrawal

✕ **Noryang,** last battle

1875 | **1880** | **1885** | **1890** | **1895** | **1900** | **1905** | **1912**

...876, Wearing of swords banned to all ...ut armed servcies

✕ **1877 Saga Rebellion** quelled. Satsuma Rebellion defeated at Kumamoto and Kagoshima

1894-5 Sino-Japanese War

1900, Japan helps free legations from Boxer Rebellion, China

1904-5 Russo-Japanese War

1912 Death of Meiji Emperor

SEPT	OCT	NOV	DEC	JAN	FEB

✕ **15 Sep Pyongyang**

✕ **17 Sep Yalu**

Jan 1895 Weihaiwei ✕

Feb 2-12 1895 Weihaiwei naval battle ✕

✕ **24 Oct to 19 Nov 1894 Siege of Port Arthur**

FEB	MARCH	APRIL	MAY	JUNE	JULY

✕ **8 Feb 1904 Attack on Port Arthur** Japan torpedo boats attack without declaring war

25 May 1904 to 2 Jan 1905 Siege of Port Arthur Russians surrender ✕

The battleship Shikishima, which served at Tsushima

JAN	FEB	MARCH	APRIL	MAY

21 Feb to 10 March ✕ **1905 Battle of Mukden** Russia forced back

27 May 1905 Battle of Tsushima Admiral Togo destroys Russian fleet in last of the 'Trafalgar-type' sea battles of annihilation ✕

THE NAPOLEONIC WARS

Campaigns directed by
Napoleon in person are
shown in red

1800   1801   1802   1803   1804   1805   1806   180

POLITICS

1800
18 December
League of Armed
Neutrality – Russia,
Sweden, Denmark
and Prussia ally
against Britain

24 December
Attempt to
assassinate
Napoleon by
French Royalists

1801
9 February
Treaty of Luneville
between France
and Austria

24 March
Czar Paul I
assassinated

1802
27 March
Peace of Amiens
between Britain
and France

2 August
Napoleon declared
Consul for life

1803
19 February
Act of Mediation –
The Swiss cantons
style themselves
Switzerland

20 December
Louisiana Purchase –
USA buys Louisiana
from France

1804
24 March
Napoleon's *Code
Civile* promulgated

18 May
Napoleon
proclaimed
emperor

1805
9 August
Third Coalition
completed when
Austria allies with
Britain and Russia

26 December
Treaty of Pressburg
between France
and Austria

1806
12 July
Confederation of the
Rhine established

6 August
Holy Roman
Empire abolished

180
7–9 July
Peace of Ti
between Fr
and Russia

EUROPE

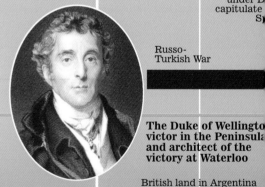

The British
Heavy Brigade
charges the
French
Cuirassiers at the
Battle of
Waterloo
18 June 1815

Hohenlinden, 3 Dec:
Moreau defeats
Austrians

War of the
Second Coalition

Marengo, 14 June:
Napoleon narrowly
defeats Austrians

Italian
campaign

5 Sept: Malta
surrenders to British

War of the Oranges between
Spain and Portugal

Jean Lannes
rose through
the ranks
from a
volunteer
to become
one of
Napoleon's
most
trusted
marshals

Archduke Charles
Austria's
outstandi
Field
Marsha
inflict
rare
defea
Napo
but v
then
whel
Wagra

British
with D

Ulm, 15 Oct:
Austrians
capitulate

Austerlitz, 2 Dec: Napoleon
defeats Austrians and Russians

Napoleon's Ulm, Jena
and Polish campaigns

Jena and Auerstedt,
14 Oct: Napoleon
crushes Prussia

Eylau,
7–8 Feb:
Napoleon draws
with Russians

Fried
14
Nap
de
Rus
conclu

Caldiero, 31 Oct

Maida, 4 July:
British defeat
Reynier's
French

Austrians and
French fight in Italy

British land in Calabria

Baylen, 2
A French
under D
capitulate
S

**Napoleon directing
his victory at Wagram,
1809**

Russo-
Turkish War

COLONIAL

Napoleon's 'dear child of victory',
the talented Marshal André
Masséna

Serb revolt against
Ottomans

The Duke of Wellingto
victor in the Peninsula
and architect of the
victory at Waterloo

British land in Argentina

The
greatest
of British
naval
heroes
and
victor of
Trafalgar,
Vice-
Admiral
Horatio Nelson
shattered French and Spanish
navies, giving Britain
supremacy of the seas.

French in Haiti: Leclerc's troops attempt to suppress
slave revolt. Despite capturing Toussaint L'Ouverture,
the French are defeated by the rebels

June: British capture
St Lucia and Tobago

20 Sept: British
capture Demerara

Assaye, 23 Sept:
British defeat Sindhia

Agra, 31 August:
Holkar defeats British

British in India

Argaum, 29 Nov:
British defeat Sindhia

Furruckabad, 17 Nov:
British defeat Holkar

Buenos Aires, 7 Jv
British under Ger
Whitelocke surren

10 July: Vellore mutiny
against British

18 Jan: British take Cape
of Good Hope from Dutch

NAVAL

Copenhagen, 2 April:
Britain destroys
Danish fleet

Algeciras, July: two
battles between
British and Franco-
Spanish fleet

One of the
greatest R.N.
admirals of his
time, John
Jervis, Earl St
Vincent

USA attacks
Barbary Pirates

Cape Finistere, 22 July: a drawn
battle between Calder's British
and Villeneuve's Franco-Spanish

San Domingo,
6 Feb:
Duckworth
defeats
Laissaque

Dardane
19 Feb t
March:
fleet
bombar
Ottoma
without

Trafalgar, 21 Oct:
Nelson defeats Villeneuve

Lemnos, 30 June: Seniavin's
Russian fleet defeats Ottomans

1800   1801   1802   1803   1804   1805   1806   180

wars of Napoleon were part continuation of the conflict that had started with the French Revolution, part the ambitions of the
ch emperor to build an empire and dominate Europe. A series of coalitions opposed him, inspired by the implacable hostility of
ain. At one time or another, almost all the nations of Europe were in arms against the French, and the warfare was continued across
oceans of the world. The peak of Napoleon's career, after a run of glittering triumphs on the battlefield, is generally thought to have
e in 1807. Thereafter the long-running Peninsular War (the 'Spanish Ulcer') was a constant drain on French resources, while Britain
inated the seas after Trafalgar. The Moscow campaign of 1812 was the 'step too far' that led inexorably to Napoleon's downfall.

The young Napoleon Bonaparte

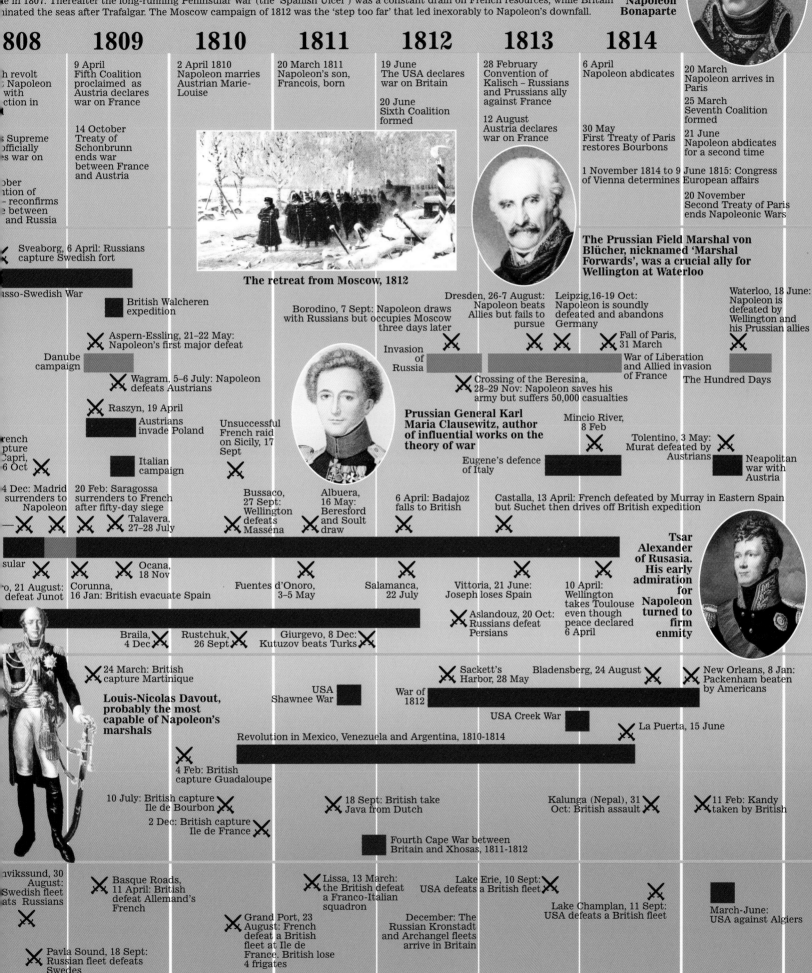

808 1809 1810 1811 1812 1813 1814

h revolt
Napoleon
with
ction in

s Supreme
officially
es war on

ober
tion of
reconfirms
between
and Russia

9 April
Fifth Coalition
proclaimed as
Austria declares
war on France

14 October
Treaty of
Schonbrunn
ends war
between France
and Austria

2 April 1810
Napoleon marries
Austrian Marie-
Louise

20 March 1811
Napoleon's son,
Francois, born

19 June
The USA declares
war on Britain

20 June
Sixth Coalition
formed

28 February
Convention of
Kalisch – Russians
and Prussians ally
against France

12 August
Austria declares
war on France

6 April
Napoleon abdicates

30 May
First Treaty of Paris
restores Bourbons

1 November 1814 to 9
of Vienna determines

20 March
Napoleon arrives in
Paris

25 March
Seventh Coalition
formed

21 June
Napoleon abdicates
for a second time

June 1815: Congress
European affairs

20 November
Second Treaty of Paris
ends Napoleonic Wars

Sveaborg, 6 April: Russians
✗ capture Swedish fort

sso-Swedish War

The retreat from Moscow, 1812

**The Prussian Field Marshal von
Blücher, nicknamed 'Marshal
Forwards', was a crucial ally for
Wellington at Waterloo**

✗ British Walcheren
expedition

Dresden, 26-7 August:
Napoleon beats
Allies but fails to
pursue

Leipzig,16-19 Oct:
Napoleon is soundly
defeated and abandons
Germany

Waterloo, 18 June:
Napoleon is
defeated by
Wellington and
his Prussian allies

Borodino, 7 Sept: Napoleon draws
with Russians but occupies Moscow
three days later

✗ Aspern-Essling, 21–22 May:
Napoleon's first major defeat

Danube
campaign

Invasion
of
Russia

✗ Fall of Paris,
31 March

War of Liberation
and Allied invasion
of France

The Hundred Days

Crossing of the Beresina,
✗ 28–29 Nov: Napoleon saves his
army but suffers 50,000 casualties

✗ Wagram, 5–6 July: Napoleon
defeats Austrians

✗ Raszyn, 19 April
Austrians
invade Poland

Unsuccessful
French raid
on Sicily, 17
Sept

**Prussian General Karl
Maria Clausewitz, author
of influential works on the
theory of war**

Mincio River,
8 Feb ✗

Tolentino, 3 May:
Murat defeated by
Austrians ✗

rench
pture
Capri,
6 Oct ✗

Italian
campaign

Eugene's defence
of Italy

Neapolitan
war with
Austria

**Tsar
Alexander
of Rusasia.
His early
admiration
for
Napoleon
turned to
firm
enmity**

4 Dec: Madrid
surrenders to
Napoleon

20 Feb: Saragossa
surrenders to French
after fifty-day siege ✗ Talavera,
27–28 July

Bussaco,
27 Sept:
Wellington
defeats
Masséna

Albuera,
16 May:
Beresford
and Soult
draw

6 April: Badajoz
falls to British

Castalla, 13 April: French defeated by Murray in Eastern Spain
but Suchet then drives off British expedition

sular

o, 21 August:
defeat Junot

Corunna,
16 Jan: British evacuate Spain

Ocana,
18 Nov

Fuentes d'Onoro,
3–5 May

Salamanca,
22 July

Vittoria, 21 June:
Joseph loses Spain

✗ Aslandouz, 20 Oct:
Russians defeat
Persians

10 April:
Wellington
takes
Toulouse
even though
peace declared
6 April

Braila,
4 Dec ✗

Rustchuk,
26 Sept ✗

Giurgevo, 8 Dec:
Kutuzov beats Turks ✗

**Louis-Nicolas Davout,
probably the most
capable of Napoleon's
marshals**

✗ 24 March: British
capture Martinique

✗ Sackett's
Harbor, 28 May

Bladensberg, 24 August

✗ New Orleans, 8 Jan:
Packenham beaten
by Americans

USA
Shawnee War

War of
1812

USA Creek War

✗ La Puerta, 15 June

Revolution in Mexico, Venezuela and Argentina, 1810-1814

✗
4 Feb: British
capture Guadaloupe

10 July: British capture
Ile de Bourbon ✗

2 Dec: British capture
Ile de France ✗

✗ 18 Sept: British take
Java from Dutch

Kalunga (Nepal), 31
Oct: British assault ✗

✗ 11 Feb: Kandy
taken by British

Fourth Cape War between
Britain and Xhosas, 1811-1812

aviksssund, 30
August:
Swedish fleet
eats Russians
✗

Basque Roads,
11 April: British
defeat Allemand's
French

Lissa, 13 March:
the British defeat
a Franco-Italian
squadron

Lake Erie, 10 Sept:
USA defeats a British fleet ✗

Lake Champlan, 11 Sept:
USA defeats a British fleet

March-June:
USA against Algiers

✗ Pavla Sound, 18 Sept:
Russian fleet defeats
Swedes

Grand Port, 23
August: French
defeat a British
fleet at Ile de
France. British lose
4 frigates

December: The
Russian Kronstadt
and Archangel fleets
arrive in Britain

COLONIAL WARS

1475	1500	1525	1550	1575	1600	1625	1650	1675	1700	1725	1750

AFRICA

The Battle of Omdurman, 2 Sept 1898. The Mahdi's soldiers, known as dervishes, attack British troops

● 1618: British settle along the Gambia

● 1672: Royal Africa Co established

1662-84: British control Tangier

175_ Kepp_ captur_ Goree fro_ the Fren_

Led by the Highland Briga_ the British overrun Egypt_ nationalists at Tel-el-Kebi_ 1882

The Mahdist commander, the Emir Mahmoud, under guard of Sudanese soldiers following his capture by the British during the Omdurman campaign of 1898

1659: French establish St Louis ● in Senegal as major base

✕ 1677: French capture Goree

● 1482: Portuguese found Elmina on the Gold Coast

1572: Portugese expedition to Zambezi destroyed

1637: Dutch ✕ sack Elmina

● 1652: Dutch settle at the Cape

1698: Portuguese defeated at Mombasa by Imam of ✕ Oman

✕ 1505: Mombasa sacked by Portuguese

● 1507: Mozambique occupied by Portuguese

● 1575: Luanda founded, Angola colonised by Portugese

1641-8: Dutch invade Angola

ASIA

Spains's two great conquistadors. Left, Hernàn Cortés (1485-1547), who overcame the Aztecs of Mexico; and (right) Francisco Pizarro (c.1470-1541) who conquered the Incas of Peru. Both fought against seemingly impossible odds.

✕ 1612: British defeat Portuguese off India

Jask, 1618: British defeat Portuguese

✕ 1621: British capture Ormuz

✕ 1640: British establish Fort George (Madras)

● 1600: British East India Co founded

1686: East India Co campaign against Bengal

Plassey, 1757: Clive smashes Daula's army

Wandewash, 1760: British defeat French

1766-9: 1st Mysore W_

● 1609: French East India Co founded

●1674: Pondicherry colonised

✕ 1715: French take Mauritius

● 1638: French established on Reunion

1746: Capture of Madras from British and victory at St Thome ✕

✕ 1630: 2nd Portuguese expedition ✕ against Kandy defeated

Macao, 1557: Portuguese ✕ fort established

● 1604: Dutch colonies on Borneo established

✕ 1656: Dutch capture ✕ Colombo from Portuguese

✕ 1662: Dutch expelled ✕ from Taiwan

'Clive of India' – a clerk who became a fine soldier

176_ Du_ occ_ Ka_

1503: Fort at Cochin ● built by Portuguese

✕ 1508: Portuguese ✕ capture Ormuz

1594: Portuguese expedition against Kandy defeated ✕

● 1619: Dutch establish Batavia, on Java

✕ 1663: Cochin ✕ seized by Dutch

1510: Portuguese ✕✕✕ 1511: Portuguese seize Goa ✕✕✕ take Malacca

1598: Dutch ● settle Bantam

✕ 1641: Dutch ✕ seize Malacca

1518: Portuguese ✕ invade Ceylon

● 1571: Spanish found Manila

1623: Dutch massacre British at Amboina

✕ 1703: Russia conquers ✕ Kamchatka

● 1689: Treaty of Nevchinsk established border between China and Russia

AMERICAS

1508: Spanish invade Puerto Rico

● 1509: Spanish invade Jamaica

1519-21: Cortez conquers Mexico

● 1607: Jamestown founded ●

1612: Bermuda colonised ●

● 1624: Barbados colonised

✕ 1655: British take ✕ Jamaica from Spanish

✕ 1711: British attack ✕ Montreal and Quebec B_

1493: ● Spanish establish Hispaniola

1524-39: Pizarro conquers Peru

1622: Jamestown destroyed by Indians ✕✕

✕ 1664: British seize ✕ New Amsterdam (New York)

1730: British attack ✕ on Cartagena fails

1532-42: Conquest of Guatemala

1629: British attack Quebec ✕

1494: ● Treaty of Tordesillas divides New World between Portugal and Spain

1543-8: Irala conquers Argentina

1564: French colony in Florida ✕ destroyed by Spanish

● 1608: French found Quebec

1642-53: French war with the Iroquois

1760: French surrender Canada_

1754-63 French and Indian War_

1540-61: Valdiva and Mendoza capture Chile

1635: Colonies on Martinique and Guadeloupe established ●

1684-9: French fight Iroquois in Canada

1755: Braddock defeated at Monogahela_

1759: Wolf_ takes Quebe_

1562-75: Spanish expedition into New Mexico

1779: Sp_ take Baton _ and Fort Ma_

1568: Spanish defeat Hawkins at San Juan de Ulloa ✕

1628: Piet Heyn seizes Spanish treasure fleet off Cuba ✕✕✕ 1634: Dutch capture ✕ Curaçao from Spanish

1500: Portuguese ● establish colony in Brazil

1567: French colonists expelled from Brazil by Portuguese ✕

1620-54: Portuguese defeat Dutch in Brazil

1475	1500	1525	1550	1575	1600	1625	1650	1675	1700	1725	1750

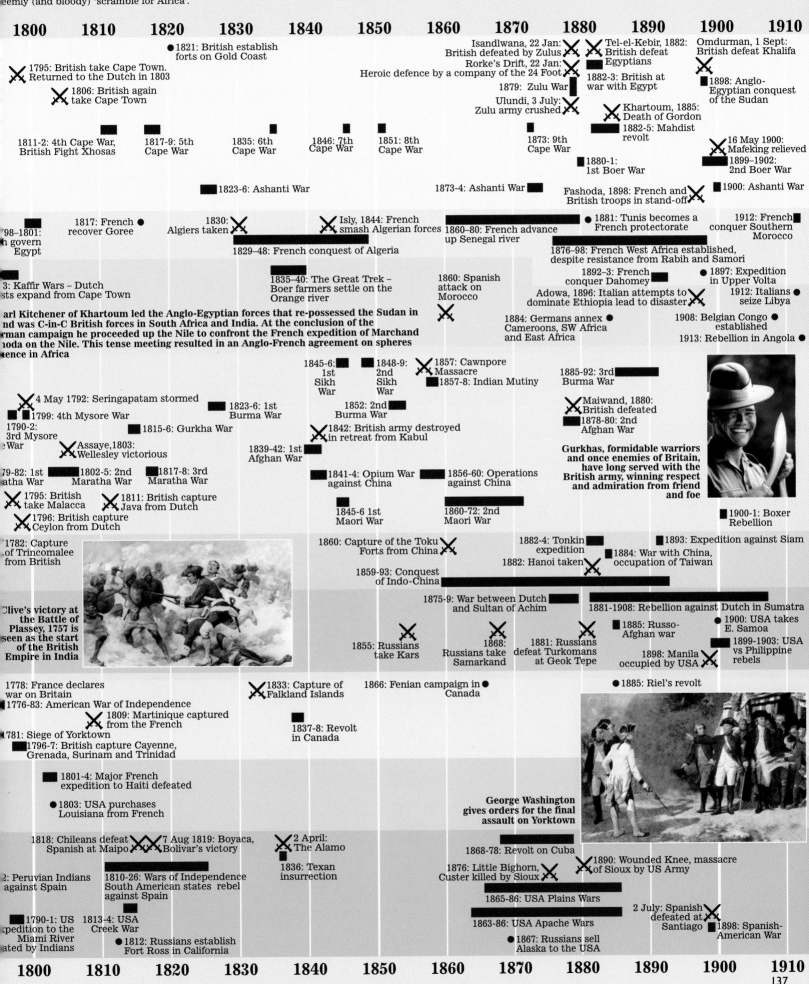

...he end of the sixteenth century, the population and prosperity of Western Europe was rising dramatically, and the maritime nations of the Atlantic seaboard were soon in ...petition for the global resources opened up by improvements in ship construction and in navigation. Europe was by now technologically far superior to the natives of the ...ds they invaded, making the conquest of empires by relatively small numbers of Europeans almost a commonplace. South America was dramatically mastered by the ...nish and Portuguese, and North America provided a new arena for Anglo-French rivalry. Later in the nineteenth century the lure of mineral deposits in particular led to an ...eemly (and bloody) 'scramble for Africa'.

| 1800 | 1810 | 1820 | 1830 | 1840 | 1850 | 1860 | 1870 | 1880 | 1890 | 1900 | 1910 |

1821: British establish forts on Gold Coast

1795: British take Cape Town. Returned to the Dutch in 1803

1806: British again take Cape Town

Isandlwana, 22 Jan: British defeated by Zulus
Rorke's Drift, 22 Jan: Heroic defence by a company of the 24 Foot

Tel-el-Kebir, 1882: British defeat Egyptians

Omdurman, 1 Sept: British defeat Khalifa

1879: Zulu War

1882-3: British at war with Egypt

1898: Anglo-Egyptian conquest of the Sudan

Ulundi, 3 July: Zulu army crushed

Khartoum, 1885: Death of Gordon

1882-5: Mahdist revolt

1811-2: 4th Cape War, British Fight Xhosas

1817-9: 5th Cape War

1835: 6th Cape War

1846: 7th Cape War

1851: 8th Cape War

1873: 9th Cape War

16 May 1900: Mafeking relieved

1880-1: 1st Boer War

1899-1902: 2nd Boer War

1823-6: Ashanti War

1873-4: Ashanti War

Fashoda, 1898: French and British troops in stand-off

1900: Ashanti War

...98-1801: ...h govern Egypt

1817: French recover Goree

1830: Algiers taken

Isly, 1844: French smash Algerian forces

1860-80: French advance up Senegal river

1881: Tunis becomes a French protectorate

1912: French conquer Southern Morocco

1829-48: French conquest of Algeria

1876-98: French West Africa established, despite resistance from Rabih and Samori

...3: Kaffir Wars – Dutch ...sts expand from Cape Town

1835-40: The Great Trek – Boer farmers settle on the Orange river

1860: Spanish attack on Morocco

1892-3: French conquer Dahomey

1897: Expedition in Upper Volta

Adowa, 1896: Italian attempts to dominate Ethiopia lead to disaster

1912: Italians seize Libya

...arl Kitchener of Khartoum led the Anglo-Egyptian forces that re-possessed the Sudan in ...nd was C-in-C British forces in South Africa and India. At the conclusion of the ...rman campaign he proceeded up the Nile to confront the French expedition of Marchand ...hoda on the Nile. This tense meeting resulted in an Anglo-French agreement on spheres ...ence in Africa

1884: Germans annex Cameroons, SW Africa and East Africa

1908: Belgian Congo established

1913: Rebellion in Angola

1845-6: 1st Sikh War

1848-9: 2nd Sikh War

1857: Cawnpore Massacre

1885-92: 3rd Burma War

1857-8: Indian Mutiny

4 May 1792: Seringapatam stormed

1823-6: 1st Burma War

1852: 2nd Burma War

Maiwand, 1880: British defeated

1799: 4th Mysore War

1878-80: 2nd Afghan War

...1790-2: ...3rd Mysore ...e War

1815-6: Gurkha War

1842: British army destroyed in retreat from Kabul

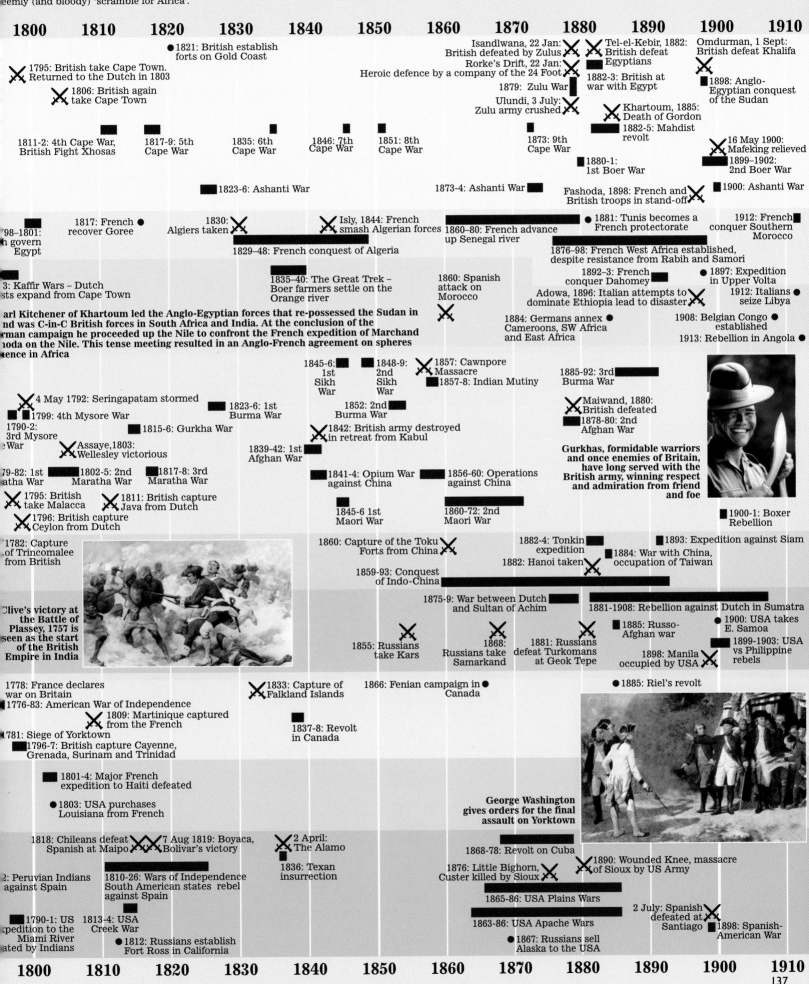
Gurkhas, formidable warriors and once enemies of Britain, have long served with the British army, winning respect and admiration from friend and foe

Assaye, 1803: Wellesley victorious

1839-42: 1st Afghan War

...79-82: 1st ...atha War

1802-5: 2nd Maratha War

1817-8: 3rd Maratha War

1841-4: Opium War against China

1856-60: Operations against China

1795: British take Malacca

1811: British capture Java from Dutch

1900-1: Boxer Rebellion

1796: British capture Ceylon from Dutch

1845-6 1st Maori War

1860-72: 2nd Maori War

...1782: Capture ...of Trincomalee ...from British

1860: Capture of the Toku Forts from China

1882-4: Tonkin expedition

1893: Expedition against Siam

1884: War with China, occupation of Taiwan

1882: Hanoi taken

1859-93: Conquest of Indo-China

...live's victory at the Battle of Plassey, 1757 is seen as the start of the British Empire in India

1875-9: War between Dutch and Sultan of Achim

1881-1908: Rebellion against Dutch in Sumatra

1885: Russo-Afghan war

1900: USA takes E. Samoa

1855: Russians take Kars

1868: Russians take Samarkand

1881: Russians defeat Turkomans at Geok Tepe

1899-1903: USA vs Philippine rebels

1898: Manila occupied by USA

1778: France declares war on Britain

1833: Capture of Falkland Islands

1866: Fenian campaign in Canada

1885: Riel's revolt

...1776-83: American War of Independence

1809: Martinique captured from the French

...781: Siege of Yorktown

1837-8: Revolt in Canada

1796-7: British capture Cayenne, Grenada, Surinam and Trinidad

1801-4: Major French expedition to Haiti defeated

1803: USA purchases Louisiana from French

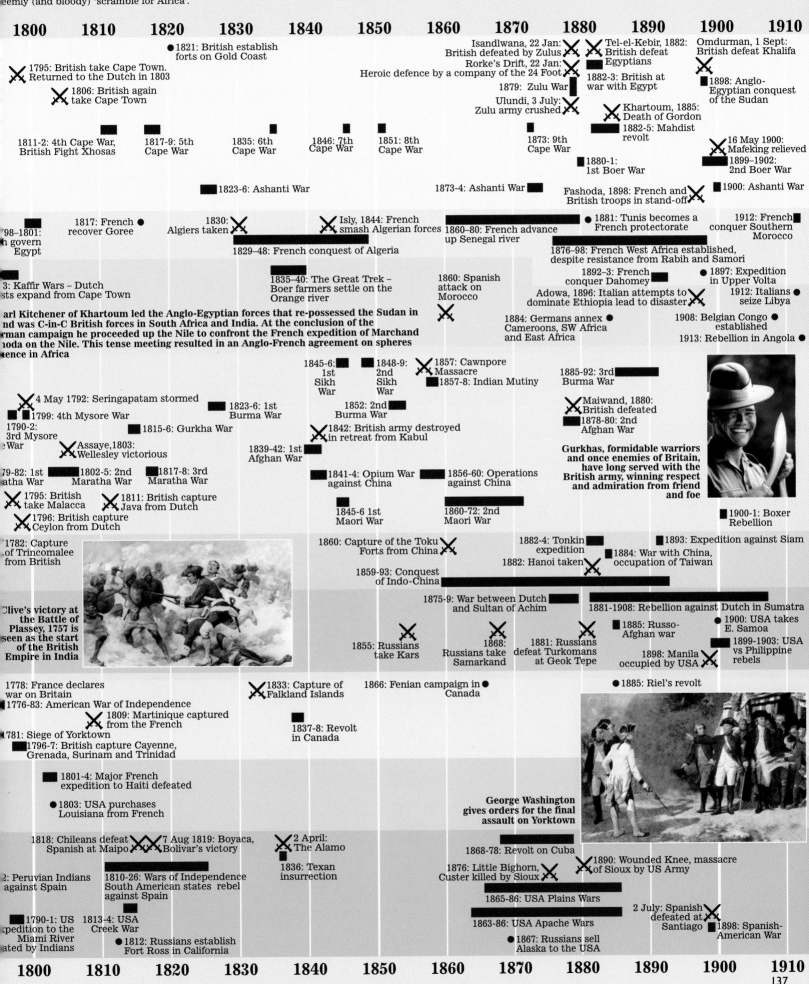
George Washington gives orders for the final assault on Yorktown

1818: Chileans defeat Spanish at Maipo

7 Aug 1819: Boyaca, Bolivar's victory

2 April: The Alamo

1868-78: Revolt on Cuba

1890: Wounded Knee, massacre of Sioux by US Army

1876: Little Bighorn, Custer killed by Sioux

1836: Texan insurrection

...2: Peruvian Indians ...against Spain

1810-26: Wars of Independence South American states rebel against Spain

1865-86: USA Plains Wars

2 July: Spanish defeated at Santiago

1790-1: US ...pedition to the Miami River ...ated by Indians

1813-4: USA Creek War

1863-86: USA Apache Wars

1898: Spanish-American War

1812: Russians establish Fort Ross in California

1867: Russians sell Alaska to the USA

| 1800 | 1810 | 1820 | 1830 | 1840 | 1850 | 1860 | 1870 | 1880 | 1890 | 1900 | 1910 |

THE AMERICAN CIVIL

The greatest of wars between the Napoleonic period and the First World War, the American Civil War caused some 600,000 deaths. The opposing sides were uneven matched: the mainly urban, industrialised North (Union) with a population of 23 millions versus the largely agrarian, plantation-dominated South (Confederacy), with b 9 millions. The war was fought on two fronts. In the east, between the two capitals the Army of Northern Virginia, under the inspirational leadership of Robert E. Le proved more than a match for a series of Union generals. In the west, the capture of Vicksburg enabled the Union to split the South, leading to Sherman's 'March to th Sea' through the heart of the exhausted Confederacy.

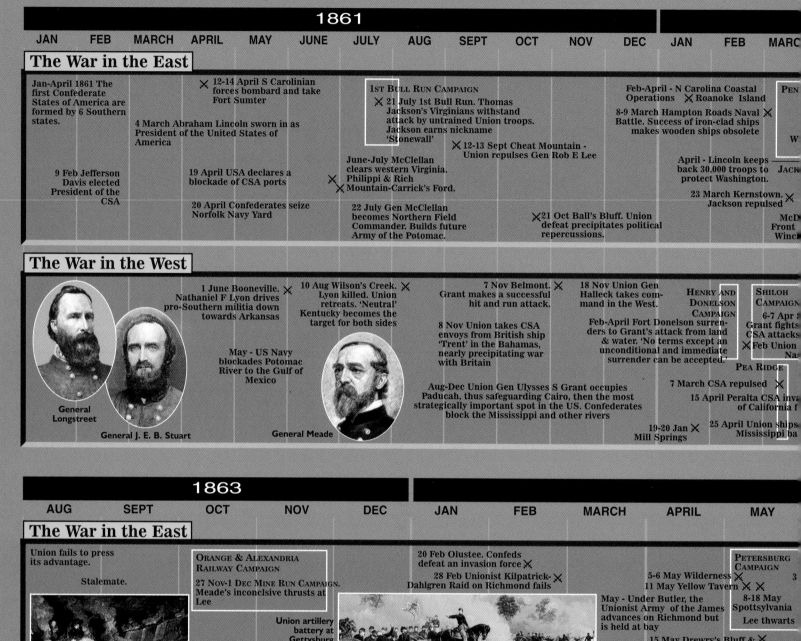

1861

| JAN | FEB | MARCH | APRIL | MAY | JUNE | JULY | AUG | SEPT | OCT | NOV | DEC | JAN | FEB | MARC |

The War in the East

Jan-April 1861 The first Confederate States of America are formed by 6 Southern states.

✕ 12-14 April S Carolinian forces bombard and take Fort Sumter

4 March Abraham Lincoln sworn in as President of the United States of America

9 Feb Jefferson Davis elected President of the CSA

19 April USA declares a blockade of CSA ports

20 April Confederates seize Norfolk Navy Yard

1ST BULL RUN CAMPAIGN
✕ 21 July 1st Bull Run. Thomas Jackson's Virginians withstand attack by untrained Union troops. Jackson earns nickname 'Stonewall'

✕ 12-13 Sept Cheat Mountain - Union repulses Gen Rob E Lee

June-July McClellan clears western Virginia. Philippi & Rich
✕ Mountain-Carrick's Ford.

22 July Gen McClellan becomes Northern Field Commander. Builds future Army of the Potomac.

✕ 21 Oct Ball's Bluff. Union defeat precipitates political repercussions.

Feb-April - N Carolina Coastal Operations ✕ Roanoke Island

8-9 March Hampton Roads Naval ✕ Battle. Success of iron-clad ships makes wooden ships obsolete

April - Lincoln keeps back 30,000 troops to protect Washington.

23 March Kernstown. ✕ Jackson repulsed

PEN

JACK

McD Front Winc

W

The War in the West

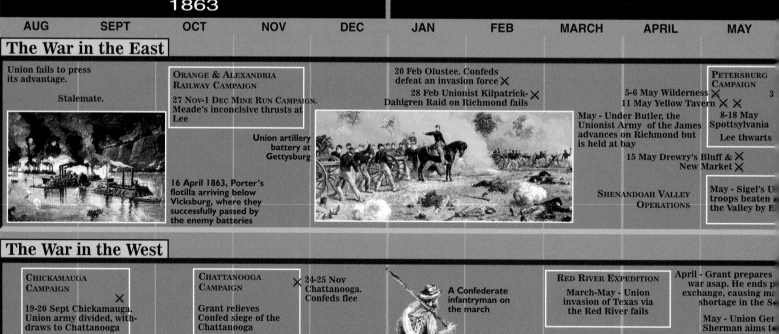

General Longstreet

General J. E. B. Stuart

General Meade

1 June Booneville. ✕ Nathaniel F Lyon drives pro-Southern militia down towards Arkansas

10 Aug Wilson's Creek. ✕ Lyon killed. Union retreats. 'Neutral' Kentucky becomes the target for both sides

May - US Navy blockades Potomac River to the Gulf of Mexico

7 Nov Belmont. ✕ Grant makes a successful hit and run attack.

8 Nov Union takes CSA envoys from British ship 'Trent' in the Bahamas, nearly precipitating war with Britain

Aug-Dec Union Gen Ulysses S Grant occupies Paducah, thus safeguarding Cairo, then the most strategically important spot in the US. Confederates block the Mississippi and other rivers

18 Nov Union Gen Halleck takes command in the West.

HENRY AND DONELSON CAMPAIGN
Feb-April Fort Donelson surrenders to Grant's attack from land & water. 'No terms except an unconditional and immediate surrender can be accepted.'

19-20 Jan ✕ Mill Springs

SHILOH CAMPAIGN
6-7 Apr S Grant fights CSA attacks
✕ Feb Union Na

PEA RIDGE
7 March CSA repulsed ✕

15 April Peralta CSA inva of California f

25 April Union ships Mississippi ba

1863

| AUG | SEPT | OCT | NOV | DEC | JAN | FEB | MARCH | APRIL | MAY |

The War in the East

Union fails to press its advantage.

Stalemate.

ORANGE & ALEXANDRIA RAILWAY CAMPAIGN
27 Nov-1 Dec MINE RUN CAMPAIGN. Meade's inconclsive thrusts at Lee

Union artillery battery at Gettysburg

16 April 1863, Porter's flotilla arriving below Vicksburg, where they successfully passed by the enemy batteries

20 Feb Olustee. Confeds defeat an invasion force ✕

28 Feb Unionist Kilpatrick- ✕ Dahlgren Raid on Richmond fails

May - Under Butler, the Unionist Army of the James advances on Richmond but is held at bay

15 May Drewry's Bluff & ✕ New Market ✕

SHENANDOAH VALLEY OPERATIONS

PETERSBURG CAMPAIGN
5-6 May Wilderness ✕ 3
11 May Yellow Tavern ✕ ✕
8-18 May Spottsylvania
Lee thwarts

May - Sigel's U troops beaten the Valley by E

The War in the West

CHICKAMAUGA CAMPAIGN
✕
19-20 Sept Chickamauga. Union army divided, withdraws to Chattanooga

EAST TENNESSEE CAMPAIGN
17 Oct Grant given overall control in West

CHATTANOOGA CAMPAIGN
Grant relieves Confed siege of the Chattanooga

✕ 24-25 Nov Chattanooga. Confeds flee

✕ Nov - CSA besiege Knoxville
6 Dec - Sherman relieves the city

A Confederate infantryman on the march

22 Feb Okalona. ✕ CSA Gen Forrest halts Union raid

RED RIVER EXPEDITION
March-May - Union invasion of Texas via the Red River fails

Mar-April - Forrest ✕ raids Kentucky. Captures Fort Pillow

April - Grant prepares war asap. He ends p exchange, causing ma shortage in the S

May - Union Ger Sherman aims t destroy Johnstone Tennessee Army

ATLANTA CAMI
27 June Ke Mountain. Sh re
Hood repulsed draws to A

WAR

General Grant General Lee General Sherman General Bragg General Burnside

1862

MAY   JUNE   JULY   AUG   SEPT   OCT   NOV   DEC

1863

JAN   FEB   MARCH   APRIL   MAY   JUNE   JULY

...MPAIGN
- 4 May Seige
...town
... Union
...advances

12-15 June Stuart's cavalry raid on Union stores

✗ 25 June to 1 July Seven Days Battles. Union forced to withdraw

✗ 31 May-1 June Seven Pines (Fair Oaks)

ANTIETAM CAMPAIGN

✗ 14 Sept S. Mountain

✗ 14-15 Sept Harpers Ferry

✗ 17 Sept Antietam. The bloodiest day of the war sees Lee's 1st invasion of the North halted

FREDERICKSBURG CAMPAIGN
Army of the Potomac drives towards Richmond

✗ 13 Dec Fredericksburg. Despite 14 charges, Union fails to overrun Jackson

CHANCELLORSVILLE CAMPAIGN
Army of the Potomac attacks Lee's smaller forces

1-6 May Chancellorsville. ✗ A resounding victory for Lee, but he loses Jackson, shot by his own men while reconnoitring.

9 June Brandy Station

13 June ✗ Winchester

GETTYSBURG CAMPAIGN

✗ Lee moves N

✗ 1-3 July Gettysburg
The greatest battle ever in the USA came from an unexpected clash. 'Pickett's Charge' fails. Lee retreats.

...LEY CAMPAIGN
...son pushes back
...00 Unionists.
→ ✗ ✗✗
✗
June - Cross Keys & Port Republic

2ND BULL RUN CAMPAIGN
Jackson & Lee circle N. to trap Union army

✗ 29-30 Aug 2nd Bull Run. Jackson throws Union back

✗ 31 Aug Chantilly. Jackson held at bay

Confederate infantry in action

STONES RIVER CAMPAIGN

8 Oct Perryville. ✗ CSA fails to press its advantage

July-Oct Confed Gen Bragg invades Kentucky

31 Dec to 3 Jan Stones ✗ River. A tactical draw but a strategic victory for the North

7 April Charleston. Union fleet bombards harbour

✗ OPERATIONS AGAINST PORT HUDSON

TULLAHOMA CAMPAIGN

2 July Union takes Chattanooga.

...TURE OF NEW ORLEANS

COMBINED OPERATIONS AGAINST VICKSBURG

✗ 9 May Plum Point

✗ 6 June Union boats take Memphis

General Hancock

✗ 19-20 Sept Iuka

✗ 3-4 Oct Corinth Union holds on to Corinth and Memphis

29 Dec ✗ Chickashaw Bluffs After 3 days of assault, Union withdraws.

✗ 7 Dec Prairie Grove. Union takes Arkansas

VICKSBURG CAMPAIGN
Jan-April Grant & Porter move troops and gunships

18 April-3 May ✗ Grierson's Raid ✗

1 May Port Gibson ✗

7-19 MAY BIG BLACK RIVER CAMPAIGN.

16 May Champion's Hill ✗

Grant's brilliant actions cover 200 miles and 5 separate victories

4 July Capture of Vicksburg after siege by Grant ✗

...64

JULY   AUGUST   SEPT   OCT   NOV   DEC

1865

JAN   FEB   MARCH   APRIL

...5-18 June
...etersburg battle
... siege by Grant

30 July Battle of the Crater. Union blows up the city defenses but mismanages the attack. A fiasco

✗ 14-20 Aug Deep Bottom

18 Aug Globe ✗ Tavern

✗ 25 Aug Reams Station

✗ 29 Sept Chaffin's Bluff. Union takes Ft Harrison

Grant destroys Petersburg's railroad lines

27 Oct Boydton Plank Road. CSA defends last rail link

2 April Assault on ✗ Petersburg. Lee evacuates and forces his way West

25 Mar Fort Stedman. Lee's ✗ surprise attack finally repulsed

✗ 9 April Lee surrenders at Appomattox Court House

14 April Lincoln shot

...8 June Union troops
...a bridge to cross the
...es

...2 June Trevilian
...ion

3 Feb - Lee appointed supreme Confed commander

6 Apr Sayler's ✗ Creek

April-May - All Confed forces surrender

2 July - 19 Oct EARLY'S VALLEY CAMPAIGN

✗ 9 July Monocacy. Early marches on Washington

2 July Early's Confeds invade Maryland

✗ 19 Sept Opequon Creek

✗ 22 Sept Fisher's Hill

✗ 19 Oct Cedar Creek
Sheridan pushes Early back & takes the Valley

2 March Waynesboro
Gen Custer overruns Early

29-31 March ✗ Dinwiddie Courthouse & White oak Road

✗ 1 April Five Forks

...August Mobile Bay.
...Union takes harbour
...ite minefield. Union
...ral Farragut: 'Damn the torpedoes!'

...ine Brice's Cross Roads.
...est
...s off Union

✗ 14-15 July Tupelo. Forrest repulsed

19 Oct Lexington. CSA Gen Price invades Missouri

23 Oct Westport. Price repulsed. End of ✗ major operations W. of Mississippi

Aug-Oct Forrest's raids ✗ against Sherman

HOOD'S TENNESSEE CAMPAIGN

30 Nov ✗ Franklin. Hood balked

15-16 Dec ✗ Nashville. Hood beaten decisively

✗ 13-15 Jan Fort Fisher. Last Confed sea gate, falls

2 April Selma. Union cavalry under ✗ Wilson take the town. Forrest escapes

...7 July Hood replaces Johnstone

✗ 22 July Atlanta. Hood pushed back

✗ 20 July Peachtree Creek

✗ 31 Aug Atlanta falls to Union

MARCH TO THE SEA
Nov-Dec - Sherman marches 300 miles from Atlanta to the coast

21 Dec Confeds evacuate Savannah

CAROLINAS CAMPAIGN
Sherman takes cities

✗ 17 Feb Columbia

✗ 22 Feb Wilmington

✗ 19-20 March Bentonville. Sherman drives off CSA attack

The first of the two cataclysmic conflicts of the twentieth century, World War I took the lives of nearly eight million combatants, plus those of unknown numbers of civil[...]
It was the first truly 'modern' war fought with a terrible new arsenal of weapons that revolutionised warfare. Firearms, including machine-guns, and artillery dominated[...]
land battlefield, above which aircraft were beginning to play a role that later in the century would become decisive. Poison gas added to the horror of stalemate battle-fr[...]
where living conditions for the troops were hellish. At sea the battleship was nearing the peak of development, but new threats from above and below the seas were alr[...]
hastening its obsolescence.

1914   1915
A S O N D J F M A M J J A S O N D J F M A M J

POLITICS & WORLD AFFAIRS

14 SEPT: VON FALKENHAYN SUCCEEDS VON MOLTKE AS GERMAN C-IN-C

15 MAY: BRITISH FORM COALITION GOVERNMENT

1 JUNE: 1st ZEPPELIN RAID ON LONDON

8 SEPT: TSAR TAKES PERSONNAL CONTROL OF RUSSIAN ARMY

11 OCT: GERMANS EXECUTE NURSE EDITH CAVELL

3 DEC: JOFFRE BECOMES FRENCH C-IN-C.
12 DEC: HAIG SUCCEEDS JOHN FRENCH AS BRITISH C-IN-C

24 APRIL: EASTER RISING IN DUBLIN

2 JUNE: KITCHEN[...] DROWNS WHEN [...] HAMPSHIRE SIN[...]

WESTERN FRONT

4 AUG: BATTLE OF THE FRONTIERS BEGINS

2-6 SEPT: 1st BATTLE OF THE MARNE

13-27 SEPT: 1st BATTLE OF AISNE

20 DEC-17 MAR: 1st BATTLE OF CHAMPAGNE

22 APRIL-25 MAY: 2nd BATTLE OF YPRES

25 SEPT-6 NOV: 2nd BATTLE OF CHAMPAGNE

FEB-APRIL: GERMANS WITHDRAW TO HINDENBURG LINE

22 APRIL: 1st USE OF POISON GAS ON WESTERN FRONT BY GERMANS

21 FEB-18 DEC: BATTLE OF VERDUN

EASTERN FRONT

26-30 AUG: BATTLE OF TANNENBERG

9-14 SEPT: THE 1st BATTLE MASURIAN LAKES

7-21 FEB: 2nd BATTLE MASURIAN LAKES

2 MAY-27 JUNE: GORLIC-TARNOW, GERMAN BREAK-THROUGH

31 JAN: GERMANS MAKE 1st USE OF POISON GAS IN WAR

JULY-SEPT: RUSSIAN WITHDRAWAL

18 MARCH-14 APRIL: BATTLE OF NAROCH[...]

4 JUNE-END OF AUG: BRUSILOV OFFENSIVE

General (later Field Marshal) Haig

SERBIA / SALONIKA FRONT

12-21 AUG: 1st AUSTRIAN INVASION OF SERBIA

7 SEPT: 2nd AUSTRIAN INVASION OF SERBIA

NOV-DEC: 3rd AUSTRIAN INVASION OF SERBIA

EARLY OCT: CENTRAL POWERS INVADE SERBIA

END OF NOV: SERBIA OVERRUN BY CENTRAL POWERS

9 OCT: SALONIKA FRONT ESTABLISHED

The UK's Lancashire Fusiliers readying for action

General Ludend[...]

ITALIAN FRONT

Austrian howitzer in use: more casualties were caused by artillery than by any other single weapon

3 MAY: ITALY DECLARES WAR ON THE CENTRAL POWERS

23 JUNE-7 JULY: 1st BAT-TLE OF ISONZO

18 JULY-3 AUG: 2nd BAT-TLE OF ISONZO

18 OCT-4 NOV: 3rd BATTLE OF ISONZO

10 NOV-2 DEC: 4th BATTLE OF ISONZO

15 MAY-17 JUNE: ASIAGO OFFENSIVE

11-29 MARCH: 5th BA[...] OF ISONZO

British howitzers

MESO-POTAMIA FRONT

NOV-DEC: BRITISH IMPERIAL TROOPS LAND AND ESTABLISH A BRIDGEHEAD AT BASRA

JAN-MAY: 1st BRITISH ADVANCE

24 JULY: BATTLE OF NASIRIYA

27-28 SEPT: 1st BATTLE OF KUT

22-26 NOV: BATTLE OF CTESIPHON

7 DEC: SIEGE OF BRITISH AT KUT BEGINS

29 APRIL: TU[...] TAKE KUT

PALESTINE FRONT

British battlecruisers under fire at Jutland

14 JAN: TURKS ADVANCE ON THE SUEZ CANAL

2-3 FEB: TURKS ATTACK ON SUEZ CANAL REPULSED

Kaiser Wilhelm

Trench warfare

WAR AT SEA

28 AUG: 1st BATTLE OF HELIGOLAND BIGHT

22 SEPT: HMSs ABOUKIR, CRESSY & HOGUE SUNK BY U9

1 NOV: BATTLE OF CORONEL

8 DEC: BATTLE OF FALKLAND ISLANDS

24 JAN: BATTLE OF DOGGER BANK

7 MAY: LUSITANIA SUNK

31 MAY: BATTLE OF JUTLAND - INDECISIVE. BRITISH MATERIAL DEFEAT BUT STRATEGIC VICTORY

THE FIRST WORLD WAR

N ..., STÜRGKH, ...NATED

...V. WILSON ...LECTED US ...SIDENT

7 DEC: LLOYD GEORGE SUCCEEDS ASQUITH AS BRITISH PREMIER

21 NOV: AUSTRIAN EMPEROR, FRANS JOSEPH, DIES. SUCCEEDED BY CHARLES I

15 FEB: HUGHES BECOMES AUSTRALIAN PREMIER

MARCH: RUSSIAN REVOLUTION

3 MAY: PÉTAIN BECOMES FRENCH C-IN-C
20 MAY: UNITS OF FRENCH ARMY MUTINY

16 MARCH: TSAR ABDICATES

7 OCT: OCTOBER REVOLUTION IN RUSSIA

17 DEC: BORDEN BECOMES CANADIAN PREMIER

14 JAN: CAILLAUX, FORMER FRENCH PREMIER ARRESTED FOR TREASON

UK Prime Minister Lloyd George

16 JULY: TSAR & FAMILY EXECUTED

11 NOV: ARMISTICE

8 NOV: BATTLE ...SOMME

15 SEPT: THE BRITISH ARE THE FIRST TO USE TANKS IN COMBAT

27 AUG: ROUMANIAN ...OFFENSIVE

AUG-END OF DEC: ROUMANIA OVERRUN BY CENTRAL POWERS

9 JULY-15 APRIL: BATTLE OF ARRAS/VIMY RIDGE

7-14 JUNE: BATTLE OF MESSINE

31 JULY-6 NOV: 3rd BATTLE OF YPRES

The air war increased in intensity as the war progressed

Tsar Alexander of Russia

SEPT: RIGA OPERATIONS

JULY: KERENSKY OFFENSIVE

12 DEC: RUSSIAN ARMISTICE

20 NOV-3 DEC: BATTLE OF CAMBRAI

21 MARCH-17 JULY: FIVE SEPARATE GERMAN OFFENSIVES ALONG THE FRONT

15 JULY-7 AUG: 2nd BATTLE OF THE MARNE

26 SEPT-11 NOV: MEUSE/ARGONNE OFFENSIVE

British troops capture Montauban

London Scots on the march

A French howitzer in action

Armoured cars proved increasingly useful as the war progressed

29 SEPT: BULGARIAN ARMISTICE

Close-quarters fighting as French infantry attack

AUG: 6th BATTLE OF ISONZO

14-26 SEP: 7th BATTLE OF ISONZO

10-12 OCT: 8th BATTLE OF ISONZO

1-14 NOV: 9th BATTLE OF ISONZO

12 MAY-8 JUNE: 10th BATTLE OF ISONZO

18 AUG-15 SEPT: 11th BATTLE OF ISONZO

24 OCT-7 NOV: BATTLE OF CAPORETTO

15-22 JUNE: BATTLE OF PIAVE

4 NOV: AUSTRO-ITALIAN ARMISTICE

24 OCT-4 NOV: BATTLE OF VITTORIO VENETO

LATE SEPT: 2nd BRITISH ADVANCE BEGINS

22-23 FEB: 2nd BATTLE OF KUT

11 MARCH: BRITISH TAKE BAGHDAD

27-28 SEPT: BATTLE OF RAMADI

US General Pershing

General Hindenburg

4 AUG: BRITISH OCCUPY BAKU ON CASPIAN COAST

14 SEPT: BRITISH ABANDON BAKU UNDER TURKISH PRESSURE

NOV: BRITISH RE-TAKE BAKU

NOV: BRITISH TAKE MOSUL OILFIELDS

Marshal Joffre

8-9 JAN: BATTLE OF MAGRUNTEIN

26 MARCH: 1st BATTLE OF GAZA

17-18 APRIL: 2nd BATTLE OF GAZA

31 OCT: BATTLE OF BEERSHEBA

13-14 NOV: BATTLE OF JUNCTION STATION

8 DEC: BRITISH TAKE JERUSALEM

Marshal Foch

1 OCT: DAMASCUS IS TAKEN BY BRITISH

19TH SEPT: BATTLE OF MEGIDDO

17 NOV: 2nd BATTLE OF HELIGOLAND BIGHT

The German fleet being led to Scapa Flow, and surrendour

Pioneering German air ace Max Immelmann

A long-range railway gun opens fire

SECOND WORLD WAR

The middle of the twentieth century sa[w]
greatest war yet, with the added horr[or]
mass 'industrialised' murder of milli[ons]
Jews and other civilians. Bombing of
brought civilians into the front-line. Air

	1939	**1940**	**1941**	
	S O N D	**J F M A M J J A S O N D**	**J F M A M J J A S O N D**	**J F M**

THE ATLANTIC

17 SEPT: RN CARRIER COURAGEOUS SUNK

13 DEC: BATTLE OF THE RIVER PLATE. GERMAN POCKET BATTLESHIP GRAF SPEE SCUTTLED, 17 DEC

5 NOV: GERMAN POCKET BATTLESHIP ADMIRAL SCHEER SINKS BRITISH ARMED MERCHANT CRUISER JERVIS BAY

23-25 SEPT: ALLIED EXPEDITION TO DAKAR FAILS

24 MAY: GERMAN BATTLESHIP BISMARCK SINKS BRITISH BATTLECRUISER HOOD

27 MAY: BISMARCK SUNK BY BRITISH FORCES

8 MAY: BRITISH DESTROYER BULLDOG CAPTURES U110 WITH SECRET ENIGMA CODES

27 SEPT: US LAUNCHES FIRST LIBERTY SHIP

26 SEPT: FIRST ARCTIC CONVOY LEAVES BRITAIN FOR USSR

11-13 FEB: 'CHANNEL DASH' GERMAN BATTLECRUISERS SCHARNHORST AND GNEIS[ENAU] RETURN TO GERMANY

WAR IN THE AIR

4 SEPT: 1ST RAF RAID ON GERMANY

15 SEPT: WARSAW DEVASTATED BY LUFTWAFFE AND ARTILLERY BOMBARDMENT

4 MAY: ROTTERDAM DEVASTATED BY LUFTWAFFE

25/26 AUG: RAF BOMB BERLIN FOR FIRST TIME

7 SEPT: BLITZ BEGINS

15 AUG-31 OCT: BATTLE OF BRITAIN GERMAN ONSLAUGHT REPULSED

17 SEPT: OPERATION 'SEALION', GERMAN INVASION OF GREAT BRITAIN, POSTPONED INDEFINITELY BY HITLER

11-12 NOV: RN AIR ATTACK ON TARANTO HARBOUR

10/11 MAY: BLITZ ENDS

20 MAY: GERMAN AIRBORNE ASSAULT ON CRETE BEGINS

7 DEC: JAPANESE AIR RAID ON PEARL HABOR

18 APRIL: DOOLITTLE RAID ON JAPANESE MAINLAND

24 APRIL: ST. BAEDEKER [RAIDS] ON BRITISH PROVINCIAL

WESTERN FRONT

9 APRIL TO 8 JUNE: NORWAY CAMPAIGN. GERMANY INVADES NORWAY AND REPULSES ALLIED INTERVENTION

THE 'PHONEY WAR' OR 'SITSKRIEG' - THE ENEMY FORCES WATCH EACH OTHER ACROSS THE BORDERS

10 MAY TO 25 JUNE: GERMAN BLITZKRIEG CONQUEST OF BELGIUM AND FRANCE.

26 MAY TO 3 JUNE: DUNKIRK EVACUATION OF BRITISH EXPEDITIONARY FORCE

14 JUNE: GERMANS TAKE PARIS

27 FEB: BRUNEVAL RAID. BRITISH COMMANDOS CAP[TURE] GERMAN RADAR STATION

27 MARCH: ST NAZAIRE RAID. BRITISH COMMAND[OS] DESTROY DOCK

British Churchill tank, well armoured, but poorly armed when compared with German tanks

EASTERN FRONT

1 SEPT: GERMANY INVADES POLAND

17 SEPT: USSR INVADES POLAND

27 SEPT: POLAND SURRENDERS

30 NOV: USSR INVADES FINLAND. 6 DEC: ATTACKS FINNISH MANNERHEIM LINE

12 MARCH: PEACE TREATY

Soviet infantry dressed in winter camouflage

6-8 APRIL: GERMANY AND ITALY INVADE YUGOSLAVIA

17 APRIL: YUGOSLAVIA SURRENDERS

20 APRIL: GREECE SURRENDERS

8 JUNE-14 JULY: ALLIES CAPTURE SYRIA

22 JUNE: OPERATION BARBAROSSA - GERMANY INVADES USSR

16 JULY: SMOLENSK FALLS TO GERMANS

19 SEPT: GERMANS TAKE KIEV

2 OCT: GERMANS LAUNCH OP[ERA]TION TYPHOON AGAINST MOS[COW]

24 OCT: KHARKOV FALLS

28 AUGUST: ALLIES CAPTURE IRAN

THE MEDITERRANEAN

11-12 NOV: RN ATTACK TARANTO AND CRIPPLE ITALIAN BATTLE FLEET

3-6 JULY: RN ATTACK VICHY FRENCH FLEET AT MERS-EL-KEBIR

12 SEPT: ITALIANS INVADE EGYPT

6 FEB: BRITISH CAPTURE BENGAZI

9 DEC: BRITISH DEFEAT ITALIANS AT SIDI BARRANI

28 MARCH: RN VICTORY AT BATTLE OF MATAPAN

20 MAY: GERMANS CAPTURE CRETE

18 NOV: OPERATION CRUSADER, ALLIES RELIEVE TOBRUK

21 JUNE: [AXIS] FORCES C[APTURE] TOBRUK

SOUTH-EAST ASIA AND THE PACIFIC

Churchill, Roosevelt and Stalin at the Yalta conference, 1945

USS Seadragon. The USN waged a highly successful campaign of unrestricted submarine warfare against Japan

7 DEC: JAPANESE ATTACK ON PEARL HARBOR

Admiral Yamamoto, the man behind Japan's early strategy

10 DEC: JAPANESE INVADE THE PHILIPP[INES]

18 APRIL: DOLITTLE

27 FEB: JAPA[NESE] NAVAL VICTO[RY] BATTLE OF J[AVA SEA]

POLITICS AND WORLD EVENTS

3 SEPT: BRITAIN AND FRANCE DECLARE WAR ON GERMANY

27 MARCH: FRASER BECOMES PRIME MINISTER OF NEW ZEALAND

10 MAY: CHURCHILL BECOMES PRIME MINISTER OF BRITAIN

10 JUNE: ITALY DECLARES WAR ON BRITAIN AND FRANCE

22 JULY: SPECIAL OPERATIONS EXECUTIVE SET UP TO ORGANIZE RESISTANCE IN OCCUPIED EUROPE

5 NOV: ROOSEVELT ELECTED TO 3RD TERM AS PRESIDENT OF THE USA

29 DEC: ROOSEVELT DECLARES USA TO BE THE 'ARSENAL OF DEMOCRACY'

10 MAY: RUDOLF HESS FLIES TO SCOTLAND ON UNOFFICIAL PEACE MISSION

9-12 AUG: ALLIES' PLACENTIA BAY CONFERENCE

7 OCT: CURTIN BECOMES PRIME MINISTER OF AUSTRALIA

22 DEC -14 JAN: ALLIES' ARCADIA CONFERENCE AT WASHINGTON

8 DEC: USA AND ALLIED NATI[ONS] DECLARE WAR ON JAPAN. 11 D[EC] GERMANY DECLARES WAR O[N USA]

16 [APRIL] MALTA [AWARD]ED G[EORGE CROSS]

to reign supreme, while German U-boats threat-
to starve Britain into surrender, and armoured vehi-
ominated the battlefields, ushering in a new period
anoeuvre. The last act of war introduced what
ed to be the ultimate weapon – the nuclear bomb.

The USAAF B-17 Flying Fortress (left)
and the RAF Avro Lancaster (right) heavy
bombers bore the brunt of the bombing
campaign against Germany.

31 DEC: BATTLE OF THE
BARENTS SEA. HITLER
ABANDONS USE OF
SURFACE SHIPS
AGAINST ALLIED
CONVOYS

15-19 MARCH: CONVOYS
HX229 AND SC122 MARK
CLIMAX OF THE BATTLE
OF THE ATLANTIC

26 DEC: BATTLE OF
NORTH CAPE. BRITISH
FLEET SINKS GERMAN
BATTLECRUISER
SCHARNHORST

12 NOV: GERMAN
BATTLESHIP TIRPITZ
FINALLY SUNK, AFTER
MANY ATTACKS, BY
RAF BOMBERS

A Hunt Class destroyer of
the Royal Navy

Y PQ17

Field Marshal
Montgomery

27 JAN: FIRST RAID OF
THE US 8TH AF

17 AUG: 8TH AF RAID
SCHWEINFURT & REGENSBURG
INDUSTRIAL AREAS
RAF RAID ON PEENEMUNDE V-
WEAPON RESEARCH SITES

18 FEB: RAF RAID
AMIENS PRISON

13 FEB: RAID ON DRESDEN

16 MAY:
DAMBUSTERS RAID

13 JUNE: FIRST V-1
FLYING BOMB LAUNCHED
AGAINST ENGLAND

8 SEPT: FIRST V-2
ROCKET LAUNCHED
AGAINST ENGLAND

9/10 MARCH: TOKYO
DEVESTATED BY
INCENDIARY RAID

AF Supermarine
pitfire

30 AUG: FIRST RAF 1,000 BOMBER RAID ON GERMANY

18 NOV: BEGINNING OF
AERIAL BATTLE OF BERLIN

24/25 MARCH: RAF SUFFER SEVERE
LOSSES DURING NUREMBERG RAID

24 NOV: FIRST USAAF
B-29 AIR-RAID ON JAPAN

D-DAY - 6 JUNE: IN THE GREATEST
AMPHIBIOUS INVASION EVER
MOUNTED, ALLIED FORCES
FIGHT THEIR WAY ASHORE IN
NORMANDY

PARIS: 19 AUG PARIS RISING. 25 AUG GERMANS
SURRENDER THE CITY

17-26 SEPT: AIRBORNE OPER-
ATION 'MARKET GARDEN' -
ALLIES FAIL TO FORCE A
RHINE CROSSING

7-31 MARCH: ALLIES
CROSS THE RHINE

OV: GERMAN AND
IAN FORCES OCCUPY
HY FRANCE. FRENCH
T SCUTTLES AT
LON ON 27 NOV

1-31 JULY: OPERATIONS 'COBRA'
AND 'GOODWOOD' - ALLIED
BREAKOUT FROM THE BEACH-
HEAD. LARGE PART OF THE GER-
MAN ARMIES TRAPPED IN THE
'FALAISE POCKET'. BY 21 AUG
FORCED TO SURRENDER

3 SEPT:
BRUSSELS
LIBERATED

APRIL: ALLIED ARMIES
ADVANCE ON BROAD
FRONT INTO GERMANY

25 APRIL: WEST AND
EAST ALLIED FRONTS
MEET AT TORGAU

German anti-tank
gunners in action

: DIEPPE RAID BY CANADIANS AND BRITISH
MANDOS REPULSED WITH HEAVY LOSS

15 AUG: OPERATION 'DRAGOON' -
ALLIES LAND IN SOUTH OF FRANCE

16 DEC-28 JAN: 'BATTLE OF THE BULGE' -
GERMAN ARDENNES OFFENSIVE FAILS,
THEIR LAST BIG ATTACK IN WEST

SURRENDERS:
4 MAY LUNEBURG
HEATH [N. GERMANY,
DENMARK,
HOLLAND].
7 MAY RHEIMS
SURRENDER TO
EISENHOWER.
8 MAY BERLIN
SURRENDER
CEREMONY.

GERMANS
OPERATION
THRUST
S THE
US AND
RAD

2 FEB: GERMAN
ARMY TRAPPED AT
STALINGRAD
SURRENDERS

5 JULY: START OF
BATTLE OF KURSK
- GREATEST TANK
BATTLE IN HISTO-
RY. GERMANS ARE
DEFEATED

6 NOV:
USSR
RETAKES
KIEV

27 JAN:
END OF THE
SIEGE OF
LENINGRAD

1 AUG - 3 OCT:
2ND WARSAW UPRISING.
BUT WARSAW FALLS TO
USSR ONLY ON 17 JAN

16 APRIL - 2 MAY:
BATTLE OF BERLIN -
SOVIET FORCES
TAKE POSSESSION
OF THE GERMAN
CAPITAL

19 APRIL: 1ST
WARSAW UPRISING

23 AUG: USSR
RETAKES KHARKOV

10 APRIL: USSR
RETAKES ODESSA

AXIS
Y AT

23 OCT-4 NOV: ALLIED
VICTORY AT EL
ALAMEIN

19 FEB: AXIS FORCES
SEIZE THE
KASSERINE PASS

3 SEPT: ALLIES INVADE MAINLAND ITALY
8 SEPT: ITALY SURRENDERS
9 SEPT: SALERNO LANDINGS

4 JUNE: ALLIES
ENTER ROME

14 OCT: BRITISH
ENTER ATHENS

4 OCT: CORSICA
LIBERATED

22 JAN: ANZIO LANDINGS

NOV: OPERATION TORCH, ALLIED
ANDINGS IN NORTH AFRICA

3 MAY: TUNIS
FALLS AND THE
AXIS SURRENDER
TO THE ALLIES

10 JULY-17 AUG: ALLIES
INVADE AND TAKE SICILY

1 FEB: BATTLES FOR
MONTE CASSINO BEGIN

29 APRIL: GERMAN FORCES
IN ITALY SURRENDER

14 AUGUST: JAPAN
SURRENDERS

19 FEB: BATTLE OF
IWO JIMA BEGINS

13 FEB: FIRST CHINDIT OPERATION

21 MARCH: US LAND ON
ISLAND OF NORTH GEORGIA

2 MARCH: SECOND
CHINDIT OPERATION

19-20 JUNE: US NAVAL VICTORY AT
BATTLE OF PHILIPPINE SEA

6 & 9 AUG: ATOMIC BOMB-
ING OF HIROSHIMA AND
NAGASAKI

BATTLE OF CORAL SEA

20 OCT: US
INVADES THE PHILIPPINES

15 JUNE: STRATEGIC BOMB-
ING OF JAPAN BEGINS

20 NOV: BATTLE
OF TARAWA

1 APRIL: BATTLE OF
OKINAWA BEGINS

7 AUG: US LAND ON GUADALCANAL

3-5 MARCH: BATTLE
OF BISMARCK SEA

15 MAR: BATTLE OF
IMPHAL-KOHIMA

23-26 OCT: US NAVAL
VICTORY AT BATTLE OF
LEYTE GULF

JUNE: US NAVAL VICTORY
BATTLE OF MIDMAY

12 APRIL: DEATH OF ROOSEVELT.
TRUMAN BECOMES PRESIDENT OF THE USA

DEATHS OF THE DICTATORS
28 APRIL: MUSSOLINI SHOT.
30 APRIL: HITLER SUICIDE

25 JULY: FALL OF MUSSOLINI.
BADOGLIO BECOMES PRIME
MINISTER OF ITALY

13 OCT: ITALY DECLARES
WAR ON GERMANY

18 JULY: FALL
OF JAPANESE
PREMIER TOJO

20 JULY: BOMB PLOT FAILS TO
ASSASSINATE HITLER

26 JULY: ATTLEE BECOMES PRIME
MINISTER OF BRITAIN

LL

ALIN

OW

14-24 JAN: ALLIES'
SYMBOL CONFERENCE
AT CASABLANCA

19 APRIL:
ALLIES' MEET
ON BERMUDA

11-25 MAY:
ALLIES' TRIDENT
CONFERENCE
AT WASHINGTON

ALLIED CONFERENCES
17-24 AUG: QUADRANT AT QUEBEC.
23-26 NOV AND 3-7 DEC: SEXTANT AT
CAIRO.
28 NOV-1 DEC: EUREKA AT TEHRAN

1 JULY:
ALLIES'
BRETTON WOODS
CONFERENCE
BEGINS

ALLIED CONFERENCES 12-16 SEPT: OCTAGON AT QUEBEC.
21 SEPT: DUMBARTON OAKS. 9 OCT: TOLSTOY AT MOSCOW.
30 JAN-11 FEB ARGONAUT AT MALTA AND YALTA. 17 JULY-
2 AUG: TERMINAL AT POTSDAM.

143

WAR IN THE AIR

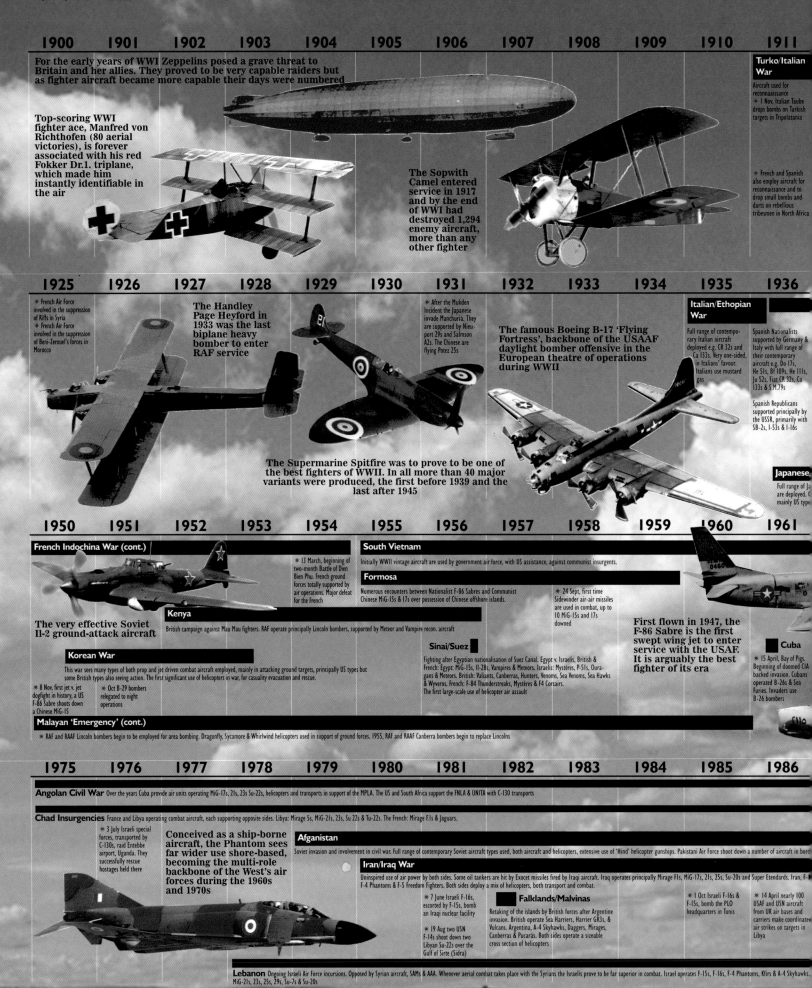

1900	1901	1902	1903	1904	1905	1906	1907	1908	1909	1910	1911

For the early years of WWI Zeppelins posed a grave threat to Britain and her allies. They proved to be very capable raiders but as fighter aircraft became more capable their days were numbered

Top-scoring WWI fighter ace, Manfred von Richthofen (80 aerial victories), is forever associated with his red Fokker Dr.1 triplane, which made him instantly identifiable in the air

The Sopwith Camel entered service in 1917 and by the end of WWI had destroyed 1,294 enemy aircraft, more than any other fighter

Turko/Italian War
Aircraft used for reconnaissance
✷ 1 Nov, Italian Taube drops bombs on Turkish targets in Tripolatania

✷ French and Spanish also employ aircraft for reconnaissance and to drop small bombs and darts on rebellious tribesmen in North Africa

1925	1926	1927	1928	1929	1930	1931	1932	1933	1934	1935	1936

✷ French Air Force involved in the suppression of Riffs in Syria
✷ French Air Force involved in the suppression of Beni-Zerouel's forces in Morocco

The Handley Page Heyford in 1933 was the last biplane heavy bomber to enter RAF service

✷ After the Mukden Incident the Japanese invade Manchuria. They are supported by Nieuport 29s and Salmson A2s. The Chinese are flying Potez 25s

The famous Boeing B-17 'Flying Fortress', backbone of the USAAF daylight bomber offensive in the European theatre of operations during WWII

The Supermarine Spitfire was to prove to be one of the best fighters of WWII. In all more than 40 major variants were produced, the first before 1939 and the last after 1945

Italian/Ethiopian War
Full range of contemporary Italian aircraft deployed e.g. CR 32s and Ca 133s. Very one-sided, in Italians' favour. Italians use mustard gas

Spanish Nationalists supported by Germany & Italy with full range of their contemporary aircraft e.g. Do 17s, He 51s, Bf 109s, He 111s, Ju 52s, Fiat CR 32s, Ca 133s & S.M.79s

Spanish Republicans supported principally by the USSR, primarily with SB-2s, I-53s & I-16s

Japanese
Full range of Ja are deployed. C mainly US types

1950	1951	1952	1953	1954	1955	1956	1957	1958	1959	1960	1961

French Indochina War (cont.)
✷ 13 March, beginning of two-month Battle of Dien Bien Phu. French ground forces totally supported by air operations. Major defeat for the French

The very effective Soviet Il-2 ground-attack aircraft

Kenya
British campaign against Mau Mau fighters. RAF operate principally Lincoln bombers, supported by Meteor and Vampire recon. aircraft

Korean War
This war sees many types of both prop and jet driven combat aircraft employed, mainly in attacking ground targets, principally US types but some British types also seeing action. The first significant use of helicopters in war, for casualty evacuation and rescue.
✷ 8 Nov, first jet v. jet dogfight in history, a US F-86 Sabre shoots down a Chinese MiG-15
✷ Oct B-29 bombers relegated to night operations

South Vietnam
Initially WWII vintage aircraft are used by government air force, with US assistance, against communist insurgents.

Formosa
Numerous encounters between Nationalist F-86 Sabres and Communist Chinese MiG-15s & 17s over possession of Chinese offshore islands.
✷ 24 Sept, first time Sidewinder air-air missiles are used in combat, up to 10 MiG-15s and 17s downed

Sinai/Suez
Fighting after Egyptian nationalisation of Suez Canal. Egypt v. Israelis, British & French: Egypt: MiG-15s, Il-28s, Vampires & Meteors. Israelis: Mystères, P-51s, Ouragans & Meteors. British: Valiants, Canberras, Hunters, Venoms, Sea Venoms, Sea Hawks & Wyverns. French: F-84 Thunderstreaks, Mystères & F4 Corsairs.
The first large-scale use of helicopter air assault

First flown in 1947, the F-86 Sabre is the first swept wing jet to enter service with the USAF. It is arguably the best fighter of its era

Cuba
✷ 15 April, Bay of Pigs. Beginning of doomed CIA backed invasion. Cubans operated B-26s & Sea Furies. Invaders use B-26 bombers

Malayan 'Emergency' (cont.)
✷ RAF and RAAF Lincoln bombers begin to be employed for area bombing. Dragonfly, Sycamore & Whirlwind helicopters used in support of ground forces. 1955, RAF and RAAF Canberra bombers begin to replace Lincolns

1975	1976	1977	1978	1979	1980	1981	1982	1983	1984	1985	1986

Angolan Civil War Over the years Cuba provide air units operating MiG-17s, 21s, 23s Su-22s, helicopters and transports in support of the MPLA. The US and South Africa support the FNLA & UNITA with C-130 transports

Chad Insurgencies France and Libya operating combat aircraft, each supporting opposite sides. Libya: Mirage 5s, MiG-21s, 23s, Su 22s & Tu-22s. The French: Mirage F.1s & Jaguars.

✷ 3 July Israeli special forces, transported by C-130s, raid Entebbe airport, Uganda. They successfully rescue hostages held there

Conceived as a ship-borne aircraft, the Phantom sees far wider use shore-based, becoming the multi-role backbone of the West's air forces during the 1960s and 1970s

Afghanistan
Soviet invasion and involvement in civil war. Full range of contemporary Soviet aircraft types used, both aircraft and helicopters, extensive use of 'Hind' helicopter gunships. Pakistani Air Force shoot down a number of aircraft in border

Iran/Iraq War
Uninspired use of air power by both sides. Some oil tankers are hit by Exocet missiles fired by Iraqi aircraft. Iraq operates principally Mirage F1s, MiG-17s, 21s, 25s, Su-20s and Super Etendards. Iran, F-4 Phantoms & F-5 Freedom Fighters. Both sides deploy a mix of helicopters, both transport and combat.
✷ 7 June Israeli F-16s, escorted by F-15s, bomb an Iraqi nuclear facility
✷ 19 Aug two USN F-14s shoot down two Libyan Su-22s over the Gulf of Sirte (Sidra)

Falklands/Malvinas
Retaking of the islands by British forces after Argentine invasion. British operate Sea Harriers, Harrier GR3s, & Vulcans. Argentina, A-4 Skyhawks, Daggers, Mirages, Canberras & Pucarás. Both sides operate a sizeable cross section of helicopters

✷ 1 Oct Israeli F-16s & F-15s, bomb the PLO headquarters in Tunis

✷ 14 April nearly 100 USAF and USN aircraft from UK air bases and carriers make coordinated air strikes on targets in Libya

Lebanon Ongoing Israeli Air Force incursions. Opposed by Syrian aircraft, SAMs & AAA. Whenever aerial combat takes place with the Syrians the Israelis prove to be far superior in combat. Israel operates F-15s, F-16s, F-4 Phantoms, Kfirs & A-4 Skyhawks. MiG-21s, 23s, 25s, 29s, Su-7s & Su-20s

1913	1914	1915	1916	1917	1918	1919	1920	1921	1922	1923	1924

Mexican Revolution

✴ Aircraft bombs government gunboats
✴ Nov, first dogfight in history, using revolvers, between Phil Rader and Dean Lamb

World War One

Aircraft initially used purely for reconnaissance, but pilots exchange shots with handguns etc
✴ During autumn numerous targets across Belgium and Northern France bombed by Zeppelins
✴ 30 Aug, Paris bombed by German Taube
✴ 22 Sept, Zeppelin sheds at Düsseldorf and Cologne bombed by RNAS on 21 Nov
✴ 22 Dec, Dover is bombed by a single German aircraft

During this year aircraft begin to be armed with machine guns
✴ 19 Jan, Zeppelin bombs Great Yarmouth. This initiates the Zeppelin campaign against Great Britain
✴ 31 May, Zeppelin bombs London for the first time
✴ 6 June, Zeppelin LZ37, while in flight, is destroyed by hand launched bombs by Flt Sub-Lt Warneford (RFC)
✴ Summer. The 'Fokker Scourge'. Fokker monoplanes, with forward firing synchronised machine-guns, dominate the skies
✴ Aug, Fokker E.III enters service
● Oct, F.E.2B

✴ Spring, the Allies gain aerial dominance
✴ Autumn, the Germans regain aerial dominance with introduction of Oswald Boelke's superior tactics
● Feb, D.H.2
● April, Sopwith Pup & Nieuport 17
● July, SPAD 7
● Sept, Albatros D.II
● Nov, Handley Page 0/100 bomber

✴ 'Bloody April', British suffer 50% casualties during month
✴ 13 June, Gotha bombers begin raids on London. Zeppelin raids have ceased
✴ Summer, the Allies regain aerial dominance with improved tactics, training and equipment
● Jan, Sopwith Triplane
● Feb, Albatros D.III & Gotha G.IV
● April, Bristol Fighter
● May, S.E.5a
● June, Sopwith Camel & Albatros DV
● July, Pfalz D.III
● Aug, Fokker Dr.I Triplane
● Sept, SPAD 13

✴ March, large German air offensive in support of Ludendorff's offensive, intensive air to ground attack. Temporary German air superiority, but Allies maintain dominance for remainder of year
✴ Paris bombed by German Gothas
✴ 21 April, von Richthofen, the war's premier ace, is shot down and killed
● 1 April RAF formed by uniting RFC & RNAS
● 13 May, British form Independent Force for strategic bombing
● May, Fokker D.VII

3rd Afgan War

✴ Operational use of RAF units on NW Frontier for reconnaissance and bombing
● Bristol F.2b, D.H.10 & D.H.9 primary aircraft deployed

Russia Civil War

✴ Poles employ Fokker D.VII fighters in fighting

✴ RAF V/1500 bomber attacks Kabul

✴ RAF become involved in the suppression of revolts in Iraq

The Boeing F4B carrier-borne fighter entered service with the US Navy in 1929. One example was sent to China for demonstration purposes, where it became the first US fighter to shoot down a Japanese aircraft, during the Chinese/Japanese conflict.

1938	1939	1940	1941	1942	1943	1944	1945	1946	1947	1948	1949

...War

The Focke-Wulf 190 proved to be Germany's finest fighter of WWII

becomes part of WWII

World War Two

Aircraft vital part of 'Blitzkrieg' tactics
✴ 15 Sept, Warsaw heavily bombed by Luftwaffe

✴ 10 April, German cruiser Königsberg, is the first major warship to be sunk by aircraft, RN Skua dive-bombers
✴ 10/11 May, largest air-raid on London, marks end of 'Blitz'
✴ 10 May, successful German airborne assault on forts of Eben Emael, Belgium
✴ 14 May, centre of Rotterdam devastated by Luftwaffe
✴ Summer, Battle of Britain, triumph for RAF
✴ London and Berlin first bombed, (7 & 9 Sept.)
✴ 11 Nov, RN aircraft successfully attack Italian Fleet at Taranto
✴ Autumn/winter, 'Blitz' night bomber offensive against UK cities

✴ 6 April, Luftwaffe heavily bomb Belgrade
✴ 20 May, successful German airborne assault on Crete
✴ 7 Dec, Japanese carrier aircraft attack on Pearl Harbor
✴ 10 Dec, British battleships Repulse & Prince of Wales sunk by Japanese bombers in South China Sea

✴ Spring, Luftwaffe begins 'Baedeker' raids against UK provincial cities
✴ 22 March, Japanese aircraft bomb Darwin, Australia
✴ 18 April, Doolittle raid on Tokyo
✴ 8 May, Battle of Coral Sea, first carrier v. carrier
✴ 30/31May, first RAF 1,000 bomber raid, against Cologne
✴ 4/6 June, carrier v. carrier Battle of Midway, decisive US victory
✴ 24/26 Oct, carrier Battle of Santa Cruz
✴ Winter, Stalingrad, failure of Luftwaffe airlift

✴ 27 Jan, first USAAF mission against Germany, Wilhelmshaven
✴ 16/17 May, RAF 'Dambusters' raid
✴ 5 March–10 July, Battle of the Ruhr, RAF offensive against German industrial cities
✴ 24 July–3 Aug, RAF & USAAF raid on Hamburg 40,000 killed in firestorm
✴ 1 Aug, USAAF raid on Ploesti oilfields in Roumania
✴ 17 Aug, disastrous USAAF raids on Schweinfurt and Regensburg

✴ 31 Feb, first USAAF raid on Berlin
✴ 30/31 March, disastrous RAF raid on Nuremberg
✴ 13 June, first V-1 flying bomb strikes UK
✴ 19/20 June, carrier v. carrier Battle of Philippine Sea, US victory
✴ 8 Sept, first V-2 rocket strikes UK
✴ 17 Sept, failed airborne operation 'Market Garden' launched
✴ 25/26 October, 4 Japanese carriers sunk, Cape Engano
✴ 12 Nov, RAF bombers sink the battleship Tirpitz

✴ 13/14 Feb, RAF & USAAF raid on Dresden, over 50,000 killed
✴ 9/10 March, first major incendiary raid on Japan
✴ 6 Aug, atom bomb attack on Hiroshima
✴ 9 Aug, atom bomb attack on Nagasaki
✴ 24 Nov, first B-29 raid on Japanese mainland

French Indochina War

French air force and naval aircraft, principally of US types, e.g. F-6 Hellcats, F-8 Bearcats, and B-26 bombers, operate in support of ground forces operating against liberationists

Berlin Airlift

29 June 48 – 19 May 49, Soviet blockade of the city is successfully broken by a major Western airlift of food and fuel

Cold War (1947-90)

✴ Strategic intelligence gathering employ many types of aircraft e.g. Canberras, U-2s, RB-47s and SR-71s. Approximately 40 Western aircraft are shot down during four decades of activity

Chinese Civil War

Nationalist Chinese use US types, e.g. P-51s, P-47, B-25/26s

Malayan 'Emergency'

RAF support of ground forces successful struggle against communist guerrillas. Early years see the employment of such types as Spitfires, Hornets and Brigands.

1963	1964	1965	1966	1967	1968	1969	1970	1971	1972	1973	1974

FU-460

G-15 and 17 s were the ay of the and her uring the nd 1970s. G-17 below with the an Air Force

US Air Force, Navy & Marine aircraft with South Vietnam Air Force in ongoing support of ground forces against Viet Cong and North Vietnamese forces. Full range of US aircraft types deployed, principal examples F-4 Phantoms, F-105 Thunderchiefs, F-100 Super Sabres, B-57 Canberras, A-4 Skyhawks & Skyraiders. Massive use of transport helicopters and helicopter gunships. USAF and USN aircraft see aerial combat with North Vietnamese MiGs, which prove to be more than competent in combat. Aerial campaign also include Laos and Cambodia. (Between 1962 to 1973 USAF lose over 2,250 aircraft of all types)

✴ After the Gulf of Tonkin Incident, 2 Aug, direct US involvement increases dramatically, particularly RB-57 Canberras, F-100 and F-105 jet fighters and naval aircraft operating offshore

✴ 2 March, start of Operation 'Rolling Thunder', bombing of N. Vietnam.
✴ 18 June, B-52 bombers make first attacks on S. Vietnamese targets

Indo/Pakistan War

✴ Inconclusive conflict over Kashmir. Air combat and ground attack was carried out by both sides. Indian operating principally MiG-21s, Hunters, Gnats, Mysteres, Ouragans & Canberras. Pakistan, F-104 Starfighters, F-86 Sabres & B-57s. In air combat the PAF is generally considered to have performed better than the IAF

✴ 12 April, B-52s employed for first time to attack targets in N. Vietnam.

Six-Day War

✴ Overwhelming land and aerial victory by Israel over Egypt, Syria, Jordan and their allies. Israel operating principally Mirage IIIs, Super Mystères, Mystères, Ouragans & Vautours. Egypt, MiG-21s, 19s, 17s, 15s, Il-28s & Tu-16s. Syria, MiG-21s, 17s, 15s & Il-28s. Jordan, F-104 Starfighters, Hunters & Vampires

1 Nov, bombing of N. Vietnam ceases

✴ 5 June onwards, strikes on N. Vietnam occur from time to time

War of Attrition

✴ Fought between Egypt, with Soviet assistance, & Israel along the frontier. Egyptian losses of the Six Day War have been replaced, plus the addition of Su-7 ground-attack fighters. Israel is supplied with US F-4 Phantoms & A-4 Skyhawks. Soviet 'volunteer' pilots also fly against the Israelis. The Israelis tend to maintain the upper hand

Indo/Pakistan War

✴ Initiated by the fighting for independence of East Pakistan (Bangladesh). India operating principally MiG-21s, Sukhoi Su-7s, Maruts, Hunters, Gnats, Canberras & Navy Sea Hawks. Pakistan, Mirage IIIs, Shenyang F-6s, F-104 Starfighters, F-86 Sabres & B-57s. In air combat, as in 1965, the PAF is generally considered to perform better than the IAF

✴ 6 April, resumption of aerial attacks on N. Vietnam. US aircraft opposed by N. Vietnamese MiG-17s, 19s, 21s and SAMs & AAA
✴ 18-30 Dec, Operation 'Linebacker' a period of intensely heavy bombing of N. Vietnam
✴ 15 Aug, bombing of Cambodia stops

Yom Kippur War

✴ 6 Oct large-scale attack on Israel by Egypt & Syria. Israel initially suffers heavy aircraft losses mainly to SAMs & AAA, but manages to maintain air superiority. Israel comes out militarily on top. Aircraft types used are the same mix as during War of Attrition.

Cyprus

✴ 20 July, Turkey begins her invasion of the island supported by F-104 Starfighters & F-100 Super Sabres in ground-attack role. No aerial combat with Greek aircraft

South Africa

1966 to late 1980s South African Air Force carries out air strikes into Angola, Namibia and Mozambique. Use Canberras, Buccaneers, Mirages and Impalas. Puma, Super Frelon and Alouette helicopters support ground operations

1988	1989	1990	1991	1992	1993	1994	1995	1996	1997	1998	1999

✴ 4 Jan two USN F-14s shoot down two Libyan Mig-23s over the Med

Kuwait/ Desert Storm

✴ Coalition v. Iraq. The expulsion of Iraqi forces from Kuwait. The Coalition air offensive is intense and sees the extensive use of hi-tech weapons and the full range of Western aircraft.

Bosnia-Hercegovina

NATO air patrols and air-strikes in support of the peacekeeping forces in the area. Has involved the use of major types operated by the alliance. An F-16 and a Sea Harrier are shot down

The F-16 has inherited the Phantom's role of being the West's main combat aircraft during the 1980s and 90s, being in service with a dozen and more air forces around the world

Kosovo Air War

Successful NATO air campaign to get Serbian ground forces to vacate Kosovo. Only one aircraft is lost during a mission, an F-117 Stealth fighter. A small number of Serb aircraft are shot down

Iraq: Operation Desert Fox

Starting on 16 Dec, 4 nights of air strikes by US and British aircraft, because Saddam Hussein will not co-operate with UN weapons inspectors

Kashmir

Tactical air strikes are carried out in support of ground forces during the ongoing clashes between India and Pakistan over the disputed border

WAR TODAY — AND TOMORROW

More than half a century since the last World War, tensions continue around the world. The Cold War between the Eastern bloc and the West ended in 1989/90, but several old-style Communist regimes continue in power. Most conflicts are internal rather than wars of conquest, occasionally reaching crisis point and provoking intervention by the major powers, as in Kosovo in 1999. The United Nations remains the fulcrum for international relations, but the United States, as the remaining superpower, and Europe are the only countries with the means to intervene worldwide. Europe is united in name only, and the armed forces of the constituent nations have not yet coalesced into one military organisation, so that NATO remains the principal agency of US–European military activity.

Chechnya
Tensions remain in Russian breakaway republic

Russia
Political, economic and social instability cause concern in view of large remaining arsenal of nuclear weapons

North Korea
Last Stalinist-style regime still developing long-range missiles and ongoing tension with South Korea

Afghanistan
Fundamentalist Taleban provides base for extremist Islamic organisations

Kashmir
India and Pakistan teeter near war over disputed border. Nuclear arms race between them continues

Burma (Myanmar)
Military government continues to deny power to democratically elected government

Taiwan (Formosa)
Major tension with mainland China. Ongoing provocations by Chinese armed forces

Spratly Islands
Disputed between most surrounding countries

East Timor
Provides focus for protest in destabilised Indonesia

Former Yugoslavia
Major NATO operations 1999 in Kosovo following Serb atrocities and expulsion of Albanians. NATO peacekeeping force now in place but Milosevic government still in power in Belgrade

Northern Ireland
Peace process in danger. Possibility of return to terrorism

Colombia
Ongoing drug wars

Iraq
Saddam Hussein regime continues to pose threat to neighbouring countries

Kurds
Continuing tension over Turkish/Iraqi areas

Arab-Israeli
Ongoing tension over Palestinian lands

Cyprus
Greek-Turkish tension over the disputed and divided island

Ethiopia
Major civil wars continue. The world continues to ignore

Sri-Lanka
Tamil Tigers continue rebellion

Ir[an]
Islamic republic continues to be unsta[ble] and government remains anti-West

Congo
Civil war continues with active involvement of Angolan and Zimbabweans

Falkland Islands
Tension still exists in view of Argentina's claim to the islands

Gibraltar
Tension continues between Spain and Britain over sovereignty

CHOKE-POINTS
Strategic areas through which major trade routes run. The security of these zones would be of the very greatest importance in a world war.

MAJOR HISTORIC BATTLE ZONES

A The Low Countries: the 'Cockpit of Europe'. Fought over more than any other part of Europe, especially in modern times. Major medieval wars included the Hundred Years War. Belgium was the invasion route for Germany at the outset of World Wars I and II.

B North Italy. Fought over especially in medieval times, with repeated expeditions mounted by Holy Roman Emperors. Subsequently major battleground in the wars of Charles V and Francis I of France in the 16th century.

C Balkans. Major 'fracture zone' between Islam and Christianity. This was the Ottoman Empire's foothold in Europe and the scene of many campaigns. With the dissolution of the Turkish Empire at the end of the 19th and beginning of the 20th century, small nations sprang up with substantial minority groups across borders. Racial and religious tensions remain. The Yugoslavian dissolution is part of this.

D Palestine. The Holy Land, precious to three of the world's great religions and the strategic crossroads between Europe, Asia and Africa. Constantly in conflict since Ancient times: campaigned over by Assyrians, Egyptians, Greeks, Romans, Arabs, Christian Crusaders and then part of the Ottoman Empire. Subsequently Arab-Israeli conflict.

E Mesopotamia. Battleground for the first empires of Ancient times. Subsequently the route for a series of invaders from Asia. Now an area of tension because of the unstable regimes in the regio[n] the West's dependence on its oil reserves.

F 'North-West Frontier.' Heartland for a series of empires inc[luding] that of Timur. In nineteenth century an area of potential co[nflict] between Russia and British India, leading to the 'Great Gam[e]' a series of adventures and misadventures in Afghanistan.

G China's northern frontier. Site of the Great Wall, built and enlarged by Chinese Emperors to keep out various raiders including the Hsiung-nu in Ancient times.

146

FUTURE WAR TECHNOLOGIES UNDER DEVELOPMENT OR EVALUATION

- **Cruise missiles** are now at the forefront of the West's armoury. These 'fire and forget' munitions can be fired from a range of platforms, including submarines. With global satellite positioning (GSP) and TV cameras to monitor the final stage of approach to impact, they have a range of up to 1,000 miles. They are vastly expensive – half a million dollars apiece – but they have the enormous advantage in politically sensitive times of being pilotless, so there is no risk to the attacker. Flying at up to 550mph, they can be vulnerable to anti-aircraft fire. Two basic Tomahawk variants deploy alternative payloads: a unitary 700lb explosive charge; and a submunitions warhead with 166 combined effect bomblets, each weighing 3.3lb. The former provides the spot-on accuracy that made the television news coverage of the Gulf War so amazing, and theoretically minimises the risk of collateral damage. The latter release the bomblets 200 yards from the target and scatter them over a 100- by 400-yard area.

- **ERGMs** (Extended Range Guided Munitions) may revolutionise conventional artillery. With a range of up to 70 miles, these take advantage of GSP for guidance to the target.

- **Multi-launch rockets**, already deployed to devastating effect during the Gulf War, may well lead to the phasing out of conventional artillery. By 2006, it is said, the British Royal Artillery may be completely converted to the new weapons.

- **Trimaran** warships have been under consideration for some time as part of the discussion concerning the question of hull shapes for warships, which are generally considerably narrower than for merchant ships. Speed and manoeuvrability are essential to most warships, but long narrow hulls tend to afford relatively unstable platforms. The answer may lie with the trimaran, which promises enhanced performance, with speeds for frigates up to more than 40 knots, and a most useful increase in deck area.

- **Ultra-silent submarines** are possible by means of a new system whereby the propulsion machinery is suspended in a submarine's inner hull by electromagnets, the gap between the inner and outer casing minimising sound transference.

- **MOB** (Mobile Offshore Base) is the concept of huge, self-propelled platforms as bases for offshore units. Aircraft carriers, with all their capabilities, are vastly expensive, and only the USA can afford to maintain big, nuclear-powered attack carriers (France is building one, but is encountering many problems). One such structure under consideration, SeaBase, is a mile-long semi-submersible structure, with a top deck landing strip and five or so decks below this for the accommodation of stores, personnel, etc. The cost, however, is estimated at $6–10 billion.

- **Objective Individual Combat Weapon** (OICW) is a light-weight modular weapon that provides the individual soldier with a 95% accuracy up to 500 metres. With two magazines and two barrels, it fires 5.56mm bullets and 20mm exploding rounds, with the effect of a small grenade. Computerised controls are linked to a video night sight and laser rangefinder. It can lock on to a moving target and calculate the range, and can even, effectively, 'fire around corners', the range being fed to the projectile fuze to explode at a given range. Under US government development, the quoted price per rifle is $12,000.

- **Remote controlled rifles** such as the TRAP (Telepresent Rapid Airming Platform) offer the ability to snipe by remote control via a video link and joystick.

- **Personal radar** is under development to give individual soldiers 'x-ray' vision. A video display on a helmet-mounted visor will make it possible to see through obstacles even several feet thick. The system uses very low frequency radiation from a hand-hand scanner. Soon, for the enemy, there will be literally no place to hide.

- **Camouflage** may be revolutionised by the application of the principle of interference, which makes the iridescence seen on some more exotic types of butterfly. Special multi-layered fibres will be adjusted electronically to change colour, giving individual soldiers, tanks and vehicles the possibility of becoming 'invisible', perhaps in the way depicted in the sci-fi movie *Predator*.

- **Casualties** in war generally depend for their survival upon the speed with which they can be transported to a medical facility for surgery. One of the latest developments that may aid combat injury survivability is a type of bandage that clots blood instantly, so that the casualty does not need to die of blood-loss before he or she can be evacuated.

- **Plastic tanks** made of toughened plastic laminate armour will be coated with chameleon crystals to change colour at will, and a stealth coating that will deflect radars. The Vickers 'Modifier' tank is one such development, but this looks fifteen years into the future.

- **The Command Post of the Future** is being developed by the US Defense Advanced Research Projects Agency, which plans to have it operational by 2002. Huge display screens and three-dimensional battlefield representations, including holographic displays, will give future commanders the ultimate in control and command facilities, with computers constantly updating scenarios and options.

- **Recruitment** to the armed forces is changing. Quite apart from the old-fashioned, but still necessary demands of physical fitness, stamina and discipline, an ability with computer game-playing is now seen as increasingly relevant. Many of the weapons coming into service rely upon computers for their operation; the recruit who is good at computer games may have just the skills the armed forces need.

- **Training for war** has for long been seen as the vital preparation that makes the difference between competence on the battlefield and dismal failure. The use of lasers and computers in exercises makes training ultra-realistic. The TES (Tactical Engagement System) makes use of lasers on rifles, with sensors on the helmets and bodies of participating troops, so that 'kills' can be realistically registered. Fieldcraft can thus be more like a 'live' situation and improves dramatically.

- **Virtual battle simulators** using computer-generated battle environments present super-realistic settings for training all branches of the armed forces – without the risk or expense of using actual machines in live conditions.

- **CRW** (Canard Rotor Wing) hybrid aircraft are under investigation by Boeing's Phantom Works. They will be able to take off and land vertically by means of two-bladed rotors, and convert to conventional fixed wing configurement for level flight. With a top speed of 450mph (much faster than a conventional helicopter) they will be exceptionally manoeuvrable.

- **UCAV** (Unmanned Combat Aerial Vehicle) is a concept for replacing nuclear missiles on some US submarines with tiny unmanned aircraft. Lockheed Martin have researched three systems launching from amphibious assault vehicles, destroyers and from Trident submarines. Launch is accomplished by means of a modified ballistic missile, rocket boosters lifting the UCAV out of the water, when it unfurls wings and heads for the target, where it can release small smart bombs using GSP. These vehicles will even be recoverable, though the idea sounds fanciful: like flies, they will be caught by a Velcro-type of substance on a raised platform.

- **UAVs** (Unmanned Aerial Vehicles) are already deployed but are constantly being improved upon. Flown from a virtual command centre, new versions will be vast improvements on the 'drone' technology currently available. The surrender of a party of Iraqi troops to an unmanned aircraft during the Gulf War is a foretaste of the future. UCAVs (Uninhabited Combat Air Vehicles) will be controlled either from the ground or from an aircraft in the area. The advantages of these technologies are several: there is no pilot to risk his life; the aircraft is cheaper; weight is reduced, affording more potential weapons carriage; and such an aircraft will be able to perform manoeuvres at high speeds that would cause a human pilot to black out.

- **Miniature spy robots**, based on the technology of the recent Mars Sojourner rover, are being developed. With video cameras on board, and sensors to detect chemicals, mines, booby-traps, etc., these would be used in groups to move ahead of troops and sweep areas. Encrypted radio signals would link them to the operator with the advancing troops. A new chemical sensor no bigger than a small pea would be fitted to swarms of 'robobugs' scouring areas for chemical traces.

- **Robot insects**, perhaps a third the size of a credit card, are under investigation. Powered by vibration to fly or hop, and equipped with various sensors, they could be on the battlefield within ten years.

- **STAR** (Satellite Tracking using Ambient Radio frequency) is a Lockheed Martin/USAF development that makes use of FM signals to track objects.

- **Death rays** Lasers in space may soon be more than a dream. China is thought to be researching blowtorch-like weapons firing laser beams hundreds of miles into space to destroy satellites. Indeed, satellite war is a major area for research. The US MIRLC laser, tested at White Sands missile range, is for shooting down satellites with a laser beam travelling at 186,000 miles per second.

- **IW** (Information Warfare) seeks to destroy an enemy's information gathering system. Destroying means of communications becomes a central part of modern warfare. If the enemy cannot see or talk to its troops, it is fighting in the dark and at a crucial disadvantage. Individual elements can also be immobilised and disabled, especially since increased sophistication in weapons design and overall warfare systems makes for greater vulnerability. The best tank in the world today, the M-1 Abrams, relies on some fifty interdependent microprocessors. Disrupt them and the tank is just useless metal.

- **WBOM** (War By Other Means) is receiving increasing attention, the idea being to close down a potential enemy's infrastructure, crashing telephone and communications networks and triggering various sorts of non-military disasters. The potential exists to actually prevent war by making the enemy impotent.

- **Cyberspace warfare** against a country's economic base and other vital infrastructure elements is now taken very seriously. The US has a Critical Assurance Office to protect against this, the open nature of modern democratic countries and increased dependence on computerised networking systems making penetration an increasing risk.

BIBLIOGRAPHY

A GUIDE TO FURTHER READING

Adam-Smith, Patsy. *The ANZACs.* 1978

Adams, James. *The Next World War: The Warriors and Weapons of The New Battlefields in Cyberspace.* 1999

Allen, W. and Muratoff, P. *Caucasian Battlefields. A History of the Wars on the Turco-Caucasian Border, 1828–1921.* 1953

Allmand, C. T. *The Hundred Years War, England and France at War c.1300–c.1450.* 1988

Archibald, E. H. H. *The Fighting Ship in the Royal Navy 897–1984.* 1984

Armitage, Sir Michael, *The Royal Air Force.* 1993, 1999

Arnold, James R. *Ardennes 1944.* 1990

– *Tet Offensive 1968.* 1990

– *Chickamauga 1863.* 1992

– *Shiloh 1862.* 1998

Atkinson, C. T. *Marlborough and the Rise of the British Army.* 1921

Austin, Paul Britten. *1812: The March on Moscow.* 1993

– *1812: Napoleon in Moscow.* 1995

– *1812: The Great Retreat.* 1996

Badsey, Stephen. *Normandy 1944.* 1990

– *Arnhem 1944.* 1993

Ballard, C. *The House of Shaka.* 1988

Banks, Arthur. *A Military History and Atlas of the First World War.* 1975

Barker, A. J. *Afrika Korps.* 1978

Barnett, Corelli. *Marlborough.* 1974

– *The Swordbearers: Studies in Supreme Command in the First World War,* 1981

Barthop, M. *The Zulu War.* 1980

Bateson, C. *The War with Japan.* 1968

Baynes, John. *The Forgotten Victor.* 1950

Beeler, J. *Warfare in Feudal Europe, 730–1200.* 1971

Beevor, Anthony. *Stalingrad.* 1998

Bennett, Geoffrey. *The Battle of Jutland.* 1964

– *Naval Battles of the First World War.* 1974

Bennett, Matthew. *Agincourt 1415.* 1991

Bidwell, S. and Graham, D. *Firepower.* 1982

Bin, Alberto et al. *Desert Storm.* 1999

Binns, C.T. *The Last Zulu King: The Life and Death of Cetshwayo.* 1963

– *Dinuzulu: The Death of the House of Shaka.* 1968

Black, J.M. *A Military Revolution? Military Change and European Society 1550–1800.* 1991

Black, Jeremy. *European Warfare 1660–1815.* 1994

– *The Cambridge Illustrated Atlas of Warfare: Renaissance to Revolution, 1492–1792.* 1996

– *Maps and History.* 1997

– *War and the World: Military Power and the Fate of Continents, 1450-2000.* 1998

Blond, Georges, trans. Marshall May. *La Grande Armée.* 1995

Bloomfield, R. *Sebastien le Prestre de Vauban.* 1938

Blumentritt, General Günther. *Von Rundstedt, the Soldier and the Man.* 1952

Boatner, M. *The Civil War Dictionary.* 1959

Bond, Brian. *Victorian Military Campaigns.* 1967

Bourke, Joanna. *An Intimate History of Killing: Face to Face Killing in 20th-Century Warfare.* 1999

Bowyer, C. *For Valour – the Air V.C.s.* 1978

– *History of the RAF.* 1979

Breasted, J. *Ancient Records of Egypt.* 1906

Brett-Smith, Richard. *Hitler's Generals.* 1976

Brown, David, Shores, Christopher and Macksey, Kenneth. *The Guinness History of Air Warfare.* 1976

Bruce, J. *British Aeroplanes 1914–1918.* 1969

Bryant, Anthony. *Sekigahara 1600.* 1995

Bulpin, T.V. *Shaka's Country.* 1952

Burleigh, Bennett. *The Khartoum Campaign.* 1899

Burne, A. H. *The Art of War on Land.* 1944

– *Battlefields of England.* 1950

– *More Battlefields of England.* 1952

– and Young, P. *The Great Civil War: a Military History of the First Civil War.* 1959

C. E. Crutchley. *Machine Gunner, 1914-1918.* 1975.

Caesar, Julius. trans. S. A. Handford. *The Conquest of Gaul.* 1956

Caffrey, K. *The Lion and the Unicorn: the Anglo–American War 1812–15.* 1978

Callwell, Colonel C. E. *Small Wars: Their Principle and Practice.* 1895, 1976

Calvocoressi, P. *Top Secret Ultra.* 1980

– and Wint, Guy. *Total War: Causes and Courses of the Second World War.* 1972

Carver, M. *El Alamein.* 1962

– *War since 1945.* 1980

Castle, Ian. *Aspern & Wagram 1809.* 1994

– *Colenso 1899.* 1995

– *Majuba 1881.* 1996

– *Eggmühl 1809.* 1998

– and Knight, Ian, *Fearful Hard Times: The Siege and Relief of Eshowe, 1879.* 1994

Chandler, David G. *A Travellers Guide to the Battlefields of Europe.* 2 vols. 1965

– *The Campaigns of Napoleon.* 1967

– *Marlborough as Military Commander.* 1973

– *Napoleon.* 1974

– *The Art of War in the Age of Marlborough.* 1976

– *Dictionary of the Napoleonic Wars.* 1979

– *The Military Maxims of Napoleon.* 1987

– *Austerlitz 1805.* 1990

– (ed.). *Great Battles of the British Army.* 1991

– *Jena 1806.* 1993

Christiansen, E. *The Northern Crusades: The Baltic and Catholic Frontier 1100–1525.* 1980

Churchill, Winston S. *The Story of the Malakand Field Force.* 1898

– *The River War.* 1899

– *Marlborough, His Life and Times.* 6 vols. 1933–38

– *The World Crisis, 1911–1918.* 1923–31

– *The Second World War.* 6 vols. 1948–53.

Citino, Robert Michael. *The Path to Blitzkrieg: Doctrine and Training in the German Army, 1920-1939.* 1999

Clarendon, Earl of. *The History of the Rebellion and Civil War in England.* 1702

Clark, Allan, *Barbarossa: The Russian-German Conflict 1941–1945.* 1995.

Clausewitz, Carl von. *On War.* 1832

Cloughley Brian. *A History of the Pakistan Army.* 1999

Clowes, William Laird. *The Royal Navy – A History from the earliest times to 1900.* 1997

Connaughton, R. *The War of the Rising Sun and Tumbling Bear.* 1988

Contamine, P. *War in the Middle Ages.* 1984

Corbett, J. S. *England in the Seven Years' War.* 2 vols. 1907

Costello, J. *The Pacific War, 1941–45.* 1981

Craig, G. A. *The Battle of Königgrätz.* 1964

Crawford, Mark. *Encyclopedia of the Mexican-American War.* 1999

Creasey, E. S. *The Fifteen Decisive Battles of the Western World.* 1851

Creasy, Sir Edward. *The Fifteen Decisive Battles of the World.* 1852

Creveld, M. van. *Supplying War.* 1977

Crompton, Samuel Willard. *100 Battles That Shaped World History.* 1997

– *100 Wars That Shaped World History.* 1997

– *100 Military Leaders Who Shaped World History.* 1999

Cross, Robin (ed.) *The Guinness Encyclopedia of Warfare.* 1991

Cruttwell, C. R. M. F. *A History of the Great War 1914–1918.* 1934

Davies, David. *Fighting Ships – Ships of the Line 1793–1815.* 1996

Davis Hanson, Victor. *Wars of the Ancient Greeks.* 1999

Davis, Brian L. *Nato Forces: Organisation and Insignia.* 1988

Davis, Paul K. and Lee, Allen. *Encyclopedia of Warrior Peoples and Fighting Groups.* 1999

Dear, I. C. B. (ed.). *The Oxford Companion to the Second World War.* 1995

Delbrück, H. *History of the Art of War.* 4 vols. 1900–20. English translation 1975–85

Devries, K. *Medieval Military Technology.* 1992

Doherty, Richard. *A Noble Crusade: The History of Eighth Army, 1941 to 1945.* 1999

Douhet, G. *The Command of the Air.* 1943

Duffy, Christopher. *Borodino and the War of 1812.* 1972

– *The Army of Frederick the Great.* 1974

– *Austerlitz, 1805.* 1976

– *The Army of Maria Theresa.* 1977

– *Fire and Stone: The Science of Fortress Warfare 1660–1860.* 1996

Dupuy, R. E. and T. N. *The HarperCollins Encyclopedia of Military History.* 1991

Dupuy, T. N. *Understanding War: History and Theory of Combat.* 1987

Dupuy, T. N., Curt Johnson and David L. Bongard. *The Harper Encyclopedia of Military Biography.* 1992

Earle, E. M. (ed.) *Makers of Modern Strategy: Military Thought from Machiavelli to Hitler.* 1943

Eggenberger, D. *A Dictionary of Battles.* 1967

Elliott, Major-General J. G. *The Frontier, 1839–1947.* 1970

Elliott-Wright, Philipp. *Gravelotte–St Privat 1870.* 1993

Ellis, John. *The Social History of the Machine-Gun.* 1976

Ellis, Major L. F. et al. *Victory in the West, vol. I, The Battle of Normandy.* 1962

Emerson, Barbara. *The Black Prince.* 1976

Emery, Frank, *The Red Soldier: Letters from the Zulu War, 1879.* 1977

Erickson, John. *Stalin's War with Germany: Volume I: The Road to Stalingrad,* 1975.

– *The Road to Berlin.* 1983

Eshel, D. *Chariots of the Desert.* 1989

Esposito, V. J. and Elting J. R. (editors). *A Military History and Atlas of the Napoleonic Wars.* 1964

Essame, H. *The Battle for Europe, 1918.* 1972

Falls, Captain Cyril. *Hundred Years of War.* 1953

– *The Art of War from the Age of Napoleon to the Present Day.* 1961

– *The First World War.* 1960

– *Armageddon 1918.* 1964

Farrar-Hockley, A. H. *The Somme.* 1964

– *The British Part in the Korean War.* 1990

Farwell, Byron. *Queen Victoria's Little Wars.* 1973

Featherstone, Donald. *Bowmen of England.* 1967

– *Colonial Small Wars.* 1973

– *Victoria's Enemies.* 1989

– *Khartoum 1885.* 1993

– *Tel-el Kebir 1882.* 1993

– *Omdurman 1989.* 1995

Ferril, A. *The Fall of the Roman Empire: The Military Explanation.* 1986

Firth, C. H. *Cromwell's Army.* 1902

Fletcher, Ian. *Salamanca 1812.* 1997

Foch, Marshal F. *The Memoirs of Marshal Foch.* 1931

Foote, Shelby. *The Civil War.* 1963

Fortescue, Hon. Sir John. *History of the British Army.* 1899–1920

Forty, George. *Afrika Korps at War.* 2 vols 1978

– *Tank Commanders, Knights of the Modern Age.* 1993

– *Land Warfare: The Encyclopedia of 20th Century Conflict.* 1997

Francis, D. *The First Peninsular War, 1702–13.* 1975

Frankland, N. *The Bombing Offensive against Germany.* 1965

Franks, N. and Bailey, F. *Over the Front*. 1992
– and Duiven, R. *The Jasta Pilots*. 1996
– and Guest, R. *Above the Lines*. 1993
Franks, N. Giblin, H. and McCrery, N. *Under the Guns of the Red Baron*. 1995
Fraser, David. *Knight's Cross*. 1993
Frere-Cook, Gervis, and Macksey, Kenneth. *The Guinness History of Sea Warfare*. 1975
Friedman, Colonel Richard S. et al. *Advanced Technology Warfare*. 1985
Fuller, J. F. C. *The Foundations of the Science of War*. 1926
– *War and Western Civilisation, 1832–1932*. 1932
– *The Decisive Battles of the Western World and their Influence on History*. 3 vols, 1954–56
– *The Conduct of War 1789–1961*. 1961
– *A Military History of the Western World*. 1967
– *Armament and History: The Influence of Armament on History from the Dawn of Classical Warfare to the End of the Second World War*. 1999
Gardiner, Samuel R. *History of the Great Civil War, 1642–1649*. 1893
Geraghty, Tony. *Who Dares Wins – The Special Air Service, 1950 to the Falklands*. 1980, 1992
Giap, Vo Nguyen. *People's War – People's Army*. 1961
Gibbon, Edward. *The History of the Decline and Fall of the Roman Empire*. 1776–88
Gibbons, F. *The Red Knight of Germany*. 1927
Gilbert, Martin. *The First World War*. 1944
Glantz, David M., and Mary E. *Zhukov's Greatest Defeat: The Red Army's Epic Disaster in Operation Mars, 1942*. 1999
Glover, M. *The Peninsular War, 1807–14: A Concise Military History*. 1974
Goodspeed, D. *Ludendorff – The Genius of World War I*. 1966
Gorlitz, W. *History of the German General Staff, 1675–1945*. 1953
Gravett, C. *German Medieval Armies 1300–1500*. 1985
Gray, Randal. *Kaiserschlacht 1918*. 1991
– with Argyle, Christopher. *Chronicle of the First World War*. 2 vols 1990, 1991
Greenhalgh, Peter. *Pompey: The Roman Alexander*. 1980
Griffiths, J. *The Conflict in Afghanistan*. 1987
Gunston, Bill (ed.). *The Encyclopedia of World Air Power*. 1980
– *Military Helicopters*. 1981
Hackett, General Sir John (ed.). *Warfare in the Ancient World*. 1989
Hankey, Lord, *The Supreme Command 1914–1918*. 1961
Hankinson, Alan. *First Bull Run 1861*. 1991
– *Vicksburg 1863*. 1993
Harbottle, T. B. *Dictionary of Battles*. 1901
Harrington, Peter. *Culloden 1746*. 1991
– *Plassey 1757*. 1994
Hastings, M. *Overlord – D-Day and the Battle for Normandy*. 1984
– *The Korean War*. 1987
– and Jenkins, S. *The Battle for the Falklands*. 1983
Haythornthwaite, Philip J. *The Alamo and the War of Texan Independence, 1835–36*. 1986
– *The Napoleonic Source Book*. 1990
– *Gallipoli 1915*. 1991
– *The World War One Source Book*. 1992
– *The Armies of Wellington*. 1994
– *The Colonial Wars Source Book*. 1995
– *Who Was Who in the Napoleonic Wars*. 1998
Healy, Mark. *Kursk 1943*. 1992
– *Midway 1942*. 1993
– *Qadesh 1300BC*. 1993
Heathcote, T. *The Afghan Wars, 1839–1919*. 1980
Henshaw, T. *The Sky Their Battlefield*. 1995
Herzog, Chaim. *The Arab–Israeli Wars*. 1982
– and Grichon, M. *Battles of the Bible*. 1997
Hibbert, Christopher. *Agincourt*. 1964
Hickey, Michael. *The Korean War: The West Confronts Communism, 1950–1953*. 1999
Hiro, D. *The Longest War*. 1989
Hobart, F. W. A. *Pictorial History of the Machine-Gun*. 1971
– *Fortress: A History of Military Defence*. 1975

Hofschroer, Peter. *Leipzig 1813*. 1993
– *The Waterloo Campaign: Wellington, His German Allies and the Battles of Ligny and Quatre Bras*. 1998
Hogg, Ian V. *A History of Artillery*. 1974
– *Illustrated Encyclopedia of Artillery*. 1987
– and Weeks, John. *Military Smallarms of the Twentieth Century*. 1973 and subsequent editions
Holder, P. A. *The Roman Army in Britain*. 1982
Hollister, C. W. *The Military Organisation of Norman England*. 1965
Holmes, Richard (ed.). *The World Atlas of Warfare*. 1988
Hooton, E. R. *Eagle in Flames – The Fall of the Luftwaffe*. 1997
Horne, Alistair. *To Lose a Battle – France 1940*. 1979
Horward, D. (ed.). *Napoleonic Military History: A Bibliography*. 1986
Houseley, N. J. *The Italian Crusades: The Papal Angevin Alliance and the Crusades against Christian Lay Powers, 1254–1343*. 1982
Howard, Michael E. *The Franco-Prussian War*. 1961
– *War in European History*. 1976
Howarth, David. *Waterloo – A Near Run Thing*. 1972
Hughes, Major-General B. P. *Firepower – Weapon Effectiveness on the Battlefield*. 1974
Hughes, Q. *Military Architecture*. 1974
Irving, David. *The Trail of the Fox*. 1977
– *Goering*. 1989
Ito, Masanori. *The End of the Imperial Japanese Navy*. 1986
Jackson, Robert. *The German Navy in World War II*. 1999
Jackson, W. *Withdrawal from Empire*. 1986
Jackson, W. G. F. *The Battle for Italy*. 1975
– *The North African Campaign 1940–43*. 1975
James, W. *The Naval History of Great Britain from the Declaration of War by the French Republic in 1793 to the Accession of George IV*. 1837
Jentz, Thomas L. (ed.) *Panzer Truppen*. 1996
Johnson, Air Vice-Marshal J. E. *Full Circle – The Story of Air Fighting*. 1964
Johnson, J. H. *Stalemate! – The Great Trench Warfare Battles of 1915–1917*. 1995
– *1918: The Unexpected Victory*. 1997
Jomini, A-H. *Summary of the Art of War*. 1838
Jones, A. *The Art of War in the Western World*. 1987
Jones, H. A. *The War in the Air*. vol. II, 1928; vol. III, 1931; vol. IV, 1934
Jones, R. V. *Most Secret War*. 1979
Josephus, Flavius, trans. G. A. Williamson. *The Jewish War*. 1960
Judd, D. *The Crimean War*. 1975
Kai Ka'us Ibn Iskandar. *A Mirror for Princes*. 1951
Katcher, Philip. *The American Civil War Source Book*. 1992
Kaye, Sir John. *History of the War in Afghanistan*. 1874
Keegan, John (ed.). *The Times Atlas of the Second World War*. 1989
– *A History of Warfare*. 1993
Keen, M. H. *The Laws of War in the Late Middle Ages*. 1994
Kennedy, Frances H. (ed.) *The Civil War Battlefield Guide*. 1990
Kennedy, Major Robert M. *The German Campaign in Poland (1939)*. 1956
Kennedy, Paul. *The Rise and Fall of the Great Powers*. 1988
Kilduff, P. *Germany's First Air Force, 1914–1918*. 1991
– *Richthofen: Beyond the Legend of the Red Baron*, 1993
Kinglake, A. W. *The Invasion of the Crimea*. 9 vols. 1868
Knight, Ian, *The Zulus*. 1989
– *Brave Men's Blood: The Epic of the Zulu War*. 1990
– *British Forces in Zululand, 1879*. 1991
– *Zulu: The Battles of Isandlwana and Rorke's Drift, 22/23rd January 1879*. 1992
– *The Anatomy of the Zulu Army: from Shaka to Cetshwayo*. 1994
– *Colenso 1899*. 1995
– *Nothing Remains But To Fight: The Defence of Rorke's Drift, 1818–1879*. 1995
– *Rorke's Drift: Pinned Like Rats in a Trap*. 1995
– *Zulu, 1816–1906*. 1995

– *Great Zulu Battles 1838–1906*. 1998
– and Castle, Ian. *Zulu War 1879*. 1992
– and Castle, Ian, *The Zulu War: Then and Now*. 1994
Kohn, G. *Dictionary of Wars*. 1986
Konstam, Angus. *France 1940*. 1996
– *San Juan Hill 1898*. 1998
Koop, Gerhard and Schmolke, Klaus-Peter. *Battleships of the Scharnhorst Class*. 1999
Kostyal, K. M. *Stonewall Jackson: A Life Portrait*. 1999
Laband, John, *Fight Us In The Open: The Anglo-Zulu War Through Zulu Eyes*. 1985
– *The Battle of Ulundi*. 1988
– *Rope of Sand: The Rise and Fall of the Zulu Kingdom in the Nineteenth Century*. 1995; also published 1997 under the title *The Fall of the Zulu Nation*
– and Matthews, Jeff, *Isandlwana*. 1992
– and Thompson, P. *Kingdom and Colony at War*. 1990
– and Wright, John, *King Cetshwayo kaMpande*. 1980
Lachouque, H. *Waterloo*. 1975
– *The Anatomy of Glory*. Tr. by A. S. K. Brown. 1978
Laffin, J. *Brassey's Battles*. 1986
– *Western Front Companion 1914–1918*. 1994
Lambert, Nicholas. *Sir John Fisher's Naval Revolution*. 1999
Lamberton, W. *Fighter Aircraft of the 1914–1918 War*. 1960
Laur, Timothy M. et al. *The Army Times, Navy Times, Air Force Times: Paperback Encyclopedia of Modern U.S. Military Weapons*. 1998
Lavery, Brian. *Nelson's Navy – The Ships, Men and Organisation 1793–1815*. 1989
Lewin, R. *Ultra Goes To War*. 1978
Lewis, C. *Sagittarius Rising*. 1936
Lewis, Michael. *The Spanish Armada*. 1960
Liddell-Hart, B. H. *The Ghost of Napoleon*. 1933
– *A History of the World War, 1914–1918*, 1934
– *The Other Side of the Hill*. 1948
– *The Real War, 1914–1918*. 1964
– *History of the First World War*. 1970
– *History of the Second World War*. 1970
Liu Ji. *Lessons of War*. 1989
Livesey, A. *The Viking Atlas of World War I*. 1994
Lloyd, A. *The Zulu War 1879*. 1974
Lock, Ron, *Blood on the Painted Mountain: Zulu Victory and Defeat, Hlobane and Khambula*. 1995
Lomas, David. *Mons 1914*. 1997
– *First Ypres 1914*. 1999
Longford, E. *Wellington, the Years of the Sword*. 1968
Longmate, N. *The Home Front*. 1981
Longstreet, S. *War Cries on Horseback – The History of the Indian Wars*. 1970
Lord, Walter. *Incredible Victory: The Battle of Midway*. 1968
Lucas, James. *War in the Desert: The Eighth Army at El Alamein*. 1982
– *Last Days of the Reich: The Collapse of Nazi Germany, May 1945*. 1986
Lucas Phillips, C. E. *Alamein*. 1962
Lyon, David. *Sea Battles in Close-Up: The Age of Nelson*. 1996
Lyon, Hugh. *Modern Warships*. 1980
Macdonald, P. *GIAP, The Victor in Vietnam*. 1993
Machiavelli, Niccolo. *The Art of War*. 1965
Macksey, Kenneth. *The Guinness History of Land Warfare*. 1973
– *Military Errors of World War Two*. 1987
– *From Triumph to Disaster: the Fatal Flaws in German Generalship from Moltke to Guderian*. 1996
Macksey, P. *The War for America, 1775–83*. 1964
Mahan, A. *The Influence of Sea Power upon History 1660–1783*. 1890
Mann, Golo. *Wallenstein*. 1971
Manstein, Field Marshal Erich von, ed. and trans. by A. G. Powell. *Lost Victories*. 1982
Mao Tse-tung. *Selected Military Writings*. Peking, 1967
Marley, David F. *Wars of the Americas*. 1998
Marshall, S. L. A. *Night Drop – The American Airborne Invasion of Normandy*. 1986

Marshall-Cornwall, J. *Napoleon as Military Commander.* 1967

Marwick, A. *Britain in a Century of Total War* 1968

– *The Home Front* 1976

Mattingly, Garrett. *The Defeat of the Spanish Armada.* 1965

McCarthy, Chris. *The Somme – The Day by Day Account.* 1993

McElwee, William. *The Art of War – Waterloo to Mons.* 1974

McKay, D. *Prince Eugene of Savoy.* 1977

McMichael, S. *Stumbling Bear.* 1991

Meier, Christian. *Caesar.* 1982

Mercer, Patrick. *Inkermann 1854.* 1998

Messenger, Charles. *Trench Fighting 1914–18.* 1972

– *World War Two Chronological Atlas.* 1989

– *The Second World War in the West.* 1999

Middlebrook, Martin. *The Kaiser's Battle: 21 March 1918.* 1978

Moltke, H. von. *Strategy: Its Theory and Application: The Wars for German Unification, 1866–71.* 1971

– *The Franco-German War of 1870–71.* 1992

Montgomery of Alamein, Field Marshal Viscount. *A History of Warfare.* 1968

Morris, D. *The Washing of the Spears.* 1966

Morrissey, Brendan. *Boston 1775.* 1995

– *Yorktown 1781.* 1997

Mueller, Joseph N. *Guadalcanal 1942.* 1992

Napier, W. F. P. *History of the War in the Peninsula.* 1832–40

Nash, D. B. *Imperial German Army Handbook, 1914–1918.* 1980

Nebenzahl, K. (ed). *Atlas of the American Revolution.* 1974

Nicolle, David. *The Normans.* 1987

– *The Crusades.* 1988

– *Attila and the Nomad Hordes: Warfare on the Eurasian Steppes, 4th to 12th Centuries.* 1990

– *Hattin 1187.* 1993

– *Yarmuk 636AD.* 1994

– *The Janissaries.* 1995

– *Fornovo 1495.* 1996

– *Medieval Warfare Source Book.* 1995

– *Lake Peipus 1242.* 1996

– *Sassanian Armies. The Iranian Empire early 3rd to mid-7th centuries AD.* 1996

– *Granada 1492.* 1998

– *Arms & Armour of the Crusading Era 1050–1350: Western Europe and the Crusader States.* 1999

Nofi, Albert A. *The Gettysburg Campaign.* 1996

Norman, A. V. B., and Pottinger, Don. *English Weapons & Warfare, 449–1660.* 1966

Oman, Sir Charles. *History of the War in the Peninsula.* 1902–30

– *A History of the Art of War in the Middle Ages.* 1924

Overy, R. *The Air War 1939–1945.* 1980

– *Goering: The Iron Man* 1984

Padfield, Peter. *The Battleship Era.* 1972

Pakenham, T. *The Boer War.* 1979

Panzeri, Peter. *Little Big Horn 1876.* 1995

Parkes, Dr. Oscar. *British Battleships.* 1957

Peers, C. J. *Ancient Chinese Armies, 1500 to 200BC.* 1990.

– *Medieval Chinese Armies, 1260 to 1520.* 1992.

– *Imperial Chinese Armies (1), 200BC to AD589.* 1995.

– *Imperial Chinese Armies (2), AD590 to 1260.* 1996.

– *Late Imperial Chinese Armies, 1520 to 1842.* 1997.

Pemsel, Helmut. *Atlas of Naval Warfare.* 1977

Perrett, Bryan. *A History of Blitzkrieg.* 1983

– *Desert Warfare.* 1988

– *Last Stand! Famous Battles Against the Odds.* 1991

– *The Battle Book.* 1992

– *At All Costs! Stories of Impossible Victories.* 1993

– *Seize and Hold: Master Strokes on the Battlefield.* 1994

– *Against All Odds: More Dramatic 'Last Stand' Actions.* 1995

– *Iron Fist: Classic Armoured Warfare Case Studies.* 1995

Pfanz, Harry W. *Gettysburg – The Second Day.* 1987

Pickles, Tim. *Malta 1565.* 1998

Pimlott, John, and Badsey, Stephen (eds). *The Gulf War Assessed.* 1992

Pitt, Barrie. *1918 – The Last Act.* 1962

– and Pitt, Frances. *The Chronological Atlas of World War II.* 1989

Polybius. *The Rise of the Roman Empire.* 1987

Pope, Stephen, and Robbins, Keith. *The Cassell Dictionary of the Napoleonic Wars.* 1999

Price, A. *The Hardest Day* 1979

Price, Anthony. *The Eyes of the Fleet – A Popular History of Frigates and Frigate Captains, 1793–1815.* 1990

Prior, P. and Wilson, T. *Command on the Western Front,* 1992

Procopius. *A History of the Wars.* 1929

Quimby, R. *Background of Napoleonic Warfare.* 1957

Ranitzsch, K-H. *The Army of Tang China.* 1995.

Ready, J. *World War Two, Nation by Nation.* 1995

Rickenbacker, E. *Fighting the Flying Circus.* 1967

Riley-Smith, Jonathan. *The Atlas of the Crusades.* 1991

Robertson, B. *Air Aces of the 1914–1918 War.* 1959

Robinson, H. Russell. *Oriental Armour.* 1967

Robson, Brian. *The Road to Kabul: the Second Afghan War 1878–1881.* 1986

Rogers, Colonel H. C. B. *Napoleon's Army.* 1974

– *The British Army in the 18th Century.* 1976

Rommel, Erwin. *The Rommel Papers,* ed. B. H. Liddell Hart, 1953

– *Infantry Attacks!* 1990 (English trans of *Infanterie Greift An,* written by Rommel in the 1930s)

Rothenburg, G. E. *The Art of War in the Age of Napoleon.* 1965

Ruge, Friedrich. *Rommel in Normandy.* 1979

Runciman, S. *A History of the Crusades.* 1994

Russell, F. H. *The Just War in the Middle Ages.* 1975

Ryan, Cornelius. *The Longest Day.* 1960

Saxe, M. de. *My Reveries Upon the Art of War: Roots of Strategy.* 1985

Shepperd, Alan. *France 1940.* 1990

Shores, Christopher. *Ground Attack Aircraft of World War II.* 1977

Siborne, H. T. (ed). *The Waterloo Letters.* 1891

Sixsmith, E. K. G. *Douglas Haig.* 1976

Smith, Carl. *Chancellorsville 1863.* 1998

Smith, Digby. *The Greenhill Napoleonic Wars Data Book.* 1998

Smith, E. D. *Counter-Insurgency Operations: Malaya and Borneo.* 1985

Smith, Peter C. *Impact! The Dive-Bomber Pilots Speak.* 1981

Smurthwaite, David. *The Ordnance Survey Complete Guide to the Battlefields of Britain.* 1989

Sokolovsky, V. *Soviet Military Strategy.* 1975

Spurr, R. *Enter the Dragon.* 1989

Stevens, Norman S. *Antietam 1862.* 1994

Strawson, J. *The Italian Campaign.* 1987

Sturkey, Marion F. *Bonnie-Sue: A Marine Corps Helicopter Squadron in Vietnam.* 1999

Summers, H. Jnr. *On Strategy: The Vietnam War in Context.* 1981

Sun Tzu, trans. R. D. Sawyer. *Art of War.* 1994.

Suskind, Richard. *The Crusades.* 1962

Sweetman, John. *Balaclava 1854.* 1990

Tacitus, Cornelius, trans. Michael Grant. *The Annals of Imperial Rome.* 1959

Tan Qixiang (ed), *The Historical Atlas of China* (8 vols). 1981 onwards

Terraine, John. *Impacts of War, 1914 & 1918,* 1970

– *The Great War, 1914–1918.* 1977

– *To Win a War, 1918 – The Year of Victory.* 1978

– *The Smoke and the Fire: Myths and Anti-Myths of War, 1861–1945.* 1980

– *White Heat – The New Warfare, 1914–18.* 1982

Thomas, H. *The Spanish Civil War.* 1961

Thompson, E. A. *The Goths in Spain.* 1969

Thompson, L. *The US Army in Vietnam.* 1990

Thucydides. *The History of the Peloponnesian War.*

Tilberg, Frederick. *Gettysburg.* 1962

Travers, T. *The Killing Ground,* 1987

– *How the War was Won,* 1992

Tsouras, P. *Changing Orders: Evolution of the World's Armies, 1945 to the Present.* 1994

Tucker, John and Winstock, Lewis S. (eds). *The English Civil War: A Military Handbook.* 1972

Tunney, C. *Biographical Dictionary of World War II.* 1972

Tunstall, Brian. *Naval Warfare in the Age of Sail.* 1990

Turnbull, Stephen. *The Samurai: A Military History.* 1977

– *The Book of the Samurai.* 1982

– *The Book of the Medieval Knight.* 1985

– *Samurai Warriors.* 1987

– *Samurai Warlords: The Book of the Daimyo.* 1989

– *Samurai: The Warrior Tradition.* 1996

– *The Samurai Source Book.* 1998

Turner, John Frayn. *D-Day Invasion 1944.* 1974

Urban, M. *War in Afghanistan.* 1990

US Military Academy. *The West Point Atlas of American Wars.* 2 Vols. 1959

Vachée, A. *Napoleon at Work.* 1914

Vegetius. *The Military Institutions of the Romans.* 1965

Verbruggen, J. F. *The Art of War in Western Europe during the Middle Ages.* 1977

Walter, John. *The Kaiser's Pirates: German Surface Raiders in World War One.* 1994

Ward, S. G. P. *Wellington's Headquarters.* 1957

Warner, Oliver. *Great Sea Battles.* 1963

– *The Navy.* 1968

Warner, Philip. *World War One: A Chronological Narrative.* 1981

Watts, Anthony J. *The Royal Navy: An Illustrated History.* 1994

Webster, Graham. *The Roman Imperial Army.* 1969

– and Dudley, Donald R. *The Roman Conquest of Britain.* 1973

Wedgwood, C. V. *The Thirty Years War.* 1938

Weller, J. *Weapons and Tactics.* 1966

– *Wellington in the Peninsula, 1808-1814.* 1962

– *Wellington at Waterloo.* 1967

– *Wellington in India.* 1972

Williams, John. *France, Summer 1940.* 1969

Wilson, T. *The Myriad Faces of War,* 1988

Wilson, W. *The Ideals of the Samurai: Writings of Japanese Warriors.* 1982

Winsor, S. *The American Revolution.* 1974

Winter, D. *Haig's Command: A Reassessment.* 1991

Wise, S. *Canadian Airmen and the First World War.* 1980

Wise, Terence. *The Wars of the Crusades 1096–1291.* 1978

Wood, Tony, and Gunston, Bill. *Hitler's Luftwaffe.* 1977

Woodman, H. *Early Aircraft Armament: The Aeroplane and the Gun up to 1918.* 1989

Woodward, D. *Lloyd George and the Generals,* 1983

Wootten, Geoffrey. *Waterloo 1815.* 1992

Wu Ch'i. *The Art of War.* 1944

Yang Hong, *Weapons in Ancient China.* 1992

Yoshida, Mitsuru. *Requiem for Battleship Yamato.* 1999

Young, Desmond. *Rommel.* 1950

Young, P. *Napoleon's Marshals.* 1973

– and Holmes, E. R. *The English Civil Wars.* 1974

Zaloga, Steven. *Bagration 1944.* 1996

Zhuge Liang. *The Way of the General.* 1989

Zhukov, Marshal Georgi, et al. *Battles Hitler Lost – and The Soviet Marshals Who Won Them.* 1988

MILITARY MUSEUMS

AND PLACES OF INTEREST

AUSTRALIA

Australian War Memorial
Treloar Crescent, Campbell,
ACT
Tel: (02) 6243 4211
Fax: (02) 6243 4325
http://www.awm.gov.au/

AUSTRIA

Sammlungen Schloß Ambras
Collections of Schloß Ambras
Schloßstr. 20, 6020 Innsbruck
Tel: (512) 34 84 46
Fax: (512) 36 15 42
info.ambras@khm.at

**Heeresgeschichtliches
Museum**
(Museum of the history of the
Austrian army)
Ghegastr., Arsenal
A-1030 Wien (Vienna)
Tel: (01) 79561
Fax: (01) 5200 17707
bmlv.hgm@magnet.at
http://www.bmlv.gv.at/

Kunsthistorisches Museum
Maria-Theresien-Platz, 1010
Wien
Tel: (01) 525 24-401
Fax: (01) 523 27 70
info@khm.at
http://www.khm.at/

BELGIUM

**Nationaal Scheepvaartmu-
seum**
(National Maritime Museum)
Steenplein 1, 2000 Antwerpen
TEL (03) 2320850
Fax: (03) 2208657

**Musée Royal de l'Armée et
d'Histoire Militaire**
Parc du Cinquantenaire, 3
1040 Bruxelles (Brussels)
Tel: (02) 7334493

Musée de la Porte de Hal
Porte de Hal, Bd de Waterloo
1000 Bruxelles
Tel: (02) 5381834

Le Musée d'Armes de Liège
Quai de Maestricht, 8
4000 Liège
Tel: (04) 2219416
Fax: (04) 2219401

BULGARIA

**Nacionalen voenno-istoriceski
muzej**
(National Museum of Military
History)
bul Skobelev 23, Sofija
Tel: (02) 521596

CANADA

**Canadian Military Heritage
Museum**
347 Greenwich Street

Brantford, Ontario
Tel: (519) 759-1313
cmhm@bfree.on.ca

Canadian War Museum
General Motors Court
330 Sussex Drive
Ottawa, Ontario, K1A 0MS
Tel: (819) 776 8600
Fax: (819) 776 8623
http://www.warmuseum.ca

**Canadian Warplane Heritage
Museum**
Hamilton Airport
9280 Airport Road, Mount
Hope
ON, L0R 1W0
http://warplane.com/
museum@warplane.com

Museum of the Regiments
4520 Crowchild Trail S.W.
Calgary, Alberta
T2T 5J4
Tel: 974 2850
http://nucleus.com/~regi-
ments/

The Naval Museum of Alberta
1820 24 Street S.W.
Calgary, Alberta, T2T-0G6
Tel: (403) 242-0002
http://navalmuseum.ab.ca/

**The Naval Museum of Mani-
toba**
HMCS Chippawa, 51 Navy Way
Winnipeg, MB, R3C 4J7
http://www.naval_museum.mb.
ca/

**Royal Canadian Air Force
Memorial Museum**
8 Wing Trenton
Astra, Ontario, K0K 1B0
Tel: (613) 392 2140
http://aero-
web.org/museums/ont/rccafm
m.html

CZECH REPUBLIC

Národni muzeum v Praze
(National Museum)
Václavské nám 68
115 79 Praha 1 (Prague)
Tel: (02) 24230485
Fax: (02) 24226488

Vojenské muzeum
(Military Museum)
u Památniku 2, 130 05 Praha
Tel: (02) 62790972721
Fax: (02) 6279096

DENMARK

Nationalmuseet
(National Museum)
Prinsens Palais
Frederiksholms Kanal 12
1220 Kobenhavn K (Copen-
hagen)
Tel: 33134411 (no area code)
Fax: 33473330

Orlogsmuseet
(Royal Danish Naval Museum)

Overgaden Oven Vandet 58
DK-1415, Kobenhavn K
Tel: 32546363 (no area code)
Fax: 32542980
http://www.kulturnet.dk/homes
/orlm/

Tojhusmuseet
(Royal Danish Arsenal
Museum)
Tojhusg 3, 1214 Kobenhavn K
Tel: 33116037 (no area code)
Fax: 33937152

FINLAND

Military Museum of Finland
Maurinkatu 1
00170 Helsinki
Tel: (9) 1616380

FRANCE

Musée de l'Armée
Hôtel des Invalides
75007 PARIS
Tel: (1) 44423772
Fax: (1) 44423764

Musée de la Marine
Palais de Chaillot
17 place du Trocadéro et du 11
Novembre
75116 PARIS
Tel: (1) 45533170
Fax: (1) 47274967

GERMANY

**Deutsches Historisches
Museum, Berlin**
(German Historical Museum,
Berlin)
Unter den Linden 2
D-10117 Berlin
Tel: (030) 203040
Fax: (030) 20304 509

**Kunstsammlungen der Veste
Coburg**
Veste Coburg, 96450 Coburg
Tel: (09561) 8790
Fax: (09561) 87966

**Staatliche Kunstsammlungen
Dresden**
Rüstkammer
Zwinger, Sophienstrasse.
01067 Dresden
Tel: (0351) 4914626
Fax: (0351) 4914629

Historisches Museum
Saalgasse 19
60311 Frankfurt am Main
Tel: (069) 21235599
Fax: (069) 21230702

**Bayerisches Armeemuseum
im Neuen Schloss**
Paradeplatz 4 Neuen Schloss
85049 Ingolstadt
Tel: (0841) 93770

Badisches Landesmuseum
Schloss, 76131 Karlsruhe
Tel: (0721) 926 6514
Fax: (0721) 926 6537

**Germanisches Nationalmu-
seum**
Kartäusergasse 1
90402 Nürnberg (Nuremberg)
Tel: (0911) 13310
Fax: (0911) 1331200

Wehrgeschichtliches Museum
(Museum of Military History)
Schloss, 76437 Rastatt
Postfach 1633 76406 Rastaat
Tel: (07222) 34244
Fax: (07222) 31958

Deutsches Klingen Museum
Klosterhof 4
42653 Solingen-Gräfrath
Tel: (0212) 59822
Fax: (0212) 593985

Waffenmuseum
Friedrich-König-Str 19
98527 Suhl
Tel: (03681) 20698
Fax: (03681) 21308

GREAT BRITAIN

Cabinet War Rooms
King Charles Street
London, SW1A 2AQ
Tel: (0171) 930 6961
http://iwm.org.uk/cabinet.htm

Duxford Aviation Museum
Duxford
Cambridgeshire, CB2 4QR
Tel: (01223 835 000)
http://www.iwm.org.uk/duxford
.htm

Glasgow Museum
Kelvingrove
Glasgow, G3 8AG
Tel: (0141) 287 2699
Fax: (0141) 287 2690

HMS Belfast
Morgan's Lane, Tooley Street
London, SE1 2JH
Tel: (0171) 940 6300
http://iwm.org.uk/belfast.htm

Imperial War Museum
Lambeth Road
London, SE1 6HZ
Tel: (0171) 416 5000
Fax: (0171) 416 5374
mail@iwm.org.uk
http://www.iwm.org.uk/london.
htm

National Army Museum
Royal Hospital Road
Chelsea, London, SW3 4HT
Tel: (0171) 730 00717
Fax: (0171) 823 6573
http://www.failte.com/nam/

National Maritime Museum
Romney Road, Greenwich
London, SE10 9NF
Tel: (0181) 858 4422
Fax: (0181) 312 6632
http://www.nmm.ac.uk

**Portsmouth Historic Dock-
yard**
College Road, HM Naval Base
Portsmouth, PO1 3LJ

Hampshire
Tel: 01705 861512
Enquiries@flagship.org.uk
http://www.flagship.org.uk/

Royal Air Force Museum
Grahame Park Way
Hendon, London, NW9 5LL
Tel: (0181) 205 2266
Fax: (0181) 200 1751
http://www.rafmuseum.org.uk

**Royal Armouries at HM Tower
of London**
HM Tower of London
London, EC3N 4AB
Tel: (0171) 480 6358
Fax: (0171) 481 2922

Royal Armouries Museum
Armouries Drive
Leeds, LS10 1LT
Tel: 0113 320 1999
Fax: 0113 320 1955
enquiries@armouries.org.uk

**Royal Navy Submarine
Museum**
Haslar Jetty Road, Gosport
Hampshire, PO12 2AS
Tel: (01705) 510354
Rnsubs@submarine-
museum.demon.co.uk
http://www.rnsubmus.co.uk

The Tank Museum
Bovington, Dorset
BH20 6JG
Tel: 01929 405096
Fax: 01929 405360
http://www.tankmuseum.co.uk/
education@tankmuseum.org

Wallace Collection
Herford House, Manchester
Square
London, W1M 6BN
Tel: (0171) 935 0687
Fax: (0171) 224 2155
admin@wallcoll.demon.co.uk
http://www.demon.co.uk/herita
ge/wallace

World Naval Base
Chatham Historic Dockyard
Chatham, Kent

GREECE

National Historical Museum
Stadiou Street
105 61 Athinai (Athens)

HUNGARY

Hadtörténeti Múzeum
(War Historical Museum)
Tóth Árpád sétány 40
1014 Budapest
POB 7 1250 Budapest
Tel: (01) 1561575
Fax: (01) 1561575

Magyar Nemzeti Múzeum
(Hungarian National Museum)
Múzeum krt. 14-16
1088 Budapest
Tel: (01) 1382122
Fax: (01) 1777806

IRELAND

National Museum of Ireland
Kildare Street and 7-9
Merrion Row
Dublin 2
Tel: (01) 6618811
Fax: (01) 6766116

ITALY

Museo 'Bardini'
Piazza dei Mozzi 1
50125 Firenze (Florence)
Tel: (055) 2342427
Fax: (055) 288049

Museo Nazionale del Bargello
Via del Proconsolo 4
50122 Firenze
Tel: (055) 23885

Museo Stibbert
Via F. Stibbert 26
50134 Firenze
Main office:
Via di Montughi, 7 Firenze
Tel: (055) 475520
(Information)
Tel:/Fax: (055) 486049
(Management)
http://www.vps.it/propart/
stibbere.htm

Museo Poldi Pezzoli
Via Manzoni 12
20121 Milano (Milan)
Tel: (02) 794889
Fax: (02) 8690788

Museo Nazionale di Capodimonte
Palazzo Reale di Capodimonte
80136 Napoli (Naples)
Tel: (081) 7441307
Fax: (081) 7418325

Museo Nazionale del Palazzo di Venezia
Via del Plebiscito 118
00186 Roma
Tel: (06) 6798865

Museo Nazionale di Castel Sant'Angelo
Lungotevere Castello 1
00193 Roma (Rome)
Tel: (06) 6875036
Fax: (06) 6822903

Armeria Reale
Piazza Castello 191
10123 Torino (Turin)
Tel: (011) 543889
Fax: (011) 549547

Museo Storico Navale
Campo S. Biagio 2148
Riva degli Schiavoni
30122 Venezia (Venice)
Tel: (041) 5200276

Palazzo Ducale
San Marco 1
30124 Venezia
Tel: (041) 5224951

JAPAN

National Museum of Japanese History
117 Jonai-cho, Sakura City
Chiba Prefecture 285
Tel: 043-386-0123
http://www.rekihaku.ac.jp/

MALTA

The Palace Armoury
Valletta
Tel: 338247/250026

NETHERLANDS

Rijksmuseum Afd. Nederlandse Geschiedenis
Stadhouderskade 42
POB 50673
1007 DD Amsterdam
Tel: (020) 732121

Rijksmuseum "Nederlands Scheepsvaartsmuseum"
Kattenburgerplein 1
NL-1018 KK Amsterdam
Tel: (020) 523 2222
Fax: (020) 523 2213

Legermuseum
Korte Geer 1
2611 CA, Delft
Tel: (015) 150500
Fax: (015) 150544

Royal Netherlands Army Museum
Korte Geer1
2611 CA, Delft
Tel: (015) 150500
Fax: (015) 150544

NORWAY

Marinemuseet
Karljohansvern
Box 21, N-3191 Horten
Tel: (33) 033397
Fax: (33) 033505

Forsvarsmuseet
(Norwegian Armed Forces Museum)
Akershus, 0015 Oslo 1
Tel: 22403582
Fax: 22403190

POLAND

Muzeum Historyczne m. Krakowa
(History Museum of the City of Cracow)
Rynek Glowny 35
31-011 Kraków (Cracow)
Tel: 229922

Muzeum Narodowe w Krakowie
(National Museum in Cracow)
ul Józefa Pilsudskiego 12
31-109 Kraków
Tel: (012) 221528
Fax: (012) 225434

Muzeum Wojska Polskiego
(Polish Army Museum)
Al Jerozolimskie 3
Warszawa 43 (Warsaw)
Tel: (022) 295271

PORTUGAL

Museu Militar
Largo do Museu de Artilharia
1100 Lisboa (Lisbon)
Tel: (01) 8882135
Fax: (01) 8884305

ROMANIA

Muzeul National Militar

Str Stefan Furtuna 125-127
77116 Bucuresti (Bucharest)
Tel: (01) 6373830

RUSSIA

Central Museum of the Armed Forces
Sovetskoi Armii 2
127157 Moskva
Tel: (095) 2815601

Gosudarstvennyj istoriceskij muzej
(State Historical Museum)
Krasnaja pl. 1/2
103012 Moskva (Moscow)
Tel: (095) 2922269
Fax: (095) 2922269 (i.e. same number)

Oruzejnaja palata Gosudarstvennye muzei Moskovskogo Kremlja
(Kremlin Armoury)
Kreml', 103073 Moskva
Tel: (095) 2023776

Central Naval Museum
Vasilevskii ostrov
Pushkina pl 4
St Peterburg (English spelling: St Petersburg)

Gosudarstvennyj Ermitaz
(State Hermitage Museum)
Dvorcovaja nab. 36
191186 St Peterburg
Tel: (812) 2129545

Voenno-istoriceskij muzej artillerii, inzenernych vojsk I vojsk svjazi
(Museum of Artillery, the Signal Corps and Corps of Engineers)
park im V.I. Lenina 7
St Petersburg

SPAIN

Museo Naval
Paseo del Prado no 5
28014 Madrid
Tel: (91) 3795299
Fax: (91) 3795056

Real Armeria
Palacio Real
Calle Bailén
28071 Madrid
Tel: (91) 2487404 ext 442

Museo del Ejército
(The Spanish Army Museum)
Calle Méndez Núñez 1
28014 Madrid
Tel: (91) 5211285

SWEDEN

Militärmuseet Skansen Kronan
Risåatan
413 04 Göteborg (Gothenburg)

Marinmuseum
(Naval Museum)
Amiralitetsslätten
371 30 Karlskrona
Tel: (0455) 84000
Fax: (0455) 84071

Malmö Museer
(Malmö Museum)
Malmöhusvägen
Box 406, 201 24 Malmö

Tel: (040) 341000
Fax: (040) 124097

Kungl. Armémuseum
(The Royal Army Museum)
Riddargatan 13
Box 14095, 104 41 Stockholm
Tel: (08) 7889560
Fax: (08) 6626831

Livrustkammaren
(The Royal Armoury)
Kungl. Slottet
Slottsbacken 3
111 30 Stockholm
Tel: (08) 6664466
Fax: (08) 6664489
livrustkammaren@lsh.se

Vasamuseet
Statens Sjöhistoriska Museer
Galävarvsvägen 14
Box 27131, 115 21 Stockholm
Tel: (08) 6664800
Fax: (08) 6664888

SWITZERLAND

Bernisches Historisches Museum
Helvetiapl 5, 3000 Bern, 6
Tel: (031) 431811
Fax: (031) 430663

Musée d'art et d'histoire
2, rue Charles-Galland
1211 Genève 3
Tel: (022) 3114340
Fax: (022) 211706

Kantonales Museum Altes Zeughaus
Wehrhistorisches Museum
Zeughauspl 1, 4500 Solothurn
Tel: (032) 233528
Fax: (032) 214387

Schweizerisches Landesmuseum
Museumstr 2
Postfach 6789, 8023 Zürich
Tel: (01) 2186511
F (01) 2112949

UNITED STATES

Cleveland Museum of Art
11150 East Blvd
Cleveland, OH 44106
Tel: (216) 421 7340 and 7350
Fax: (216) 421 0411
info@cma-oh.org
www.clemusart.com

American Airpower Heritage Museum
Midland International Airport
9600 Wright Drive
Midland, Texas 79711
Tel: (915) 567-3009
Fax: (915) 567-3047
http://www.avdigest.com/
aahm/

Gettysburg National Military Park
97 Taneytown Road
Gettysburg, PA 17325
Tel: (717) 334-1124
http://www.nps.gov/gett/

Guilford Courthouse National Military Park
2332 New Garden Road
Greensboro
North Carolina 27410-2355
Tel: (336) 288-1776
http://www.nps.gov/guco/

Higgins Armory Museum
100 Barber Ave.
Worcester, MA 01606-2444
Tel: (508) 853 6015
Fax: (508) 852 7697

Metropolitan Museum of Art
1000 Fifth Av.
NewYork, NY 10028-1098
Tel: (212) 879 5500
Fax: (212) 570 3879
http://www.metmuseum.org/

National Infantry Museum
Fort Benning, Georgia
Tel: (706) 545-6762
http://www.benningmwr.com/m
useum.htm

National Warplane Museum
Elmira-Corning Regional Airport
17 Aviation Drive
Horseheads, New York 14845
Tel: (607) 739-8200
http://www.warplane.org

Navy Museum
901 M St. S.E.
Washington, D.C. 20374-5060
Tel: (202) 433 4882
Fax: (202) 433 8200
http://www.history.navy.mil/bra
nches/ngcorg8.htm

Palm Springs Air Museum
745 North Gene Autry Trail
Palm Springs, California 92262
Tel: (760) 778-6262
sales@air-museum.org
http://www.air-museum.org/

Saint Louis Art Museum
Forest Park, Saint Louis
MO 63110
Tel: (314) 721 0067
Fax: (314) 721 6172

Shiloh National Military Park
1055 Pittsburg Landing
Shiloh, TN 38376
Tel: (901) 689 5696
http://www.nps.gov/shil/

United States Air Force Museum
Wright-Patterson Air Force Base
near Dayton, Ohio
45433-7102
Tel: (937) 255-3286
http://www.wpafb.af.mil/muse
um/

Vicksburg National Military Park
3201 Clay Street
Vicksburg
MS 39183-3495
Tel: (601) 636-0583
vick_interpretation@nps.gov
http://www.nps.gov/vick/

YUGOSLAVIA

Vojni Muzej Jugoslovenske Narodne Armije
(Military Museum of the Yugoslav People's Army)
Kalemgadan 69
11000 Beograd (Belgrade)
Tel: (011) 620722